THE
MURDER
OF JACOB

MARY ELLEN JOHNSON

*THERE ARE MANY DIFFERENT KINDS OF
MURDER*

VOICES
PUBLISHING

ISBN 0-9655668-0-3

First Edition/February 1997

FOREWORD/MARY ELLEN

Jacob Ind is my friend. Jacob has also been my profound teacher. Not only has he taught me things I would rather not know about—murder, abuse, the prison system, and our criminal courts—he has taught me about the many faces of love.

Where do I begin? Jacob has taught me so much. To be grateful for the little things in life that aren't so little—the touch of someone's hand, a smile, kind words in a letter, kind words during a visit, a hot shower, hamburgers for lunch. Jacob has taught me that someone who was abused from the day he was born can retain a purity of soul that is as endearing as it is mystifying. He has taught me that even a person who, by all objective standards, should never have "bonded" and therefore cannot be capable of any "positive" emotions, IS capable of love.

Jacob taught me, "Chains don't break the spirit. The spirit breaks the chains." That the only real prison is the prison of the heart. He taught me to have faith in God because in the prison of our lives we have no one else to turn to. Now if only I can remember... If only I can practice those truths...

I am not saying that Jacob chose the proper "solution" to his "dilemma" by killing his parents, or that he has no emotional problems. Others would paint you a picture of a very different Jacob. His prosecutors saw a cold-blooded murderer. Many people consider him to be a blemish on the face of this community and best forgotten. Department of Corrections regards him as a troublemaker, a possible or actual psychopath who exists to give them grief. Self-help and psychology books explain why someone like Jacob was doomed from the time he was in his mother's womb.

But none of the afore-mentioned factor in several important intangibles—Jacob's soul, God's healing power, and the difference that love can make. That word again. I believe love is the premiere power in the universe—God's love, agape love, the love between a man and woman, the love between a parent and a child, the love between friends. Jacob is my paradigm. Is love enough? Can love literally move mountains, as I believe? If so, why do I doubt that it can heal the heart of one abused child? Or that it hasn't already?

Because of my emotional involvement with Jacob, I make no claim that I am an unbiased observer in *The Murder of Jacob*. I did my best to give a balanced account of Jacob's life and to recount events objectively. I tried very hard to be fair with teachers, counselors, agencies and those involved in the criminal justice system, letting their actions speak for themselves. In a society that expresses compassion for battered women, I find it tragic that that same compassion does not extend to its children. Particularly if the crime occurs in Woodland Park. Particularly if that child's name is Jacob Ind.

However, I did not try to whitewash who Jacob is. I did not try to mitigate the impact of his crime. Nor do I blame people who are unsympathetic to him

and his act. I understand their horror and revulsion. But I would ask that law and order enthusiasts also keep an open mind when reading this. Because, in the end, *The Murder of Jacob* isn't really about murder. It is about the crime of abuse and how it can destroy a soul. Several souls. Abuse is the twisted DNA running through the backgrounds of Jacob's mother and stepfather, as well. A crime that corrupts generations. By punishing Jacob, we can temporarily bury the problem, but it is not going to go away.

It is also my fervent hope that those who are hostile to Jacob and/or me will not obfuscate the issues I raise by focusing on me personally. As this manuscript edged toward publication, the voices grew louder. "Just who is she, anyway? What are her motives?" I've tried not to respond to personal criticisms.

I am not the issue.

Child abuse is.

Pedophilia, and how we refuse to deal with it, is.

Especially if these child-rapists and soul murderers possess money, power, and prestige. Especially if they are well-educated, well-spoken, handsome, pretty, charming, and intelligent. Unless these people look and act like the monstrosities they are, we all too often refuse to believe their victims. (Even when they look the part, their punishment is usually minimal. Again, the unspoken message: Children are unimportant.) Jacob understood that. So do all the other Jacobs. That's why most never tell. They know they won't be believed. Or they will be blamed. Or ignored. Or returned to their abusers. Or sent to foster homes or institutions where they will be subjected to yet more soul damage.

In addition, I am still looking for the answers to the following questions. Did Jacob Ind receive a fair trial? Is justice served by locking children such as Jacob forever behind bars? Why were Kermode and Pamela Jordan given free rein to emotionally, physically and spiritually rape their sons? Why was Jacob the only one who finally stood up to them, saying, "This stops here?" Why do we refuse to deal honestly and fairly with Jacob?

Most importantly...

If Jacob Ind is to be held accountable for his actions, why aren't the teachers who failed to report the abuse, the neighbors and friends who ignored the Ind brothers' cries for help, Department of Social Services, which failed to properly investigate the Jordans, and law enforcement officials, who repeatedly visited the Jordan residence and/or knew about the abuse? Why was Jacob Ind made the scapegoat for the sins of an entire community?

Tell me.

Explain why you and I aren't responsible when so many of us knew, when so many of us turned away...

When so many of us continue to turn away.

◊   ◊   ◊

Much yet remains unknown about the events surrounding December 17, 1992. Because Jacob's case is still under appeal, I have had great difficulty in gaining access to Discovery, which supposedly contains every scrap of paper, every snapshot, every morsel of information regarding this case. I wrote the District Attorney four different times and personally visited the D.A.'s office trying to obtain all relevant documents. My inquiries were ignored. Such indifference lends credence to several people who told me that they contacted the D.A., as well as prosecutor Bill Aspinwall, at different times—including during Jacob's trial—with information helpful to his case, and that their phone calls or inquiries were also ignored. My inquiries to Jacob's defense attorneys concerning Discovery never elicited a response either. Jacob's appeals attorney, Barbara Blackman, who always returns calls and answers letters, believes that Shaun Kaufman still has Discovery. I have also been told that it is a matter of public record, available for me or anyone else to view at my leisure. If true, I am looking forward to that opportunity.

I do know far more about the Ind case than I included in *The Murder of Jacob*. Some is too sensational to print without irrefutable proof. Hopefully, funds from this project will provide for the first thorough investigation of the events surrounding December 17, 1992—at least from a defense standpoint. None of us yet knows the entire truth concerning the Jordan murders. To echo someone from Gabrial Adams's defense, "This is the most complicated case I've ever been involved in.' Nothing is as it seems." I agree. The only thing I can say with absolute certainty is that Kermode and Pamela Jordan are dead.

What do I hope to accomplish by telling Jacob's story? I'm not asking for much. Public awareness. Legislative changes. " Battered children" to be placed on equal footing with "Battered women." Harsher punishments for the Kermode and Pamela Jordans of the world. Treatment, instead of incarceration, for children like Jacob.

And yes, I want my friend to be physically freed.

What are my odds? Jacob Ind is the youngest person in the history of Colorado to receive life without parole. Generally, in cases of parricide these children receive prison sentences but few, if any, have been subjected to punishment as draconian as Jacob's. Barring a miracle, Jacob will remain locked away until the day he dies.

But I do believe in miracles.

FOREW0RD/JACOB

When this book was still in the draft process I made sure to get a copy of the manuscript to make sure that it is as factual as it could be. To what I can personally vouch for it is completely true, though I cannot say I'm 100% positive that the events I didn't witness with my own eyes are true. I trust that they are. I am adamant that only the absolute truth be told by me or anybody who speaks for me. Lies, deceptions and distortions can only do harm but the truth will "set me free." I am not concerned that the truth may condemn me. This life isn't what's important. If the complete truth is known and I don't find physical freedom I'll know that it is my purpose to be here in physical prison and I'll work my whole life to fulfil that purpose...

I honestly can't say whether or not I'd react the same way if I could go back in time (to December 17, 1992.). Thank God I can't, and thank God I'll never be placed in a situation or environment that I was raised in again. But I want to make one thing clear. I am not a victim. Sure, my childhood sucked. Being raped and forced to perform oral sex on my mom and Kermode sucked. Being beaten sucked. But what does wallowing in grief and self pity accomplish? I see people all the time on talk shows with "poor me" syndrome. Their victimization feeds them. They peel the scabs so the wounds won't heal. I don't want to be pitied. Understood would be a closer word but still inadequate. If it was up to me the stories of abuse wouldn't be well known. That's not something that feels good for it to be known. But unfortunately it is necessary to expose if I don't want to die in a cesspool of iniquity (prison)...

Prison isn't that bad though. I have freedoms and have found happiness and growth. The hardest part about prison is sticking with God and staying on His path in the midst of constant unyielding temptation. It seems as if the longer I'm here the harder it gets to stay half way godly. My faith carries me but when I stumble, I hit hard. When I eventually get out (I believe I will one day) I will be a strong man of God so these are the times I should be thankful for. If I am freed, I plan to start my own contracting/restoration business, hopefully with my dad if he's still alive. Prison has drawn me closer to him and let me see who my true friends and family are. I also want a wife, kids and a normal life. I just hope that God has that planned for my life.

I know most likely there aren't any kids who are in a situation like I was who are reading this but in case there are, I have to say this. I know that no matter what, you're going to do what you're going to do. Still, think about your actions seriously--whether it's to continue your silence, escape into drugs, run away, or even suicide or killing--consider your options. Go to somebody. Try every way to get out of the situation without doing something stupid that's going to hurt you or perpetuate the problem.

For those of you who've lived through it, there's only one way to be completely healed and able to get on with your life. It's not through mental

health. Nor is the solution within you. It's Jesus, the Ultimate Healer. He can and wants to heal all the pain and hurt that's deep within you. All you've got to do is receive the free gift He's offering. Ask for it and you'll receive it.

I'm not sure what it is that I want this book to accomplish but it just seems right that it should be written. Maybe somebody's life will be touched. Maybe it'll shed some light upon the problem of child abuse. Maybe people will learn that the worst possible thing you can do to your children is to be verbally and emotionally cruel to them. Whatever this does, I just hope it does God's work and I must thank him for giving me such a dear and close friend, Mary Ellen, who would take the time, effort and (have the) courage to stick by me. Thank you God, thank you Mary Ellen and I thank my friends and family who have supported me.

ACKNOWLEDGMENTS

A word about the manuscript itself. Jacob edited the original copy, at least where it dealt with information gathered in our private interviews. He was extremely brutal on himself and his motives. Where there are differing versions of events, such as disparities between Jacob's account of sexual abuse and his brother's, I included both. I have also included any discrepancies, such as the Lofthouse Incident, that occur between one person's version of an event and another's. No two people viewing or personally involved in an incident will remember it in exactly the same way. Since the prosecution barred me from Jacob's trial and transcripts were not available, I reconstructed the proceedings from the copious notes of fellow writer Lynn Bliss. For Lynn's cooperation I offer my heartfelt thanks. The courtroom scenes were severely edited, of course, and real attorneys will probably scoff at some of the questions I constructed, though I trust they were faithful to the lawyers' intent. Witnesses' answers were as close to verbatim as possible. Whenever I gave a person a pseudonym I marked that with an asterisk. (*) As far as individuals' surnames, many had several different spellings in newspaper accounts. Generally, I chose one and carried it through the entire manuscript. To preserve the privacy of innocent people and to make sure that nothing I write will adversely affect Jacob's case in the courts, I will issue the caveat that some details have been altered. These do not affect any larger "truths."

Most of the information about Jacob's childhood was provided via court testimony, interviews with Jacob, his brother Charles and Godmother Lupe Thorson. A special thanks to Lupe, who has also become a good friend. I cherish our continuing connection. I interviewed many people off the record, which added to my understanding of Jacob and of the way things work in Teller County. I wish I could print more. Maybe someday. I never interviewed Jacob's accomplice, Gabrial Adams. I do not know the truth about Gabrial. I know that his parents love him, believe in his innocence and trust that someday God will release their son.

The ladies at the Woodland Park Library have been wonderful in supplying me with all sorts of arcane books over the years. I thank my family and my friends for being so patient with me as I struggled through this project, and through Jacob's conviction. Many people have helped me gather information and have been so supportive that as I began listing them I was so afraid of leaving someone out that I deleted individual names. This is a generic thanks to all of you. You know who you are. I could not have survived without your friendship, support, prayers and advice.

Desktop publishing has made the business of book production far easier, but one still has to be semi-computer literate. I'm not. Many thanks to Judy Simpson, Jim Thiele and Tom Gallo, who patiently helped me get my new program up and running. Also, a major thank you to Jeanette Holtham, who

took time out of her very busy schedule to help me do a final polish, and give the manuscript a more professional look.

I would also like to thank three business owners. Beth O'Neal of Eon's Books, 601 W. Midland Avenue, Woodland Park, will keep a permanent supply of *The Murder of Jacob* on hand. A visit to Eon's, which will include meeting Francis, Beth's golden retriever, will be well worth the scenic drive. To view Jacob's art work, a photo of which is in the back of *TMOJ,* visit Yolanda's Botanica in the Historic Manitou Spa Building, Manitou Springs. Jacob's "Prison Bars" is on permanent display there, thanks to my good friend, Yolanda Gonzalez.

If you are as impressed with my cover as I am, the credit goes to Brandon Lewis. Brandon did a first-rate job and I hope to see his name on many other book jackets. He is a struggling artist, can be reached through Voices Publishing, and is a joy to work with. He is also my nephew, so, yes, I am happy to give him free advertising. He deserves it.

My grateful appreciation to everyone.

THE MURDER OF JACOB was not an easy book to write. Nor will it probably be an easy or enjoyable book to read. The language can be crude and the events graphic. But I figure if Jacob lived it, I can write it and you can read it.

Which is why I dedicate this book, not just to "my" Jacob, but to all the Jacobs out there, who even now are crying in their beds, hiding in their closets, hoping against hope that "someone" will miraculously rescue them. All too often, their hopes remain just that. Vain fantasies. Wishful thinking. Unanswered prayers.

Please.

We must give them a way out.

We must care.

We must help all the Jacobs.

Sweet and cloying through the air
Falls the stifling scent of despair.

~T.S. Eliot
Murder in the Cathedral

PART ONE
MURDER
Chapter 1

Fall 1992

Jacob the Favored. Jacob the Adored. Many family members and friends assumed that it was Jacob, rather than his older brother, Charles, who was Kermode and Pamela Jordan's favorite. In a way that was true. Stepfather Kermode Jordan had been obsessed with Jacob from the moment he first saw him. But Jacob had turned 15 on September 26, 1992. He was no longer the precocious four-year-old that Kermode had fallen in love with.

Now when Kermode studied his youngest stepson he saw only traces of the beautiful child Jacob had been. The once blond hair had gone dark and his cheeks had thinned, especially over the past few months. That sturdy boy's body had shot up to six feet and filled out until Jacob was one of the largest players on Woodland Park High School's freshman football team. Still those remarkable black eyes hadn't changed, nor had that radiant smile.

But how seldom Jacob smiled these days. What was he thinking? What rebellions was he plotting? Jacob didn't talk back, not like his eighteen-year-old brother. The occasional defiant look and flare of temper were there, but there didn't seem to be much need to worry about him yet. From infancy onward, Jacob had been a remarkably obedient child, wanting only to please. He had been easy to control.

And Kermode Jordan was a master at control. An engineer at Digital Equipment Corporation in Colorado Springs, Kermode was also a student of human nature. In his extensive private library he stocked hundreds of books on dominance, brainwashing and mind control. Although Kermode's great love was the philosophy and philosophers of Ancient Greece, he was also an aficionado of World War II. He especially admired two of that era's most famous dictators, Stalin and Hitler. Throughout the eleven years of his marriage to Pamela Ind, Kermode had ruled his household like a dictatorship. And it had worked. Hadn't it?

In many ways Kermode had indeed achieved success. He enjoyed a good paying, prestigious job. He lived in one of the nicest homes in Sunnywood Manor, an affluent subdivision outside the picturesque Colorado mountain town

of Woodland Park. He was blessed with a trophy family consisting of two handsome stepsons and an attractive wife sixteen years his junior.

Pamela Jean Jordan, whom he referred to as his "magnificent star," was the "finest woman he'd ever known." Or so he liked to tell Jacob. Kermode and Pam complemented each other in many ways. She was dark where he was light. Small and quick where he was a tall man with a deliberate manner. Pam was moderately political whereas he styled himself a "revolutionary."

Still, Kermode and Pamela were alike in the important things. Both were bright and ambitious. Both were control freaks. Both had similar philosophies on raising children. That philosophy had served them well. Their sons were good students, polite to their elders and obedient to their parents. To the outside world, the Kermode Howard Jordans appeared to be the perfect family...

But all was not well inside the Jordan household. By the fall of 1992, Kermode and Pamela were drowning in a sea of debt and despair. Digital had begun laying off hundreds of its employees. Pam worked as an assistant at Care & Share, a non-profit organization that distributed food to the needy. Care & Share might be a politically correct job for someone of the Jordans' liberal persuasion, but Pam had gone from a high paying position at California's Pacific Bell to barely cracking twenty grand a year. The Jordans' combined salaries still neared ninety thousand, but that was a forty thousand dollar annual drop in the five years they'd lived in Colorado. Pamela had been forced to cash in her stocks. Every credit card was maxed out. Most frustrating of all, the family was attempting to sell their residence at 120 Ridge Drive during one of the worst real estate markets in twenty years.

Far worse than the debt, however, was the despair. The Jordans guarded their privacy so fiercely that few people knew what was really happening behind their closed doors. Kermode and Pamela had spun their web of lies so skillfully that they had fooled just about everyone. For a long time, they'd even fooled themselves. But a gaping hole had been torn in their web. That hole filled them with despair. The despair of forever having to pretend to the outside world and to oneself that life was perfect and the Jordan family was perfect and they themselves, unlike the rest of society's parents, were perfect. Kermode and Pamela knew better. Masters at denial, they could no longer deny the hole in their web. It even had a name. Charles Ind.

Husky and good looking, the All American kid with All American grades, Charles had reached "a certain age." He was rebellious. No, he was worse than rebellious. He was impossible. He also had a mouth on him. Who was Charles talking to? Was he confiding the family secrets? That was Kermode and Pamela's biggest fear. What would he tell? And who would he tell it to?

The Jordans had spent a lifetime training their sons never to speak to anyone about anything that happened inside their domain. Largely, they'd succeeded. Maybe the boys had mentioned an occasional "incident" to their

friends, but nobody believed children.

So far, Jacob, in particular, had adhered to the Jordan code. While Kermode and Pamela had always castigated their youngest son for his "bad attitude," it was one thing to bring home an S- on a report card and quite another to blurt family secrets to a concerned teacher or a friend's sympathetic mother. That possibility increased with each year. But Jacob was still young enough to be malleable. They had time with their baby. But with Charles time had run out...

Kermode the Philosopher, Expert at Mind Control, understood that a definite shift in power had occurred within the Jordan household that last summer. For eleven years Kermode had enjoyed total dominance. Every time Kermode did those terrible things to Charles, he said, "I'll break your neck if you tell," and Charles had always bowed to his stepfather's threat.

But now it was Charles who could have snapped Kermode's neck. Charles was nearly as tall as his stepfather, with the powerful legs and arms of a football player, whereas Kermode possessed the stringy muscles of an alcoholic. Although Kermode had once been a Golden Glove boxer, at fifty-seven he wore dentures, his hands were covered with liver spots and his face turned lipstick red when he drank. Every time Kermode looked at Charles he must have wondered whether Charles would tell the secret. Those past months, even as the family structure crumbled and the physical and emotional violence escalated, Kermode had largely refrained from taunting Charles. Toward the end he did not so openly profess his contempt of "queers" and "fags" around his oldest stepson. Toward the end the word "blackmail" hovered unspoken between them. Toward the end Charles did not silently take the beatings, but fought back. Toward the end it was Kermode who cowered like a frightened rabbit.

The Jordan household completely exploded in September of 1992. That was when Charles Ind moved out.

◊ ◊ ◊

One day Charles was there; the next he was gone. His departure was as quiet as a sigh. He scribbled a note to his mother which he left on the kitchen counter. "Moved out early. Will call when I get a phone."

Jacob had known for a while that Charles was leaving. He even ratted his brother off. He enjoyed seeing his parents bash Charles instead of him. Jacob joined in the criticism. In "a weird, twisted way" he felt he was being a "son" by doing this.

The day Charles left, Jacob was at Jan's Cafe, where he held down a summer dishwashing job. His parents arrived at the restaurant, located off Woodland Park's main street, and pulled him aside. Basically, all they said was, "Your brother moved out. You can have his room."

3

Jacob guessed they gave him the bigger room as a reward for tattling.

For a few short days or even a week, Jacob's life was actually better. Forgetting about his real or imagined shortcomings, Pamela focused her anger on Charles's betrayal.

"He's going to be sorry," she railed. "He's nothing but an ungrateful bastard and when he comes crawling back I might not even let him return."

Charles's betrayal made Jacob happy. With his older brother out of the way, nothing could interfere with him being a son. Except Jacob wasn't exactly sure what "being a son" meant. Especially regarding his mother. While she had a phony-sweet public face, in private she was relentlessly critical. To Jacob, it seemed she hated him for his very existence. Always she had compared him unfavorably with his older brother.

"Why can't you be like Charles?" she'd say, in that hate-filled voice she reserved only for him.

But now she turned that question around and used it as an insult. "You're acting just like Charles!"

What did that mean? What did his parents expect from him? Jacob wanted to please both Kermode and Pam, but how could he? Even if he did something right, they made him feel as if it were somehow wrong and as if HE were somehow defective.

Still, maybe things would change for the better. It seemed that way, since Charles had turned into the hated one.

When Pam said, "Charles will never make it on his own," Jacob concurred.

Pam continued, "All he has is his loser job at Wendy's and that piddly allowance your dad sends him. How's he going to pay for rent and food and school? I sure won't help him."

Jacob agreed. Agreeing with his mother felt good, as if they finally had something in common. He wanted to be her ally. In addition, he was truly infuriated at Charles for hurting her. Pam actually cried over her first-born's departure, something she seldom did.

When Jacob saw the pain in his mother's eyes, he longed to comfort her, but he didn't know how. In addition, he had to wrestle with his own private pain. Outsiders might think that Pamela favored Jacob, but Jacob knew the truth. If HE had moved out, Pam would have said, "Good riddance." She would never even have asked him to return. The reason was simple enough. His mother hated him.

Jacob was perceptive enough to realize that his parents were upset by Charles's leaving for a second reason. For the first time Kermode and Pamela had totally lost control of one of their children, and, according to Jacob, "That scared the hell out of them." Pam in particular hated having to relinquish dominance. "She raised us for her to win." One of her's and Kermode's favorite stories involved the donkey, the carrot and the stick. Only with the boys there were never any carrots. After Charles turned seventeen and he was finally

allowed to get a driver's license, Pam had used his battered VW bug as a weapon. If he displeased her, she took his car keys. Plain and simple. Charles got mad and argued, but she always won. Family and friends regarded Charles as the stronger brother, but Jacob considered his rebellions "stupid." He knew it was a no-win situation. "Mom always won. Always."

Until the day Charles walked.

As the 1992-93 school year began, Jacob was enthusiastic about the future. Hoping to contrast favorably with the fallen favorite, he launched into "Being-a-Son mode." He developed all sorts of optimistic plans for making his parents proud. He would do all the household chores, study ever harder, be even more cooperative. He would "prove" he was better than Charles, that they didn't need their oldest child. By being the "good son" who stayed, maybe his parents would love him.

All too soon that particular fantasy got "shot to hell."

All too soon Jacob realized that, rather than things changing for the better, he was completely at his parents' mercy.

Now it was just Jacob and his tormentors.

Now they three were alone in the house where he would soon kill them.

Jacob never liked 120 Ridge Drive. He had no idea that the structure he called "home" had always been an unhappy place. The imposing three story had a troubled history. It was built in the early 1980's by a couple who erected it as their "dream home." After they moved in, misfortune quickly followed. A neighbor molested one of their children. Their previously harmonious marriage collapsed, ending in an acrimonious divorce. Following that family's departure, the property remained vacant save for an occasional tenant until the Jordans purchased it in 1987.

Jacob didn't care much about material things, so Ridge Drive didn't impress him. It sure enough impressed his parents, though. His stepfather acted as though it was his own private fiefdom. And Kermode ruled over his subjects, particularly Jacob and his brother, not like a mere lord, but like a king. Outsiders generally considered the Jordans to be polite but aloof. Jacob understood why. His parents hoarded their privacy the way a miser hoards gold. They had to. Because of the secrets.

In many ways, 120 Ridge Drive reminded Jacob of his family. Perched high on a hill, the house was close enough to the road so that passersby could see the decks and cedar siding, but far enough away so that one could only glimpse the wall of windows facing Pikes Peak's jagged north profile. Like its inhabitants, the residence revealed just enough of itself to impress onlookers. Yet its steep driveway, which Jacob shoveled after every snowstorm, warned, "Come near, but do not enter."

A motor home was parked in a prominent spot. That motor home was an unsubtle reminder that the Kermode Howard Jordans were a family that in an affluent neighborhood numbered among the most comfortable.

Jacob's parents were big on appearances. Inside their 4,000 square foot house a gallery of pictures lined the upper bedroom hallway. Smiling faces of Jacob and his brother--opening Christmas presents, skiing, running along a California beach, posing for a group portrait with their parents. So many smiling faces. The minute Kermode pointed his camera at them, the boys knew they'd better smile. The Chinese tapestry in the dining room, an antique, was worth a million dollars—at least according to his mother.[1]

Recently, to ready the house for sale, Jacob's parents had redecorated every room. They enjoyed showing off the patio furniture in the solarium, the family area with its gleaming, newly refinished wood floor and the dining room, which was dominated by a magnificent berlywood table that Jacob loved to polish. Generally, Jacob didn't think much about the furniture or the expensive Southwestern art or the ceramic figurines beyond the fact that he had to clean everything. What he noticed most about the house was the atmosphere, which was cold and that, when he and his parents inhabited the same room, it was filled with hatred toward him. The only time the house seemed warm and welcoming was when his pets were there.

In fact, if Jacob were being truthful, his feelings about his residence went beyond dislike. Ridge Drive terrified him. When he was alone he sensed someone following him. Often, even when his parents were at work, Jacob carried a gun to feel powerful, as if a weapon could provide him with some measure of control over his fate. He also carried the gun "for protection."

Protection from what? Jacob has no idea. Could this have had something to do with his dabbling into the occult? In his quest for power Jacob had used the incantations from *The Black Arts*, one of Kermode's well-worn books, to call forth demons. After perceiving a presence behind him, the frightened teen had stopped.

But the panic had preceded Jacob's brush with Satanism. For as long as he could remember, he'd felt the eyes. As he lay in bed pretending to sleep, he sensed someone in the room or watching him from the doorway. Yet upon opening his eyes he was alone. When Jacob showered, especially early in the morning, he locked both bathroom doors, but once they were unlocked and he faced the thought of going up the dark staircase, panic seized him until he could hardly breathe. Heart hammering, he'd race back to the safety of his bedroom.

Sometimes Jacob could grasp, at the edge of his consciousness, the

---

[1] A more realistic appraisal, taken before the Jordan auction in September 1993, valued the tapestry at $600.00

6

identity of his demons. In the fall of 1992, after his brother moved out, he began to realize that his demons came in human form.

Jacob's demons were his parents.

In the real dark night of the soul, it is always three o' clock in the morning, day after day.

> ~ F. Scott Fitzgerald
> "The Crack Up"/*The Crack Up*

Chapter 2

September-November 1992

When Jacob once again discovered himself on the front lines in the Jordan Wars, he was dismayed to realize that all the heavy artillery was aimed at him. Without Charles everything was double—double the tension, double the arguments and double the chores. Jacob had already endured a difficult summer. Kermode's drinking had worsened and tensions had escalated until even the most innocuous situation was potentially explosive. In fact, a drinking bout, later referred to as "The Lofthouse Incident," is what had precipitated Charles's leaving.

Since that episode in early September, Kermode was officially "on the wagon." When the family dined out he ordered iced tea instead of his usual beer, though his newfound sobriety did not prevent Pamela from buying a six pack every other day and drinking it in front of him. It wasn't the first time Kermode had vowed to quit drinking. Perhaps Pam didn't feel like altering her lifestyle to accommodate his—especially when she figured any change would be temporary.

Kermode's vow wasn't something that Jacob necessarily considered a plus either. A drunken Kermode was familiar. Jacob knew what to expect. Bad as it was, there were few surprises. Without alcohol, his stepfather was like a baby without a pacifier.[2] Unusually tense and easily angered, Kermode used Jacob for his verbal and physical punching bag more frequently than before.

It wasn't that his stepfather had never hit him. But since Jacob was his favorite, Kermode's attacks hadn't been as frequent as Pamela's. And afterward he would sometimes do nice things to make up. Besides, Jacob didn't mind the beatings so much. The first blows hurt quite a bit, but after awhile they just felt "real hot with a sting." Like Kermode's drinking, being hit was something he was accustomed to. He'd been "disciplined" from infancy onward. He regarded it as "normal."

Numbing the mind, however, was harder than numbing the body. Kermode's brutal remarks had escalated with Charles's departure, with his private struggle to conquer chemical addiction. Kermode constantly referred to Jacob as "motherfucker," "asshole," "punk" or "faggot." The fifteen-year-old found it increasingly difficult to heed his older brother's oft-repeated advice, "Ignore them." For Jacob, "The garbage dump was becoming increasingly full."

Jacob tried to retreat to his earlier method of coping with his parents. He.

---

[2] Toxicology reports at the time of Kermode's death revealed that he had been drinking. Jacob didn't know this.

8

disappeared. Maybe they'll forget all about me, he thought, hopefully. Jacob had nearly perfected the art of invisibility, but with Charles gone, the rules had changed. He no longer had any cover. Somehow, no matter how quiet he was, how he stayed out of Kermode and Pam's way, how deeply he withdrew into himself, his parents always managed to notice him--with all its attendant consequences.

For awhile, high school football provided an outlet for Jacob's frustrations. He was a left tackle offense, and right tackle defense on Woodland Park's freshman team. WPHS's freshmen were okay, not great, but they were better than the varsity, which hadn't won a game since 1988. Jacob didn't care about winning or losing. He enjoyed the physical contact. The slamming, tackling and roughhousing helped him take out his aggressions in a healthy manner.

Still, there were circumstances surrounding football that distressed him. He refused to take showers with the rest of the players. "I was modest," he says simply. But Jacob's girlfriend, Stephanie Endsley, saw bruises on his body.

"What are those?" she asked, pointing to the marks.

Jacob shrugged. "Just football injuries."

Stephanie thought they were in pretty peculiar places, but when she pressed him, he changed the subject.

Jacob was shy about exposing his naked body. The very idea of showering with a bunch of males filled him with panic, though he had no idea why. Was it simply because, as he said later, "Every kid feels inadequate with his equipment at that age?"

Jacob also hated the way the coach and teammates put their arms around him or patted his butt. At their touch a chill went through him and he had to force himself to keep from jerking away. Jacob again attributed his squeamishness to modesty. He had always hated getting physicals, and hernia checks were an agony. Nor could he urinate in public restrooms. He didn't know whether all guys felt the way he did. Maybe it had something to do with the way Kermode called him "faggot," when he was really angry, and Jacob's hatred of homosexuals. Maybe it had to do with something else, something that Jacob didn't dare remember...

As with everything in Jacob's life, he paid a price for being allowed to play football. For one thing, Kermode and Pamela insisted on picking him up after practice rather than allowing him to car pool or ride his bike. No big deal? Just another example of conscientious parents? Not the way Jacob saw it. To him, they were snatching away more of his all too rare moments of freedom.

On the way home from football practice, the Jordans generally stopped off at Banana Belt Liquors. While one parent went inside to purchase a six-pack, the other launched into a monologue of Jacob's shortcomings on and off the field. When parent #1 returned, the monologue became a "dialogue," with Kermode and Pam doing all the talking. The words and phrases, which in some form he'd heard all his life, blended together in a meaningless jumble.

Throughout the four mile ride home, Jacob looked out the window of the Dodge Ram and tried to think himself far away. He imagined himself running through the woods like in *LORD OF THE FLIES*, or escaping as a hermit, a tramp or a hobo. To be alone, without all the voices, all the anger and putdowns, was his idea of the "Ultimate Freedom." Jacob had always had a fertile imagination. It was reality he had trouble dealing with. And reality, in the form of his parents' hatred, was becoming impossible.

◇ ◇ ◇

Concerned, involved parents that they were, the Jordans attended every one of Jacob's football games. Kermode carried a megaphone and Pamela brandished a cowbell in order to command Jacob's attention on the field. He felt like Pavlov's dog. When he heard that tinkling bell he was supposed to listen attentively to their shouted comments. Although he was embarrassed by his parents' behavior, Kermode and Pam considered themselves to be cheerleaders.

"Did you hear us? We really got the crowd into it," they'd say, proud of their school spirit.

Actually, many bystanders disapproved of Pamela's behavior. She screamed at Jacob and called him "Stupid," causing the other mothers, who considered her comments to be more cruel than encouraging, to keep a safe distance away.

Sometimes Jacob fantasized taking his mother's silly cow bell and jamming it down her throat. Still, he tried to look responsive while ignoring his parents. That didn't work. Once they were alone, Kermode and Pamela told him, "You should hear us yell at you and do what we say."

On the way home they recounted a list of Jacob's athletic errors. "You were too slow... too clumsy... didn't hit hard enough...don't know what you're doing... dumb...worthless..."

Jacob knew everything they said must be true. He just didn't know what to do about it. If only he could figure out a way to please them. But everything he did was wrong. What was he going to do? How was he going to survive?

It was during this time that limbo, which psychologists later described as major depression, became an important part of the fifteen-year-old's life. Jacob describes limbo as "unconscious consciousness. It is also an emotion, maybe depression, but whatever it is, it's very addictive, like being on drugs."

In this condition, hate, love, anger—all the normal emotions—ceased to exist, or at least faded until they were manageable. As did Jacob's fear of rejection and having people disappointed in him, which along with worry, were the worst feelings imaginable.

Throughout 1992 Jacob had periodically experienced limbo, but as fall edged toward winter, he spent more time there. His world became distorted. It seemed to be slowing down. He even talked and moved more slowly. Sometimes

10

he couldn't struggle out of his torpor when he was with his parents and they noticed his peculiar behavior. Instead of questioning him, they belittled him.

"You have a tough guy attitude. When're you gonna straighten up?"

Which was the way it always was. If he was acting good or bad or neutral or if he was in the throes of a nervous breakdown, Kermode and Pamela attributed it to his attitude.

So long as Jacob had the physical outlet of football, he managed to cope. Unfortunately, football ended the last week of October. After that Jacob's life didn't just spiral downward. It crashed.

Jacob's days consisted of school, homework, cleaning, and fighting with his parents—sometimes it seemed until the very walls shook. Jacob became a prisoner in his own house. Kermode and Pamela's domain was the middle floor, primarily the kitchen, which provided a perfect view of the steps and Jacob's room. During weekdays he wasn't allowed downstairs. Kermode and Pamela wanted him upstairs so they could keep an eye on him. Should Jacob venture onto the main level, they said, "What're you doing down here?"

If Jacob needed to go to the bathroom, which was located in the hall, he had to sneak out. He'd inch open the door and dart across the corridor, looking toward the kitchen as he did so. When Pamela caught him, she hollered, "You're stalling. Get back to your homework."

Monday through Friday was totally devoted to school. Saturday was generally relegated to housework. Sometimes Pam donned her "Bitch Outfit," meaning sweats, and disinfected the refrigerator or did other deep cleaning, while Jacob scoured counters, dusted, washed lamp shades and vacuumed floors. On his hands and knees he scrubbed the sunroom, stairs, entryway, bathrooms, kitchen and hardwood floors. Then he vacuumed everything again. If Pamela spotted a rock on the floor or if anything met with her disapproval, he had to repeat the entire process. All the while, Kermode sat at the kitchen table smoking cigarettes or he and Pam cheered the San Francisco 49'ers on TV.

Jacob was granted minimum communication with the outside world. His real dad, Frank Ind,(*) who lived in Illinois, called once a week. His parents allowed them a twenty minute conversation, though they confined his weekday conversations with classmates to five minutes.

"You've got homework to do," they'd say, if anybody was foolhardy enough to call. "The phone's not a social thing. It's a tool."

Jacob could only contact friends long enough to say, "Let's get together," as though he were conducting business. While Kermode and Pam were at work, however, he was able to talk until he heard the Dodge Ram coming up the drive.

"Gotta go now," he said, slamming down the receiver. Awaiting his parents' arrival, Jacob's heart raced, his face flushed and his skin turned clammy

in all the classic symptoms of a panic attack. Even though he put the phone back in place and busied himself with some acceptable activity, he always figured they'd somehow "know" he was being disobedient.

Jacob was astute enough to understand that his parents didn't really care so much about the telephone. They were simply reminding him who was in command. Jacob also grasped the fact that other battles, separate from his, were being waged in the Jordan household. Increasingly, he sensed a silent power struggle raging between his parents. Pamela wanted total control; Kermode refused to relinquish it. The division of power in the Jordan marriage had always been as rigid as everything else involving Kermode and Pamela. Pam dictated things on the outside, like grocery shopping and social functions. Kermode dictated everything inside the home. During the last few months, someone appeared to be trying to change the rules.

Jacob had no idea what was happening between his parents. All he knew was that their conflict occasionally worked in his favor. If he wanted to go for a hike or visit his friend, Jeremy Watson(*), Kermode would ask, "Are you done with your homework?"

"More or less."

"No, he's not finished with his homework," Pam said. "He needs to review."

Regardless, Kermode occasionally allowed Jacob to go. Pam's features would sharpen, but she didn't directly dispute her husband. Instead she said, "Be back by four." Since it would already be noon that stipulation made any outing virtually impossible. Kermode might overrule her, or simply return to his smoking. When that happened, Jacob returned to his room.

◊ ◊ ◊

As October slipped into November, tensions escalated even further. No doubt about it, Kermode's job was in serious jeopardy.[3] While angry and fearful, he couldn't use alcohol to blunt his emotions the way he had in the past. So he used Jacob.

Pam feared an old ulcer had returned. Too much stress caused it to act up, so she left more of the "discipline" to her husband.

When the fights between Kermode and Jacob became too raucous, she even warned, "Keep it down."

Frustrated, Kermode gave his stepson a dirty look. Jacob hurriedly

---

[3] Neither Ind brother knew until the trial that Kermode had already been terminated from Digital.

12

withdrew to the relative safety of his bedroom. Arguments became hit and run maneuvers—hurl insults and retreat. Not that Pamela totally relinquished the war zone. In fact, she discovered a new method of corporal punishment. Rather than whack Jacob with her hand, which hurt HER, she began whacking him with her shoe. If he was beyond her reach, she threw it at him.

Limbo became Jacob's constant companion. Of course, he had no idea why he was so depressed. He was dumping memories from his mind as quickly as they occurred. Jacob was an expert at not remembering. That was how he'd survived the last eleven years. No, that was how he had survived his entire life.

Still, at school he remained capable of pretending that he was a boy like any other boy. While his grades had dropped and he was in danger of bringing home two C's, he still managed to laugh with his friends and argue good naturedly with his teachers and carve the name of his true love, Lila, on his desk. In fact, Jacob could do a nearly flawless imitation of all the other fifteen-year-olds who attended Woodland Park High School. But he wasn't like them and he brooded upon the horror of his existence to the exclusion of eating, sleeping, combing his hair, showering and doing his homework.[4]

Yet, while Jacob's mind twisted and turned endlessly, he could think of no escape. He mistrusted grownups, anyone in a position of authority, and though he'd hinted about the abuse he didn't dare elaborate to teachers or counselors. His parents had always said, "No one will believe you."

Besides, he didn't think he had anything much to complain about. Jacob defined physical abuse as breaking someone's jaw or locking them in a closet or throwing them through the wall, so being hit with a belt, a shoe or a hand didn't seem like any big deal. Corporal punishment wasn't necessarily a bad thing, he rationalized. It just depended on how it was administered. And what was so horrible about name calling? The authorities would ridicule him and tell Kermode and Pamela, making his life that much worse.

Only as Thanksgiving neared, Jacob wasn't sure how it could get much worse than it already was.

---

4 Jacob indignantly insists he showered nightly. He just didn't use deodorant. Everyone else disagrees.

There is no old age for a man's anger.
Only death.

~Sophocles
Oedipus at Colunus

Chapter 3

Jacob confessed to schoolmates that he was miserable. He didn't say much about what was literally happening in his household. A lifetime of training held him back. Instead he spoke in code. "I really hate my parents," he told teachers and fellow students. "I wish they were dead."

If anybody bothered to probe, Jacob said Kermode and Pam were mean. Beyond that, he largely kept silent.

"Can I come live with you?" He asked his two closest friends, David Mabie and Armando Lee.

But even as the three teenagers discussed the possibility, Jacob understood any respite would be temporary. Kermode and Pamela would just yank him back. What about Department of Social Services? They were supposedly there to help abused kids. Weekly, workers from DSS, the high school and the Woodland Park Police Department met to discuss problem students and situations. Why not go to them?

Jacob knew better. The police department had been to the Jordan household several times over the years. According to them, everything was perfectly okay.[5] And Teller County Department of Social Services was a joke. David Mabie, an abused child, had lots of experience with DSS.

"They don't help," David told him. "They only make things worse." In David's case, Social Services had actually returned him to his persecutors.

What else? Jacob considered running away, but where could he hide in a small town like Woodland Park? He fantasized living out in the forest, and only returning home when his parents were gone in order to pick up supplies. But it was the middle of the winter and his parents seemed as omniscient and omnipotent as God. They would know—and thwart—any move before he could execute it.

Nor was Charles a viable option. His brother lived in a cabin the size of the Jordan living room and was working full-time in addition to school, while subsisting on food stamps. According to Charles and others, Jacob had always

---

[5]Although the trial did not bring out extensive police involvement, a member of the Teller County Sheriff's Department informed me of the incidents. This person's position is that no abuse occurred since the investigations uncovered nothing. "If there had been abuse it would have been reported," I was told, in direct contradiction to the experience of many unfortunate children in our community.

turned to his older brother for help. According to Jacob, he'd NEVER done that. It didn't do any good. Whatever the truth, Jacob knew he had to figure something out on his own. Even if he decided to move in with Charles that would be the first place Kermode and Pamela looked.

Jacob felt so helpless. Increasingly, for him there seemed to be no way out. Ever.

◇ ◇ ◇

Thanksgiving was only days away. Then the Christmas season. Jacob dreaded this time of year. The holidays were inevitably marred by Kermode's drinking. And the contrast between the community's celebratory mood and his family's private behavior was more than he could bear.

When Jacob was alone, he began carrying a loaded shotgun, as much out of defiance, since guns were something he wasn't supposed to touch, as for protection. Plus, knowing that he could instantaneously end anybody's life, his own included, exhilarated him. Kermode's shotgun provided him with something he wasn't used to—a sense of power. As he held it, he fantasized being a soldier or cop, burglar or assassin.

By this time, a part of him had begun to realize a gun would be his instrument of rage.

Only Jacob's rage was still turned more inward than outward. Sure, he would like to see his parents dead, but that was more a fantasy like, "Someday I'd like to play pro-football," than a decision to be acted upon.

He remained paralyzed. And afraid. Increasingly, he felt as if he didn't really know anything until and unless his mother told him. He was never certain whether he might be breaking one of the rules Pamela had just made up or what the consequences might be. But something was starting to stir inside, a flicker of rebellion, the idea that something had to be done.

Occasionally, he even questioned his mother about a "rule" such as, "You can lock the bathroom door," vs. "Don't you dare lock the bathroom door."

"Why can't I lock the door? I like my privacy."

"What're you trying to hide?" She'd say in her "I-utterly-despise-you" voice.

"But you told me last week I could lock it."

"It's not like I haven't seen it all before. Just leave the goddamned door unlocked and quit arguing."

"This makes no sense," he cried, in desperation. "There's no logic to it."

"It's totally logical because I say it is."

Pamela's eyes burned with hatred whenever Jacob was "disciplined" or during their "discussions." He dreaded those looks, not because he loved his mother because by this time he swore he didn't. But he so much wanted her to love him, even when he knew she never had. Never would.

15

It was sometime around Thanksgiving, Jacob can't remember an exact date, when a shift in his thinking occurred. Instead of hoping for Divine Providence to intervene on his behalf, or deciding to implement his plan to kill himself, Jacob reached a monumental decision. He listed all the reasons his life was so terrible, why suicide seemed the only solution. When he pondered the list, he discovered everything on it had to do with his parents. Then the revelation came. Instead of killing myself, he thought, why not kill Mom and Kermode?

Yes!

It wasn't as if he hadn't contemplated such a thing before. His friend, David Mabie, had talked about eliminating them for years. Though David was nearly two years older than Jacob, he was also a freshman. Tall, blond, Aryan handsome with blue eyes that seemed to stare right through people, David came from an environment similar to Jacob's, only without the money. Three years previously David had first suggested that Jacob's parents should die. Over the years he'd periodically brought up the subject. Jacob didn't know what to think of David and his B.S. talk. In the beginning Jacob didn't hate his parents. Well, maybe he did, but not to the extent of killing them. Still, he let David plan the murders and sometimes even contributed ideas. Talking about it made Jacob feel better, as if he really had a way out. But eventually, the subject was dropped and Jacob shoved the conversations in the back of his mind.

That last summer, the summer of 1992, Jacob and David had burgled a house where David had previously seen a .22 caliber pistol. David hid the pistol in the woods near his family's trailers.

David suggested, "We should use this to kill your parents."

At that time, Jacob was more obsessed with killing himself. He thought constantly about burying a bullet in his brain. He began playing Russian Roulette with Kermode's .357, sometimes with two bullets in the chamber. When he pulled the trigger and heard the click he felt an incredible rush. Suicide seemed much easier, more logical than coping with Kermode and Pamela.

Until now.

Jacob approached David when they were walking back from lunch at Loaf and Jug. Usually he and a couple of friends left WPHS's campus for one of several nearby fast food places. In addition to lunch they sometimes took a few hits off a pipe, generally provided by David.

Jacob took his friend aside and asked, "Would you kill my parents?"

David got real excited. Days later, he returned the stolen .22, which he had cleaned and polished. He hid the gun inside his brightly striped sweatshirt and presented it to Jacob at school. Jacob put the .22 in the bottom of his backpack. Knowing he carried a gun made him feel good, like "Billy Bad Ass."

After that, David and Jacob discussed their plan whenever possible over the phone, using code words like "trumpet." For Jacob, talking reassured him

that life would soon get better. But could he ever actually transform all this talk into reality?

The incident with the microwave cart provided the answer.

◊ ◊ ◊

Jacob can't remember exactly when the "microwave cart incident" occurred. He knows his parents were watching the 49'ers in the family room. The family room was huge, with a tiled wet bar and hardwood floors that Jacob had cleaned more times than he could count. It opened onto the sunroom with the weight lifting bench where Kermode had once tried to kill Charles and the hot tub that nobody ever used. On this particular Sunday Kermode and Pamela were relaxing in their matching pair of blue recliner rockers.

Jacob had been doing his homework, but decided to take a break.

"Quit stalling," Pam said when he came downstairs. "Go back to your room and don't come out until you're finished."

Jacob countered with something, he doesn't remember what. Then he turned his back on his parents and headed for the steps leading to the main level.

He heard Pam say, "Don't give me dirty looks," but he didn't hear Kermode get out of his recliner. Nor did he hear his stepfather come up behind him "like a coward." Kermode pushed him. Jacob slammed against a nearby microwave cart. His thigh hit a corner, smashing to the bone.

"Don't you ever talk to your mom like that!" Kermode screamed, spraying spittle on Jacob's face.

As Jacob walked up the stairs, he whispered through tears, "Okay, Motherfucker. I was going to spare you, but no. Fuck that. You're dead, Motherfucker."

◊ ◊ ◊

Charles returned home for Thanksgiving dinner. Although he'd only been gone three months, the eighteen-year-old noticed a definite change in the atmosphere, "an electric charge in the air." It was almost as if all the players in the drama were positioning themselves for the tragedy that was to come, maneuvering themselves into their parts, readying for the moment when Death, in the form of Jacob's hired executioner, would race across the frozen earth to claim them.

Those last weeks Kermode especially must have wondered whether his house was a refuge or a prison. He'd tried so hard to make it his monument, his symbol to the world and to himself that he was a success. How hollow that all seemed, now that he was about to be laid off and his entire future was in jeopardy. And not only because of Digital. Because of Charles. And Jacob? Did

17

Kermode, who had spent so much time trying to mold his youngest stepson, sense the change? Had Kermode begun to realize that, while 120 Ridge Drive might be his castle, the insurrection was in danger of starting from inside the castle walls?

Or did he perceive that the enemy was already within, plotting the overthrow of the king and queen?

All other ways are closed to you
Except the way already chosen

~T.S. Eliot
Murder in the Cathedral

Chapter 4

Mid-December 1992

Sometime in early December, Jacob found his executioner. He decided he didn't want his friend, David Mabie, to do the deed. Instead, he approached Gabrial "Major" Adams, a seventeen-year-old martial arts expert. Although small and slight, Gabrial enjoyed something of a reputation. Rumor had it he was into Satan worship, though his big love was the military. He believed himself to be a reincarnated Vietnam War vet and had a small "army" of followers, with whom he played "war games." Major even claimed he knew how to levitate, ninja-style.

Jacob first approached Major on the school bus. He saw the Senior, who often wore a dark trenchcoat and either black or camouflage garb, flipping through a ninja catalog.

Jacob sat down next to Gabrial. He asked, "Do you kill people for money?"

"Depends. Who?"

"My parents."

"I'll come home with you after school and we'll talk."

With very little problem, the deal was struck. Two thousand dollars for two dead bodies. Jacob's instructions were simple. "I don't care what you do, as long as it's quick and painless."

Gabrial came up with a couple of different plans. First, he decided that Kermode and Pamela should be poisoned.

"The easiest way to do that is, we'll contaminate every jar of their favorite brand of coffee at City Market. Other people will buy the coffee besides your parents, but when people start dropping dead, that'll be good cuz it'll deflect attention from the real targets."

Jacob wasn't sure whether this was a viable plan, but something had to be done. He couldn't eat, he couldn't sleep, his mind wouldn't shut off. For hours on end, he went over the misery of his life, and how it had to stop. He was too depressed, his thinking too convoluted, to be able to think past the fact that his parents had to die. So, as outlandish as Major's plan might have seemed under other circumstances, Jacob went along with it.

Plan number one was discarded when a new shipment of coffee with different expiration dates arrived at City Market.

"The plan's too dangerous now," Gabrial said.

19

Move along to plan number two. A bomb.

"Why don't we blow up your parents' car?" Major suggested. "I'm a bomb expert."

Ultimately, nothing came of that idea either. Then Major decided to snap Pamela and Kermode's necks. Jacob wasn't sure how a 5'5" kid was going to break the neck of a 6'2" man. Most likely Kermode would shake him off the way a German Shepherd would a Chihuahua, especially since both Jacob's parents were unusually strong. But Major, martial expert that he was, insisted.

One Sunday Major spent a couple of hours at the Jordan residence. He decided to come up behind Kermode and then Pam, taking them by surprise. That didn't work out because the pair never separated long enough to allow him to put his idea into action.

Third plan: Chop off their heads. One swift slice for each. Jacob expressed skepticism.

"I saw a cop show where something similar was tried and the blade got stuck in the bone. I sure don't want that to happen."

"I can do it," Major said. "And it'll be quick and painless, just like you said."

That weekend when Jacob was in his bedroom, his parents called up the stairs, "You have a visitor."

The next thing he knew Gabrial was inside, holding a rusty machete in his hands.

Appalled, Jacob asked, "What're you doing with that?"

"I'm going to kill them right now."

"No way! Not in broad daylight. Get that outta here."

Besides, about the only thing that old machete could do was give them lockjaw. Or Kermode would wrest it away from Major and jam it down his throat. Then he'd come after Jacob and that'd be the end, for sure.

The machete incident should have been a pretty strong indication that Major didn't know what he was doing and that Jacob had better call the whole thing off. But he couldn't survive if his parents did, so he continued pressing Gabrial.

On Friday, December 11, Jacob thought they'd cemented their scheme. Gabrial had said he would do the deed that weekend, but Jacob said, "Absolutely not. My parents' schedules are too erratic."

They had agreed that Major would kill Kermode and Pamela on a weekday, though Gabrial said he'd have to talk to his "mentor" first, lest the killings somehow "unbalance the universe." Jacob didn't know what the hell Major was talking about. He babbled on about the "negative metaphysical," about how it was impossible to go back in time, but that it was possible to SEE back in time. The vibes had to be right and the executions couldn't proceed until Gabrial had received some sort of package from this mysterious guru. But he assured Jacob all that had been taken care of.

December 15 arrived. Both boys concurred, "Tonight will be the night." Jacob ingested a bunch of pills out of the main medicine cabinet in order to help him sleep so that when he awakened, the act would just somehow have happened without having anything to do with him. Kermode and Pamela would simply be gone. No pain. No mess.

The following morning, after struggling awake from what could most accurately be described as a blackout, he listened for the sound of his parents' breathing. Despite the fact that they were two doors away, Jacob could still hear them. The knowledge that his parents remained alive filled him with despair.

Jacob repeated the scenario the night of December 16th. Pills, blacking out, awakening to find that nothing had changed. That morning, after going to school, he waited in the hallway before first hour for Major.

Christmas break would occur in two days, and the mood at Woodland Park High School was festive. Santa and his reindeer, courtesy of Mr. Makris's shop class, readied to take off from the roof of the main building. Holiday signs and decorations cluttered the walls. Even the hall lights had been covered with construction paper containing Christmas cut outs, though the result, far from merry, had made the area unusually gloomy.

As Jacob searched for Gabrial among the skaters and jocks, druggies, cowboys and preppies, David Mabie walked over.

"Did Major come last night?" David asked.

"No."

David, who still insisted that he wanted to execute Kermode and Pamela, said, "Just get the gun back, and I'll do it. If he doesn't come tonight, get the gun back."

Once David left, Jacob continued searching for Gabrial. He finally spotted his would-be partner, dressed in his usual camouflage outfit.

After motioning him over, Jacob said, "We need to talk." On the way to the bus stop, he had spotted Major's footprints in the snow outside his house. Gabrial was famous for stalking people. Had this just been another of his bizarre military games? Why hadn't Major done what he promised?

Jacob asked, "Why didn't you come last night?"

"I did. Kermode stayed up all night on Monday and last night there were cops all over the place. I'll come tonight."

The first bell rang. As Jacob headed toward Honors English he felt total hopelessness. He knew that Major was lying, that he wasn't going to come. Nobody was going to. Now, what was he going to do?

◇ ◇ ◇

Jacob drifted through Honors English and gym. He recalled nothing about those classes beyond the fact that he complained to friends about Counselor Greathouse wanting to send him to Cedar Springs, a treatment facility for juveniles. The previous week Charles had made him sit down with David

21

Greathouse, their high school counselor, for a ninety minute conference about what had been happening in the Jordan household.

"Jake, answer me one question," Charles had said, "Have you ever wanted to hurt Kermode and Mom?

"Yes," Jacob had replied, but realizing his admission, he quickly added, "Not any more."[6]

Greathouse had mentioned Cedar Springs as a possible solution, but Jacob feared going to a juvenile home or mental institution even more than he feared staying with his parents. At least he knew what to expect in his present world. Everyone he knew who'd been "in the system" agreed state-run facilities were as dangerous and as abusive as his home environment.

Throughout that last day of Kermode and Pamela's life, Jacob went through the motions. He remembered very little about his classes or what was happening around him. Increasingly, time seemed to be playing tricks on him. Sometimes hours passed like minutes and minutes lasted an eternity. Often Jacob blacked out and awoke having no idea what had happened or where he was. Hard enough to keep it together at school, with others giving him strange looks or asking where his head was at. At home, Kermode and Pamela accused him of being spacy, which was a "tough guy attitude."

"You haven't done your homework yet," they'd charge.

No longer capable of pretense, Jacob just gave them an empty look, which caused more screaming. He couldn't even control his posture around them anymore. Away from 120 Ridge, Jacob liked to slouch, but something was happening inside when he couldn't remember how, when, or where he was supposed to act a certain way. "Sit up!" they'd snarl, and fear coiled around Jacob's heart because he was slipping up and all the boundaries were blurring...

Drafting was third hour. His teacher, Victor Smith, a tall, strongly-built football coach in his forties, knew Jacob's older brother Charles better than he knew Jacob.

Smith considered Charlie to be a responsible, personable young man who helped out the less talented kids in the class. Smith wasn't sure what to think of Jacob, who he'd only known since the beginning of the school year. Sometimes Smith regarded Jacob as the most obnoxious kid he'd ever been around, and sometimes he could be extremely insightful and caring. Jacob was just so erratic. He could be a model student or totally disruptive. Smith's class was self-paced, allowing a fair amount of freedom. He allowed students to communicate, but Jacob went to extremes. Often he talked just to be talking. When Smith ordered him to stop, he would look at him and say, "Okay, I'll knock it off. I won't talk anymore. I'll just sit here and be really quiet." That might last and it might not.

---

[6] Charles remembers this as, "Do you ever want to hurt Mom?" "Sometimes."

Yet, on Smith's birthday, Jacob said, "For your birthday present I'm not going to say a word." And he didn't.

That day, December 16, Smith had another altercation with the fifteen-year-old. Smith was helping a student in an area separate from the classroom.

Before departing, he instructed one of his pupils, Ronnie (*), "Write down the names of anyone who's disruptive."

Ronnie took his admonishment seriously. When Jacob leaned back in his chair, Ronnie said, "All right. That'll be ten pushups."

Jacob laughed. "No way."

A little later Jacob threw a paper airplane in the trash can. Ronnie wrote him up.

Upon returning, Smith received an account of Jacob's transgressions. Smith warned Jacob, who was talking incessantly, to behave but Jacob ignored him. There seemed to be "no calming him."

Finally, the exasperated teacher said, "This is totally, one hundred percent unacceptable. I want to know what the hell the problem is."

He ordered Jacob into his office. During the past few weeks Smith had noticed a definite deterioration in Jacob's physical condition. He was gaunt and disheveled. Sometimes when sitting at the drafting table, he suddenly jerked, as if zapped by an electric shock. Smith wondered whether Jacob might be on drugs. Several times he'd noticed the fifteen-year-old's face flush or turn pale and glossy and sweat dripped from his face.[7]

Whatever was going on in Jacob's head, Smith was certain of one thing. He'd had enough.

Realizing he'd misjudged his drafting teacher, Jacob was extremely nervous. What if Smith called his parents? Jacob was so out of touch with reality he hadn't even correctly gauged the extent of Smith's displeasure. He'd just been agitating him for something to do and he, who was always so watchful and wary, had misread the resultant signs.

Smith said, "Is your mom at work? This has been going on more than it should. You're just not on task the way you normally are."

Jacob was horrified when Smith picked up the receiver. If Kermode and Pamela were contacted, their retribution would be a million times worse than

---

[7] Smith misinterpreted what psychologists would later label panic attacks as a reaction to drugs. During these attacks Jacob would turn alternately hot and cold. He timed his pulse at between 170-180 beats a minute. The attacks had been commonplace since he'd repeated eighth grade and nearly constant over the last several weeks. Disconnected from his emotions, Jacob didn't feel conscious fear. He felt something in the depths of his mind, but simply labeled the experience a "rush" and endured it as best he could.

any punishment the school meted out.

"Please don't call my mom," he begged.

Though sympathetic, Smith insisted. Jacob was obviously distraught but Smith felt he was over-reacting. Smith knew and liked Kermode and Pamela. Kermode was very quiet, the kind of person you'd never notice in a crowd. Smith had been impressed when, during Charles's Sophomore year, Kermode had pulled him aside after a banquet and expressed his appreciation for the time Smith had spent with Charles.

Smith did realize that there were problems in the Jordan household. As a coach, he often received the confidences of players, and Charles complained about Kermode's drinking and incessant disapproval. He'd even charged that he and Jacob were mentally abused. But the way Smith saw it Kermode and Pam simply wanted their sons to be super human beings. The Jordans were affluent-type people and they expected their children to succeed. What was wrong with that? If the Jordans were strict, well, parents today were too easy on their kids.

Smith did remember one disturbing incident involving Kermode. This is part of what was later referred to as the Lofthouse Incident.

"That summer Charlie had gotten his ear pierced. Kermode had driven over to the high school to pick up Jacob after football. Upon spotting Charlie's earring, he'd humiliated him in front of his friends and forced him to remove it. He also refused to give Charlie a ride home, so I picked him up. Charles basically poured out his heart, telling me how miserable he was and how mean his parents were."

Smith had been concerned enough to contact Pamela, who was always reasonable. She explained, "Kermode and I talked to Charlie about getting his ear pierced and the problem is not the earring so much as the fact that Charlie is not being open and honest with us. Kermode and I are very discouraged about that."

During other phone calls, Smith had also expressed concern over the way Pam and Kermode constantly took away Charles's driving privileges. Pamela always promised that they would discuss and possibly re-evaluate the situation.

Smith ended each conversation feeling that Pam was really listening to him, that when making decisions about her boys she, unlike many parents, actually considered his advice. And her thoughtful, considered explanations further underscored Smith's belief that the Jordans were a caring family. Charles might feel persecuted, but Smith concluded he was feeling sorry for himself.

Today when Smith called Pamela wasn't in her office at Care & Share. Jacob was granted a temporary reprieve. Smith felt sorry for the poor kid, who was obviously "on pins and needles." He tried to make Jacob feel better by complimenting him on his intelligence, forensics ability and drafting skills, which were good enough to take him to the college level or even beyond.

Jacob wasn't used to praise. He could hear a thousand curses without flinching, but when someone was kind, he became emotional. Tears came to his

24

eyes and he put his head down.

Smith was touched by Jacob's show of vulnerability. He couldn't renege on his promise to call, but he could soften the blow.

"When I talk to your mom, I'll tell her that I've just been so harsh on you, that she needs to be gentler. Do you think that it would help if I talk to Kermode and tell him that we've resolved this and you see your errors?"

Jacob shook his head. "No, that won't do any good at all."

Near the end of class Smith finally made contact. After explaining the situation, Pam responded, "We're having so much trouble with Jacob. We're at such odds with each other. We just can't bridge that communication gap."

She sounded concerned and reasonable, but remembering Jacob's fear, Smith added, "I've really reamed him out. He just needs some support from you. He needs you guys to be behind him a little bit. It's taken care of. I see no problems at all. If you want to come in, you and Jacob, we can sit down and talk about some things, but at this point I think he feels a lot better."

Pam thanked him and hung up. As always she was sweet as syrup, though in reality she disliked Smith, his teaching methods and the way he meddled where he didn't belong. She was especially furious at her son, whose bad attitude had once again caused attention to be focused on their private lives. Damn Jacob! They were having a problem bridging the communication gap, all right. And Pamela Jean Jordan would see to it that she would take care of this particular communication gap the minute she and Kermode got home.

Death has a hundred hands
and walks by a thousand ways
He may come in the sight of all
he may pass unseen, unheard.
Come whispering through the ear
or a sudden shock on the skull.

~ T.S.Eliot
Murder in the Cathedral

Chapter 5

December 16-17, 1992

Jacob dreaded the sound of the garage door opening. He knew what was going to happen the moment Kermode and Pamela arrived from work. And it did. His mother hurried up the basement stairs primed for action.

This fight followed the usual pattern, starting out mellow with cruel tones.

"I got a call from Mr. Smith today. What did we tell you about getting calls? HUH?"

As Pam continued, her anger grew. Soon, her censure spread from Jacob to Smith, which was a relief. Hoping to keep her focused on the drafting teacher rather than him, Jacob added his own condemnations.

But Pamela wasn't long diverted. All too soon she returned to Jacob's shortcomings. She was obsessed with seeing that her boys got the education she felt she lacked, and Jacob damn sure better quit crossing her. Eventually, Kermode joined in. This too followed a familiar pattern. Pamela usually started the fights, at least around school issues. When Kermode took over, the arguments really escalated.

Jacob had heard similar lectures thousands of times so he largely blanked his parents out. He was only really afraid when Pam hollered directly in his face. Then he cringed, waiting for the expected blow.

There are two different versions of what happened next. Jacob, who tends to minimize his parents' cruelties with the passage of time, maintains his parents yelled at him for awhile, and then it was over. Immediately after the murders, he said they beat him that night.

In Jacob's first version, they used their favorite weapon, "Billy Belt," a leather belt with an Aztec buckle left over from Kermode's hippie days. Despite the fact—or maybe because of it—that Billy Belt was used to inflict pain, Jacob usually wore it to school.

Jacob originally said his mother administered the corporal punishment that last evening. Pamela's beatings generally hurt worse than Kermode's because her aim was so bad. Up until the time he was thirteen, his parents made him strip. Kermode usually hit Jacob on his legs and backside so that the marks

26

wouldn't show, but Pamela hit him on his tailbone and upper torso. Jacob didn't think his mother really meant to hit him there. He just figured her aim was bad.

Following either his parents' tongue lashing or their beating, Jacob ate his final supper—one barbecued pork rib. Instead of dining at the kitchen table, he took his plate into his bedroom. In the past his parents would never have allowed him to eat alone, but since Thanksgiving he had virtually holed up in his room and they'd barely commented on his absence.

Rather than eat, Jacob generally stuffed his meal in the bottom of his trash or flushed it down the toilet. Once Pamela had noticed the food and questioned him, but he'd given some lame answer that she hadn't pursued. Pam couldn't have helped but notice that Jacob had lost nearly twenty pounds in the past month, especially when Charles called to question her. Pam shrugged off her oldest son's concern, saying, "He's just going through a phase."

Jacob gave his leftover ribs to his cat, Gungha, who generally followed him around like a dog. Then he returned to the kitchen area to say good night. Despite the escalating tensions, there were times during those final days when he felt nostalgic toward his parents. Each time they three were together, he thought, This will be the last meal I eat with them. Or, This will be the last time I hear their voices; this will be the last time I'll see them watch TV. This is the last time I'll hear my mom laugh, the last time she'll bitch at me. This is the last thing she'll ever cook. He would think, Go ahead, enjoy your last meal.

On one of those last three nights, Jacob can't remember which, he even kissed his parents both good night. He wanted to do that because they were going to die. He had never gotten to say good-bye to the dogs and cats in his life who died, so he wanted to say goodbye to his parents. He kissed each one on the lips, just the way they had made him do thousands of times, and said, "I love you."

And Jacob figured he probably did love them. He loved Kermode because his stepfather could be kind, though he loved who his Mother "could potentially be more," as he later phrased it. Jacob often thought, If I could be a son Mom might be lovable. Once again, the fault was his, not his mother's.

It was so hard to explain, this business of love. Yeah, Jacob would have to say he definitely DID love his parents—if love was Kermode and Pamela's definition, a feeling mixed with rage and pain and hatred and all sorts of black things. Because Kermode and Pamela always told him and Charles they loved them, so love was combined with beatings, tongue lashings, emotional humiliations and things so twisted that Jacob tried not to remember them. But they clutched his soul like barnacles clutch the hull of a ship...

Jacob withdrew to his bedroom, his favorite place. With the door closed he felt warm, safe and isolated, as if nothing existed beyond the oasis of those four walls. That wasn't exactly true because twice, as punishment, Pamela had removed his door from its hinges, allowing Jacob absolutely no privacy. Trying to shield himself from his parents' prying eyes he'd dressed in the closet, but

27

often when he looked up, one or both of them would be watching from the hallway.

And once Pamela had eradicated everything of a personal nature from his room except for his dresser and bed. It was that attitude of Jacob's again. She'd kept his tapes, stereo, and personal effects locked away for nearly a year.

Kermode and Pamela also had the unsettling habit of flinging open the door for no reason, as if expecting to find him doing God knows what. In addition, his mother periodically conducted raids in which she threw away anything that Jacob had collected. Pamela accused her son of being a pack rat, as if that were some character flaw that must be corrected. She rummaged through his dresser drawers, the drawers beneath his bed and in the bowls atop his stereo table searching for offending bones, buttons, shells, rocks or coins.

"Legally these things belong to me," she'd say, while confiscating them.

Jacob always cried because the only things he had were the things in his room, but it made no difference. She still threw them away.

Recently Jacob had taped three Iron Maiden posters on his bedroom wall. Pam hadn't said anything, which gave him a glimmer of hope. Maybe life was improving. Little gestures like the posters lifted his hopes. But a slap or a snarled command always yanked him back to reality—which was that truces were simply that—interludes in the Jordan War.

Jacob slipped the Doors Greatest Hits into his tape recorder and did his homework. Or tried to. His mind didn't want to focus. He fiddled with a wicked scab on his arm from where he had recently mutilated himself. Odd that pain sometimes felt good. Not when his parents hurt him, but when he could control it by inflicting it upon himself.

In geometry a few weeks previously he had seen a fellow student, Brad March, carve an X—for Malcolm X—in his hand. Fascinated, Jacob had carved a tattoo on his own arm. The moment he finished, he knew that it was the stupidest thing he'd ever done. If his parents found out he wouldn't be able to sit down for a week. Jacob had tried to get rid of the tattoo by scrubbing it with a fingernail brush. While it had hurt like a son of a gun, the feeling had also been cleansing--as if all his frustrations were coming out with the pain.

When Jacob finished, his arm had a nasty scab several inches across. By the time Pam finally noticed, he explained that he'd scraped it against a wall and she hadn't pressed him.

Sometime around nine o'clock Jacob heard his parents retreat to their master bedroom. He was always alert to the sound of them walking in the hallway, so for the first time that evening he relaxed. Every moment of every day he knew exactly where Pamela and Kermode were in the house and what they were doing.

Jacob decided that it was time to risk leaving his sanctuary. Two weeks previously, his dogs, Pike and Chaka, had escaped via a hole in their pen. Their absence still bothered him. Maybe now he could check to see whether they

might have miraculously returned.

Jacob peered down the hallway. His parents' door was never closed because of the cats, but neither adult was visible. He hurried downstairs to the main level, his bare feet whispering on the brindle-carpet. After opening the outside door, he gazed into the night, hoping for a glimpse of his wolf/German Shepherd or his Newfoundland/Great Dane. He assumed Pike and Chaka must have been picked up by one of the dogcatchers patrolling Sunnywood Manor, but when he'd called the shelter earlier in the day his pets hadn't been turned in. He missed them and worried about them. His dogs were kind to him and when he buried his face in their fur, he could sense how much they, at least, loved him.

As Jacob sneaked back to his room, he suddenly felt so overwhelmed. The blackness of the night was nothing compared to the blackness of his despair. He felt as if he were moving through a dream, as if his soul had shattered and been imperfectly glued back together. Gabrial Adams would never come. What was he going to do?

Jacob stripped down to his underwear and readied for bed. After scooping two pain killers off the top of his painted white dresser, he gulped them down. During his recent session with David Greathouse, the counselor's solution to Jacob's deteriorating condition had been to order the teen, "Get more sleep." Ever obedient to adults, Jacob had started taking cold medication, cough medicine, pills, anything that could knock him out.

Jacob's radio clock displayed the time, 9:30. Once beneath the covers, he pulled the blankets and flimsy plaid bedspread beneath his chin. He waited for the pills to kick in, hoping that the effect would be similar to previous nights, when he'd suddenly felt as if he'd just run into a brick wall and the next thing he knew, four hours had passed. He'd wake up, woozy and groggy, but there was no other way that Jacob was capable of resting. His mind wouldn't allow it. All night he'd lay awake, recalling the day's events, going over conversations, real and imagined, making up both parts, listening to music, thinking about his parents and how he just wanted it all to end.

Jacob generally took showers when the house was quiet, after Kermode and Pam were asleep, around two or three in the morning. As the water poured over him, he thought about his parents and panic gripped him, a panic he didn't understand, for it seemed to come up from nowhere. But it didn't. Because the wee hours of the morning was the time when Kermode prowled the house, when he roused Charles and ordered him to entertain him with readings from Socrates and Plato. Jacob and Charles could never really sleep because they never knew when they would be jolted awake by a drunken Kermode, or by their mother, ordering Jacob to remove a mouse that one of the cats had carried inside.

Always something.

And there were other times, buried deep in Jacob's psyche, when Kermode had ordered his tiny stepsons to clean themselves off in the shower because they were "so fucking dirty..."

As the pills took effect and Jacob drowsed, he had no idea that his hour was finally at hand.

Or that, even at this very moment, his executioner was slipping toward him through the darkness.

◊ ◊ ◊

The numbers on the clock in Gabrial "Major" Adams's bedroom inched toward midnight.[8] Gabrial rested, still as death. The minutes stacked up, his neighbors slept or settled in for Late Night with David Letterman, and Gabrial waited patiently for the proper time. Gabrial had trained his body to do his bidding, and, if he so chose, he could lay in perfect repose. Major was a practitioner of ninjitsu, the art of stealth, and ninjas had nearly superhuman control over their bodies. Once warlords had hired men like him to sneak into enemy territory and uncover the secrets of the opposition. Sometimes the warlords had even hired ninjas to assassinate their enemies. Did Gabrial think of Jacob Ind as a warlord? He had hired Major to assassinate his enemies, after all.

At the appointed time, Gabrial rose fluidly from the bed. Dressed in dark pants, dark turtleneck and vest, he blended perfectly with the blackness of his bedroom. After sticking the .22 caliber pistol Jacob had given him inside his waistband and Jacob's hunting knife, Mrs. Ed, inside the sheath attached to his belt, Major concealed two swords inside the long black trenchcoat that was an indispensable part of his attire.

Gabrial crossed to a large wooden-frame window. The lock had been broken several years—and many reconnaissance missions—ago. It was a simple matter to edge the window open ever so carefully on its tracks, to remove the screen, and lean it against the outside wall. Gabrial's bedroom was at ground level so he need only swing his legs over the ledge in order to step out into the night.

A crust of snow covered the ground. The temperature hovered around zero and Gabrial's breath puffed in front of him, but he didn't mind the cold. Cold,

---

[8] This portion is reconstructed from testimony at both trials regarding Gabrial's character, the route he is alleged to have taken to the Jordans, the murder scene and witness accounts. It is also based on private interviews. Gabrial's version of events, which varies from this account, is detailed in the chapter reconstructing his trial. Gabrial and his parents maintain he is innocent.

heat, rain, snow—they were just challenges to overcome. A ninja could roll into a ball, giving the appearance that he was a stone. He could cling lizard like to a wall for hours, or position himself so that he was indistinguishable from the limb of a tree. Ninjitsu could also be translated as the art of invisibility, and Gabrial had spent long hours of practice, blending in with the landscape.

Gabrial moved silently through the snow, which was inches deep in some places and leaf thin in others. The air is rare here at eight thousand feet, the blackness of the Colorado sky, alleviated only by an occasional ragged cloud, more intense. Columbine Village, where he lived, consisted of a cluster of duplexes surrounded by open fields and a handful of houses. Few lights were on, but Gabrial often staged maneuvers in the dark and Highway 67 ran only yards to his left. Occasionally a car passed, momentarily catching the ragged tops of fences or illuminating the individual needles on a Lodgepole pine. Clumps of buffalo grass stood out against the ghostly ground. The half moon cast just enough light to guide him along the path, but not enough for betrayal. The stars were as cold and white as the moon.

Gabrial passed darkened houses and pine trees with billowing shadows. Snow lay deep in the gullies. Ahead were the lights of Paint Pony, one of the oldest subdivisions surrounding Woodland Park. He had planned his route well, taking short cuts and poorly traveled roads to Sunnywood Manor, his destination.

The houses grew increasingly large and isolated. Rock formations and stands of aspen loomed around him. Gabrial reached Ridge Drive, a dirt road, and followed it. The Jordan residence was located at one of the highest points in the development. A light was on in the Smith house directly opposite and at the Sandusky house to the east, but the night remained absolutely still. While every house he'd passed claimed at least one dog, not one had marked his passing. Could that be interpreted as an omen proclaiming the rightness of his mission?

Reaching the Jordans' driveway, Gabrial crept up the steep rutted road toward the house. He swung around the garage area and up the railroad tie steps toward the front door. An airlock covered the original entrance. He eased open both doors and stood for a long moment inside, orienting himself. The foyer was large and spacious, with a hall tree directly to his left. He glimpsed his reflection in its mirror.

Removing his swords, Gabrial carefully placed them on the polished hardwood floor. After slipping off his shoes, he moved upstairs. A bleached cow's skull, the centerpiece of an objet d'art, gazed blindly at him. As he approached the master bedroom door, the whisper of his fatigues was the only sound. .22 in hand, Gabrial stepped inside.

A mirrored dresser was located to his left; a tall chest in the far corner. Directly to his right was the four poster bed. Gabrial pointed the barrel at Kermode, who was half-propped up against a mass of pillows. The plan was to

fire execution-style into Kermode's head. Then, before Pamela has a chance to fully awaken, do the same to her. Both deaths would be quick and painless, exactly the way Jacob had insisted.

Gabrial aimed for Kermode's temple.

Bam! Bam!

Two bullets slammed into Kermode's face. One penetrated above Kermode's right eye, the second below it. But instead of succumbing peacefully to death, Kermode began howling and cursing. He grabbed at the gun barrel, trying to wrestle it away from Gabrial. Pamela bolted upright with an earsplitting scream. Gabrial quickly pumped two more shots into Kermode, hitting him in the shoulder and right arm. Then he swung the .22 at Pamela. One bullet tore through her right deltoid, a second grazed her left shoulder. But Pamela continued yelling like a madwoman and Kermode continued fighting and Gabrial couldn't get away long enough to reload and finish the job. Only one thing left to do.

Gabrial reached for his knife.

Jacob woke out of a sound sleep. His digital clock read 1:10. What had awakened him? Then he heard it again—the pop of gunshots. How many he couldn't tell, but there were several. More than there should have been. The murders must be going down. Heart racing, he swung his legs over the side of the bed and held his head in his hands. Damn it, Major, hurry up! Something was horribly wrong. What was all that noise? Why was his mother screaming?

"Jacob! Jacob!" Pamela didn't sound frightened. She sounded royally pissed, as if he'd better get his butt in there right away.

Jacob stumbled into the hall. In the doorway to the master bedroom he saw Kermode grappling with Major. He had the seventeen-year-old in a combination headlock/choke hold. A music stand and planter crashed to the floor, followed by a ceramic figurine.

Seeing his stepson, Kermode yelled, "I've been shot!" He sounded the way he did when he was drunk. Blood trickled down his face from one of his wounds.

Gabrial's left arm, which held Mrs. Ed, was extended. Pam was squatting, trying to retrieve the knife. Jacob knew that, if his mother succeeded, Gabrial would be dead.

"Let go, Mom!"

Jacob tried to pry Pam's fingers away from Major's wrist, but she remained locked like a pit bull.

"Mom, Let me get it. Let go!"

"Get the swords!" Gabrial hollered.

Jacob had no idea what he was talking about. Maybe Major was referring

to Jacob's sword. He raced back to his room. Spotting a can of bear mace, which the family used to repel stray dogs, Jacob grabbed it and ran back to the master bedroom.

Kermode was still wrestling with Gabrial. Pamela just stood, not doing much of anything, though she could have fled out the sliding glass doors leading to the deck.

Jacob yelled, "I'm going to spray!"

"Okay!" Major buried his face in the carpet.

Despite Kermode's weakened condition, Jacob was most afraid of him, and maced him first. Kermode collapsed, coughing and choking, against the bathroom doorway. Jacob sprayed his mother, who had started toward the master bath where the family guns were kept.

After finishing the spray, Jacob ran into the bathroom, slammed the door and, since the lock was broken, leaned his entire weight against the wood. The mace burned his throat and lungs. Pamela kept yelling, "Jacob! Jacob!" Why wouldn't she shut up?

He opened the door. Gabrial had turned Mrs. Ed on Pam.

"Slit her throat!" Jacob yelled before slamming the door again. Soon the entire neighborhood would be racing up the driveway.

Somebody tried to enter the bathroom. Jacob pushed in the opposite direction. This had to stop. His gaze fixed upon the linen shelf directly in front of him. Kermode's .357 was kept there, nestled inside a red back pack. With shaking fingers, Jacob reached for the pistol and the bullets attached by a velcro pouch to the holster.

He slipped one bullet in the chamber and opened the door.

Kermode was still slumped against the cherrywood dresser. His legs, clad in blue sweats, sprawled in front of him.

Spotting Jacob, his mother yelled, "Shoot him! Shoot him," referring to Major.

Gabrial's eyes bugged. Was he thinking that Jacob would obey her? But if Jacob shot his partner and his parents survived, he would never get away from them. In a way he dreaded his mother more than Kermode. She would make him feel so guilty, even in prison which was where he was bound to end up. Or if he didn't go to jail he would be sent back into this hellhole where both of them did unspeakable things to him and he'd never ever be safe.

Jacob stood by the medicine cabinet in the bathroom and aimed at Kermode's head, no more than 1-1/2 feet away.

Bam!

The noise from the .357 reverberated like thunder. Kermode's head slammed away from the impact. Jacob's ears rang from the gunshot. He couldn't hear anything. Yes, he could. Pamela yelled, "Not him! Not him!" As if he had screwed up once again and he couldn't even get this right.

Jacob re-loaded the pistol. Pam was kneeling at Kermode's feet. Jacob

33

wasn't sure where Gabrial was, just someplace behind his mother. When Jacob pointed the barrel in her direction, she must have figured he was going to shoot Gabrial. Jacob squeezed the trigger. The bullet missed Pam, slamming into the wall behind. The smell of gunpowder stung his nostrils.

Time seemed to slow as Jacob fumbled for a third bullet. His hands trembled so badly that an eternity passed before he managed to slip another bullet into the chamber. He pointed the barrel at his mother.

Pamela's eyes widened. For the first time she really appeared to understand that Jacob hadn't made a mistake, that he had meant to kill Kermode and that he meant to kill her.

"Why?" she asked.

In concert with the bullet that smashed through his mother's brain, Jacob replied, "Because you were cruel to me."

The Lords of Hell are here,
They curl round you, lie at your feet,
swing and wing through the darkness

~T.S. Eliot
Murder in the Cathedral

Chapter 6

Pamela's head hit the floor like a cabbage. Jacob had tunnel vision, only seeing bits and pieces of everything--her hair, her legs, her feet, which twitched like a rabbit's. Jacob didn't like that at all. He'd killed animals before at his friend, Mondo's, ranch, and had witnessed their death throes. This was just the same, only it wasn't the same at all. This wasn't some ground squirrel, this was his mother...

Jacob turned his back on his parents. Echoes from the final gunshot still rang in his ears. "Do you think anybody heard?" he asked Major.

"Just the whole fucking neighborhood," Gabrial responded, moving toward the bodies.

Soon the Smiths and Bridgemans and Mitchells and the elderly couple that lived across the street would be knocking on the door. Then the police would arrive with their lights flashing, guns drawn, and Jacob didn't care. How had this happened? Nice and neat it was supposed to have been. Jacob would just wake up some morning and his parents would be gone. No blood, no screams, no pain.

"I didn't want to be involved," he said. "You fucked up."

"It was the gun. The gun."

"Why didn't you slice her throat?"

"It was the knife," Major said, referring to Mrs. Ed. "Leave it to you to give me a defective knife."

Jacob would hear his mother's screams forever.

Gabrial seemed to be searching for something but Jacob was suddenly anxious to flee the master bedroom, the bodies sprawled on the floor and his fellow executioner. If he looked around, he would see things he didn't want to see. Blood everywhere. On the walls and floor and furniture...

"Do you have any ammo for this?" asked Gabrial, holding up the murder weapon.

Jacob handed him the box of shells and walked out.

◊ ◊ ◊

Jacob sat on the edge of his bed. He felt sweaty all over, as if he'd just completed a five mile race. He stared into space. It had really happened. The house was finally his. He had his freedom. But it didn't feel like freedom. What

did it feel like?

Jacob lay down. His throat hurt from the mace and his hands were clammy. He heard the sound of running water from the master bath. Major must be washing off the blood. Silence. Jacob had no idea how much time passed or what had happened to Major. Nor did he care.

Jacob wanted to rest, to erase the last hour from his mind, but he didn't feel sleepy. What was he feeling? He couldn't say, which was hardly unusual. Jacob had long ago ceased being able to label his emotions. When he was little, Pamela had said, "Don't you dare get angry." "Toughen up." "Don't cry." When Jacob couldn't turn off his tears on cue, she slapped him and screamed, "Stop it!" Kermode chimed in, "No use crying over spilled milk." If Jacob couldn't respond to the wisdom of a saying he didn't understand, Kermode clarified his point with his fist. Sometimes they'd have to slap him several times before he managed to switch off his feelings—at least in their presence.

But Jacob's sadness had leaked out in other ways. He cried when Charles and stepbrother Cameron teased him about being "China Jacob" because the corners of his eyes slanted, especially when he smiled. He cried when they sang, "Flipper, the Hooker," because Flipper was his favorite show and he didn't want anyone making fun of his beloved dolphin. In fact, no matter how hard Jacob tried, he still found himself crying over a lot of inappropriate things. Maybe it was because he wasn't allowed to cry over things that really hurt. Well, he HAD cried when the sorrow welled up from the very core of his being and he couldn't control the pain, but those times had become increasingly infrequent. Sometimes after turning fourteen, Jacob had finally mastered the trick. No more tears.

Jacob heard Gabrial outside his room. He stood. His partner entered the bedroom and switched on the light. His eyes were bright, excited. What had he been doing in the master bedroom?

Gabrial crossed to Jacob's white dresser. "I think I may have lost a glove." He held up his covered hand. "When you go back in the room to discover the bodies be sure and get my glove before you call the cops. I locked the door. You'll have to kick it down."

He didn't seem nervous or upset, more like exhilarated.

"Better wipe that off," he said, pointing to a bloody fingerprint that he'd left on the dresser's surface.

Jacob complied, rubbing the blood onto his underpants. Major said something about meeting tomorrow in order to fashion an alibi. Then he stepped out into the hallway. Like the polite young man his parents had raised him to be, Jacob escorted Major to the door.

"I can't pay you the full two thousand dollars," Jacob said, watching him put on his boots. "I didn't want to be involved in it."

"I know. I'll settle for a thousand."

For the first time Jacob noticed that both the air lock and front doors were

wide open. How long had that been the case? What was wrong with Major? Jacob suddenly remembered his cats. What had happened to them? Had they wandered outside?

Gabrial picked up his samurai swords. So that's what he'd meant when he yelled for the swords. Major shrugged into his black overcoat, repositioned the weapons inside and readied to leave.

Jacob didn't further pursue tomorrow's meeting, though they'd have to come up with a hell of an alibi since Gabrial had fouled everything up so bad.

Jacob's partner faded quietly into the night. Now the fifteen-year-old had the house all to himself. He could do anything he wanted, but he didn't have any idea what he wanted to do. For the first several minutes he expected to be discovered. The Smiths were right across the road, the Sanduskys just up the street and there were houses in back. Sunnywood Manor was always so quiet. In the stillness screams, shouts and gunshots would carry a long way, wouldn't they? But incredible as it seemed, no one came knocking.

Jacob decided to play some thrash music. When discussing assassination plans with David or thinking about the murders, initially he'd played a lot of it, particularly D.R.I., Dirty Rotten Imbeciles. The thrash group's words, which emphasized death and violence, were kind of like a preparation, helping him bolster his courage. With David, he would think, Okay, I can go along with this. So many times he didn't know whether he'd have the strength to end their lives. He knew he had to, but sometimes he just couldn't face it. But as the lead singers yelled and the drums slammed and the guitars shrieked, Jacob's resolve hardened.

D.R.I. sang, "You seriously ask for my autograph. I can't help but laugh. Just leave me alone, Why don't you go home? Go die! GO DIE NOW!" The words didn't sound so terrific tonight. He put on Exodus. "We're going to take your life. Kick in your face and rape and murder your wife."

Jacob quickly clicked off the stereo. After picking up his guitar he strummed Claire de Lune and some blues-boogie style music. It didn't feel right. Nothing felt right. He put on a Doors tape that his friend Mondo had lent him. These past few weeks he'd been listening to a lot of Doors. Maybe he should turn up the volume full blast. Now nobody would scream, "Turn that off!" Or take his tapes away. But he didn't want the neighbors to hear and somehow the idea didn't give him any satisfaction.

Jacob returned his guitar to its case. The house seemed eerily quiet. It creaked and moaned the way it always did, and the electric furnace came on with a tick-tick-ticking whisper, but there were no human noises, or any of the feelings that always accompanied the presence of his parents. Kermode and Pamela need but step into a room and the atmosphere crackled with tension. Tonight it was almost benign. But his parents weren't really there. Technically they were, he guessed, but not in any dangerous way. He was finally safe from them if he didn't think about his mother with that strand of dark hair fanning

37

across her face and that river of blood leaking onto the floor like some ghastly nose bleed...

What to do? Jacob decided to take a shower in the downstairs bathroom. First, he walked around the house, turning on the light as he entered each room. Jacob had always been afraid of the dark. He wasn't sure why, only that he had to chase away the darkness in order to chase away his terror. He couldn't even put a label to his fear. He just felt like a mouse cowering in a corner. Even now that he was older, he still preferred leaving the lights on when he was writing, daydreaming or reading. Occasionally, when he'd be concentrating on something totally unrelated, the phrase, 'Fear of the dark is fear of the unknown,' would pop into his head. He could never figure out why.

Jacob didn't think it was really fear of the unknown. What was it then?

He finished his tour of the house. It was after two o'clock. From the sunroom windows Jacob could see the Smith's house, blazing with thousands of outdoor Christmas lights—colored ones, plain ones, winking ones and ones that looked like fireflies. The Smiths always made a big deal out of holidays. In addition to Christmas, Jacob watched the family gathering Easter eggs on Easter Sunday, and on the first day of every school year the parents took pictures of their children. Jacob didn't know how to feel about all that family togetherness. He sure didn't want his parents doing anything with *him*, but in a way he envied the Smiths. It would have been nice if the Jordan family could have enjoyed at least one event without fighting. Nice to have had parents who bought thoughtful presents and fussed over him and Charles and offered encouragement instead of abuse when they strung Christmas lights and didn't mind if the tree wasn't flawlessly decorated. Why couldn't something be done without criticism and complaint? Christmases with his real dad were a lot better. Frank didn't care if Jacob put two silver balls right next to each other and he gave Jacob fun presents like computer games.

Jacob did remember one Christmas when Kermode and Pamela had gone all out.The tree looked perfect and the presents looked perfect, at least according to the photos that Pamela had meticulously placed in the family album. There were pictures of the boys opening presents with wrapping paper and bows strewn all around, and of them clustered around Kermode as he strummed a guitar. But Christmas wasn't Christmas without alcohol. Jacob never knew when either parent's mood would turn ugly, shattering the festive atmosphere. Over the past several years his mother had decided that Christmas wasn't worth the bother unless company was expected. Only then would she and Kermode put on a huge phony display and pretend that they were indeed the All-American family.

That act was wearing thin. Last year, 1991, the Jordans had arranged a big get-together. Kermode and Pamela had purchased a grocery cart full of liquor which Kermode had largely drunk by himself and he and his eighteen-year-old natural son, Cameron, had gotten into a fistfight in front of the other relatives.

This season the decorations remained in the storage shed. Pamela's shopping had consisted of a couple of shirts and pairs of pants for Kermode and Charles. She'd also bought Charles a microwave. Charles always got the best presents.

Jacob decided that he would take a shower. Despite the fact that he was alone, he locked both bathroom doors. Afterward, he returned to his bedroom. He couldn't sleep. His room seemed lonely. Jacob figured he should feel safe, but instead, he felt...uneasy. His thoughts kept returning to that locked door behind which his dead parents were sprawled.

Jacob unplugged his clock radio and went downstairs. After retrieving a blanket from the bathroom closet, he made a bed for himself on the family room couch. The couch was contemporary in style, with a tan background and a splotchy pattern and individual cushions that made for a comfortable fit when he stretched out upon it.

In the far corner of the room was a wood-burning stove surrounded by a large moss rock hearth. Because electricity was so expensive, the stove was often used to warm the house, though not tonight. Still, Jacob's woolen blanket kept him warm. Off the family room was a fifth bedroom which Kermode had converted to his study. One of his stepfather's most prized possessions was a set of antique leather bound books dealing with Greek philosophy. Jacob had occasionally read from the books because he hoped to understand what Kermode found so fascinating about that ancient time period and to better argue a point during political discussions. Such things had been part of Kermode's molding process. Kermode had tried to inculcate his own ideas into Jacob's brain, thereby creating a miniature version of himself. His stepson: Revolutionary, Philosopher, Scientist, Genius. Kermode had molded Jacob after the fashion of Greek elders mentoring their students. Mentored him in ways that Jacob could only faintly remember, like the echo of a gunshot, the ghost of a sob...

Jacob lay in the darkness, staring up at the ceiling. His parents' bodies were above him, resting atop the plywood and carpeting. Jacob didn't like to think about that. He felt the same way as when he'd done something wrong and he knew he was in really big trouble. Only now the feeling was intensified a thousand times.

From out of the shadows, Hops, Jacob's favorite cat, appeared. She leapt upon his bare chest and he stroked her silky fur. Jacob particularly loved Hops because he'd watched her being born. Hops's mother had crawled up on Jacob's pillow and delivered her litter right in front of him. Hops purred and burrowed against him as if she knew that something was wrong. Gradually while comforting his pet, Jacob's own dread disappeared. He felt perfectly calm, at peace with himself. As he contemplated his life, he was surprised to realize that this was the best he'd ever felt. Finally, finally he was safe.

Once Hops left, so did Jacob's contentment. He retrieved an old Bible from the study and began looking up anything to do with murder. He didn't know much about the Bible but he hoped it would say something like, 'If you do it it's

39

all right.' It didn't. Instead it warned, 'If you do such and such it's just as bad as murder...' 'If your hand does something in sin, cut it off.'

And emphatically, 'Thou shalt not murder.'

Jacob didn't like that at all. There was no getting around it. He was in serious trouble.

How was he ever going to get out of this mess? He really only had one choice. Jacob began to pray.

"It's been a long time since I actually talked to You," he told God. "I fucked up."

Jacob prayed for an hour or two. He ended his prayer by promising God that he would see Him the next day.

Now that Jacob had made up his mind to commit suicide, he had to figure out the details. He probably should go to school. He would skip first hour so he could explain to his best friend Mondo what had happened. He would tell Mondo that he loved him like a brother. Then he'd go back home and write letters to his friends. He planned to give half of his pot to Lila and half to his friend Jeremy. Then he would call 911.

"I killed my parents and now I'm going to kill myself," He would say and hang up.

Immediately, Jacob would retrieve the twelve gauge shotgun from the closet, take it out on the deck, put it to his forehead and pull the trigger.

The prospect of dying didn't frighten him. For as long as he could remember Jacob had been consumed with thoughts of death. Not that he believed anything would happen. He just expected an explosion, dazzling lights. Annihilation.

Jacob finalized his suicide plans. Then he slept.

'Would you know my name, If I saw you in heaven? Would you feel the same, If I saw you in heaven?'

At 6:45 Jacob awakened to the sounds of Eric Clapton's, "Tears In Heaven." Of all the songs, Jacob thought. Either this is supreme irony or God has a sense of humor.

Sleep hadn't refreshed him. Even as he'd dozed, a part of him had remembered the bodies, the deed, the fact that in a few hours he would be seeing his parents. Only they wouldn't be meeting in heaven.

Jacob returned to his bedroom. His room looked uncharacteristically sloppy with its unmade bed and discarded clothes, but Jacob didn't bother to tidy up. He put on a pair of blue jeans and his diamond-patterned tie-dye shirt. Now he could wear anything he wanted. Maybe he should go all out with bellbottoms, flowered polyester shirt and the road runner necklace he'd purchased at Goodwill. Either that or wear some of his political buttons that bore slogans like

"End U.S. Aid to El Salvador," and "Support the Police: Beat Yourself Up." In the past he'd often worn his "good clothes"—meaning those his mother approved of like dockers, turtlenecks, and sweaters—to the bus. Then on the way to school he'd change into something more to his liking. But if he appeared looking like a flower child, he might draw attention to himself. Not that that really made any difference.

Time seemed to drag. The bus arrived around 7:20. Jacob was ready to go by seven. He descended the stairs to the kitchen and sat at the table. He didn't think about his parents, about what might be happening to their bodies. That didn't seem real in a way, yet in a way it did. It was so hard to explain what he was feeling and thinking.

After awhile, Jacob decided that maybe he needed something to drink. His parents kept their liquor in the cabinet above the refrigerator. He removed a full bottle of Scotch and took a long drink. The whiskey burned going down and caused his empty stomach to rebel. He was afraid he'd vomit. Jacob closed his eyes and waited until the urge subsided. The liquid left a bad taste and did nothing to assuage his anxiety. With each passing moment, his nervousness intensified. In a few hours he would go out on the deck, sit down on one of the benches, take one last look at Pikes Peak surrounded by the brilliant Colorado sky, pull the trigger, and none of it would matter anymore.

Jacob put food and water out for his cats. He didn't want to think about what would happen to them when he was gone. Everything was just so screwed up. He'd never wanted any of it to turn out this way, but there was no going back now.

Finally, Jacob put on his Levi jacket with a fur collar, stuffed Major's missing glove, which he found in the mud room, in his pocket, and left for the bus stop. He was the first to arrive. After the others drifted from their houses, they chatted about inconsequential things. Nobody mentioned that they'd heard strange noises in the middle of the night or seen anything out of the ordinary.

Several kids discussed their plans for the holidays. In two days Jacob was supposed to fly out to Rockford, Illinois, to spend some time with his real dad. He'd nearly forgotten about that. Well, that was never going to happen now. Jacob concentrated on the next few hours—what he would say to Mondo, and about his own impending suicide. The more he thought about killing himself the less he liked the idea. Still, what choice did he have?

On the bus he sat next to fifteen-year-old Jeremy Watson (*). Jeremy, a blonde-haired, blue-eyed skater/stoner type, was one of Jacob's best friends. Last summer they'd spent a lot of time together and Jeremy had helped Jacob get a dishwashing job at Jan's Cafe.

"You bring it?" Jeremy asked, referring to some pot Jacob had promised.

"Nope." Jacob had decided to give his entire stash to Lila. Turning, Jacob surveyed his fellow passengers, looking for his partner in crime. Major wasn't on the bus.

41

"Why didn't you bring it?" Jeremy asked.

Jacob kind of wanted to tell his friend about what was locked away in the master bedroom. Maybe verbalizing would make last night seem real, or make it disappear. If only locking away his parents could somehow lock away the deed. But it couldn't, so he talked about pot instead.

"I need it. Why don't you ask Dave?" he said, referring to David Mabie.

While the bus bounced along, Jacob sang part of the Doors' *L.A. Woman*, repeating the chorus, "Mr. Mojo Rising, Is your mojo rising?"

Jeremy later recalled that Jacob seemed to be in a good mood, but Jacob was an expert at pretending. Show one face to the world, and never let anybody know the truth. For as long as he could remember his parents had warned, "What goes on behind these walls is nobody's business," and he hadn't dared disobey them. Once, at age nine, he'd threatened, "I'm going to call the cops." Kermode and Pamela had taunted him, saying, "Go ahead. Nobody will believe you," and Jacob's resolve had crumbled. He'd always had a terrible fear of being called a liar--maybe because Pamela stretched the truth so much and he didn't want to be anything like her. Well, he wasn't like her, was he?

But in a few hours, he would be. Yes, Jacob thought, as the bus lurched down Kelly Road. In a few hours he would be as stiff and cold and dead as his mother.

And (Jacob) was afraid, and said,
How dreadful is this place."

~ Genesis 28:17

Chapter 7

Surrounded by the noise of the other riders, the coldness inside Jacob began to dissolve. He could almost believe that this was just another day, but as the bus neared the school, he began to shake. He clasped his legs and hands together until the trembling passed.

The school buses parked in the elementary school lot below WPHS. Jacob's breath plumed in front of his face as he and Jeremy and the others strode up a short incline to the middle and high schools--a sprawling length of buildings connected by a glass commons. Snow heaped against the brick walls, upon the winter dead lawn and around a wrought iron sculpture of a panther, the school mascot. One more day until Christmas vacation. One more day until Jacob would have boarded a plane to his dad's. As if that would have solved anything. Even if he'd told, Pamela had often said that there was no legal way Frank could ever get custody, so why bother? Frank could only provide a temporary reprieve. Jacob liked his dad okay and Frank tried to be a real father, but Pamela had warned that Frank would never get custody, so there was no point in confiding anything. Besides, Jacob only saw his real dad a few times a year and their relationship was superficial. Kermode had been too rough and Frank was too much like another kid, so in a way Jacob felt as if he didn't have a dad.

Once inside the main building, Jacob looked first for Mondo. When he couldn't find his best friend, he headed for Major's locker, but his partner didn't show. Major had promised they'd concoct an alibi. Where the hell was he? Wasn't he going to come to school? What did his absence mean?

Before first hour, counselor David Greathouse sought out Jacob. Greathouse, a bearded man in his early fifties with a lean runner's body, had been a guidance counselor for five years, working with students bearing last names beginning A-K. Greathouse had worked closely with Charles after he'd expressed a desire to leave home. Charles wanted to be emancipated, which at eighteen was no problem, but Greathouse had discouraged him primarily for financial reasons. Charles had revealed something about the turmoil in the home, his stepfather's drinking and the verbal abuse. He even expressed fear for Jacob and worried that by moving out he was abandoning his younger brother. Greathouse also suspected that Jacob might be at risk, but like everyone else the boys turned to for help, he never filed any sort of report or attempted to verify Charles's allegations. He did speak to Pam several times about her eldest son's move and arranged for Charles to remain covered under the family health plan. During their conversations, Pam was very guarded about her relationship with

her boys, only alluding to "conflicts."

As for Jacob, Greathouse and he had only discussed possible problems that previous week.Greathouse later said he'd initiated the session after Jacob threatened another teen with scissors. Jacob and Charles agree that Charles approached Greathouse expressing concern over his younger brother's deteriorating condition. Jacob certainly hadn't wanted to talk to David Greathouse or anyone else. What if his parents found out?

Once in the counselor's office, Charles had done most of the talking, though Jacob admitted that he'd had difficulty eating and sleeping. Jacob also said,"I spend as much time as I can at school without getting into trouble... We haven't eaten a meal together since Thanksgiving." Greathouse noted that the fifteen-year-old looked tired, ill, unkept, depressed, and "very tormented."

Following the meeting, Charles's impression was that Greathouse was unresponsive and arrogant. With all the discussion of violence and emotional abuse, it does seem reprehensible that Greathouse, in his capacity as counselor, didn't take steps to immediately defuse the situation. He did arrange for an intake specialist from Penrose-St. Francis Hospital to speak with Jacob, though he did not make this an urgent priority.

When Greathouse spotted Jacob on December 17, he reminded him that the specialist would be available first hour. Jacob responded appropriately enough, though he'd actually forgotten all about seeing the woman. In this instance, his upbringing served him well. He just reacted automatically, the same way he had all those times when people asked about bruises, tears or various physical ailments, such as stomach aches or high fevers or vomiting. Blame it on everything except the cause. You want me to see somebody? All right. I can do that. I can do anything except reveal the truth.

7:50. Minutes away from first hour. Jacob saw David Mabie. He pulled his friend over near a restroom, away from other students.

In a loud whisper, Jacob said, "The music played," referring to their code. "But I did it. It was all fucked up."

David's expression was the same as when they plotted something—a calm look, but with a gleam in his eyes. "Are you serious?"

Jacob looked around nervously. "Yes." He ran his fingers through his thick black hair. "Do you know where Mondo is? I'm tempted to just go home now and shoot myself."

David didn't say anything.

"Major went into the room and shot the .22 six times. I shot the .357. Three times. Two shots hit him...them. One missed."

David stared at him.

The bell rang and both teenagers parted for first hour.

44

Jacob met with the intake specialist, but didn't say much of anything. His mind sometimes had difficulty functioning properly, but he managed to pretend that things were one way when they were actually another. In response to a question about his parents, Jacob replied that they were at work and that everything was fine. Following that meeting he went to gym and shot hoops. Then he participated in a forensics debate. Fellow students remember that he gave a spirited presentation.

Between second and third hour, Jacob finally found Armando Lee. Mondo is a short quiet young man with deep set Indian eyes and a sweet smile. His family lives fifty miles outside of Woodland Park on a huge chunk of land that is isolated from just about everyone and everything. Jacob loved going to Armando's, tearing around in one of his dad's many vehicles, killing ground squirrels and just enjoying being free. Mondo's parents were gentle and kind, the sort of parents Jacob wished he had. In the weeks preceding the murders Jacob had asked the Lees if he could come live with them. But even as he'd asked, he knew Kermode and his mom would never have allowed him to stay.

Jacob and David had talked to Mondo about killing the Jordans, but Mondo had dismissed it as a stupid idea. Now, when Jacob started telling his friend about the murders, he became agitated.

"I can still hear my mother screaming," Jacob said, pacing in front of Armando. "I think I'm just going to go home and kill myself."

Mondo expressed his horror, but Jacob pressed him for the best way to accomplish the deed. Mondo knew a lot about guns. His family kept weapons in virtually every room of their house. Jacob wanted his death to be quick and neat. Every time he'd previously contemplated suicide he'd worried that Charles would have to clean up the mess and he didn't want his brother to have to deal with something really bloody and awful.

"If I put the shotgun between my eyes, that'll work, won't it?"

Mondo didn't answer.

"That'll work, won't it?"

"Yes, it'll work." Mondo said in an anguished voice."Look, do you want me to call the police for you?"

The bell rang for third hour.

"We'll talk during lunch," Mondo promised.

◇ ◇ ◇

Jacob arrived at Victor Smith's drafting class near the end of third period, following his forensics debate. Smith was annoyed.

"I've marked you absent. You were supposed to check in at the beginning of the day to let me know your plans."

"Oh, okay. I guess I'd better go to the office."

To Smith Jacob seemed "internally calm, emotionally controlled... He

45

appeared to be free from whatever mental pressure had been troubling him." In hindsight Smith wondered whether Jacob's deterioration, along with his changes in skin color, his sweatiness, and hyperactivity, might all have been indications of a nervous breakdown.

Smith also later reflected on the differences between Jacob and Major Adams, whom he taught in two classes. Jacob struck Smith as a moral young man, the kind who wouldn't steal, for example, whereas Major often ended up with other people's things. And when Smith entered a room he would immediately discard someone like Jacob, but he'd never discard Major. Although Gabrial was a quiet kid, Smith always assigned him a seat in the front of the room. Major made him uneasy, in the sense that he didn't know what he was capable of doing. Smith suspected that Major might be violent. He carried *The Anarchist's Cookbook* around and talked incessantly about martial arts. Despite his small size, he could be menacing. Major spoke so knowledgeably about Vietnam that Smith decided he had either read a heck of a lot of books on the subject or there might be something in his claim of being a reincarnated Vietnam vet.

After exchanging a few more words with Smith, Jacob left drafting and walked outside to his geometry class, which was located in a modular behind the high school. His geometry teacher, Cindy Meyer, who has long silky blonde hair, a strong face and forthright manner, considered Jacob to be one of her favorite students. In geometry he was generally the center of attention, but in a positive way. He always asked such interesting and thought provoking questions, and his smile, well, everyone agreed that Jacob's smile could light up any room. Cindy had long suspected that things weren't terrific in Jacob's life, but he was guarded in his remarks. She couldn't help but notice, however, that his sleeping habits had changed because he started falling asleep in class.

When she asked him about it, he said, "I just can't sleep."

"Well, you're either going to have to get more sleep or stay home."

Today, his fellow students didn't notice anything different about Jacob. He actually seemed in a better mood than in the past weeks, and scored a "B" on a pop quiz. But while Jacob tried to concentrate on the various formulas, a part of him expected someone from the central office to appear, or a message to be sent or a phone call made. Jacob knew that he was about to be found out. He wasn't sure how it would happen or who would tell, but he was certain that his time was nearly up. And he was right.

◊ ◊ ◊

At ll:15, David Mabie entered Greathouse's office.

"I'm concerned that a friend of mine killed his parents. I'm afraid something terrible happened at Jacob Ind's house last night.

Counselor Greathouse hurried to Charles's classroom, only to find that

46

Charles had called in sick. Greathouse went outside to Cindy Meyer's portable classroom. Meyer explained that she would send Jacob to his office as soon as he was finished with his test.

The minute Jacob spotted Greathouse he figured his time was up. He just didn't know whether it was about the "shrink" or the murders.

After returning to the main building, Greathouse saw David Mabie following principal Jim Taylor into his office.

Once the door was closed, an excited David repeated his story. "I think Jacob Ind might have done something to his parents."

Jim Taylor, a tall, big boned man with thinning brown hair, a plain face and a stern manner, had been a principal at WPHS for five years. The school year of 1992-93 was shaping up to be one of his most challenging. The recent defeat at the polls of two important initiatives, a tax limitation amendment and a one cent sales tax that would have increased funding for public schools, was especially frustrating. Hundreds of thousands of dollars would have to be cut from Woodland Park's budget at a time when the community was the third fastest growing in the state. Enrollment had topped seven hundred, and new students arrived almost daily. With the advent of gambling in nearby Cripple Creek, poor people had flocked to the area, hoping for decent paying jobs in the casinos. Big money also poured in from states like California. These children brought with them a host of big city problems—guns, gangs, but Taylor had never dreamed that he might be facing something as serious as murder.

Uncomprehending, Taylor looked from David to Greathouse. "What do you mean, 'Done something?'"

"I think maybe Jacob Ind's parents are dead."

Taylor was shocked. Charles and Jacob were bright kids and good students, and Pamela was a dream parent—active in school activities like science and forensics.

Taylor tried to think back over what he knew about Jacob Ind. The Jordans had insisted that Jacob repeat the eighth grade despite the fact that his grades were excellent, which was peculiar. Pamela had worried that Jacob was too immature for high school. But Jacob's friend Mondo Lee had also repeated, so in a way her decision made sense. "I don't want to separate them," she said. Jacob hadn't appeared resentful. In fact, the extra year had probably done him good. He appeared to have adjusted well to high school. Any discipline problems had been minor. Recently, there had been an incident involving a couple of other kids. Jacob had supposedly threatened to kill one of them with a pair of scissors, but when Taylor investigated, he found that the circumstances had been overblown, that there had been plenty of guilt to go around. After David Mabie finished his bizarre story, Taylor and Greathouse discussed a plan of approach-- Taylor would call Kermode and Greathouse would call Pam. Hopefully, the couple would answer their respective phones and everything would prove to be some macabre joke.

47

When Greathouse returned to the counseling center area, Jacob was slumped in a chair beside the secretary's desk, waiting.

"I have a couple of phone calls to make and then I'll be right with you," said Greathouse.

After disappearing into his office, he called the Jordans' home phone number. Busy. He then called Care & Share in Colorado Springs. The first person on the line said, "Pam hasn't arrived yet." A second worker expressed her concern. "Pam always calls if anything is wrong."

Increasingly alarmed, Greathouse asked Jacob to come into his office. He studied the youth. Jacob looked normal enough, though he appeared tired. Greathouse tried to decide upon the best way to approach the subject. Maybe he should ease into it and try to gauge Jacob's reactions. Greathouse talked about first hour and Jacob's counseling session with the intake specialist.They discussed treatment for his depression. Intently watching Jacob's face, Greathouse mentioned that his parents would be involved in any therapy.

Jacob simply said, "That won't be a problem."

At 11:30, Jim Taylor, who'd unsuccessfully tried to contact Kermode at work, arrived. Greathouse decided it was time to directly confront Jacob.

He recounted what Mabie had said before bluntly finishing, "We have a report you killed your parents."

Jacob paused, lowered his eyes, nodded and seemed to relax in his chair. Sliding down he rested his head on the back of the cushion. "I shot them with a .357."

That admission opened up something inside Jacob. "They hit me, they hit me," he cried, "and I couldn't take it any more."

"Where are they? At home?"

"In the house."

"In the house?" one echoed.

"In their bedroom."

"We have to talk to the police."

Taylor and Greathouse didn't ask many questions. They didn't have to. Jacob talked and talked, jumping incoherently from subject to subject in some crazy chronology that neither man was capable of following. Jacob was obviously distraught and disbelieving of what had happened. He seemed to need to purge himself of the sights and sounds of the previous night and kept returning to the murders. When he talked about being awakened and going into the master bedroom, he started crying.[9]

"My mother was screaming, she was screaming," he said.

Jacob explained how his parents had been shot several times but weren't

---

[9] Jacob disagrees with this version of the testimony. "I didn't cry until later when my brother came in and said he understood why I had killed them."

dead.

"Unfortunately," he said, "I had to finish them off."

Taylor and Greathouse's eyes met. Taylor studied the fifteen year old. His body language and attitude betokened one word, "Despair."

Jacob babbled about how unhappy he and Charles were, and how with his parents out of the way they could sell their house and go to college. None of it made a heck of a lot of sense to the two men, but he wanted to get everything "off his chest."

Greathouse and Taylor pressed Jacob for the identity of his accomplice. Fearful for his own safety, Jacob refused. Gabrial had warned him that he better not cross him, and Jacob believed he would carry out his threat. If Jacob told and they never captured Major, not only would he be at risk, but so would his brother.

"I can't tell you who it is," he said, though in no time at all the identity of his accomplice was all over school.

Jacob then turned his attention to his missing dogs. "Kermode ran them off," he said. Jacob would later say that he would never have killed his parents if Kermode hadn't been so mean to Pike and Chaka, just as he said he wouldn't have killed them if his mother had put up a Christmas tree, just as he said so many things. Jacob never realized that with each word, every added detail he was writing his death sentence. Had he refused to confess or cooperate, his defense would actually have been stronger. Police might say, "If you confess, it'll go easier on you," but what they really mean is it will make their job easier.

While Greathouse stayed with Jacob, Jim Taylor returned to his office. After contacting the Woodland Park Police Department, he phoned the central office, a crisis team in the building and organized a faculty meeting for after school. Things were already going crazy. Word was getting out and he had to figure out a way to keep matters under control. His priority was the safety of his students. Gabrial Adams was a worry. Where was he? There were so many scary stories nowadays of people going crazy and picking victims off from rooftops or towers or trees. Could Major even now be outside the school watching and waiting and readying to kill again? It was hard to believe, but no harder to believe than the fact that Kermode and Pamela Jordan had been executed by their own son.

◊　◊　◊

Jacob's feeling of relative well being abruptly ended when his brother entered the room. Charles hadn't gone to school that morning. According to him, he had the flu and had been home sick in bed when he got the phone call. Charles looked extremely pale, and as he approached Jacob, Jacob saw the pain in his eyes, though as always, Charles maintained his composure.

Jacob broke down. "I'm sorry, I'm so sorry," he sobbed. Charles put his

49

hands on the back of Jacob's neck. They were icy cold. He bent over and said, "I love you and I don't blame you."

Jacob kept thinking, I killed my brother's parents. How could I have done that? How can he ever forgive me? Jacob didn't want Charles to be mad at him, and he felt so terrible because he had just made his brother an orphan.

Charles and Jacob stayed together for about ten minutes. Jacob cried and Charles soothed him. All of Charles's attention was focused on making things okay for Jacob. He couldn't break down in front of him. He had to maintain control, he had to take care of him. Throughout their lives, Charles had always tried to protect his younger brother, at first in a little boy manner, when he could only whisper, "It'll be all right," or touch his shoulder and guide him to his room. Later, he had protected him with his sarcasm, by turning the brunt of his parents' attention against himself, and allowing Jacob to slip away. Now, he swallowed back his tears so that Jacob wouldn't feel worse, so that he would understand that Charles did indeed love him, no matter what. Only after Charles left his brother did he allow himself to give into his grief. Then Charles sobbed as though his heart had broken--because it had.

Officer Glen Jardin, a juvenile and DARE officer, mirandized Jacob following Charles's departure.

"Jacob was visibly upset. He clutched a Kleenex and had obviously been crying for some time. After I mirandized him, I ordered him to remain silent."

A part of Jacob couldn't believe what was happening. Despite the tears, the strained faces of the adults and their serious demeanor, he didn't feel as if he were in a lot of trouble.

But that was about to change.

And (his brother) said,
"Is he not rightly named Jacob?"
For he hath supplanted me these two times.
He took away my birthright
and behold now he has taken away my blessing...

~ Genesis 27:36

Chapter 8

Lucinda Reed is a teacher at Woodland Park Middle School. She has variously been described as a family friend of the Jordans and/or as a friend of Charles, who was one of her forensics students. Jacob describes Reed, who has been teaching at Woodland Park for a quarter century, as being "on the bad side of middle age." A more objective description would be that Lucinda is of average height and weight with short, stylelessly cut black hair and large, expressive eyes. Reed's gestures and manner of speaking tend toward the theatrical, which is hardly surprising considering that she is a drama teacher.[10] (When one of Gabrial's defense attorneys couldn't remember Lucinda's name, he referred to her as Miss Drama.) Reed is one of those people who seems to consider herself, no matter in what capacity, as "The Star Attraction." Watching her performances on the stand throughout two trials and a suppression of evidence hearing, witnesses often commented on her overblown behavior—the throbbing voice, rolling eyes, and dramatic gestures. Spectators in both Jacob's and Gabrial's trials questioned how jurors could take her seriously. But obviously, given the verdicts in both cases, they did.

Lucinda Reed had taught both Charles and Jacob, but she was far closer to the elder Ind brother. (During Jacob's trial she testified that she was initially closer to Jacob, which he dismisses as another of her lies.) According to Lucinda, she originally knew Charles through her daughter, who had been his

---

[10] In an early morning phone call soon after I started working with Jacob, Reed threatened to sue me if I included her in my book. Also, during the summer of 1996, after a "jailhouse attorney" sent a routine request concerning Lucinda's records to the Woodland Park Superintendent's office, the convict received a letter from William Kelly Dude, whose law offices represent the Woodland Park School District, denying access. The convict was later informed that he was being investigated by the Woodland Park Police Department, which is headed by Reed's friend, Mike Rulo. All because the convict asked for files that—in any other school district, under any other circumstances—are open to the public.

friend for several years. She and Charles did not become good friends until after the tragic events of December 17, 1992.[11] Charles and "Reed", as he calls her, initially began spending time together because of forensics, a shared love. At WPHS, forensics begins in October and runs through April 15. Training is intense. Charles had participated in forensics since Junior High and he credits the poise and various acting techniques he learned with helping him through the difficult months following his parents' deaths. Reed's students will tell you that she is not only concerned with them academically, but personally, and over time Charles opened up to her. Reed was kind to him, and he grew to regard her as a surrogate mother. He even kept a photograph of her, a birthday present from "Mom," in his cabin, atop his television set. Charles has credited Lucinda with saving his life.

By Charles's Junior year he was having trouble functioning. He played football, maintained his grades and participated in forensics, but his thoughts careened from violent to suicidal. He could no longer handle his home life, the times when Kermode dragged him out of bed at two a.m. to castigate him for some real or imagined infraction, or the endless fighting. Charles coped by turning to alcohol. Lucinda, who has also struggled with a drinking problem, recognized what was happening and tried to help.

"I was tough on Charles," recalls Reed. "I warned him that unless he quit drinking he would be kicked off the forensics team."

But Reed also provided a sympathetic ear. With her quick intelligence and her ability to spice up a story, Lucinda reminded Charles of his own mother--at least when Pam was being "Mom" and not "Pam." Reed listened to his problems, offered suggestions and seemed genuinely concerned with his welfare.

As Reed tells it, around noon on the day of the murders, Barb Waas, a fellow teacher and member of Woodland Park High School's Crisis Committee, pulled Reed out of class to inform her that the Jordans might be dead. Waas singled Lucinda out, "because she knew Pamela had been my friend." After asking team teacher, Jerry Parent, to take over her class, Reed hurried through the commons, which connected the middle and high school, to the office. Once there, she discovered that Jacob had indeed confessed. Moments later she spotted Charles, who was headed for the principal's office. Charles had already been in to see Jacob. Reed rushed out to meet him and put her arms around him. Charles began sobbing.

Lucinda said, "I cannot take the pain away, but maybe I can help."

Reed and Charles retreated to the counseling room where principals Hanna and Taylor, Superintendent Fred Wall, Athletic Director Stan Dodds and

---

[11] Charles, Jacob and other witnesses date their friendship far earlier. Reed testified under oath that they became close after the murders.

Counselor David Greathouse were gathered. Although Charles wanted to leave the school, reporters had already lined up outside. Charles was in no condition to talk to the press, but he couldn't possibly exit without being seen. Woodland Park High School is located on a rise. Patches of grass are interspersed with concrete walks and two long stairways which ascend from the road and student/teacher parking. The entire area is open. Charles would have had to brave a gauntlet of reporters. Everyone was concerned with how best to get him safely out of the building. The males debated whether to order the press to leave, but Lucinda pointed out an obvious flaw.

"If we tell reporters to back off, they'll still be watching the entrance. They'll be able to figure out that the next person out the door will most likely be Charlie."

Apparently, neither Reed nor her companions remembered that there are several exits in the back of the building through which she and Charles could have discreetly exited. According to Reed, she decided that the best thing to do was to brazen it out.

"I told Charlie to put on his sunglasses, turn his hat around and we walked out as if nothing had happened."

Nobody challenged them.

While at Charles's tiny cabin, located a few blocks from the school, Reed made a list of things that must be done.

"Number one, it is imperative that you get into some kind of grief counseling. Secondly, you must contact an attorney for your brother. Third, funeral arrangements must be made."

Charles agreed, but attorneys, counseling and funeral arrangements were not uppermost on his mind.

"I have one other thing I need to take care of. I want to see Jacob."

Around three p.m. Lucinda went home. Her residence is located in the heart of the town of Woodland Park, less than a mile from Charles's cabin. Charles asked Reed to call his real father, who had recently moved from California to Illinois. Reed said that Charles didn't want to call his dad, but Jacob says Charles had a block on his phone and was unable to call long distance. Anyway, Lucinda called the Ind residence several times, only to get the answering machine. Finally, around 4:15 p.m., she reached Frank Ind with the grisly news. It took several long moments of dramatic posturing before Lucinda told Jacob's father what had happened. By that time Frank must have wondered whether everyone in his family had been wiped out. The final knowledge that his children, at least, were alive came as something of a relief. At least until reality sank in. Then Frank hung up the phone and made reservations for the earliest available flight to Colorado.

◊ ◊ ◊

While Charles remained in hiding from the media which had gathered outside his cabin, the police sent word to Officer Bud Bright, who had joined Officer Jardin with Jacob, that Pamela and Kermode's bodies had been discovered. Officer Bright immediately bagged Jacob's hands with paper bags and rubber bands to preserve evidence of gunshot residue, cuffed him and led him out the front door of WPHS. Because it was lunch hour a lot of kids were standing around. Jacob recognized some of them, looking shocked, nudging each other and pointing as if he were some sort of mutant to be studied and dissected. Jacob didn't mind. In fact, he found his situation more interesting than anything else--and actually, more familiar. A part of him had always figured that he'd end up this way, being some sort of criminal, being part a public display of curiosity and derision. All of his life Jacob had received attention for the bad things he'd done. Positive reinforcement was so rare as to seem like some exotic fruit or an elaborate game with byzantine rules beyond his comprehension. Yet he did know how to respond to negative attention. And negative attention was better than no attention at all.

The Woodland Park Police Department is situated across the street from the post office in a quiet, largely residential area of Woodland Park, less than a mile from the high school. It's located in the back of the Municipal building—a flat roofed, sprawling expanse of concrete block which houses everything from the water department to Park and Rec to the fire department.

Jacob was placed in a room adjoining the dispatcher's. Officer Bud Bright instructed him only to give his name and date of birth, but over the course of several hours, Jacob made several curious statements.

"Do you think they'll let me and my brother decide what to do with the bodies? I want them turned into fertilizer and plant a tree over it."

Jacob had always desired that for himself, as well. Then over the years his kids and grandkids could come and play on his branches, so that he and his progeny would always share a connection. In essence such an act ensured Jacob that he would never die and he found that idea comforting.

Jacob also asked, "Do you think they'll let me have a lock of my parents' hair?"

He wanted something physical of theirs, a memento that he could touch, that would remind him of them and of the good times they'd shared. He certainly didn't hate them now, though he felt relieved that his nightmare was finally over. He didn't really believe yet that he was in trouble. Because how could he be in bigger trouble than he'd been with his parents?

Even though the door was closed Jacob could hear the other officers

discussing the whereabouts of Gabrial Adams. Major hadn't yet been picked up. Police were familiar with Adams. They often saw him wandering around Woodland Park in his long trench coat and had been called to the Adams's home several times on various complaints about Major's behavior. All were leery of the seventeen-year-old.

Major was actually arrested with very little problem. When officers arrived at 790C Columbine Village Drive, Gabrial asked if they had a search warrant. Even after one was produced, he refused to open the door. Officer Curtis Rictor had to place Major on the ground and handcuff him. Inside the small townhouse the police found Gabrial's trench coat, a glove and other clothes he had been wearing the previous evening drying in the dryer. Hidden amid a pile of clothing on a plastic chair in Gabrial's bedroom, Officer Rictor found the .22, a knife, a black nylon holster and ammo carrier containing eight live rounds. He noted blood on the surface and grill of the .22, and that the weapon smelled of blood. In addition, the handle and blade of the knife contained blood stains. Rictor continued digging. Inside a pair of black jeans he located a .357 magnum, which also carried the blood smell.

After Gabrial arrived at the police station, one of the officers said, "Make sure you get photos of his hands." Major had several cuts in the webbing between his thumb and finger, some of which later required stitches.

Jacob wondered whether Gabrial might still have blood on his hands. Jacob certainly had Pamela and Kermode's blood on HIS. But Jacob was beginning to understand that no amount of water or even the passage of a thousand years could rid him of his particular stains.

Back to Lucinda Reed and her version of The Night of the Arrests. While ensconced in his cabin Charles continued to insist that he must visit Jacob. "I have to see my brother." Lucinda was concerned for Charles's well being, so she called the Woodland Park Police Department and demanded to speak with Officer Mike Rulo, a personal friend. Rulo wasn't in.

Undeterred, Lucinda informed the dispatcher, "It is imperative that Charles sees his brother."

She left a message for Rulo to call back, but when he didn't, she kept calling.

Finally, around 7:45, the dispatcher told Reed that Mike Rulo and District Attorney John Suthers, who had driven up from Colorado Springs, had discussed the matter. Suthers himself came on the line. Lucinda repeated her concern for Charles, and Suthers was "compassionate." He asked how old Charles was, and agreed that "for Charles this (seeing Jacob) was a necessity." Jacob was presently at Langstaff-Brown, Woodland Park's emergency medical

center, having tests done for gun powder residue, and hair samples and fingernail scrapings taken. He was due back at the police station around 8:15. Suthers agreed to allow Charles a visit before Jacob would be transported to Zeb Pike, a juvenile detention facility.

Here is where events become murky or unbelievable, depending on your point of view. At the suppression of evidence hearing held a year after the murders, Jacob's defense dismissed as ludicrous the idea that John Suthers—an aloof, law and order prosecutor—would act out of compassion. Suthers is particularly tough on juvenile crime, and Jacob's attorneys couldn't conceive of Suthers, who later commented that the crime scene was one of the most gruesome he'd ever seen, being sympathetic toward a confessed murderer.

Defense attorney Shaun Kaufman argued unsuccessfully that Lucinda Reed was allowed to see Jacob so that whatever information she gathered could later be turned over to authorities. Prior to being processed, a murder suspect is never allowed visitors, and certainly not someone who is a casual acquaintance. It just isn't done. Period. Even the law enforcement officials who testified at the hearing agreed that such an event was highly irregular. Lucinda insisted that she, Suthers and Rulo acted totally out of humanitarian reasons.

Whatever the truth, Lucinda and Charles[12] arrived at the police station around 8:10 p.m. They waited in the anteroom for nearly thirty minutes until Jacob returned. Detective Mike Rulo then led the pair to a room in back of his office. Upon opening the door, Rulo said, "This is not being tape recorded or video taped." Jacob doesn't remember Rulo's remark, but recalls being comforted by the knowledge that whatever occurred between him and his brother would be private—an ironic statement in light of Lucinda Reed's subsequent actions.

Reed and Charles entered a small room, no more than 10'x10.' It contained a counter with equipment on it, a metal desk and three chairs. Jacob was seated in one of the chairs. He rose. He was handcuffed and shackled and trembling, and when Charles hugged him he started crying.

"I'm sorry, I'm so sorry," Jacob kept saying.

Lucinda also hugged Jacob. All three sat at the metal table.

"Why are they doing this to me?" Jacob asked, referring to the handcuffs. "Where the hell am I going to go?"

Charles responded, "It's the law."

Lucinda started questioning Jacob about the murders. As she explained in court, "We needed to know. Charles needed to know." Which is a curious

---

[12]A third student, Sunny Freeman, accompanied them. Whether Sunny was ever interviewed I can't say, since that would be in Discovery. Apparently, Sunny waited outside during Charles's and Reed's meeting with Jacob.

assertion, considering the fact that several people, including Jacob himself, had already given Charles the pertinent information.

Ever obliging to his elders, Jacob recounted the murders. Throughout, he cried and shook. The night was bitter cold, there was no heat in the room, and Jacob was only wearing a t-shirt and jeans. Lucinda recalled for the court that nobody had any Kleenex so she leaned over and brushed the tears from his cheeks. Jacob dismisses that as another example of her "story-telling," but everyone agrees on one point. Jacob was in shock. Many people suspect that he had suffered a psychotic break. That, at the time of the murders and during the subsequent hours, Jacob was no longer fifteen years old and a freshman at Woodland Park High School. That he was once again five years old and facing the terror of coming home on quiet afternoons to be greeted by a giant who forced him into a white-tiled bathroom where unspeakable acts were performed upon his defenseless body. That Jacob was five years old and crying out to a mother who never wanted him and never loved him and who answered his pleas for protection with beatings and taunts of "You're a liar," and who performed unspeakable acts of her own.

No one ran any psychological tests on Jacob until much later so we'll never know whether a psychotic break actually occurred. Initially, Jacob's attorneys speculated that they might plead "not guilty due to impaired mental condition." Jacob agrees with that assessment, but, perhaps because they didn't lay the proper groundwork, the defense ultimately decided on "self defense."

Even Lucinda Reed, no champion of Jacob's, realized that something was definitely wrong with him that night. As she put it, Jacob "did not realize the consequences of his acts." At one point he asked whether his absences from school would be excused. He also wanted to know where he was going to live now that his parents were gone. Lucinda said, "Your real father has custody."

Jacob scooted back his chair and declared emphatically, "I can't do that. I can't live with him."

Jacob continued to recount, in disjointed sentences and non sequiturs, the murder night--including the fact that "he had gotten the belt."

Lucinda asked, "Were there any marks?"

"I don't know."

One of the last things Jacob supposedly remembered seeing was Major's bloody knife and bloody glove. In other testimony, Lucinda recalled that the glove was actually dripping blood. Jacob doesn't remember any of this, and logically, the idea of a glove so drenched in blood that droplets can be seen falling onto the floor in a darkened room, is ludicrous. Another example, according to him, of Reed's "dramatics."

Finally, after forty minutes—Jacob insists it was closer to fifteen or twenty—Mike Rulo poked his head inside. "We need to transport him now. Please say your goodbyes."

57

Jacob said, "I'm very cold."

Charles started to remove his letter jacket. Lucinda countered, "Why don't you give him your sweater?" Charles stripped off his sweater and handed it to his brother. Jacob then asked for a few minutes alone with Charles. His thoughts had centered on a stash of marijuana in his room that he hoped Charles could remove.

"I didn't want to get in trouble for having illegal drugs in my possession. Silly me! So once we were together I explained to Charles what should be done with the pot. I wasn't even worried about anything else."

Reed returned Charles to his cabin around 9:40 and stayed through the ten o'clock news. The murders and the arrests were the lead story though details remained sketchy. After a final hug and kiss for Charles, Reed went home to bed.

Upon awakening the following morning, Lucinda realized that her recollection of Jacob's "confession" was a little hazy. For example, she couldn't remember the exact time Jacob had said he'd heard the gunshots. This concerned Reed, who ordinarily "has an excellent memory."

Early in the morning of December 18, 1992, Lucinda called her friend, Athletic Director Stan Dodds, and asked him to act as a witness for what she was about to do. Realizing the importance of Jacob's statements, Reed decided to tape her recollections of their meeting. Afterward, she turned the tape over—not to Jacob's defense attorneys or to a neutral party for safekeeping—but to the police. This recording, which can only be described as hearsay, would later form the major basis for Jacob's confession.

Emancipation from the bondage of the soil
is no freedom for the tree.

~Rabin-Dranath Tagore
Fireflies

Chapter 9

After Charles and Lucinda Reed left, the police transported Jacob to the sheriff's station in Divide, a tiny town four miles west of Woodland Park. Teller County is ill equipped to handle serious crime, certainly not murder, and the deputies had to scramble for an appropriate place to put their suspect. They finally decided on the drunk tank. It was extremely hot in the cell, especially after the chill of Woodland Park's police station.

As the hours passed, Jacob realized he was hungry. He hadn't eaten since the family's last dinner more than twenty-four hours ago. Odd that all those weeks he couldn't choke down anything and now all he could think about was filling his stomach. The old guy on duty was pretty short with him, but he did round up a blanket and a meal. All in all, Jacob couldn't complain about his handling by law enforcement. Nobody had slammed him around or yelled at him or treated him the way cops supposedly treated suspects on TV. Some of the deputies actually seemed fairly compassionate.

Jacob hadn't seen Gabrial, though he understood that his partner had been taken into custody. Jacob didn't know or care much about anything beyond what was directly happening to him. He had no idea whether the media had even reported the murders. Only later did he learn that the story led both local and regional broadcasts, and was picked up by national wire services. Jacob wasn't worried about the news media or legal representation or anything else. It was one o'clock in the morning--exactly twenty four hours since the murders--and he was feeling the effects of months of insomnia. Sometimes it hit him that he was in a lot of trouble and when he'd faced Charles he'd been remorseful, but most of the time nothing much registered. All he really wanted to do was sleep.

Jacob was emotionally exhausted from everything that had happened that day. He curled up on the cot with the wool blanket wrapped around him and dozed. Around 2:00 he was awakened and told that he'd be going to Zebulon Pike, a juvenile detention center in Colorado Springs.

A deputy handcuffed Jacob and placed him in the back seat of the sheriff's vehicle. Was all this really happening? He felt so detached—and so tired. As if he could sleep for a thousand hours straight. He wasn't allowed to rest in the car, however, so he stared blankly out the window. His whole life had been turned upside down, but none of it seemed like any big deal. And the steel of the cuffs encircling his wrists, the stern faces of the officers, the wire mesh on the squad car, all of it somehow seemed every bit as familiar as his "other life." So this is where his fifteen years had been headed, toward this particular moment.

When Jacob Patrick Ind is snatched by the law and wrestled to its bosom. To be taken away from his parents and to be punished seemed appropriate somehow.

The ride down Ute Pass to Zeb Pike took approximately half an hour. As they passed Green Mountain Falls, Chipita Park and Cascade, Jacob studied the clusters of lights. The Rockies rose tall and ghostly on either side of the highway. How long would it be before he passed this way again? He needed to concentrate, to squirrel away details so that he wouldn't forget. Manitou Springs, nestled in the foothills with Pikes Peak looming in the background, looked like one of those miniature villages from holiday displays. Christmas lights, like hundreds of fireflies, decorated the shrubbery on a mansion overlooking the city.

The cruiser turned off Highway 24 toward Zeb Pike. Street lamps cast a mellow glow upon the glassy blackness of asphalt. Businesses dominated this part of the west side of Colorado Springs, and beyond the businesses people were sleeping in their beds where it was warm and everybody had enough covers and enough love and they were safe and nothing could disturb them. Dark and quiet and peaceful in those houses where fear did not exist.

But Jacob couldn't comprehend that. Mom and Dad were nice. Mom and Dad were monsters, exactly like his parents, and those peaceful-appearing homes were precisely that—"appearing." Behind the surface they were every bit as nightmarish as his own had been. Jacob could often hold two mutually contradictory thoughts. Everyone's family was as screwed up as his. Nobody's was. All kids hated their parents; all parents hated their children. No, only the Jordan family and Jacob Ind. His situation was unique. Hardly. Everyone experienced the screaming, fighting and hatred that had made Jacob disappear inside himself and never come out again. If only he could now disappear into the physical darkness of this December morning the way he had so long ago disappeared into that emotional void. But this was real. The deputies were real. His handcuffs were real. The cold was real. The deed was real. No way to go back even if he'd wanted to. But where would he go? And what choice had he had?

The cruiser headed up 21st Street on the last leg of Jacob's journey. The road was nearly deserted and he suddenly felt so abandoned. Jacob might even have been afraid, but if he was, he quickly shoved down that feeling. Just another new experience, he told himself, as the detention center came into view. Something different. Everything's okay.

Zebulon Pike Detention Center, named after the Army officer and explorer who "discovered" Pikes Peak, looks remarkably similar to a regular school. The two story sprawl of buildings, separated from the city by a desolate stretch of road and barren hills, has a lot of windows, which surprised Jacob. He guessed he'd been expecting bars and a prison atmosphere. And barbed wire, rather than the chicken mesh surrounding the enclosure.

Once inside the facility, he was placed in a tiny holding cell containing

a bed, a toilet and window. Jacob drowsed until around four a.m. when he was awakened by a staff official.

"Your lawyers are here to see you."

Jacob followed the official to the visiting room. He really hadn't given much thought to attorneys. He figured his super-responsible brother had hired them. Which was good. If it had been left to him he probably wouldn't have done anything.

Jacob was met by Shaun Kaufman and Jim Dostal. Even though Jacob was destitute, a lot of lawyers were interested in such a high profile case so he could have had his pick. But Jacob didn't question Kaufman and Dostal's credentials or expertise, and within the legal community they were generally considered to be competent attorneys.

Shaun, who would remain on Jacob's case until the sentencing, was the younger of the pair. He was dressed casually in sweats and wore his hair a bit longer than usual, perhaps a quiet statement regarding his political views and/or his love affair with the Grateful Dead. To Jacob, Shaun seemed a little better than the usual lawyer because he had a sardonic sense of humor reminiscent of Charles's. Jim Dostal, a bearded man in his early forties, was quiet and Jacob found him intimidating. Even at this early hour Dostal wore a tie.

Shaun and Jim stayed for approximately half an hour. Dostal, who took his responsibilities seriously and expected his client to do the same, warned Jacob not to talk to anybody about anything.

"This is what you tell them," said Jim. "I have a lawyer and I do not wish to speak with you about my case at this time."

They didn't ask Jacob anything much about what had happened, and it was only during another visit that Kaufman told him that he'd committed a very serious crime."You could get life." Generally, when Jacob talked to his attorneys or to Charles, he realized the enormity of his actions. Otherwise, it just didn't sink in. It was like he'd wake up the next day and get ready for school and just get on with the life he'd always had. But now he was part of a very different life.

Jacob stayed at Zeb Pike for ten days before being transferred to a "real jail." The food was good and for the first time in months he actually looked forward to meals. He found it easy to adjust to the routine. Jacob has always felt far safer with schedules and predictability. With his parents his life had depended on their whims, on whether they'd had a bad day at work or too much to drink, a phone call from Jacob's father or a "look" from himself. Here, although the rules didn't always make sense, they remained constant. And, by virtue of his crime, the other teens treated him differently. For the first time in his life, he received a certain amount of respect. Either they kept a deferential distance, as if fearful that he might go off on THEM, or they sought him out. He had no idea that "Jacob Ind, the Woodland Park youth accused of murdering his parents," was already a familiar media phrase. He hadn't read about himself or watched any of the newscasts, so he didn't realize his burgeoning notoriety. The

Gazette Telegraph had rated the murders as one of the top ten local stories of 1992. Still functioning with one foot in reality and one foot in dreamland, Jacob went through the motions and simply accepted everything that came his way without comment or question. Life just was. He didn't think about his parents or the past or about much of anything except the present moment. Beyond that and his mind simply shut down.

◊ ◊ ◊

Pamela and Kermode were buried on December 21. Family started arriving beforehand. Jacob's father visited his son as soon as a meeting could be officially arranged. Frank Ind, a good looking man whose dark hair, eyes and facial structure clearly establish his paternity over Jacob, tried desperately to make sense of his child's actions.

"Why couldn't you have waited?" Frank asked, referring to Jacob's plane ticket to Rockford. "Why didn't you ever mention what was going on, that you were so unhappy?"

Frank had no idea anything was wrong in the Jordan household, which made Jacob's murderous rampage all the more bewildering.

"Did Pam and Kermode physically abuse you?" asked Frank. "Emotionally?" "Sexually?"

Mindful of his attorneys' warning, Jacob replied to each question, "I can't talk about that, Dad."

Frank cried, but Jacob felt contempt rather than pity. "He wasn't crying for me," he later said. "He was crying for himself."

Jacob's grandparents, Daniel and Grace Wallace,(*) also visited. Jacob didn't know Daniel and Grace very well. Pamela was generally hostile toward her mother and Grace had early on expressed her disapproval of Kermode Jordan, which added to the strain. The Wallace family is a complicated web of bruised feelings, divided loyalties, ancient hurts and outright animosity. All that internecine intrigue was pretty boring to a kid so Jacob generally ignored it all. Nor was he all that interested in his parents' funeral service. He and Charles had discussed the matter somewhat over the telephone. When his brother asked what to do with Kermode and Pamela's bodies, Jacob made it short and sweet. "Burn 'em."

During their initial visit with their grandson, Daniel and Grace Wallace treated him with compassion. Daniel shook Jacob's hand and Grace hugged him. That must have been particularly difficult for Grace since she had just come from viewing her dead daughter. Although the service was to be a closed casket affair, Grace had tearfully insisted upon one last glimpse. The funeral director demurred since Pamela had not been "prettified." However, Grace, an imperious woman, was not to be denied. Immediately upon viewing her child's brutalized remains, she fainted. Charles, who had been standing nearby chatting

with friends, swivelled around, watched his grandmother fall, turned his back to her and continued talking.

Charles's coldness, at least as perceived by the Wallace clan, and comments made during this time caused some of Pamela's siblings to question whether he might have been involved in the crime. Charles, so sarcastic and "dark", seemed a far more likely suspect than his younger brother. Some of the Wallace clan were not really surprised by the murders. As one sister later observed, "I don't blame Jacob for killing Pam. I could have done the same thing." It was simply the identity of the triggerman that was so incomprehensible. Jacob and the brutal events of that night just didn't go together. There appeared to be a lot of missing pieces to this puzzle.

Christmas 1992 arrived. The staff at Zeb Pike handed out trees and decorations and conducted a contest to see which pod could do the best job of decorating their area. Jacob's pod won and was rewarded with Burger King whoppers. Christmas morning each teen was provided with a small gift. Jacob was given a travel checker player. He didn't mind Christmas in detention. In fact, it was a lot better than being at home.

"It felt like a family. There was a closeness I'd never experienced before."

One night Jacob did experience a flashback. He and his roommate slept on the floor with only a thin mat, a sheet and a blanket. As Jacob drew the sheet up around his shoulders, he smelled an odor exactly like that of bear mace. Instantaneously, he was back in Ridge Drive's master bedroom, re-living the murders. The experience unnerved him, though it wasn't the last time he would be involuntarily transported back to December 17, 1992.

Jacob's mental state remained fragile. He made several phone calls during this time. Almost everyone he talked to agrees that he appeared "out of touch with reality." One of those whom Jacob contacted was his pal, David Mabie. During these interchanges, Jacob was clearly into his prison persona. Once he asked David to kill Gabrial.

"If you get Major," he said, "they've got nothing on me."

Jacob had heard from other juveniles that his partner in crime had gotten out on bond. That was false, but Jacob was so isolated he had no way of separating fact from fiction. He was furious over the very thought that Gabrial Adams might be walking around while he had been denied bail. He also expressed concern that Major might harm Charles. When talking to David, Jacob remembered attorney Dostal's warning not to speak about his case, but he didn't think it applied to Dave. David was one of his best friends, wasn't he? David was totally loyal, wasn't he? Jacob could say pretty much what he wanted, couldn't he?

No, he couldn't.

Later, Jacob would find out just how good a friend David Mabie had been.

◊ ◊ ◊

On the afternoon of Christmas Eve, as Jacob was decorating his pod, Charles Ind was being interviewed by two officers from the Teller County Sheriff's Department. Nick Adamovich, the lead investigator, and John Falton were particularly interested in the conversation that had taken place between Jacob, Lucinda Reed and Charles at the police station. Jacob hadn't talked since then and that confession formed a major part of their case. Charles, who had no legal representation, was willing to be cooperative, but he didn't want to inadvertently hurt Jacob. A self-contained young man, Charles had no trouble setting boundaries.

"My conversation with Jacob that night is confidential," he said.

The officers immediately backed off. Charles wasn't under suspicion of anything and if he shut down, the entire interview would be wasted. Instead, Adamovich and Falton asked Charles about abuse. Both detectives were interested in what would drive a fifteen-year-old to kill his parents.

"Why did you leave home?" asked one.

Charles, who had just buried his parents two days previously and was emotionally exhausted, chose his words carefully. He mentioned some mental abuse, but didn't go into detail.

"I was tired of Kermode's drinking and I couldn't take the abuse and put downs."

"What putdowns?" John Falton, a tall cowboy-type with a friendly smile and down-home manner, asked.

"Kermode would always criticize my friends. Most of my friends didn't have nearly as much responsibility and Kermode didn't like that. Generally, I worked forty to fifty hours a week, did housework and ran errands."

Charles ran his hand over his short dark hair, which he'd recently tipped blond. The detectives waited. "My mom would say things to me like, "You cannot survive out in the real world without us. You're nothing without us."

Charles measured each word, trying to decide what to reveal and what to keep hidden. It was always difficult to think about the past, and nearly impossible to be cooperative with two men who were committed to putting his brother behind bars, possibly for the rest of his life.

"Pam (When his mother was being "bitchy," Charles often referred to her by her given name) would slap me in the face if she thought I was talking back. The last time she slapped me was two days before I moved out. I hadn't washed a fork. I said, 'I did all the rest of the dishes.' Pam hit me with an open hand across the face.

"We had no privacy. She would walk into my room whenever she wanted. I always had to study and couldn't go out with my friends. Even when I finished studying, she wouldn't believe me. She wouldn't let me do much of anything."

Charles continued, "The rule was that we couldn't take money out of the household. All our money had to be in the bank. Mom co-signed with Jacob so he couldn't get access to anything he'd earned without her approval, though I

could technically withdraw funds. One time last summer, the summer before the...this happened, I decided to buy some clothes--two pair of shorts and three shirts. They cost maybe fifty-seventy five dollars. They told me I didn't need the clothes. Then they said, 'Who the hell do you think you are spending your money without our permission?'"

None of this sounded serious to the detectives.

Adamovich, a broad-shouldered man with strong facial features and a commanding voice, asked, "Was money tight?"

"They never made it apparent that they were in debt. Finances were none of our business. I saw one of Kermode's paychecks for sixteen hundred dollars. I thought it was per month. I really didn't know."

Adomovich asked, "Do you blame Jacob for killing your mother?"

Charles lit another cigarette. "No. I'm not glad about it but we tried to get help a week prior to the murders. I went to Mr. Greathouse twice, once a week before the murders. I also went to the Department of Social Services. Jacob opened up to David Greathouse. We told him about the drinking episode in August where Kermode fell down the stairs. And we told him about the Christmas recital, when Kermode slammed Jacob around. I also went to Ralph Morris at DSS before I moved out and told him about Kermode's drinking. I thought I had given Greathouse and Ralph enough information to start an investigation." In a statement that was later contradicted, Charles claimed that he'd only contacted DSS once.

The detectives asked Charles about Jacob's companion in crime. "Gabrial Adams is a potential psychopath," Charles said flatly. He had met Gabrial, who had lived in Woodland Park two years, when they were both Juniors. At first Charles merely considered him eccentric.

"Gabrial preferred to be called Major. He told that to the entire class. The reason he called himself that was because he met a person who claimed to be an assassin for the army and was a major and so Gabrial emulated him. Gabrial often talked about war games. He said he had been a World War II soldier fighting Germans and that he was in the Vietnam War. One time he wrote an electric schematic on the board. I said, 'Hey, Major, what are you doing?' Gabrial said it was battle plans and 'It would take me six months to explain them to you.'"

"Did you ever discuss your feelings about Gabrial with Jacob?"

"Yes, last summer. I said, 'Gabrial is crazy. Stay away from him.' Jacob agreed. He told me that Gabrial had once come up to him, given him a knife and said, 'Here. Stab me.'"

Gabrial had never been to the Jordan house, at least when Charles lived there. Major did have a friend who lived close by, but the only contact Jacob and his partner had before the murders, as far as Charles knew, was while riding the same bus.

Still seeking an understandable motive for parricide, the detectives

65

continued pressing Charles about abuse.

"After I moved out all the attention I was shielding from Jacob fell on him and he couldn't handle the mental abuse. Pam and Kermode often quarreled. Jacob would eat dinner upstairs and turn the radio up so he couldn't hear them fight." [13]

"Did Jacob ever talk to you about killing your parents?"

"No. I would have stopped him. During our conversation at the police station, I said, 'Why didn't you tell me?' And Jacob said, 'Because you would have stopped me.' And he was right. I would have taken him home, packed a bag and ran my ass down to Social Services and told them, 'You have a kid here who is willing to kill his parents.'"

Jacob told Charles that he and Gabrial had been planning the murders for two weeks, and that Major had done most of the planning. During that time period, Charles had noticed that Gabrial would try to stare him down at school. He had no idea what the kid was trying to prove--at least not until after the murders.

The detectives asked how often he and Jacob had seen each other before the murders.

"Not often." Chain smoking throughout, Charles lit yet another cigarette. "The previous Saturday we had a forensics tournament at Pueblo East (approximately an hour's drive from Woodland Park) and Jake and I ate lunch together. He didn't say a lot except that he was a couple of minutes late for the trip down and Mom yelled at him. Jacob said, 'If you'd been late she would never have yelled at you.'"

The detectives returned to the night of the murders. Adamovich particularly, appeared frustrated by the course of the interview. He was trying to understand why Jacob would commit such a heinous crime, but what Charles had so far recounted sounded pretty normal.

"Jacob had to kill them," Charles said. "As far as Major was concerned, they could have bled to death. Jacob was executing almost a mercy killing. All he wanted was for the deaths to be quick and painless."

Adamovich, who believes that teachers and Social Services do a terrific job reporting abuse and helping children, again asked, "Why didn't you ask for help?"

"We tried to but nobody bothered to listen to us. We both felt trapped. I

---

[13] Jacob later said that his parents seldom fought. His assertion is contradicted by a neighbor who, during that summer, awakened between two and three in the morning in order to feed her baby. Through the open window she often heard Pamela and Kermode screaming "for what seemed like hours at a time. It was really awful stuff." While some of that might have been directed at Jacob, who wouldn't have dared raise his voice, Pam and Kermode were obviously having marital problems.

could move out because that was accessible. Jacob had three more years and that seemed like a lifetime."

"Why didn't anybody do anything?"

"Because they didn't care."

"But counselors are there for a reason," Adamovich said, apparently ignorant of the many complaints lodged against Teller County's Department of Social Services, as well as problems at WPHS.

"Yeah, but they weren't doing their job," Charles said bluntly. "Greathouse didn't do a damn thing." Charles also told his friend Lucinda Reed about Kermode's drinking during Charles's junior year, and she had "begged Pamela to get family counseling." But no one had really helped.

Charles's explanations did little to shed light upon the crime, or help the investigators understand what had precipitated Jacob's actions.They were looking for one specific act that could somehow explain this most unspeakable of crimes. Where was the motive? Adamovich, who never spoke to Jacob, later dismissed the fifteen-year-old as a psychopath. According to his way of looking at things, Jacob had deliberately faked the panic attacks, the loss of weight, had gone to the counselors merely to concoct an abuse alibi, and had disposed of his dogs in order to keep the neighbors from being alerted upon Gabrial's arrival.

"Jacob and I were like caged animals," Charles said. "It's really hard to describe the constant nitpicking, what we felt. After I left all my responsibilities were transferred to Jake and he wasn't used to it. Before, Jacob's responsibility was primarily the floor. I did everything else—the trash, the dogs, the dishes, that sort of thing. [14]

"He used to have to clean the bath, hallway, vacuum, and dust weekly. Once a month when I was home we had to scrub down all the walls with Clorox. Whenever we were cleaning, Mom and Kermode would drink beer or wine and watch TV. Mom did do the cooking," Charles added dryly.

Charles was as frustrated as the detectives with the course of the conversation. He wasn't ready to reveal the secrets—the wounds were too raw—but he hoped to make them understand that his brother wasn't a cold-blooded killer. For so many years, he and Jacob had been warned to keep their mouths shut and now he was expected to bare his soul? And to Jacob's would-be executioners? Later, during the trial, the prosecution used the interview to their advantage, saying, "If there was sexual abuse, why didn't Charles mention it at

---

[14] Jacob later contradicted Charles concerning who did what chores. And Jacob was far more of an animal lover than Charles, so Pike and Chaka were his responsibility. Family and friends spoke of the cleaning chores BOTH boys were subjected to. But whatever the truth, those close to the situation agree that after Charles moved out Jacob was a virtual slave.

that time?"

"We weren't allowed to watch TV on weekdays," Charles continued. If Pam caught Charles, she would turn it off because "You should be reading." She did allow Jacob sometimes to play Nintendo or be on the computer. Jacob was the bright one, without Charles's learning disabilities and physical flaws. Jacob was also mechanically inclined, whereas his older brother would be the first to say all he knew about computers was how to turn one on. Kermode and Pam always cultivated perfection, in whatever form. Anything less was ridiculed.

Nick Adamovich still couldn't understand what was so terrible in the Jordan household. No TV? Big deal. And every kid got slapped around and yelled at. He certainly had when he was growing up and it hadn't hurt him any. "You're going to have to help us out here," he said.

The detectives continued to press, but Charles had had enough. "I don't want to remember what went on in that house," he said flatly. "If I remember, I can't function anymore. I don't even want to think about my parents right now."

But during the subsequent months the detectives thought often about Kermode and Pamela. They had personally witnessed the carnage inflicted upon two virtually defenseless people. And Woodland Park, this prosperous mountain community with its airy homes and pristine way of life, wondered about the Jordan family. What would drive a child to murder his parents? Was Jacob simply a bad kid who killed them "because they made him take out the trash," as some asserted, or did the answer lie in abuse? "Something had to be horribly wrong in that household," others maintained. "A child doesn't kill his parents for no reason."

What then was the reason?

That is the land of lost content.
I see it shining plain,
The happy highways where I went
And cannot come again.

~ A.E. Houseman
The Welsh Marches

PART TWO
MY INVOLVEMENT

Chapter 10

Woodland Park is a picturesque community of three thousand, nestled in the foothills of the Colorado Rockies. Highway 24, which runs through the town, reveals established businesses with western false fronts, wooden porches and cracked sidewalks. Much of the new development is on the west end of Woodland Park. There are two new shopping centers, a sprinkling of restaurants and fast food chains like Wendy's and McDonald's. The houses in the heart of Woodland Park reflect its origins. They are quaint summer cabins, slapped together on weekends, most likely with the help of a couple of cases of beer. All the later subdivisions radiate from the city core like spokes from a wheel—affluent developments with names like Morning Sun, Paradise Estates and Sunnywood Manor. The architecture leans toward the dramatic, with soaring ceilings, free-flowing rooms, lots of decks, skylights and fireplaces. The exteriors are generally of wood and executed in earth tones. Since no manmade structure can compete with the magnificent scenery, builders prefer to blend in with the pines, granite rock formations, and stands of aspen.

Because Colorado Springs is only eighteen miles away, Woodland Park is primarily a bedroom community. People can live here forever without knowing their neighbors or even patronizing local businesses. Conversely, those who want to get involved with community affairs soon discover that they can make a far larger impact than in cities. And indeed the same names appear on the school board, heading the P.T.A., in the Chamber of Commerce and at city council meetings, at fund raising affairs, and working as volunteers. In Woodland Park, families can be as isolated or as involved as they choose to be.

Woodland Park has luxuries that city dwellers have long since assumed are part of a mythical American past. Businesses do not ask for identification when you cash a check. There are seldom lines at the bank or the post office and postal employees are downright helpful. The checkers are also friendly at City Market, which even sports a Deli and a bakery. The average time spent waiting for check out is under three minutes. Except at the height of tourist season, you can park right in front of any business. To get license plates one need only drive

69

to the county office building—a two minute drive from one end of the town to the other—and emerge five minutes later, plates in hand. The pace of life is slow and leisurely. Dress for both men and women runs toward plaid shirts, blue jeans, and hiking boots. Even members of the Chamber of Commerce dress casually. Jeeps are commonplace, as are pickups—often with a couple of giant dogs in the back. Until the advent of gambling, traffic jams were as rare as blizzards in July. Winters the traffic is still sparse, except on weekends, when skiers flock to the slopes and gamblers pass through on their way to Cripple Creek.

People live in Woodland Park because they want to, and it shows on their faces, in their attitudes. Few move here only because "We can make more money," or "Until we can retire," or "At least it's close to family." They live here because they can cross country ski, hike the national forests, fish the streams—or simply because they find something spiritual in the craggy mountain peaks, the rarefied air. Woodland Park has an unusually high percentage of creative types—artists, writers, sculptors, not to mention those who might best be described as spiritual seekers. The phone book lists seventeen churches as opposed to five bars. Beliefs range from hard-core Fundamentalists to New-Agers. Many people punctuate their sentences with "Praise the Lord!" and "Thank you, Jesus!" A local minister recently filed a lawsuit against the school district because the administration was allowing Greek mythology to be taught as part of a world literature class. The Reverend Skipworth complained that the district encouraged the teaching of pagan religious beliefs while refusing to teach biblical Christianity. Perhaps the best known of those who are more metaphysically inclined is author Mary Summer Rain. Mary's books detail her spiritual journey under the guidance of a blind Indian, No Eyes, and contain prophecies concerning the last days of our planet. Probably every religion known to man has adherents in Teller County. There is even talk of satanic rituals taking place near the isolated area of Manitou Lake, but most residents agree that "those types" come up from nearby Manitou Springs, which has long been rumored as a center for occult activities.

My family and I have lived in Woodland Park for seventeen years. The air is clean and pure, the sky a dazzling blue, and we enjoy some of the sweetest summers on earth. We have no humidity and few bugs, and the summer time consists largely of 78 degree weather, accompanied by gentle breezes. I live in a subdivision beyond the city limits. I have seen hawks and an occasional eagle and herds of elk grazing below in the aspen grove. Once I looked outside my bedroom window to see a black bear lumbering up the hill directly below me. At night, from our upper deck I have a view of the heavens that seems to last forever. The sky is blacker here at 8,500 feet and the stars brighter, and I love to watch the moon rise above the foothills and catch in the pines beyond our main deck. During the day I can see Pikes Peak from my front windows, and from my back a mountain range topped by a jumble of rocks known as Devil's

Head. Not a day goes by that I do not thank God that I live in Colorado.

But there is another Woodland Park, another Teller County. It has been my experience that primarily two kinds of people live here. There are those who like people well enough, but prefer them at a distance. They'll wave at their neighbors and help them if they're in trouble, but they consider their home a refuge, and aren't interested in any sort of socializing. Generally, houses, even in well established developments, are isolated from each other, either by lot size or natural barriers.

The second type seems to be one that has difficulty adjusting to life in a complex urban society. If possible, they would bow out of the twentieth century. They live on winding dirt roads backed up to thousands of acres of national forest. Sometimes, by choice, sometimes because of extreme poverty, their living conditions are primitive. Some of their dwellings have dirt floors. Some are without electricity or running water. Often mothers prefer to have their babies at home, serviced only by a midwife. While city folk might call them "characters" or eccentric, residents have more of a tendency to shrug off their lifestyle with, "It's none of my business."

Those who are disillusioned with the area, or who are associated with Social Services or various mental health professions, charge that Woodland Park is a great place for malefactors to hide. The back roads and large lots allow monsters like the Jordans to commit their atrocities in private. People who themselves like privacy are not inclined to be particularly inquisitive about their neighbors' behavior. Before Jacob's trial, several former residents said, "Jacob should never be tried in Teller County. There are too many families here with too much to hide. Do you think they're going to condemn the Jordans when they're doing the same thing?"

Teller County is also in the grip of development fever. It is one of the fastest expanding areas in the United States. Unbridled growth is increasingly an issue. Citizens complain of corruption and under-the-table dealings that would put bigger cities to shame. Two residents, former residents of Chicago, stated privately, "Cook County can't compare with what goes on here." Teller is run by good old boy Republicans and reflects the problems that come with one party providing the lone political voice. Agencies such as Department of Social Services, the county's biggest employer, wield an unusual amount of power. Parents repeatedly complain that if families are poor, DSS will take children away without provocation. If the family is well to do, nothing is done. Former DSS workers have also alleged that, should a department employee get in trouble for such things as drunkenness or malfeasance, their cases are never brought to trial. Indeed, the Woodland Park Police Department, which works closely with DSS in investigating abuse cases—especially at Woodland Park High School—have refused to file reports against DSS employees, even involving such serious matters as spousal abuse. Periodically, citizens rise up to complain against DSS, investigations are conducted, politicians arrive vowing

71

to clean up the mess, employees are shifted around, and the problem continues. As I would later find out, Jacob's case involved some of the most powerful agencies in Teller County. It is my belief that those agencies made certain that the truth surrounding December 17,1992 remains buried--even to this day.

◇ ◇ ◇

I first heard of Jacob Ind on a hazy November afternoon in 1992. I had picked up my daughter from weight lifting, as I always did. Erin was involved in a lot of sports and generally stayed after school to work out. On the way home we usually talked about what had happened at school that day. With the recent vote for gambling, Woodland Park was rapidly changing, and the school system reflected that. A large percentage of kids were arriving from big cities in California or Texas or Illinois, though gambling hadn't really altered what had always been a transient population. As a middle school principal once told me, "People come here thinking that the mountains will cure all their problems. What they don't realize is that they bring their problems with them." Parents sometimes became disenchanted and left after one rough winter or the realization that nothing had changed for them except the scenery.

As in all schools, drugs are readily available. Teachers at the high school have told me about drive-by shootings, slashed tires and broken car windows. Kids have been expelled for carrying guns and there are even a few gang member wanna-be's. Now, to look at these kids one wouldn't think of gangs or inner city kids. Woodland Park remains pretty much a white bread community, and as increasingly expensive homes are being built, an upper middle class one at that. While the parents generally love the leisurely life style, their offspring aren't so sure. We have one movie theater, an occasional teen center that closes as quickly as it opens, and a handful of organized activities. For kids used to more of a social life, Woodland Park can seem as isolated as Katmandu. Children, such as my daughter, who started kindergarten here, don't have anything to compare it with and generally tolerate the boredom--at least until they graduate. Then they, like my two sons, Eric and Terrence, vow they'll never return.

After picking up Erin, I usually asked, "How was your day?" During the four mile trip home, I got an earful about the coach she didn't like or the girlfriend she'd just gotten in a fight with, or how she'd done on her Spanish test. This particular day she started describing this weird kid in her Geometry class. He dressed like a hippie, a crime in my rather preppie daughter's eyes.

"He is SO strange," she said. "But I like him."

I talked to her in the usual parent fashion, saying how kids sometimes did odd things when they were searching for their identities, that they try on various personas until they become comfortable with who they are. I imagined Jacob as some scrawny little character, maybe 5'5" with sticks for arms and dirty

72

shoulder length hair, slouching around in his camouflage jacket, head band and platform shoes. By that time we were home and the subject was dropped. But for some reason, the conversation stuck in my mind. As did the name, though I could never have imagined in what context I would hear "Jacob Ind" again.

Or maybe a part of me knew even then...

◊ ◊ ◊

December 17, I was downtown finishing my Christmas shopping. The afternoon was bitter cold, as had been the past week or so. Crusted snow lay upon the ground, covered by a fresh layer of powder. My oldest son, Eric, an apprentice lineman, was still at work and Terrence had just returned from his freshman year at college. Evening comes early in the mountains and though it wasn't even five o'clock, I had already switched on my headlights. After parking in the attached garage, I scooped up an armful of packages and entered the foyer. The house was dark and cold and unwelcoming. Because electricity is so expensive, almost everybody heats with wood and our woodburning stove had burned low. I tossed the packages onto our antique velvet sofa and hurried to stoke the fire. Like many of the homes in Teller County, our house is open with a combination living room, dining room and loft so it doesn't take long to warm--or cool off, for that matter.

At that moment the phone rang. It was Terrence, calling from a friend's house. "Did you hear, two kids murdered somebody's parents?"

"Oh, my god. When did this happen? Do you know their names? Do we know them?"

Terrence couldn't supply many details. We didn't realize that both Jacob and Gabrial had already been taken into custody, and that in many ways, this was old news. Radio and television had already reported the story. Terrence was concerned about Erin, or Missy, as we sometimes call her, who remained at the weight room.

"I think at least one of the boys is still free," he said. "They don't know where he's at."

Always protective of his sister, Terrence decided to go to the school and pick Missy up.

"Be careful," I said. "Take somebody with you. Make sure it's safe. And come straight home."

No wandering around Woodland Park that night. Suddenly, our safe community didn't seem so safe. It seemed like all the other communities, the dozens of small towns and farms and big cities that I had so often read about in True Crime books. Not that serious crime was unknown in Teller County. In fact, the past two murders had also involved teenagers. One had killed his mother. A second had blown away a nice old lady who owned a record store. The first had gone to our church. I had bought records from the nice old lady.

But somehow those crimes hadn't touched me beyond the initial shudder and expressions of shock and horror.

Eric and my husband, Mark, arrived home. We waited anxiously for Missy and Terrence. Odds were I wouldn't know the kids who'd done this. While I always attended school plays and functions, we moved to Woodland Park to be by ourselves. I worked from the premise that teachers and the school system knew what they were doing, at least until proven otherwise, and I generally didn't get involved. I recognized Erin's friends by sight, but she was too young to date so I didn't know more than a handful of boys. Out of an enrollment of seven hundred, chances were good that Erin might not even be familiar with the suspects.

We huddled around the stove, glancing out the front window every few seconds for Terrence's approaching headlights.

Finally, Terrence and Missy walked through the front door. She was obviously shaken.

"What happened?" I immediately asked. "Do you know the kids?"

"I know one of them. Jacob Ind—"

"He's not the boy you were telling me about is he? The hippie?" For once I remembered a name.

"Yes, that's him."

And that's how Jacob came into my life.

The vilest deeds like poison wells
Bloom well in prison air
It is only what is good in man
That wastes and withers there;
Pale anguish keeps the heavy gate
And the warder is Despair.

~ Oscar Wilde
Ballad of Reading Gaol

Chapter 11

The murders were probably the biggest story to hit Woodland Park in a long time, certainly the biggest story of 1992. Over the weeks, as tales began circulating about possible abuse, I began wondering more about Jacob Ind. I imagined him in his tiny cell, frightened and alone, a child little older than my daughter. Did he regret killing his parents? Did he cry himself to sleep at night? Did he even understand what he had done? Did anyone visit him? Was he suicidal? What had Jacob's parents done to make a decent kid, by all accounts, pick up a gun and kill them? Just exactly what sort of person was Jacob Patrick Ind? Shy, a loner, exceedingly bright, witty, different. But underneath all the adjectives, to me Jacob Ind was a baby. A baby facing life in prison. He couldn't have a mature grasp of his actions or any true comprehension of what was happening to him.

I finally decided to write to Jacob. I also wrote to his attorneys, offering to help any way I could with his case. I didn't know what I could possibly do, but those familiar with the system had already told me that D.A. John Suthers was out for blood. While in many states children of Jacob's age are tried as juveniles in similar circumstances, Suthers had stated from the beginning that both Jacob and his seventeen-year-old partner would be treated as adults. (For those in law enforcement who maintain the Jordan murders were carefully calculated, the question must be asked, Why then didn't Jacob kill his parents three months earlier, when he was still fourteen? The courts would have *had* to try him as a juvenile.) No, not only was Jacob Ind to be made an example of, he was to be demonized in the process.

From the outset, everything seemed stacked against Jacob. Beyond Suther's vendetta was the problem of Jacob's defense. Jacob was indigent. While Shaun Kaufman was not a public defender, he would be paid a public defender's salary. How hard would he work for his client? How greatly would a tight budget impact any investigation?

After corresponding with Jacob for six weeks, he asked me to visit him. I procrastinated. Letters seemed enough. The very idea of prison filled me with dread. No way did I want to enter THAT world. Besides, I am a shy person.

75

What would a fifteen-year-old stranger and I possibly have in common? Still, I imagined another visiting day passing without company and how depressed and lonely Jacob would be. He had recently tried to commit suicide and after seeing him in court, his emotional fragility was obvious. As much as I would have preferred to maintain a safe emotional distance, I agreed. 'All right, Jacob,' I wrote. 'Let me know the time and date and I'll be there.'

◊ ◊ ◊

El Paso County's Criminal Justice Center is a group of slate grey and blue concrete block buildings located in a remote part of Colorado Springs. From their prison cells, inmates can glimpse a stream and cottonwoods. The surrounding area consists primarily of open fields scarred by a trailer park, a sewage treatment plant which stinks regardless of the time of year, a dilapidated auto garage and tiny houses sporting bail bonds' signs. Railroad tracks run parallel to a lonely two lane highway populated primarily by sheriffs' vehicles.

The complex was constructed in 1988. Community Service prisoners tend the various slices of lawn and maintain the interior of the center itself. The lobby is functionally impersonal with linoleum floors, clerestory windows and rows of green chairs that fill up on visiting nights. For someone who has never been involved with the underbelly of the system, just entering the building is intimidating. Here is where accused murderers, forgers, rapists, child molesters, and parole violators prepare to confront an increasingly chaotic justice system. Hidden behind metal doors and tunnels and walls are people I have read about in the Gazette Telegraph, who exist somewhere out there, a million experiences removed from my safe existence.

Visitors at CJC are only allowed access to loved ones at certain times and on certain days. Because Jacob's last name begins with an I, he can receive company on even numbered days. Children under eighteen, after displaying a birth certificate or student I.D. to confirm their relationship, are permitted one visit per weekend. I notice that those waiting to be processed generally possess a different skin color from the population of Woodland Park. One glance tells me, however, that the dividing line between them and me is not ethnicity. It is poverty. I can see it in the cheap tennis shoes, outdated clothes and defeated demeanor of the aging women standing so patiently in line, as if they've done this thousands of times before. I see it in the clusters of young men with their gang colors and tough, frightened expressions. I see it in the teenage girls sporting tight sweaters and bad bleach jobs and a white-hot sexuality. But they are trying to survive in their world the same way I, a middle-aged, middle-class woman, am trying to survive in mine. I wonder if I look as out of place to them as they look to me, or worse, whether I am indistinguishable. We do share a common bond, after all.

On this particular March day, the lobby bustles with young women

cradling infants or grasping squirming toddlers. Many of the children appear to have arrived directly from church, all scrubbed and fresh and wearing their best clothes, ready to spend thirty minutes peering at Daddy from behind a plate glass window. Their mothers look flushed and pretty in their flowered dresses and lace collars. I wonder what crimes their husbands have committed? How do they explain his absence to acquaintances? Are they ashamed to have a criminal for a spouse?

After checking in, I have to wait for an available booth. When my name is finally called, I place my car keys on the counter in order to avoid tripping the metal detector as I turn around. After being cleared, a buzzer sounds and I pass through a metal door. Up two flights of concrete stairs in a bleak, windowless area, then down a long corridor. My shoes clatter across the grey concrete floor. I reach a trio of painted doors labeled with different letters. My destination is "B", One Bravo One, where juveniles are held. As video cameras record my every move I descend two more flights, into the heart of the jail. My heart races and I feel slightly claustrophobic. The entire experience, as mundane as it probably seems to most people, unnerves me. As I make a final turn, I hear laughter from behind a door to my left. I assume prison personnel are secreted there because no inmate could possibly find anything amusing in this airless, sunless hole. Another door, which slams behind me like a clap of thunder, and I finally enter the visiting area. There are five open booths and two booths with doors on them for attorneys and other professionals, as well as a contact visiting room at the far end of the corridor. Hesitantly, I walk to my assigned booth.

I am in a place without windows, that is bathed in artificial light, that is serviced by filtered air and that contains absolutely no softness. We on the outside take for granted all the different shapes and textures of our surroundings. Here there are no curves, no padding, or any building materials other than concrete and steel. Textures range from smooth and unyielding, as in the metal bench bolted to the floor, to rough and unyielding, as in the concrete walls. The only color comes from the orange garbed prisoners waiting in the booths. They all look so painfully young and vulnerable. I pass Gabrial Adams. His hair is slicked back and his expression is bright, expectant, like a little boy readying for his first day of school. I hear Gabrial's family never misses a visit.

Then I'm face to face with Jacob. I'm struck by the beauty of his smile and by what an unusually handsome child he is. Thick dark hair, Indian eyes, high cheekbones, and that smile, which I'm already discovering, is one of life's pleasures. No doubt about it. In a few years Jacob Ind is going to be a heartbreaker.

We're separated by a thick glass partition and can communicate only by phone. Jacob's voice is surprisingly soft and reminiscent of a young boy's—hesitant, uncertain. I discern a slight twang, though I can't place any specific region of the country. Normal conversation is impossible. The

connection is poor and I have to speak loudly and place one finger in my ear so I won't be distracted by the other voices echoing hollowly through the room. We talk about light things—school, music, current events, his prison routine. We both avoid any mention of the murders. I'd been informed that the phones are monitored so nothing case-related should be mentioned. David Mabie's parents had already turned over taped conversations between Jacob and their son, as well as several of Jacob's letters to the prosecution. Shaun Kaufman had warned his client that if anyone ever appeared claiming to be a defense psychiatrist Jacob must first clear any visit with Shaun's office.

"Never trust anyone and never reveal any information unless you're absolutely certain of their credentials. The prosecution employs lots of sleazy tricks."

If Jacob should be conned, Aspinwall's people would simply say,"Your client misunderstood. We clearly informed him that we were with the prosecution."

We have a pleasant visit, though it is disconcerting to talk to someone locked in a soundproof cage. Jacob likens it to a zoo, and that's what I think of, watching monkeys in the monkey house. Before we know it, a deputy raps at the door, signaling a half hour has passed. I promise I'll return.

Over the next weeks I visited Jacob maybe six times. I had to plan my visits around his various times in lockdown. Lockdown is punishment meted out for various infractions, ranging from horseplay or disobeying a lawful order to inciting a riot. In lockdown, a prisoner is allowed "one hour out." Otherwise, he must stay in his cell without books or TV or any privileges. He can receive letters, but that's it. Visitors, of course, are forbidden. Jacob had already been in lockdown several times.[16]

Initially, lockdown was torture for Jacob. During one fifteen day stretch, he wrote, 'Here in lockdown I have been thinking, and the more I think, the more my mind wanders the depths of reality and limbo. Everything and anything I have been wondering about.' I worried about him. Soon after his suicide attempt I'd seen him in court and he'd appeared more like a ghost than a human being. Jacob has always possessed the ability to withdraw inside himself, and he'd done this so effectively that he'd almost ceased to exist. While Jacob hated having to cope with inmates who were far older and more streetwise, he equally dreaded being alone.

On April 20, 1993, soon after his release from a five day lockdown for "verbal abuse," I visited CJC. As soon as I saw him I knew something was

---

[16] Ultimately, he would spend more than a year in "Disciplinary Segregation."

wrong. I picked up the phone.

"I've just been written up again," he said. "This time for at least fifteen days."

His eyes were bright with unshed tears and I sensed his despair. I shared it. Jacob's infractions were all minor, the kind that, depending on the prisoner and the largesse of the guard, were often overlooked. I suspected that the nature of his crime might have something to do with his treatment. Hard to understand how isolating an emotionally fragile child—who was supposed to be innocent until proven guilty, no less—could be considered a positive or helpful experience.

Suddenly, Jacob started talking about his parents and about the abuse he had suffered at their hands. He spoke about Charles's leaving and how, without his brother around to deflect Pamela and Kermode's rage, the violence had escalated. Kermode had recently tried to quit drinking, which only made him meaner. He and Pamela had heaped Charles's chores on top of Jacob's own, chores that might take an entire weekend to complete. If they didn't like the results, they would make Jacob start all over again.

When Jacob paused, I said, "I don't think we should be talking about this."

I imagined deputies listening to our every word, hurrying over to the D.A. with sensational details. I didn't know how Jacob's admission could hurt him, but the law remains one of the world's great mysteries. I was entering another dimension here, embarking on an uncharted journey into the legal version of the Twilight Zone.

I said, "I really think we'd better change the subject. This could get you in trouble."

"No, it'll be all right." He rushed on, detailing a time when Charles and Pamela had gone away to a forensics tournament and Kermode had spent most of the week in bars. Outside Tres Hombres, a Tex-Mex nightclub, he had slammed Jacob against a car and threatened to crush his head in. Then he alluded to the Lofthouse Incident, when he had hidden the butcher knives and guns from a drunken Kermode, and he and his mother had fled for their lives.

I shifted nervously on the steel stool. "Jacob, I'm not sure we should do this. What about the phones?"

"Naw. That's okay. I used to cry all the time," he said, referring to his childhood. "My mom used to always tell me I had to develop a thick skin, to toughen up."

I asked him about some of the rumors I had heard, about the bruises and marks classmates had seen on his arms.

"That's true. David Mabie, Stephanie Endsley and my best friend Mondo all commented on them."

But when I questioned Jacob about the cigarette burns students had mentioned, he appeared bewildered.

79

"No, I don't think so," he finally said in that soft child's voice. "There are just so many black spaces that I can't remember."

He looked lost and frightened.

A deputy arrived and escorted Jacob back to his cell. As I left, I wondered whether I had somehow jeopardized Jacob's entire future. Some things were better left to professionals. Tales of abuse was probably one of them.

Love, pain and money cannot be kept secret.
They soon betray themselves.

~Spanish Proverb

Chapter 12

At every court hearing I had cornered Jacob's attorney to remind him that I was eager to help his client in any way he deemed acceptable. Whatever Shaun Kaufman's private misgivings, he graciously allowed me to help his investigator, Candace Delaney,(*) go through the library in the Jordan residence. Perhaps clues to his client's admittedly heinous act might be found among Kermode's thousands of books with their emphasis on mind control, esoteric religions and western philosophies.

Never having been involved in an investigation, I didn't know what to expect the first time I visited the crime scene. Yellow police tape still blocked the bottom of the Jordan driveway. A lock box on the front door served as a silent reminder that Ridge Drive was still for sale. Once inside, there was little, other than the key-wound clock in the foyer that had quit keeping time and the bullet hole in the siding outside the master bedroom, to indicate that Pamela and Kermode would never return. Even the telephones, minus the answering machine tape the police had confiscated, remained connected.

During my initial visit I noticed an unpleasant odor, which I attributed to stuffiness. After all, it was April 1993. Ridge Drive had sat vacant for four months. Later, a person familiar with crime scenes told me that the scent didn't come from a winter-closed house.

"What is it?" I asked, trying to pinpoint the elusive odor.

"Death," I was told. "Once you smell it you'll never forget it."

This person said that the smell of blood can never truly depart a house. That once the blood sinks into the plywood subflooring, no matter how diligent the scrubbing, the scent will linger like some ghastly perfume.

My initial reaction to Jacob's home was that, despite its four thousand square foot floor plan and airy sun room, it felt closed-off, even suffocating. Rooms opened into other rooms. Locks abounded. The four bedrooms, which occupied the entire upper level, were tiny and dark. After several more trips, I realized the residence was as deceptive as Kermode and Pamela had been. A medicine cabinet in the middle bathroom concealed the entrance to a secret room. The carpet in the wet bar closet hid a floor safe that remained undiscovered until after the murders. The hot tub in the solarium never once held water. The wet bar never held liquor.

When I first entered the master bedroom, only a sporadic dusting of fingerprint powder on the colonial style furniture hinted at the mayhem. I didn't know then that nearly three thousand dollars' worth of repairs had been made to the 13x15' room. Some of the damage had been caused by that December night's events. More had been caused by the Teller County Sheriff's Department

and the Colorado Bureau of Investigation. The tan carpet had been replaced with other similarly colored flooring. The bathroom door was new and the re-sheetrocked walls had been painted bone white. An indigo blue and scarlet wallpaper border matched the colors in the comforter atop the four-poster bed. Pamela's jewelry box sat on the mirrored cherrywood dresser. Her rings, chains and conservative earrings nestled in their appropriate places, as if she'd just recently placed them there.

Over my next few visits I sifted through miscellany that can be found in homes across America. Inside various dresser drawers I inspected reading glasses, photographs, belt buckles, old drawings containing Charles's, Jacob's and stepbrother Cameron's signatures, Kermode's bizarre sketches, and dozens of keys that didn't seem to fit any known locks. Most unsettling was the large gift box of cashews, candies and smoked almonds, a present from the boys, in the top drawer of Kermode's night stand. I imagined him rummaging through the box in search of a late night snack. I couldn't shake the feeling that the Jordans were expected back momentarily and that I, an unwelcome intruder, had better quickly find my way back out the door and out of their lives.

There is no doubt that such fiercely private individuals would have been indignant over all the outsiders invading their domain. Police lifted evidence, investigators examined photo albums and tax returns, and heirs hauled off mementoes. As the family's goods were readied for auction, workers wrapped crystal and gold bordered dishes and tossed worn linens in boxes, where they would eventually be sold at five bucks apiece.

Perhaps Kermode and Pamela's disapproval transcended their deaths. Those who spent any time at 120 Ridge following the murders remarked upon its oppressive atmosphere, the feeling that he or she was being scrutinized by hostile eyes.

I felt it too. After a few solitary visits, I made sure someone was always with me. But it wasn't necessarily anything "supernatural" that was most unsettling. Ridge Drive's inhabitants might have physically departed, but their residence still had disquieting tales to tell.

Even in death Kermode Jordan dominated the premises. He had picked out all the furniture. Most of the art work bore his signature. He'd taken nearly all the photographs. Almost everything of a personal nature, including the cartons of books, papers and letters that filled every available space, belonged to him. Pamela's past was relegated to a box of aging photos tucked away in a far corner of the storage shed, and the boys' to a shelf beneath the kitchen phone. 120 Ridge Drive appeared to be Kermode's shrine. Pamela and her sons seemed to be little more than ghosts, drifting through his world without leaving an imprint.

At first, nothing in Jacob's house meant anything to me--not the snapshots in the photo albums or grouped on the walls, not the Chinese tapestry in the dining room or the microwave cart in the family room. Later, after hearing

Jacob's story, I viewed his home through very different eyes. Every groove on the polished wooden floor, every piece of furniture, even the locks on the bathroom doors contained a memory.

The living room sectional? I see Jacob bent over the southwestern-style couch, with his jeans and underwear crumpled around his ankles. The surrounding decor is perfect. The tiled fireplace with stove insert doesn't contain so much as a stray ash on the hearth. The mirrors above the mantle are diligently polished. Kermode's antique tapestry rug, which has a tendency to wrinkle, is pulled taut across the wine colored carpet; his drawing of a ship on a stormy sea and an impressionistic city scape hang precisely at eye level. Circular end tables display magazines positioned exactly one-half inch apart. The only thing out of place, like stacks of newspaper or dirty laundry, is Jacob, whichever parent is readying to administer "Billy Belt," and the other who observes Jacob's punishment.

The kitchen table? I picture Pamela seated at one of the beige chairs topped by green hand towels to catch crumbs, methodically peeling the label off her Budweiser while she and Kermode inform their charge of his endless faults. I imagine Kermode seated at the patio table in the sunroom, contemplating Pikes Peak through a haze of cigarette smoke. He catches sight of Jacob and stands long enough to slam his stepson in the ribs.

Jacob bends over, coughing and gasping for breath.

"Quit coughing," Kermode yells.

When he can't, Kermode smashes him again. Ever watchful, Pam stands off to the side, smiling slightly...

All of these insights were gained over the course of a year, the time I spent working with Jacob. Little did I realize that April day in the visiting room at CJC how profoundly Jacob's hurried confidences would change both our lives.

Several days following our visit I met Candace Delaney once again at the crime scene. Jacob had written me about Ridge Drive's "secret room," which opened into the attic. He enclosed a diagram. Maybe something helpful might be found inside the room. During family arguments he had often hidden Kermode's guns and a machete there.

Candace and I found nothing except toys, old magazines and correspondence. While looking through various boxes, I mentioned my recent visit to CJC. In Candace's capacity as investigator, it certainly wasn't her duty to share information concerning anything that occurred inside the Jordan household, and she hadn't. I assumed she knew a lot, but being a professional, kept such revelations private.

Believing I would only be confirming common knowledge, I reiterated the fifteen-year-old's volatile encounters with his parents.

Candace looked at me in surprise. "But Jacob won't talk to anybody about the abuse."

It was my turn to express astonishment. "Well, I couldn't get him to shut up."[17]

A few days later I received a call from a woman identifying herself as attorney Jim Dostal's secretary.

"Mr. Dostal would like to meet with you," the secretary said.

The following week I found myself in the office of Jacob's co-counsel. I had seen Jim Dostal in court but had never spoken to him. Dostal, who would later sever his relationship from Shaun and remove himself from Jacob's case, is a dedicated defense attorney who speaks eloquently about the rights of the underprivileged. But by 1992 he had neared critical burn-out from too many long hours and frustrating battles. Unlike Shaun, who Jim correctly described as "effervescent," Dostal guards his speech and his conversation sometimes seems more like a cross-examination. It is a habit he is aware of and apologizes for.

After Dostal motioned me to a seat in his spacious office, he asked me a few questions about my involvement with Jacob.

"Does he write to you?"

"Yes."

"What do you do with his letters?"

"I keep them in a box at home."

"Why do you think Jacob killed his parents?"

"Because they abused him."

Jim swiftly got to the point. "Since Jacob's started confiding in you, will you go into the prison system as a private investigator and ferret out the physical and emotional abuse?"

I was stunned. Didn't an investigator have to have some sort of license? Apparently not, and if all I had to do was ask questions and listen, surely I couldn't screw that up too badly, could I? As Jim elaborated, I was alternately frightened and elated. I didn't know anything about the criminal justice system, but I was willing to help Jacob any way I could.

After I agreed, Shaun came in and explained the proper way to ask questions.

"Don't lead Jacob on or put ideas in his head. Press for specifics. How, when, why, where. Don't ask, 'Did they beat you,' but rather, 'How were you

---

[17] Rather than inflate my importance, Jacob says the reason he didn't talk about the abuse with anybody else is nobody really asked him. To gain the trust of an abused child, one probably has to spend far more time with that individual than the courts will ever pay for. Used to a lifetime of silence, a child is not going to tell the secrets simply because he is told to.

disciplined?'"

He suggested that I read an article in the New Yorker about false memories.[18] In closing, he warned, "Stay away from sexual abuse. Leave that to the psychiatrists."

On May 17, 1993, my younger brother's birthday, I walked into CJC with a letter from the law firm of Kaufman and Dostal stating that I was a private investigator and I was to be given unlimited access to Jacob Ind.

Which was exactly what I had.

With that casual beginning, I was introduced to an alien world—the world of the soul murdered. My education began with the murders themselves. They were undeniably gruesome and Jacob recounted them with such a lack of emotion that I sometimes wondered whether he wasn't exactly what the prosecution maintained--a heartless killer. Abysmally ignorant of abuse, I had no idea that children like Jacob must wall themselves off from their emotions in order to survive the horrors heaped upon them. Ironically, that's also how they find the courage (that some term "coldness") to destroy the bodies of those who have already conspired to destroy their souls.

Over the next several months, I spent from nine to twenty hours a week at CJC learning the story of Jacob's life.

The following details his world—and the people who inhabited it.

---

[18] The articles, which detailed the saga of a sheriff who confessed--incorrectly--to molesting his daughter, were later expanding into a book, RECOVERING SATAN.

High school with first husband, Frank Ind.

The "pretty" Pam holding Jacob that Godmother Lupe Thorson prefers to remember.

Kermode Jordan, around age 49.

Jacob around the time stepfather Kermode began raping him.

Jacob, 6, at California Beach.

Kermode & Jacob, two years into the Jordan marriage.

Kermode with his boys--Jacob, Charles, and Cameron.

Christmas at Woodmont, the Jordans' second Christmas together. (With Jacob, Charles, and Kermode's natural son, Cameron.)

House on Arabian Street, San Jose, California. Here is where Kermode's sexual abuse escalated.

Whenever Jacob got dirty, Kermode would administer one of his infamous hour-long bathes.

The many faces of Pamela Wallace/ Ind/ Jordan.

Pam the "Career Woman."

Pam of the infamous kisses.

Pam, during one of the family vacations the Jordans took to escape the city.

The Pam that the boys referred to as "the witch."

Jacob, age 17, when he worked in the print shop at Centennial
Prison in Canon City. In September 1995, Jacob was sent to
Colorado State Penitentiary, Colorado's notorious "control
unit."Before being sent to C.S.P, Centennial's warden told the
author, "Jacob can be there a short time or he can leave in a pine
box." Despite public statements that, "Inmates work their way in,
they can work their way out," there are no written guidelines for
leaving C.S.P. Some inmates have been there since its inception,
more than three years ago. These inmates have never had a write-up,
and yet they will never be allowed to leave. Each time Jacob is
promised a departure, "something happens."

The author,(sans hat), and her friend, Yolanda Gonzalez. After hearing rumors of Department of Social Services' involvement in the Ind case, Mary Ellen contacted Yolanda, with whom she had once briefly worked. Not only did that contact renew and deepen their friendship, but Yolanda indeed possessed startling information concerning events surrounding the Jordan murders. During Jacob's trial, Yolanda contacted the District Attorney's office twice. Her calls were never returned.

In my beginning is my end.

~T.S.Eliot
East Coker I

{The past} eluded us then, but that's no
matter--tomorrow we will run faster, stretch
out our arms further...So we beat on, boats
against the current, borne back ceaselessly
into the past.

~F.Scott Fitzgerald
THE GREAT GATSBY

PART THREE
THE PAST
Chapter 13

Pamela Jean Wallace was born on January 20, 1951. Her father, Donald, was an accountant at a meat packing plant in the town of Crestone, Pennsylvania. Donald is a quiet man—some would say cold—the kind of person that you could never recall at the previous night's party or ten minutes after he left the room. With his gangly build, bald head and plain, rather stern features, one wonders how he ever attracted such a beauty as his wife, Grace. Grace Wallace is exactly like her name—tall, statuesque, with elegant manners and gestures and striking, deep set eyes which betray her Sioux heritage. Whereas Donald was a nonentity, Grace always turned heads. She had a regal quality about her, reinforced by her belief that she deserved to be treated a notch above everyone else. Grace wanted to be the helpmate of a corporate executive rather than the wife of a mid-level pencil pusher with few social skills and no desire to learn. She wanted to live in a mansion in West Crestone with the millionaires and throw fabulous parties that would land her name in the society section of the Crestone Independent. Because she couldn't blaze across a larger stage, she demanded to be queen of her own household.[19]

While Donald wasn't ambitious enough for Grace, he did hold down a respectable white collar job and they lived in a nice middle class neighborhood. Although their house was on the wrong side of the tracks to impress native Crestonians, it was large—not so large as to be flashy—and their small lawn was meticulously manicured. Grace kept an immaculate home, was an excellent

---

[19] I have tried to assure family members a measure of privacy by changing names and other details of their lives. However, underlying truths that might help explain Pamela's behavior--such as the alcoholism and incest within the Wallace family--have all been verified.

cook and bore her husband six children—four girls and two boys. The Wallaces appeared to be the average middle-class family of the 1950s. Better off than their blue collar counterparts, but not quite so well off as Ward and June Cleaver. While Grace didn't wear pearls around the house they would have suited her, and her children were even better behaved than Wally and the Beaver.

So if the Wallaces were a typical family—save for Grace's obsession with dustballs—how did the Pamela Jean of Jacob's nightmares come into being? Was she an aberration? A bad seed? Hardly. While the Wallaces closely guard their secrets, clues can be garnered from the family itself--grown children who don't speak to each other, bad marriages, neuroses, substance abuse problems.

Pamela, who was the second oldest daughter, seldom talked about her childhood. She told friends that she was "Daddy's little girl," but never supplied details. On the witness stand Grace depicted Pamela as a good, dutiful daughter. Kermode had corrupted her. It was all that pervert's fault. But, while there is no doubt that Grace loved her daughter, Pamela feared and resented her mother, even as she desperately strove for her approval. In later years, when readying for a parental visit, Pam's normal fastidiousness turned into manic frenzy. She made Charles and Jacob clean out the most obscure storage areas and re-wash the walls and inside cupboard doors while she scrubbed the linoleum floors until the water was completely clear. She spent days perfecting things that were already perfect. Should Grace make a negative comment, Pam despaired.

"I don't know why I bother," she said. "I can never do anything right."

When Pam beat her boys, she justified her actions because she wasn't as brutal as her parents.

"What're you crying about? I had to get straight A's, hold down a job and clean the house, all for an allowance of five cents a week."[20]

Pam and her sisters complained that Grace was never a mother to them, though they remain conspicuously silent about Donald. Why? What was wrong? The Wallaces regularly attended First Presbyterian—and what a handsome family they were—and Grace read her Bible every day. They ate together, with Donald always at the head of the table, just the way it was supposed to be. Grace used sterling silver tableware and Noritake china and the children's manners were impeccable. Their clothes were properly starched and ironed, with every pleat in place and every button securely fastened. They were polite to their elders and did well in school. So why did Grace feel the need to retreat into the emotional haziness of prescription medicine and alcohol? Why was she a hypochondriac who always believed herself to be in danger of contracting a terminal illness? If she suffered from so much as a hangnail she fretted that it would become infected, she would develop blood poisoning and die. Her

---

[20] Other members say this was a gross exaggeration.

children charge that she always had to be the center of attention and her illnesses allowed that. Pam told Jacob and Charles that Grace's mind had been fried by Valium, which she has long been addicted to. But even with all the pills, Grace was forever on the verge of tears. When she cried, she couldn't stop.

Why was Grace so miserable? Was she simply selfish and self-centered? Or does the answer lie in statements she's made since the murders?

"If those boys were sexually abused," she confessed to the boys' godmother, Lupe Thorson, "Pamela had to know."

Just as Grace knew. Something was very wrong in her household and she wanted desperately to stop it. But how could a mother with six children, a woman who forever believed herself on the verge of dropping dead of a heart attack, support herself?

Grace tried so hard—as hard as her daughter would someday try—to pretend that everything was fine. But she knew better. For one thing, her husband was an alcoholic tyrant. Oh, Donald wasn't anything like Kermode. He didn't fall down or slur his words or hold meaningful conversations with himself. No, when Donald drank he just became more silent and deadly. His anger was cold and calculated, as bloodless as the figures he daily manipulated. When one of his children misbehaved, he took them down to the basement and tied them to a post and beat them with an electrical cord. He even beat Daddy's little girl.

In AA, recovering addicts refer to alcoholism as the elephant in the living room that everyone ignores. The Wallaces had another enormous elephant in their midst. His name was Harold. He was the oldest brother, the one nobody talks about. When Pam was a teenager, Harold virtually vanished. Some say that he joined the military, others that he went to prison, still others that he simply left Crestone in order to strike out on his own. Those closest to the family do agree on one thing. The reason Harold became the shadow brother was because he raped anywhere from one to all of his siblings, depending on who's telling the story. Pam maintained he only raped her younger sister, and that nobody else was harmed. Whatever the truth, Harold simply vanished from the Wallaces' lives. The problem was disposed of within the family circle and never discussed again.

While Pamela didn't get straight A's in school, she generally made the honor roll. She was active in school affairs, though in a class of three hundred, she didn't stand out. Despite the fact that she had a pronounced overbite, Pam grew into a pretty teenager with arresting brown eyes, long dark hair and a slender build. She joined Crestone High's Orchestra, which she differentiated from a mere band because it had stringed instruments, and pep club. Her grades were impressive enough that upon graduation she was offered a scholarship to a local university.

Pam, who would always be haunted by her lack of education, declined the scholarship, however. Instead she got married.

The name Ind is well known in the central part of Pennsylvania. Charles I, Jacob's great-grandfather, practically built the town of Crestone back in the twenties and thirties. Charles I constructed the mansions in West Crestone and paved the roads that led to the steepled churches and financed many of the businesses servicing downtown.

Jacob, who from prison has become interested in his family history, said,

"My great-Grandpa, Charles Ind I, owned a big business doing construction work. He lived in a middle-class house down the street from his son, Charles Junior, where my Grandma still lives. The house was nice, but no mansion, though the family lived well. When my dad was young, his father, Charles Junior was killed in an auto accident. The story goes that the mob killed him over gambling debts. They ran him over at night. Charles I continued running the business until he got real sick. His wife is still alive, but at the time of Charles I's death, she was in the hospital so she couldn't do much of anything. Afterward, my great-grandfather's sister and her husband ran the company and screwed it up. It eventually went out of business. My great-grandfather and grandfather's work was so good that townspeople still rant and rave about it. I'm proud of that fact."

By the time Charles Junior's only son, Frank, was born in 1950, the name Ind had faded from the advertisements on the sides of the old brick buildings and the Ind contracting business was only a billing cycle away from bankruptcy. What the mob hadn't extracted for gambling debts, family members had re-routed into their own personal checking accounts. The Inds still managed to cling to a few of the privileges they'd once taken for granted. Frank's mother belonged to the garden club and the family had a lifetime membership at Crestone Country Club--after all, Charles I had built it--where young Frank was introduced to golf, his lifelong love.

Academically, Frank Ind was an average student. He wasn't really much interested in studying. All he wanted to do was play golf. He dreamed of turning pro, of playing at the Masters and being another Arnold Palmer. He spent all of his free time on the golf course, and despite the fact that he was a handsome young man with dark, deep-set eyes and wavy black hair, he didn't have many girl friends. Golf was his love.

How Pamela ever managed to attract the shy teenager remains a puzzle. When you ask Frank, he can't think of one positive thing to say about his ex-wive, which leads to the inevitable follow up, "Why would you marry someone you hated?" But Frank has a tendency to re-write his history the same way Pamela did hers. Perhaps they were drawn together primarily because of a fluke in the gene pool. Pam and Frank shared such a striking resemblance that when one looked at the other, it was like gazing into a mirror. Pam was fascinated by

the resemblance and said that sometimes when they made love, it was like having sex with herself. The ultimate narcissist, she was titillated by the notion. Frank and Pam started going together their senior year. They went for long walks near the train station that Charles I had built and along the Clarion River running through the heart of Crestone. After school, Pam did her homework on the patio overlooking Crestone's golf course while Frank practiced. Pam vowed that she believed all Frank's dreams of golf greatness and when she spun stories of what it would be like when Frank "made it," he knew there was no way he could fail.

Like everybody else in Crestone, Pam was aware of Frank's heritage and she considered Frank Ind to be a prize catch. People could talk all they wanted about the Ind family no longer having money, but just wait until Charles Junior died. Frank would inherit everything, and Pam was convinced that "everything" would make her a wealthy woman. Throughout her life Pamela retained the ability to believe things were exactly the way she said they were, no matter what evidence to the contrary. Frank was going to give her a life such as her mother only dreamed of, the life she deserved.

Frank hated going to the Wallace house. Donald seldom said more than "Hello" and "Goodbye," and Frank wasn't used to so many kids hanging around, though the Wallace brood was so quiet they seemed more like shadows on a wall than people. Grace was generally friendly, at least when she wasn't so spaced out she didn't recognize him. At other times she seemed terribly sad, as if she'd been on a crying jag. When he questioned Pam, she denied anything was wrong and made it plain that he was not to bring up the subject again.

Passive by nature, Frank often found himself overwhelmed by his girlfriend. He loved Pam because she shared his ambition, and spoke with such conviction regarding their future. Pam was so strong and confident and she treated him well. How could he not respond to somebody who obviously adored him? Sex with her was wonderful. Even though she swore she had been a virgin, she was aggressive and uninhibited and would do anything he asked of her—and a few things he'd never dreamed of. Frank also admired the way she could walk into a crowded room and carry on a conversation with anyone. She told the most interesting anecdotes. And if they seemed a bit exaggerated, well, what was wrong with spicing up a story?

While Pam considered herself a romantic and told everyone that she was in love with Frank, the truth was more complicated. Frank was her ticket out of Crestone, her life of drudgery, away from her alcoholic father and pill-popping mother and all those bothersome siblings. She wanted somebody to take care of HER for a change. She figured her odds with Frank were pretty good. Either he'd make it on the pro-golf circuit or when Charles Junior died.

Frank would have preferred waiting until after his career was established to get married, but Pamela insisted on a June wedding. Nearly two hundred people crowded the lovely old stone Presbyterian church that Charles I had built.

90

Frank, who had just turned eighteen the week before, looked lost in his rented tuxedo. Pam was lovely in her antique white gown and veil topped by a satin bow. Her ring was a disappointment. While she'd hoped for one of the family heirlooms she was certain the Inds still possessed, Frank gave her a simple gold band. Still, her wedding day was wonderful. Traditionally, Crestonians spent lavishly on their children's weddings, and Pam had four bridesmaids and an altar filled with flowers. As she walked down the aisle, she carried in her hands a bouquet of red roses and in her heart the conviction that her past was dead the moment she said, "I do."

For the first time in her life Pamela Jean Ind believed that she was safe.

◊   ◊   ◊

Soon after marriage, Frank and Pamela moved to San Jose, California. When Frank wasn't in college, he was on the golf course. Convinced that golf would be her ticket to riches, Pam didn't mind having to work. It would only be temporary. In a year she would be cheering her husband while television cameras captured her adoring expression and the money rolled in.

Pam was hired as a telephone operator at Pacific Bell. She hated the traffic and the tacky trailer they lived in and the monotony of her job. Pam really, really didn't want to work. While the burgeoning women's movement heralded the value of a career, Pam preferred to nest. She certainly wasn't in any hurry to have children. Maybe she never would. No, she wanted to create a special space for PAMELA, to decorate her home with lots of plants, photographs and pretty furniture. She wanted to cook nice meals and watch her favorite soap operas and enjoy the peace and quiet of a house devoid of a whining mother, a tyrannical father and demanding siblings. She knew all about sacrifice. Hadn't she lived a life of it? She didn't mind postponing her dream, just as long as she didn't have to wait an unacceptable amount of time. Pam liked schedules. When she wrote something down, it became more real, somehow. It made her feel in control. And Pam's plan for her life went as follows: work two years, then retire. Buy a nice house—it could be small but it had to be in a better part of town—after three. Four years and she would have a sports car in the driveway—a Jaguar might be nice or a Corvette. On their fifth wedding anniversary they would leave San Jose all together. By that time Frank would have made a name for himself on the PGA circuit, and he would only have to play golf enough to maintain a comfortable lifestyle. They would live somewhere with lots of mountains where she never had to hear the roar of traffic or scream of sirens, where she could leave her door unlocked and her neighbors were so far away that she never had to speak to anybody unless it suited her.

Pam's life plan fell behind schedule. At the end of two years she was still working. PGA requires golf school and they couldn't afford it, which meant Frank wasn't any closer to turning pro than he'd been as a pimply-faced

91

teenager. Pam was not happy. Green fees were outrageously expensive and she was getting damned tired of bankrolling something that looked increasingly like a hobby. They began fighting over his golf, his low-paying jobs, his inability to be a hustler the way Pam thought he should be.

Frank seldom responded to Pam's criticisms with anything other than a hurt expression. His hangdog manner only served to further infuriate her. What was wrong with him? Why couldn't he stand up to her? Why couldn't he get his act together and be a man? He was nearly twenty one, for God's sake, and yet he slunk around like a frightened little boy. Didn't he know she was criticizing him for his own good?

By the third year of their marriage Pam decided that Frank ought to give up golf entirely and concentrate on finishing school. She agreed to finance his education, which she considered a major sacrifice, but he needed a degree in order to properly support her. California in the early 1970's was booming. With a business degree Frank could start his own company and really make something of himself. Frank reluctantly agreed.

"Yes, it's time to grow up," he said."Yes, I've been foolish and selfish and I'm sorry."

He promised he would change, that he would accept his responsibilities as a husband. He would do what Pam wanted.

Despite Frank's malleability, they still fought. He was just so disgustingly weak. When Pam sensed that particular flaw in another human being, she went for the jugular. Because she had felt so weak and helpless as a child, she was determined never to feel that way again, or allow anybody else in her life to remind her of that part of her past. She, who could seem as refined and ladylike as her mother, humiliated her husband with language that would make a drill sergeant blush. Increasingly, Frank retreated to his bedroom or went for long walks along a nearby bike trail.

In March of 1973, after they'd been married nearly five years, Pam became pregnant with Charles. She didn't really want a child, and Frank had pretty much decided that the marriage wasn't working, but they agreed to stay together until after the baby was born. Pam ignored the whatever-it-was growing inside her and worked until she went into labor.

After Charlie arrived, life was better. Frank was thrilled at the idea of being a dad, and awestruck by his son. Charles was a cute little thing with curly brown hair and the trademark Ind-Wallace eyes and a pudgy little body that just begged to be picked up. Pamela diligently filled out every line in Charlie's blue baby book—the first time he slept the night through, his first tooth, his first taste of formula, the guests at his baby shower.

One of the guests was Lupe Thorson, who became Pam's lifelong friend. Lupe, who, in 1973 had recently been discharged from the military, is a petite, pretty woman with large brown eyes and a vivacious personality. She was married to a carpet layer with a vision. Her husband, Chet, had plotted out their

lives. Before having children, he wanted to take a trip around the world. They did. While he made good money as a carpet layer, especially when he accepted overseas assignments, he would stay in the trade fifteen years. After that he would start his own business. He did that, as well. Unlike Pam, Chet achieved his goals.

Lupe had a son Charlie's age, so she often babysat for Pam, who she considered her best friend. Lupe is one of those people who could mother the entire world and it was easy to love Pam's son. Lupe had to agree with Pamela Jean's assessment of her husband. Frank was a sweet guy, but he was weak. He tended to blame everybody else for his failures and he had the strangest habit of always sabotaging himself just when everything seemed to be going great.

Like the way he quit college one semester short of graduation.

Frank didn't see any reason to finish. "Business degrees are a dime a dozen," he said. Plus they needed the money and he hated school.

Pam saw her husband's action differently. To her, dropping out of school was the final betrayal. Frank was supposed to be the bread winner the way her Daddy had been. He was a perpetual kid who refused to take responsibility. While he was perfectly capable of supporting a family, he worked part time in a sporting goods store, for God's sake. And now he had shattered her wife-of-successful-executive dream. Pam felt cheated. Pam felt HAD. What good was Frank? She wouldn't let him in her bed on a bet, he couldn't make a living and he was a lousy father. Sure, he spent time with Charlie.

But, as she often complained to her mother, "The minute I walk out the door he foists Charlie off on a babysitter so he can sneak off for a round of golf."

Enough was enough.

Despite Pam's aversion to work, she was a dedicated employee. Over the years she received numerous promotions. When she and her husband went to company parties she was the center of attention, whereas Frank sulked around the edges. The stories that Frank had once found so charming infuriated him. Pam was nothing but a pathological liar. She could tell him that she'd been taken hostage at gunpoint but he'd have to see footage on the evening news before he believed her. And who did she think she was fooling the way she flirted with all her bosses? Frank knew exactly how she'd obtained her promotions—on her back.

While Pam had often been unfaithful, in the past she'd been discreet. No longer. One day Frank returned to their trailer to find her in bed with some young stud who'd come by to install Cablevision. Their fights became more physical. Sometimes Pam hit him. Once he appeared on the Thorsons' doorstep with a black eye. When Pam became enraged, she literally saw red and God help anybody in her path.

As far as she was concerned, her anger was totally justified.

"Everyone knows how crazy I get when they piss me off. If they're stupid enough to get in my way they deserve what they get."

One of the reasons Pam goaded Frank so much was because she wanted her husband to fight back.

"Why can't you act like a man?" she taunted.

Once he became so infuriated he threw a chair across the room. That had been a start, but he'd never followed up.

"If he'd only show some backbone, maybe I could stomach everything else," she complained to friends.

But Frank didn't. To the very end, she considered him to be a wuss.

When Charlie was two, Frank and Pam separated. Pam rented a neat little gingerbread house in a marginal part of San Jose. Frank moved into an apartment. He had no trouble starting a new relationship, and settling into a quiet routine. He was amazed at how serene life was minus his wife. Being with Pam had been like being in the center of a tornado. He missed Charlie, but he saw him on weekends. That was enough, especially since Pam was part of any visitation.

Pam continued having affairs, mainly with men who could help her. She used sex as a weapon. When Pamela spotted an appropriate target she fulfilled his wildest fantasies in order to gain control over him. If she needed a break on her rent, she seduced her landlord. If she wanted to get rid of a female competitor, she slept with her boss and the competition was transferred or fired. Men were such fools. They thought with their dicks. Give them what they wanted and you could manipulate them any way YOU wanted. Not that Pam was looking for a long term relationship any time soon. Maybe if she could find some vice president who didn't have a bunch of ex-wives and bratty kids in his past. Otherwise she wasn't in any hurry.

Pam became pregnant by one of her bosses at Pacific Bell. She liked Victor okay, but she was clear-sighted enough to know that he would never leave his wife. Still, she had no intention of allowing him to walk, not when she was the one left with the mess to clean up. In her own way, she would make Victor pay. So she informed her lover, who was childless and desperately wanted a son, "I'm pregnant. And I'm going to get an abortion."

Pam enjoyed rubbing her lover's nose in the fact that she was fertile whereas his dried up bitch of a wife couldn't produce.

Pam asked her friend Lupe to drive her to the abortion clinic. Raised Catholic, Lupe was stunned by the callous manner in which Pam decided to get rid of her baby.

"I couldn't believe the way she acted," Lupe said later. "She was so cold. She might as well have been discussing changing the oil in her Volkswagen."

Although Pam was only three months pregnant when she terminated her pregnancy and had no idea of the sex of her dead baby, she informed Victor that it had been a boy.

Pam and Frank were separated for a year. Frank was happy in his small apartment. He had a nice girlfriend and he had started playing golf again so his

life was full. Pam hated having to juggle babysitters and work and see Frank adjust so effortlessly to being single. Never able to take rejection, she was stung by how easily her husband had exchanged her for his phony-sweet Barbie doll. At least if Frank were back she wouldn't have to pay out so much money for child care. Besides, Charlie needed a dad for "fun." After a full day's work, Pam was often too exhausted to do anything more than throw together something to eat and fall into bed.

She decided that a reconciliation was in order. "Charlie needs a full time dad," she told Frank. "Things will be better this time around." Pam showed Frank her sweet side. She quit harping on his faults and no longer called him a lazy bum, even when he lost his job at the sporting goods store. She subtly pointed out how inappropriate his Barbie doll was and played upon his guilt over being a part-time father.

"Charlie misses you so much. All he wants is for us to be a family."

Frank allowed himself to be lured back into the relationship. Marriage to Pam hadn't been all bad. And she had such a good paying job now that he could really live a lot better with her shouldering most of the living expenses. And he did love Charlie.

One month after Frank moved back in, Pamela became pregnant with Jacob.

Hush, my baby, baby don't you cry...
Mother's gonna make all of your nightmares
come true,
Mother's gonna put all her fears into you.
Mama's gonna keep you under her wing,
She won't let you fly, but she might let you sing...

~Pink Floyd
*Mothe*r

Chapter 14

Pamela was pissed when she discovered her condition. How could that even be? She and Frank only had sex once and this had been the result? It wasn't fair. Pam and her spouse had quickly fallen into the same old pattern—she yelled, he withdrew. The idea that their reconciliation would somehow miraculously change their basic incompatibility was obviously false, so now what? All she needed was another mouth to feed. But maybe, just maybe a second baby could save their marriage. Pam hated failing at anything, and she sure as hell didn't want Frank running back to Barbie. She'd keep him just so Barbie couldn't have him. Still, Pam seriously considered a second abortion. She was trying to hold down a demanding job and pregnancy took so much energy. Besides, the way she saw it, Frank squandered her money on whatever struck his fancy, and he wasn't even a dependable babysitter. Once again, Pamela felt trapped.

Pam often discussed whether she should have an abortion with Lupe Thorson, though she never revealed her true thoughts. Warm hearted, generous Lupe, or "Tia" as most everyone called her, doted on her own son, Eric, and baby Sonia. She would never have understood how much Pam hated the creature growing inside her. No, Pam had to hide her antipathy behind reason and logic.

"I'll have to buy new maternity clothes that I can't afford." "Our home is too small for four people." "How can I care for two children and hold down a full time job? "What am I going to do with two kids if Frank and I break up?"

She could never tell Lupe that she lay in bed at night with her hands pressed against her stomach, trying to will herself to miscarry. She ordered that thing that had invaded her womb to get the hell out. It was all Frank's fault. Why hadn't he used protection?

For whatever reason, Pamela ultimately decided to carry Jacob to term. She ignored her condition as long as possible, wearing regular clothing and working as hard as all the non-pregnant women in her division. She refused to put up a crib in Charlie's room or decorate the baby's corner or purchase anything for it. Charlie's cast offs were fine and if she postponed buying toilet articles and other necessities, maybe she could postpone the delivery date. Pam convinced herself that something would intervene to save her. Until the deus ex machina arrived, in whatever form, she would not allow her life to be disrupted.

96

But Pamela's dreams were filled with blackness and her thoughts with hatred. Something would happen. Something MUST. But if it didn't and the invader actually had the temerity to be born, she would make him pay.

◊ ◊ ◊

Jacob came into the world on September 26, 1977. There is a Pamela mythology surrounding his birth, just as there is around so much of his life. While other parents recount cute anecdotes about Daddy getting lost on the way to the hospital or Mommy going into labor at a Moody Blues concert, Pamela told her youngest son, "I nearly died bringing you into the world. I was in labor for an entire day."

And this wasn't an occasional contraction but hard, mortally wounding pain. Throughout she was only seconds away from meeting the Grim Reaper. The doctors despaired of saving her. Frank, who had been in the delivery room, was led away weeping. He just wasn't man enough to view his wife's suffering. When Jacob finally entered the birth canal, the obstetrician discovered he was a breach birth.

Jacob wouldn't come and he wouldn't come. Pamela later told him, "They were going to have to cut you in two in order to get you out."[20]

The truth was more mundane. Pamela's delivery was fairly routine. When she went into labor Frank drove her to the hospital and was in the delivery room most of the time. Jacob was breach, but the doctor didn't have any problems. Pam's fabrications were designed to keep the spotlight on herself where it belonged. She resented the amount of attention heaped upon the newest addition to her family. She'd suffered through nine months of heartburn, swollen ankles and a dangerous delivery, and all anyone could do was fawn over this wrinkled eight pound piece of flesh? People needed to appreciate her efforts, her pain, and if she had to exaggerate a little to be acknowledged, where was the harm in that?

Pamela decided to name her son Jacob, which means Usurper. Friends visited her in the hospital and she duly noted each guest in Jacob's yellow baby book. Pamela Jean is probably one of the few mothers in America who actually finished the baby book of a second child. In her neat, utterly characterless script—her writing looks as if it had been crafted by a machine rather than a person—she diligently entered Jacob's accomplishments—the first time he slept all night, the first time he laughed, the first time he sat up.

---

20 Early in my interviews with Jacob he recounted this statement without questioning it. Even when I pointed out that doctors never cut babies in two, my rebuttal didn't register. Perhaps because Kermode reinforced Pam by telling him, "It's California law. If the mother's life is in danger, you kill the baby."

Nowhere did she make a notation as to what was really happening in the Ind household. Jacob's presence had worsened her relationship with Frank. He treated Jacob as if he were an amusing toy—take him out and put him away when it's convenient and ignore him the other twenty hours a day. Charlie was jealous and demanded more of Pam's attention, and she was just so tired. Worst of all, Pamela could hardly stand to hold her infant son. Why? Naturally, her deficiency was actually Jacob's.

"The reason I didn't hold you that first year," she later told him, "is because you were black and blue from your delivery and you'd flinch if you were held."

When Pam looked into that tiny face, she didn't feel love. She felt rage. He was so small and helpless and Pamela did not take kindly to small, helpless things. Jacob was an unpleasant reminder of her own vulnerability.

Pam always hated Jacob. Jacob told me that. Charles told me that. When I first started visiting CJC, Jacob said, "I know my mother loved me. She just didn't know how." As we became closer, he said, "My mother never bonded with me. I didn't care because I didn't have any feelings for her. I liked seeing the hatred in her eyes."

Rather than wondering at her reaction to her baby, Pamela, Expert at Denial, Spinner of Fantasies, put the blame squarely where it belonged. Her hatred was Jacob's fault. He shouldn't cry. He shouldn't wake her up. He shouldn't be so demanding. He shouldn't be so hungry. He shouldn't be. He shouldn't be...

Mothers love their children. That's just the way it is, or the way society assumes it is. But Pam had never been able to feel honest to goodness emotion—at least not the soft ones like love, compassion, and kindness. She often felt as if she were masquerading as a human being. She mirrored others' feelings because she had no idea of her own. Friends were always telling her what an adorable baby Jacob was, how good natured and pleasant, and she agreed. Yes, he did have the most beautiful eyes. Yes, his smile was a joy to behold. Jacob was the kind of baby people just naturally wanted to cuddle. Pamela saw the way others were drawn to Jacob, how they responded to his sweetness with coos and hugs, and she felt an unreasoning anger. How could anybody love that squalling brat? They might be fooled by his act, but she wasn't. In private she let Jacob cry in his crib and when he wouldn't shut up, she shook him and screamed, "I wish you were dead. I wish you'd never been born."

But a part of her was mortified by her behavior. What was wrong that she couldn't love her son? Why was she so dead inside? Such feelings made Pam ashamed. And Pam had left shame behind on her wedding day. She wasn't about to be sorry for anything.

Always sensitive to appearances, Pamela understood the face she must show to the world. Lest she be labeled a monster, she doubled her public efforts to seem a doting parent. When people commented on Jacob's easy going nature,

she vowed she'd never had a minute's trouble with him. If they mentioned his good looks, she smiled proudly. If they wanted to compare notes as to Jacob's progress, she rattled off the date that he'd first rolled over. Grace, who adored her grandsons, was certain that little Jacob was Pamela's favorite. And who could blame her? Charlie was darling, but Jacob was....well, Jacob was Jacob, and for those who came in contact with him, that was enough to explain why he was so loved.

Months before the murders, Pamela told Charles, "I know I made a lot of mistakes with Jacob. I never bonded with him and I feel terrible about that."

If Pam was capable of loving anyone, perhaps it was Charles. Charles clung to that hope through all the years of cruelty and abuse with Kermode. Before Kermode, she had been good. It was only after...

Everyone needs to love and be loved. We especially need our parents to love us, so, whether illusion or reality, Charles had to believe that Mommy loved him. She could be horrid, no doubt about that, but sometimes he glimpsed her softness and those fleeting moments sustained him. A child will die without love. To survive, he will construct love even where it isn't. If Pamela screamed, it was because she was a tough disciplinarian and was concerned that he be the very best. If she beat him, she beat Jacob more often and harder. If she slapped him across the mouth for crying, she was only preparing him for the reality of the cruel world that he would someday have to face. If she called him "faggot," it was because she didn't want him to be a sissy. If she seldom hugged him, men weren't supposed to need hugs or physical affection. It made them weak and Pam wanted him strong.

Especially as a small child, Charlie was devoted to his mother. Whenever she left, he wailed and clung to her. While Pam pretended annoyance, she was secretly pleased. He didn't cry that way with Frank or Lupe or anybody else. He loved her best, no doubt about it. She also appreciated his serious manner. He was more like a little man than a four-year-old. He helped her around the house by vacuuming and tidying up and already preferred the company of grownups. He abhorred dirt and was so well behaved and so much brighter than his playmates that Pamela was certain he would do her proud. When people looked at Charles they would know what good parents he had.

Correction, PARENT. Because, by the time Jacob was six months old, Frank Ind was history.

◊ ◊ ◊

Jacob's earliest memory—he says it could be a dream—is of his parents fighting. As Frank and Pamela quarrel over who's going to sit on the living room sofa, Charlie takes Jacob by the hand. Jacob, who is barely walking, toddles outside where Charlie shows him a fire truck or some other vehicle with wonderful flashing lights. That memory pretty much sums up Jacob's

99

life—fighting followed by his older brother's ineffective attempts to somehow protect them both.

Frank moved from their home into an apartment which he shared with Celeste,(*) a quiet girl nearly ten years his junior. Celeste is another of those people who seem to show up so often in Jacob's life—somebody who blends in, who doesn't quite seem to exist. She is totally unremarkable—of average height and weight, with nondescript features and a complexion that blends with her flaxen hair. She looks like the librarian she is.

Pamela hated Celeste because she was so young. She told friends, "It's not surprising Frank has to rob the cradle. He can't handle a real woman." Frank needed a naive little thing with no life experience who wouldn't be able to figure out what a spineless jellyfish he really was.

Still, the contrast rankled. Sometimes Pam felt closer to one hundred than twenty eight. California was filled with beautiful young women living off their daddies or sugar daddies. They could enjoy the beach or lounge beside their swimming pools or drive around with the tops down in their convertibles or spend the day at Fisherman's Wharf without having to arrange time off. They didn't have to worry about taking care of two young kids or making the rent payment or whether they could afford a silk blouse, even on sale. Pam wanted to walk barefoot along the beach and hike in the mountains and ride a bike through Yosemite National Park and wear expensive jewelry and have a manicure whenever she felt like it. Pam wanted to LIVE, not merely exist.

After their first separation, Pamela had purchased the small house she and the boys lived in. In an uncharacteristically generous offer, she tried to negotiate what was an undeniably favorable settlement for Frank.

Lupe Thorson remembers, "Pam agreed that if Frank would quit claim the house over to her, she would forego any request for child support. The house didn't have a huge amount of equity, but Pam didn't want to have to sell it and uproot herself and the boys."

Although Frank has long protested that he never cared anything about his wife's money, there are contradictory versions of his behavior.

"Frank told Pam he wouldn't give up his portion of the equity," Lupe says. "He also wanted half of her pension from Pacific Bell. When she protested, Frank threatened to take her to court. Well, you just didn't do that to Pam. She was furious."

Pamela railed that she wasn't about to support that worthless bum forever. If Frank wanted to play rough, he would soon discover that he was no match for Pamela Jean Wallace.

By the time the divorce was granted, not only was Frank denied any part of Pam's pension, but he was ordered to pay $260.00 a month child support. Most galling of all, he had to assume their credit card debts, which included the recent purchase of a $3,000 blue flowered couch with matching valance that Frank hated. Whenever Pam allowed herself to be vulnerable and she was

100

kicked in the teeth for her efforts, she lashed back with a vengeance. She had tried to be fair, so the greedy bastard got exactly what he deserved. Even after the murders Frank was bemoaning the injustice of their divorce.

Frank's credibility is further eroded by similar incidents. A few years following their divorce, he and Celeste forged Pam's name to a credit application for furniture. Unable to handle money, Frank's credit was lousy so he decided to use his ex-wife's. He'd had to pay off that $3,000 monstrosity of Pam's, so wasn't turnabout fair? If he hadn't been saddled with her debts, he'd have been able to buy something nice for him and Celeste. Or so he rationalized his crime. Pam had no idea of Frank's actions until she and Lupe went car shopping. During a credit check her name appeared on a Sears credit card that she didn't own. Only after she threatened to call the D.A. did Frank even own up to the act.[21]

Frank was also lax about paying child support.[22] Several times Lupe Thorson heard Pamela call her ex, asking for money. $260.00 was hardly a large sum even with Frank's marginal income, but as far as Pam was concerned, the money was just another reminder that Frank was a deadbeat dad. The way she saw it, Jacob and Charlie came second behind his golf and other interests.

Still, there is no doubt that Frank loved his boys. He was proud of having fathered two such handsome children and beamed when people said Jacob looked like him. But Frank wasn't quite sure how to be a father. Pam overdid the discipline, but he ignored it. When they misbehaved, he retreated just the way he'd retreated from Pam's wrath. He liked to roughhouse with them and take them out for ice cream or to the beach, but when it came to being a day to day father he had no idea.

Frank might call Pam a money-grubbing bitch, but she never took him back to court for more child support. She often told Jacob and Charles that she could make him pay up to $2,000 a month, which is highly unlikely, but even if it were true, she never pursued the possibility. Maybe Pam simply believed in the old adage, 'You can't squeeze blood out of a stone.' Frank would never have any money and it was pointless to harass him. What Pamela needed to do was find herself an educated man, say, a vice president of a company, who could provide her with the security she so desperately craved.

---

[21] Jacob, who has become close to his father since the murders and believes Frank has taught him the meaning of love, disputes this story. "Never happened. That was a lie my mom told Charles that I overheard as a kid and I confronted my dad about it."

[22] Jacob also disputes this. "My dad sent me xeroxes of every one of his canceled checks. My mom was a pathological liar. She'd make up things or put up a phony front in order to back up her lies, but none of it's true.

Pam continued working. It wasn't easy, but Lupe helped out with babysitting. Pam really depended on her friend. After putting the kids to bed, they often retreated to the backyard patio to drink a beer or smoke a joint. Sometimes as they relaxed in companionable silence the strangest thing happened. They could somehow tap into each other's thoughts and carry on conversations without speaking. Or Lupe would frame a question in her mind which Pam answered out loud. Realizing what they'd just done, they looked at each other and burst out laughing.

That psychic closeness lasted until Pam's death. Whenever something traumatic happened in either woman's life, the phone soon rang.

"I know something's wrong," Pam would say. "What's happening?" Or Lupe called, only to hear Pam respond, "I was just thinking of you."

With all the revelations that have surfaced since Pam's death, including dark ones involving her own family, Lupe now laments, "I never knew her at all."

But Pam never shared herself with anybody. Maybe bits and pieces, but never the entire "Pamela Jean." She never allowed anyone to get that close. Perhaps Kermode, but he was the mirror of her shadow side. He understood because he was just like her. She certainly couldn't confide in Lupe, who, in many ways, was Pam's opposite. How could Pam confess that she hated her children to the original earth mother? How could she tell a woman who opened her house to the world that she clung to her possessions and considered visitors spies who must be quickly dismissed? How could she tell someone so open about her own dark feelings?

Pam often said that she and Lupe were closer than sisters, but considering how estranged Pam was from her family, that wasn't much of a compliment. And Pam was secretly jealous of her best friend. Lupe could stay home whereas Pam was running ever faster on that same old treadmill. Pam both loved and hated Lupe Thorson. How come Lupe was so lucky? What had she done to deserve such an easy life? When Lupe and her husband were having problems, Pam urged her to divorce Chet. Then she unsuccessfully tried to seduce him. But Pamela didn't stop with the attempted corruption of Lupe's husband. She committed the ultimate betrayal. And she did it with Lupe's son.

When Lupe babysat, she generally brought her son Eric and baby daughter along. Eric was a handsome black-haired green-eyed four-year-old. Once he'd been outgoing and fearless, but his behavior abruptly changed when he was around two. He quit talking and his sleep was troubled by nightmares. Lupe and Chet took him to various doctors. Some spoke vaguely of possible learning disabilities. One postulated that Eric had suffered a traumatic event in his young life, but Lupe had no idea what could have happened. She just knew that

somewhere along the way, her bright, laughing son had disappeared. He was quiet and shy, especially around Pam. Lupe sensed that Pamela didn't like him, but she ignored her intuition for nearly fifteen years, until revelations at Jacob's trial finally explained Eric's past. Until then, Lupe told herself that a grown woman couldn't dislike a child. She was just picking up on Pam's disapproval of her child-rearing methods, which her friend considered far too lax.

"You spoil your children," Pamela said. "Someday you're gonna be sorry."

Pam was a tough disciplinarian, no doubt about it. She was quick as a striking snake with her hands. One moment they'd be at her side and the next thing either Jacob or Charlie would be holding their faces, crying. She even slapped Eric once, but that was too much for Lupe.

"I wouldn't do that to your children, so don't do that to mine."

Pam backed off. She needed Lupe, both as a friend and a babysitter. Lupe was wonderful with Charlie and Jacob. She particularly loved her "little Jacob-beaner." He was just so sweet natured and he cuddled so nicely that she held him for hours at a time. Pam resented all that touching and holding. Jacob better not think that SHE was going to spend half her life fawning over him the way Lupe did. But Pamela was careful not to reveal her true feelings about her infant son. Once when Lupe helped her tuck Jacob in his crib, she gushed, "Can you believe that I actually wanted to get an abortion?"

Occasionally, the mask slipped. During one naptime, Lupe entered the bedroom to find Pamela bent over the crib, whispering between clenched teeth, "I hate you. I wish you'd die. I wish I'd had an abortion."

When Pam realized Lupe's presence, she quickly picked up her crying son. "I didn't mean it," she said, hugging Jacob. Lupe attributed Pam's actions to post-partum depression. It was a given that everybody loved Jacob. It was inconceivable that his own mother didn't.

Another of Pamela's actions was harder to explain away. Not only did she often comment on her son's "cute little dick," but several times when changing Jacob's diapers, she played with his penis and laughed, "Oh, look! He has a hard on." Lupe was disturbed by Pam's vulgarity, but in the seventies incest was something that didn't happen, and it sure didn't happen with your best friend. Pam could be way too forward when it came to sex, but Lupe figured SHE was being a prude. Besides, if Pam was doing something wrong, she wouldn't do it in front of anybody, would she? Still, when she touched Jacob that way Lupe felt as if something evil had entered that cheery little bedroom with its animal wallpaper and gauzy white curtains. Pam reminded her of some huge malevolent spider skittering toward its victim. Lupe tried to rationalize away her unease. She had been programmed by all those years of Catholic upbringing, all those nuns and priests preaching about good and evil and the devil lurking around every corner readying to leap into the hearts of men. Pam's actions might seem inappropriate, but she loved to shock people. She often teased Lupe about being repressed, and she was right. Weren't people supposed to be open and

honest about expressing their sexuality? Psychologists postulated that if parents were uninhibited around their children, they wouldn't grow up with neuroses. Lupe wasn't sure how pulling a baby's penis could help him, and she didn't know whether she agreed with current theory, but Pam didn't like being told what to do, anyway. Best just to change Jacob's diapers as often as she could, even when Pam was around, and hope that her disapproval registered.

Pamela did very well at the phone company. Despite her lack of a college degree, she became an engineer. She loved wielding power over men, wearing a hard hat, climbing around construction sites and bossing co-workers. She harped on the smallest transgression, the slightest deviation from blueprints. She spoke in harsh, clipped tones, adopted male gestures and mannerisms and was absolutely heartless to anyone in a position beneath her. Watching Pamela Jean wield power was not a pretty sight. She never lost the opportunity to publicly humiliate anyone who crossed her. Men hated her and the knowledge delighted her because there wasn't a thing they could do about it. She was running the show, and if anybody forgot, she did her damndest to see that they were fired. It was payback time, and payback could be a bitch.

Her new position meant a nice raise, but Pam was always stressed between the demands of her job and her children. Jacob had started walking and, while Lupe observed that he was a remarkably obedient child, Pam privately despaired that he was into everything. He and Charlie exhausted her. Many evenings after picking them up from the sitters, she had everybody fed and bathed and in bed by six o'clock. And, once she put them down, neither of them had better move. Sometimes Jacob didn't get it and he started hollering. Pam just wanted to stuff a pillow over his face to shut him up. She often drank, and the alcohol fueled her dislike. Black was how she felt, black as the surrounding darkness, black as the California night, black as the memories stirred by that pathetic wail. She lay in the gloom, listening to that helpless cry, trying to ignore all the conflicting emotions and images it stirred. She remembered lying in another bed, stiff and watchful, senses straining to hear the whisper of footsteps in the hall. That Pamela had been small and vulnerable and she hated her. As she hated the whisper of the opening door and that huge shadow gliding toward her...

Jacob was a reminder of how powerless she'd once been. And that, for Pamela Jean, was the most unforgivable sin of all.

◇ ◇ ◇

A year after the divorce Pamela decided that she'd had enough of motherhood. She showed up at Frank's doorstep with a sniffling Charlie by her side and Jacob in her arms.

"I don't want them anymore," she told her startled ex-husband. "You take them. I need to find myself."

With that declaration, Pamela Jean walked out of Charlie and Jacob's lives.

Children, you are very little
And your bones are very brittle.

~Robert Louis Stevenson
'Good and Bad Children'

I, a stranger and afraid
In a world I never made.

~A.E.Houseman
Last Poems

Chapter 15

Pam was happy in her spacious two bedroom apartment. It had lots of
closet space for her silk blouses and Evan Picone suits, and tile kitchen
countertops that nicely showed off her appliances. She decorated the living room
with her blue flowered three thousand dollar couch and matching valance that
Frank was still paying for. She hung photographs of her family on the walls and
ferns from the ceiling and settled into life as an unencumbered woman. The
complex primarily housed singles and Pam spent a lot of time sunbathing by the
swimming pool. She received a lot of male attention. She had those magnificent
Indian eyes and it was only in profile or when she was angry that you really
noticed her large nose, weak chin, and overbite (which she later corrected with
braces.) Pam was slender and not at all modest about showing off her figure.
Who would have guessed that somebody in such great shape could be the mother
of two? Pam herself almost forgot. It was as easy to wipe Charlie and Jacob from
her mind as it was to wipe off the water drops from the pool furniture upon
which she lounged. The intimate photographs in her apartment were for show.
They could be trotted out when she wanted to look feminine or evoke sympathy
or be petted and praised for having borne two such handsome children, but she
made it clear that Father had custody of the sons. Prospective husbands need
not worry about messy entanglements. Pamela went for days without thinking
about her boys, and weeks without seeing them. Frank was forever trying to get
her to babysit or shame her into taking them back, but she paid about as much
attention to him as she did the ants on the sidewalk.

While Pam dated a lot of men, she particularly liked Alphonso Gonzales,
a handsome, green-eyed carpet layer. Al wasn't socially acceptable. He was the
wrong race and educational background, but he pampered her and she loved it.
He was every woman's dream—attentive and helpful, the kind of guy who would
help the hostess clean up after a dinner party or ask, "What can I do?" and
genuinely mean it. Despite the fact that Al was blue collar, he made decent
money which he lavished on Pam, another plus.

The main drawback was his three children. No way she was going to get
suckered into raising somebody else's kids. They were older—Sonny and

105

Lorraine were in their early teens, though Victor was the same age as Charlie—but like all kids they were spoiled and disobedient and she detested them.

Sonny, Lorraine and Victor openly returned her dislike. They had seen Pam in action at various parties and in their opinion she was nothing but a hard-drinking, loud-mouthed slut. If Pam was with people she considered social equals, she guarded her language and acted like a lady, but watch her around their dad's friends. She was lewd and crude. Al might be fooled by her—a lot of adults were—but she never bothered to pretend with kids and the Gonzales children knew exactly what she was.

Pam had the discretion of a bitch dog in heat, and seemed to enjoy having sex where others could see or hear. Nor was she inhibited about her body, not that Sonny, in particular, thought she had much to show off. Pam was going through one of her "man" phases when she'd chopped off all her hair, and she was so thin and flat chested that she could be mistaken for a boy. And her eyes were always so mean—but maybe that's because she was looking at him. Pam had certain looks for grown ups and certain looks for children. Just the way she had different tones of voice. She addressed kids as if they were mutants without minds or feelings, whose sole purpose in existing was to infuriate her.

The Gonzales kids particularly hated Pam's hypocrisy. Pretending around their dad that she was so high class and refined when they knew different. They saw her perform at the wedding of a mutual friend. Not only did Pam get drunk, but during various breaks in the reception she and a couple of mariachi players disappeared at different times inside the back of the band's van. Sonny and Lorraine and a bunch of other kids stood outside listening to the lovemaking, watching the van rock, and cracking jokes. When Pam and the mariachi players finally finished, they got out and rearranged their clothes in front of their audience. Pam cast Sonny a look like, "I dare you to tell your dad, you little sonofabitch." Then they returned to the reception as if nothing had happened. Sonny did indeed tell Al, and his and Pam's relationship subsequently cooled. The Gonzales children were relieved that "The Bitch," as they called her, appeared to be permanently out of their lives.

Pam continued her liaisons at Pacific Bell. She found herself pregnant yet a fourth time and arranged for a second abortion. Occasionally, Charlie called. She assured her sobbing six-year-old that she would visit him and Jacob soon. The moment she hung up she forgot her promise.

Pam had almost convinced herself that she didn't even have any children beyond those smiling faces in their silver frames when she received the unfortunate news. The apartments were being turned into condominiums. Pam would have to move.

Without warning, Pamela Jean turned up once again at her ex-husband's.

"I want my boys back, " she said.

Frank gave them to her.

◇ ◇ ◇

Pam was depressed over losing her apartment and with her return to her old life. After putting the boys to bed, she often sat at the kitchen table and drowned her unhappiness in beer. Life was a bitch. Sure, she had a good job, but she still didn't make enough money and she lived in a shoebox of a house while right across the bay, in San Francisco, women her age lived in fairy castles. Sometimes Pam supplemented her income by selling drugs and her body. She liked the excitement of crossing the line into the forbidden, but the occasional cheap thrill couldn't blind her to the fact that she was nearly thirty years old, she was a divorcee with two kids, and the years stretched ahead with little to recommend them—work, nursemaiding her sons, middle age, work, old age, work, retirement, death.

Sometimes Charlie wondered whether the only reason his mother wanted him and Jacob back was to have a handy source on whom to vent her frustrations. Charlie's most vivid memory of that time is when they three visited Lupe's spacious two story. Charlie took the bookkeeping keys to one of Lupe's file cabinets. When Lupe discovered they were lost, she, Charlie and Pam hunted around the study until Pam spotted them near a book shelf. The whole episode took up maybe fifteen minutes of a two hour visit. Lupe wasn't upset and Pam, after giving Charlie a lecture on keeping one's hands to oneself, appeared to have forgotten.

On the ride home, Charlie sensed that something was wrong. His mother's face started getting that look that he and Jacob dreaded. When Pam was angry her nose got sharper. All her facial muscles tightened and her eyes bugged. She looked really gawky and tight skinned—the same way she did when she was drunk.

Charlie was frightened. He sat in the backseat with his body pressed against the door and his fingers digging into his palms, trying to think of some way to prevent what he knew was going to happen.

Once in the privacy of the house, Charlie retreated to his room. Pamela grabbed him and shoved him into her bedroom. She yanked down his pants and underwear.

"You little bastard," she yelled, reaching for the belt. "When are you going to learn to obey? When are you gonna behave yourself?"

Pam beat Charlie unmercifully, not only on his bare buttocks but on his lower back and legs.

"It seemed like she wouldn't quit. Just beat and beat me. She hit me one final time and suddenly dropped the belt and she said, 'Damn.' And she stopped."

107

Pamela had hurt her hand. Even so, Charlie couldn't sit down for many hours afterward.

When people look back on that period of the boys' lives, they often ask, "Where was Jacob?" He had already perfected the art of disappearing. Sometimes you could share the same room and not even know he was there. Jacob had learned that it was dangerous to call attention to himself and could withdraw so completely that he almost ceased to exist.[23] Even now, despite his high profile, Jacob aspires to anonymity. What better way to disappear than to be one of hundreds in a prison uniform, identified by a number instead of a name—just one male face and form among many?

By the age of two, Jacob understood that being noticed caused problems. The only time his mother paid any attention to him was when he'd done something wrong. While Pamela was hard on Charles, she reserved a wooden spoon for Jacob. After breaking the spoon over his bare buttocks, she replaced it with a cutting board.

If Jacob cried or laughed too loud, slammed the door or sat the wrong way, out came the bread paddle—at least till she broke it—or Dr. Stick, a switch which hung on the side of the refrigerator.

Jacob was terrified of his mother and her implements of torture. He tried so hard to be quiet and good, though he was never sure quite what he'd done to upset Mommy. Whatever it was he didn't want to do it again. He lived in dread of seeing that awful expression on her face. He had nightmares about witches, in the form of his teachers at Action Day Pre-School, tying him up and throwing him in a big kettle and eating him alive.

Grace and Dick had moved closer to Pamela so they could visit more frequently. Grace was concerned for the boys. Pam was under such a lot of stress and she seemed to take it out on Jacob. It was hard being a single parent and Grace didn't want to criticize, but one time she went over to the house to find Jacob trying to hide from Pamela behind some curtains and crying his heart out.

Grace suggested, "Perhaps you should get some sort of counseling. Or at the very least get Frank to spend more time with Jacob and Charlie so you can have a break. The boys shouldn't suffer because you're so unhappy."

What Grace couldn't understand was how her daughter could ever be mean to Jacob. She tried to believe that everything was fine and Pamela Jean was a wonderful mother, but she couldn't ignore the fear in Jacob's eyes, or the way both boys were more like robots than children. Pamela said something and those boys did it, no questions asked. Grace was all for discipline, but this seemed extreme. After observing her daughter's interaction with her youngest son, she assured herself that Pamela and Jacob had a normal relationship. But her heart

---

[23] Kermode had the same facility. He could be dominant and arrogant and a commanding presence, or he could fade away.

told her something else.

Pam was not the kind of woman that any child would naturally seek out for maternal warmth or attention. There was nothing soft or yielding or gentle about Pamela Jean. But Jacob was desperate for affection. He wanted so much for her to stroke him and treat him nice. His dad was good to him, as were his grandparents and his Tia, who rocked him and sang *Puff the Magic Dragon*. But he needed his Mommy's love. Sometimes he stood in front of her, looking up at her with those huge brown eyes. He ached for her to hold him, but he didn't dare raise his arms. She'd merely slap them away.

Pam would scowl down at him. "Get out of here. Leave me alone." She shoved him. "Go to your room."

Jacob did as he was told. Crying only made things worse so he picked up his legos and began constructing imaginary space ships.

Jacob was a bright boy. He soon figured out that asking for Pamela's attention was futile, so he convinced himself that he never needed it in the first place. But what Jacob never figured out was the nature of his terrible sin. What was wrong with him, what evil had he committed that had made him so unworthy of his mother's love?

It was around this time that Pamela and Al Gonzales decided to move in together. Pamela hated the idea of having to put up with Al's three kids, but Sonny and Lorraine were old enough to be built-in babysitters and housekeepers. It was an added plus that Al and his children got along well with Charlie and Jacob. The Gonzales's enjoyed both boys though Charlie could be irritating. He was a mama's boy, which they could never understand, and, despite the fact that he was seven years old, always wanted to hang around grownups. But J.J., as everybody called him, was adorable. He was just learning to really talk and he said the cutest things. Al and his kids chuckled at everything he did. After his baths, J.J. loved to run around naked. They all laughed at his pudgy legs and arms and his delighted giggles as they swatted his behind or chased him. J.J. was really something special. You couldn't help but love him.

I interviewed Al several months after the murders. Because of the gag order and the intervening distance, he hadn't heard about the deaths. As his second marriage crumbled, he had even fantasized about a reconciliation with Pam, who had been the love of his life. It was impossible to believe that little J.J. would have done such a terrible thing, though the knowledge did nothing to diminish Al's love.

"Jacob was irresistible," Al explained. "He was a beautiful child, and so sweet-natured. He was so affectionate that you couldn't help but be affectionate in return."

Jacob used to crawl up in Al's lap and snuggle against him. Jacob, who likened Al to a giant teddy bear, remembers burrowing against that enormous chest and how safe he felt. Twelve years later, he was stunned to discover that he towers over Al and there is no evidence of either a huge chest or belly.

But, as Lorraine said, "J.J. only came up to our ankles, so he looked upon everybody as huge!"

J.J. hated fighting and dissension. He wanted everybody to get along. If he could make them laugh to defuse the tension, that's what he did. Even then he had a delightful sense of humor and after coaxing a grin out of someone, his own face beamed like a cherub's. When the Gonzaleses saw Jacob smile in the courtroom, all the intervening years dropped away. If only for a few moments, their little J.J. was back.

Al only remembers two disquieting things concerning the boys. One night after going into Jacob's bedroom to check on him, Jacob threw his arms around Al's neck. "I feel safe when you're here," he said.[24] Al also remembers returning home from work to find Jacob and Charlie hiding in the back yard behind some trees. When he finally persuaded them to come out they were terrified but they never explained why.

Other than that, his and Pam's relationship was idyllic. She was a good woman—intelligent, sensitive, hard working, and a devoted mother. Sure, she was tough on Charlie and Jacob but that's because she wanted the best for them. The only unsettling thing Al remembered was the way she'd suddenly appear in the bathroom when he was taking a shower. He would look out and she'd be standing in front of the glass door, staring at him. It scared the hell out of him. And it was odd how after they moved in together their lovemaking virtually stopped. They were more like some old married couple than lovers. Sometimes he had the feeling Pam didn't even like sex, though that seemed impossible. When they were dating, she'd been insatiable. But for Pam, sex was ever about wielding power, not about love. After that, it was dispensable--just as friendships, babies, out-dated clothing and a chipped dinner plate were dispensable.

Al's children hated "The Bitch." Even after a decade they remember her cruelty and expressed no surprise over the murders. They just couldn't believe that J.J. would have been the one to pull the trigger.

"I don't blame Jacob for killing her," Sonny said. "Somebody should have a long time ago."

Pamela was careful to save different parts of herself for different people. Al got her good side. The kids got the bad. Charles and Jacob were okay to trot

---

[24] Jacob scoffs at the notion. "A little boy would never use a term like 'safe,'" he says.

out at certain times, when she wanted to impress Al with her mother act. Otherwise they were shadow children. She wanted nothing to do with them beyond, "Hi, Kids, I'm home." A couple of minutes of obligatory chatter and that was enough. After that they'd better disappear, or she would reach for Dr. Stick.

She was mean to Al's kids, but seldom in his presence. She was careful never to touch his two oldest, mainly because teenagers weren't safe. Sonny was big and tough enough to hit back, though Lorraine, with her soft eyes and motherly ways was no threat. Pam called Lorraine, "Fatso!", harassed her about her weight, and treated like her personal slave. She was meanest to Victor, who at six, was vulnerable. She poked him in the chest with her finger, called him names, pinched and slapped him.

When Al's children tried to tell their father, he, like so many adults in Pamela's life, sided with her. She was such a convincing liar. Who would believe that someone so seemingly sweet could suddenly turn into a demon? For the most part the Gonzales children, like all the children Pamela tormented, suffered in silence. Sometimes Sonny stomped around in the sand and mud in the front yard and tracked it inside on the dark shag carpet. Then he jumped all over her lovely furniture. Surprisingly, Pam, who seemed to have a sixth sense about dirt, never noticed.

Pam saved her worst punishments for her own children. They were little. They were well trained. She didn't have to worry about them striking back or tattling. She could do what she wanted with them, and she did. She was forever hitting and humiliating them. When she slapped them—her favorite punishment—her face was transformed. She looked absolutely evil.

Pam often beat Jacob on his bare bottom with a ping pong paddle.[25] Should Charlie and Jacob do something she disliked she invariably ordered them to go to their rooms. Oftentimes, she washed Jacob's mouth out with soap beforehand. Should she later find evidence of soap or saliva on his bed coverings, she slapped him or repeated the entire process. If the boys didn't retreat to their bedrooms quickly enough, Pamela yanked them off the ground by their arms with enough force to dislocate their shoulders. As they flailed helplessly in the air, she smacked their bottoms several times and pushed them into their rooms. Both boys were terrified of the dark. She made them stay there with the shades shut, the lights turned off and the door closed. They always sat in the darkest corner of the room, where the shadows were deepest and most threatening and they didn't dare move because she would hear if they shifted the chair so much as an inch on the wooden floors.

After work Pam and Al usually polished off a bottle of Blue Nun and

---

[25] The prosecutor called this normal discipline. The jury agreed.

locked themselves away in their bedroom. Sometimes Jacob needed his mommy, and stood outside their door, crying for her. If Al was home, she'd respond. If not, the door stayed closed. Lorraine sometimes got up and carried him back to bed. Or Jacob cried himself to sleep and she found him there the next morning, curled up in a ball. It was always Lorraine and never his own mother who scooped Jacob in her arms and returned him to his room.

During this time Charles had to have a series of operations on his leg to correct a congenital deformity. If left untreated he would have been crippled. Charles was required to wear a brace and perform special exercises. When I made disparaging remarks about Pamela's mothering skills, Jacob referred to this episode to show that Pam loved Charles, at least.

"Mom nursed Charles back to health," he said. "She helped him with all his exercises and did everything for him. She actually cried over Charles."

Jacob didn't really remember the operations or their aftermath. He is simply repeating another Pamela myth. The truth is Pamela never took any time off from work to assist Charles and in the evenings left most of the caretaking to others. Frank Ind swears that HE was the one who nursed Charlie. Al and his kids agree that Al generally tended to Charlie's needs. Occasionally, the seven-year-old lost control of his bowels, which disgusted Pam. Imperfection of any sort, even in her own children, aroused contempt rather than compassion. It was Al who cleaned him up afterward. The only thing Pamela did for Charlie was make him repeat third grade because he'd missed so much school. His grades were fine and the teachers thought that he should be passed, but Pam insisted.

While Al's memories of Pam have become romanticized, even he admits that during their time together Pam had several affairs. Face it. Al was a stopgap lover. He was Mexican, he was blue collar and he didn't make a six figure salary. Not good enough. But Al and Lupe's husband had recently received job offers in Saudi Arabia, which meant that her imperfect lover would soon be making lots of money. So, as Al readied to take off for Saudi Arabia, Pamela asked him to marry her.

Fall, 1981. Ronald Reagan was president, home mortgage rates hovered around 15% and AIDS was a disease nobody had ever heard of. 'Dallas' was the number one rated television show, Pink Floyd's, The Wall, topped the charts, Ted Kennedy divorced his wife of twenty-two years, Prince Charles married Lady Diana Spencer, and Pamela Jean Ind was engaged to be married. Her fiance had been gone a couple of months. Pam and Al made long distance preparations over the phone for their wedding upon his return the following year.

Jacob missed Al. He'd always wanted a daddy, and Al had been the closest

he'd ever had. But Charlie assured Jacob Al would soon be back. Then they'd have a new daddy forever.

While Pam was officially engaged, and had a respectable diamond to prove it, she still picked up men. What Al didn't know wouldn't hurt him. Besides he'd been gone more than two months. Did he seriously expect her to be celibate?

One night Pam went to an Irish pub in downtown San Jose where professionals hung out. Later, when retelling the myth of her introduction to husband number two, she falsely claimed that Lupe accompanied her. Pam generally went bar hopping on her own. The last thing she needed was competition, or some prude like Lupe reminding her that she was engaged and she should be staying home in her dinky, dreary house writing letters to Al rather than out enjoying herself.

The bar had dark mahogany paneling, lots of brass and red flocked wall paper. A haze of cigarette smoke hung over the booths and tables, largely filled with couples or groups. While Pam ordered a beer, she checked out the possibilities. One look and she could pretty much determine from a man's dress, haircut, jewelry and the way he carried himself whether he possessed enough money to interest her.

As the evening progressed, the place filled with Saturday night prowlers and pub crawlers. Pam was feeling good. She'd had enough to drink to make her loose and guys were falling all over themselves trying to pick her up. Sometime during the evening she noticed a distinguished looking man sitting alone at a nearby table. He was obviously older, maybe in his forties, which meant that he was established, and he was wearing a suit. Pam caught the gentleman staring at her a couple of times, so she flashed him one of her lovely smiles. When he didn't approach her, she went over to his table, plopped down on his lap and introduced herself.

A few minutes with the stranger and Pam's head was reeling. She was really onto something here! Not only was he tall and handsome, but he was obviously well educated, waving big words around as casually as he waved his cigarette. He was the president of his own company, Jordan Engineering, and he wasn't shy about revealing the fact that he made one hundred thousand dollars a year.

One hundred thousand dollars! When Pam looked into the gentleman's green eyes she saw dollar signs—lots of them. He was everything she'd ever wanted in a man. The fact that he was sixteen years older only added to his appeal. That was the perfect age difference. A man in his forties was reaching the peak of his earning power. Forget Al and his three bratty kids and his embarrassing accent and his calloused hands and his high school education.

By the evening's end Pamela knew that she was in love. And the lucky gentleman's name? Kermode Howard Jordan.

Doc Holliday:	"A man like Ringo has a great empty hole right through the middle of him. He can never kill enough or steal enough or inflict enough pain to ever fill it."
Wyatt Earp:	"What does he need?"
Holliday:	"Revenge."
Earp:	"For what?"
Holliday:	"For being born."

~Val Kilmer and Kirk Russell
Tombstone

Chapter 16

What was Kermode thinking when he met Pamela? For one thing, at 46, he must have been flattered that someone nearly two decades his junior, would find him attractive. Not that Kermode had ever had any difficulty attracting women. The first love of his life had been his mother, Thora, a tall angular woman with a hatchet face and a cap of badly dyed black hair. Thora adored her only child, Kermie. Kermode was breast fed until he was three, and there was no doubt that the number one man in Thora's life was not her husband but her son. Thora saved all Kermie's drawings, school programs, report cards, even scraps of paper with one or two words on them. Convinced her son would grow up and accomplish great things, she hoarded his childhood mementos as if they were precious jewels. Kermode returned Thora's love with slavish devotion. Should one of his wives make a negative comment about her mother-in-law, Kermode responded with a tongue lashing or a beating. He even emulated Thora's drinking problem and adopted her excuse to explain away his staggering and slurring.

"My mother's side of the family has Indian blood, which makes us allergic to alcohol. We don't drink very much, no more than anybody else, but that condition makes any alcohol have an exaggerated effect on our nervous systems."

Thora was what today some people call a "New Ager." Her letters to her son are filled with positive affirmations and spiritual teachings from gurus, Christian mystics, Scientologists and just about anyone who was a little outside the mainstream. "We are what we think." "We need only desire something and put that desire out to the universe and it will be fulfilled." "All things are possible." "We create our own happiness, just as we create our own sorrow." Thora never lost an opportunity to tell Kermode what a special person he was, what a unique and blessed being. If he would only take her principles to heart he would achieve the full potential God intended.

The Jordans were ranchers and miners from around Cortez, Colorado.

Kermode spent part of his childhood on a farm, which accounts for many of the stories he told Jacob about having sex with animals. Like Pamela, he didn't talk much about his childhood, though it was obviously violent. While beating Charlie and Jacob, he taunted, "What're you crying about? My father used to beat me with a knife-sharpening strap."

Kermode had his first real sexual experience when he was eight years old. He and the neighbor girl, an older woman in her early teens, touched and fondled each other. Hoping for more, the girl tried to bribe Kermode with chocolate chip cookies, but "he was too young to do anything." Not for long. By the time he and Pamela met, he had been married four times and had enjoyed many affairs. 120 Ridge Drive contained hundreds of letters, many from various romantic liaisons spanning thirty years. In the early sixties, when abortion was still illegal, he persuaded two girlfriends to terminate their pregnancies. Both wrote of their fear, unhappiness and pain when Kermode cast them aside afterward. He even reneged on a promise to pay for one's abortion.

It is impossible to know how much Thora realized concerning Kermode's promiscuity. Blinded by love, she generally only saw the best in her son. She blamed all those awful women for chasing Kermie and when the relationships turned sour, THEY were responsible. Occasionally, a certain amount of disapproval does slip through. In a letter from the 1970's she accused Kermode of being sick and perverted. 'You treat women shamefully. You're cruel and your morals are disgraceful. You're dishonoring the Jordan name. You must get help or you'll end up in the gutter...'

She didn't specifically state what he had done to so disgust her, but it apparently involved a much younger woman. Kermode was between wives at the time. Wife number one had suffered through numerous infidelities and his indifference to their baby girl, Justine. Kermode only saw his daughter once or twice a year. In a conversation with Charles after the murders, Justine remembered watching her father try to strangle her mother. [25]

Wife number two termed herself the classic battered wife. Kermode tried to kill her after she made a comment about his mother. Barbara Turrentine also had a baby boy that Kermode sometimes acknowledged as his and sometimes didn't. That son is now in prison. Wife number three is a mystery. Wife number four, Shannon, bore Cameron, Kermode's only son. Shannon was great in bed but stupid out of it, according to Kermode, and that marriage only lasted a few years.

During and between his many marriages he had a string of girlfriends-- almost exclusively with dark hair. He also frequented strip joints and porno

---

[25] At the trial, both mother and daughter said that he was a model parent and father.

shops. He recounted a story to Jacob about spending time in the x-rated part of Tijuana, watching a naked woman on stage having sex with a Great Dane. Thora would have had much to be disgusted about.

Never having known Kermode, save through Jacob's eyes, it is hard for me to be objective. In his early years, before the ravages of booze became undeniable, he would probably be called handsome. Pictures of him taken during a stint in New York when he wanted to become an actor (he got out of the profession because there were too many "faggots"), show an almost pretty young man. His voice, which I heard on various tapes, is rather deep and pleasant. When contesting a drunk driving charge before a California judge, it is openly sarcastic, supercilious. I can imagine him lashing Charles and Jacob or anyone unlucky enough to encounter his wrath. Kermode was facile with words and he used them to wound—and wound and wound. In a tape where he is reciting his poetry, accompanied by a saxophone and various beatnik type music, he is heavily dramatic. After the poetry drifts into conversation he also sounds drunk and pompous. His voice is slightly slurred, as if he had to be wary of false teeth or inebriation. Pamela can be heard making admiring comments. She often expressed awe of Kermode's education and vocabulary. When he started pontificating, she clung to his every word the way a student would an admired professor.

After Kermode graduated from his pretty boy phase, he could probably be described as "ruggedly handsome." By the time he died, a common adjective was "professional." Kermode was tall, 6'2", with long, skinny legs and an unimpressive torso. If he was the golden glove boxer he claimed to be, it must have been through some sort of innate talent. He clearly spent little or no time working out. He had light brown curly hair and depending on the fashion of the time, generally wore it long. He often sported a beard or a mustache.

One of the most interesting things about both Pamela and Kermode was the way they changed their appearance. Many times they can't be recognized from one photograph to the other. Kermode had long hair, stylishly cut. No, unkempt and more like a bush. Here his hair is short. He's clean shaven and looks like a non-descript businessman. No, he has shoulder length hair, a full beard and would be right at home in a daguerreotype of a mountain man. Sometimes his clothing is flamboyant; sometimes it's conservative.

In the mid-sixties when Kermode was thirty, he returned to college for a master's degree in philosophy. Every campus newspaper, every term paper, every notebook from that time was boxed up inside the shed next to 120 Ridge Drive. Despite his highly touted intellect, most of Kermode's grades were C's. No professor seemed impressed with his abilities, and when reading his work, the word "pretentious" often came to mind. Kermode also dabbled in the literary, writing several chapters about a black man who was stopped by the police. The writing is pompous and windy and amateurish. "Here," he seems to be saying, "I will give you my views on authority." "Here I will give you my

philosophy of life." "Here I will give you some big words." "Here I will give you both my philosophy and big words." [26]

Studying wasn't the only thing Kermode did on the college campus of Berkeley. Lyndon Johnson was president and Vietnam was heating up. More young men were being drafted and more body bags being shipped back from Southeast Asia. Although Kermode had quietly allowed himself to be drafted into the Army back in the fifties, he was now one of millions protesting the Vietnam war. He wrote anti-war columns for the student newspaper, smoked pot, dropped acid, staged protest rallies, and helped bomb a couple of recruiting offices.

In addition to being a revolutionary and a philosopher, Kermode fancied himself a painter. His paintings are bizarre—a devilish looking figure, all angles and planes, in a dress; a picture of a skull with a rose between its teeth and a crown of thorns on its head. A sketch of a naked man with something, possibly a woman, emerging from his stomach, and oil paintings of green-headed demons. The margins of his college notebooks are filled with grotesque figures and naked women.

Sometime during his time at Berkeley Kermode also started dabbling in the occult. In one of his books, *The Black Arts*, he scribbled, 'I've tried these spells and they work.' He talked about how there is a dark side in every man and how evil is better than good. Kermode was always fascinated by the satanic, and engaged in various minor rituals over the years. Thora's belief in the metaphysical was bastardized by her son into something far darker. Although Kermode had many books in his library on Christianity, eastern religions, reincarnation, the power of mind over matter, healing and magic, whatever he was looking for, he didn't find it in the spiritual.

By the time Kermode and Pamela met, Kermode may have been able to project the image of the prosperous businessman but his success was bogus. He had been fired from various positions for drinking binges and had a checkered employment record. Even when he held down a job at various engineering firms, his performance reports were dismal. 'You are not a team player,' his superiors wrote. 'Your work is sloppy.' 'You are arrogant and uncooperative. Nobody wants to partner with you.'

As far as his statement that he was a hundred thousand dollar a year man, any union carpenter or even a manager at Burger King, made more money than Kermode Jordan. He had been through at least one bankruptcy and he was forever late on his child support payments. It seems a bad joke that while Pamela viewed Kermode as a meal ticket, he regarded her in the same light. Pamela made around fifty thousand in 1981. Kermode made half that.

---

26 In one of the many ironies of Jacob's and Kermode's relationship, Jacob is a far more naturally talented writer than his mentor.

When Lupe Thorson was first introduced to Kermode, she was appalled. Pam had raved so much about her "dreamboat," but Kermode, who was in the middle of a serious drinking binge, looked closer to sixty than forty. He had an old man's film over his eyes; he was unkept and seedy looking. Pam gushed about his salary and position and education, but all Lupe could think was, He gives me the creeps.

"What do you know about this guy?" she asked. "You met him in a bar. How do you know he isn't a pervert?"

Lupe had always stood by her friend and her decisions, but Kermode was different. He made her uneasy. "I wasn't impressed by either his degrees or his intellect. He seemed like any other drunk to me. And Pam was moving way too fast. She'd only met him a couple of nights ago and they were already talking about moving in together?"

Pamela was so angry over Lupe's negativity that she threw her friend's gifts and belongings on the front lawn and refused to speak to her for several months.

There was also the matter of Al, Pamela's fiance. What was she going to do about him? Apparently nothing. He had served his purpose. Pamela didn't owe him an explanation. She didn't owe him anything. Pam took her phone off the hook and told Lupe, "Tell him the engagement is off." She forbade the boys to ever utter his name. Charlie and Jacob were to wipe Al Gonzales out of their memories. He had ceased to exist because Pamela had said so.

After her marriage, Jacob once met Al in the supermarket. Jacob ran over to him, thrust his little hand in his, and said, "Come home with us, Al. Come home." All these years later, Al still cries when he remembers.

After receiving news of the breakup, Al returned from Saudi Arabia as soon as possible, but it was too late. Now that Pam is dead and St. Pam is being resurrected, Al maintains that they always remained friends.

"When we broke up, Pam went off to meditate for a while, and then returned to say our relationship wasn't working. We parted amicably."

The idea of Pam "meditating" over anything brings derisive snorts from those who knew her. Pam introspective? Not in this lifetime. And how she and Al could have conversed from a distance of several thousand miles is another mystery. Al's romantic version is also contradicted by his own children. In fact, he was so angry over Pamela's betrayal that he broke into her house and stole some sculptured butterflies he had given her. Only Pam's threat to call the police prompted their return.

Four days after meeting Kermode, Pamela brought him home to her small house on Woodmont Avenue. She had been reluctant to reveal the fact that she had two small sons. She didn't want anything to louse up this relationship and she worried that a man who was old enough to have grown children would react negatively to Charlie and Jacob. She was relieved when Kermode told her that he loved little boys. So many men were turned off by family responsibilities. It

further reinforced her belief that she had found someone very special.

While Kermode professed to be pleased about having an instant family, Pamela wasn't thrilled with the idea of getting stuck with a third boy in the form of Kermode's son, Cameron. Cameron's mother, who lived in San Francisco, had full time custody, so Pamela would tolerate the eight year old, but only until she'd firmly hooked her fish.

Jacob doesn't remember much about his first meeting with Kermode other than that he was big and friendly and he had a nice son. Charles was quiet, sizing Kermode up, and what he saw he didn't like.

"Kermode was just too nice. I didn't trust him."

Charles didn't really want anybody moving in on him and Jacob and his mother. The three of them were just fine, at least until Al returned. He resented suddenly having to share his mother with somebody else, and he was confused by the way he and Jacob were supposed to pretend that the past year with Al hadn't existed. Kermode was an intruder. He was making their life more difficult and Charles didn't want any part of it.

Kermode could hardly believe his good fortune. Here he had a lovely young woman, in the prime of her life. Pam was dark-haired and dark-eyed like his mother, and he felt as if he'd just met a kindred soul. She was strong the way he was strong and their outlook on the world was similar. On a multitude of levels, many of them unspoken or even unconscious, they seemed a perfect fit. Kermode always maintained that Pamela was "the most phenomenal woman that he had ever known."

But there was more to Pamela Jean than just her face and her body and her good paying job. There was also the matter of her sons. Kermode was always good with kids, especially boys, staying up half the night to play Monopoly, or taking them fishing, skiing or camping. One Christmas he and son Cameron had shot out all the Christmas tree bulbs with Cameron's Christmas present, a pellet gun. Sometimes Kermode was like a big kid himself. So why would he mind two such attractive boys? Charles, so bright and articulate, was eight years old, with dark, curly hair and a mischievous smile. Then there was Jacob, who had to be one of the most beautiful children ever created.

I often imagine Kermode's meeting with Jacob. Jacob was shy and hung back, gazing at the big man through those magnificent brown eyes.

Pam pushed him forward. "This is your new daddy," she said.

Jacob wanted a daddy more than anything. He smiled hesitantly at Kermode. He guessed it was okay to have another daddy, especially one who seemed so friendly and enjoyed picking him up and holding him close. Jacob wanted only to please everybody and to be loved, and here was this big man, touching him and being so nice.

And Kermode, what was he thinking? That he'd just died and gone to heaven. Forget Pamela. Forget Charlie. Forget everyone and everything. Four times married, a ladies' man, Kermode had his own dark secret, and that was he

lusted after little boys. He took one look at Jacob, with his blond beatle-styled hair, round cheeks, soft mouth and charming baby voice, and Kermode fell in love. Someone like Jacob came along once in a lifetime. You might glimpse him at a baseball game or in a department store toddling beside his mother, or if the gods were kind, he might move in next door. But to be able to tuck him in every night and bathe him and hold him any time he pleased, and have it all be legal... Well, it was DESTINY!

Five minutes with Jacob and Kermode made up his mind. Not only was he going to move in with Pam, he would marry her—and have unlimited access to his own private harem. Pamela and Charlie and Jacob. But the others were merely incidentals, side trips on the great journey of Kermode's life. The true object of Kermode's desire stood before him, four years old, trusting and totally unaware of the fate that was about to befall him. Kermode had just met the love of his life, and it wasn't Pamela Jean.

It was Jacob.

A survivor may leave his hometown, leave
his family, never see the abuser again.
But he cannot leave his body forever...
Eventually, awareness of the body
returns, and with it awareness of the pain and
humiliation of the past.

~Linda T. Sanford
Strong At The Broken Places

PART FOUR
SOWING THE SEEDS

Chapter 17

When I first started interviewing Jacob, he told me that he didn't remember anything between the ages of five and nine. I found this interesting because his therapists figured that he'd been molested at around five.

Soon after the murders, Jacob's court-appointed psychiatrists, Drs. David Caster and Frank Barron, visited him at the Criminal Justice Center to begin their evaluations. When they questioned whether he'd been sexually abused, Jacob turned cold, and his heart seemed to drop to the pit of his stomach.[27]

Dr. Caster asked, "What would you do if Kermode sexually abused you?"
"I'd kill him!"

Jacob was startled by his response. He had no conscious memory of being molested, but he HAD killed Kermode. Could that have something to do with his reason?

Shaun Kaufman had warned me to stay away from sexual matters, which wasn't a problem. I didn't know anything about incest and I wasn't eager to learn. Especially when it might have darkened the life of someone I cared about. Too painful. Too unspeakable. Too incomprehensible. Better to pretend it had nothing to do with the events of December 17, 1992. Or, if it had, let someone qualified deal with it.

Jacob did sometimes mention the possibility of molestation. "Even if I was sexually abused, I wouldn't want to know," he told me."Ever since the psychiatrist asked me that, I've had second thoughts about it. It's possible, but I have that memory lapse." He tapped his temple. "If it DID happen--and I think it did even though I have no proof--it probably happened all those times that Kermode and I were alone. My mom DID work and Charles was in physical and mental therapy."

For someone who had no memory, it turned out that Jacob was right on

---

[27] Dr. Caster observed that he turned pale, his heart raced, and he had a panic attack.

target.

By the end of the first week at the jail, of working as a volunteer investigator, I had already fallen into a routine that plagued me throughout my involvement with Jacob. At night I fell asleep easily enough. Just entering the Criminal Justice Center was stressful and our sessions could be draining, so I was generally exhausted. But in the wee hours I awakened, thinking of him. What should I ask about the following day? How should I handle a particularly disturbing or revealing comment? How could I best reach him?

Over the months I came up with dozens of ideas. Some of them were moderately successful. Most might not have helped his memories but they passed the time and provided a lot of interesting conversation.

I attempted story writing and asking questions I found in various textbooks like, "If you were a fly on your bedroom wall, how would you describe what you see?" I tried workbooks on abuse. Jointly we read self-help books like John Bradshaw's, *Healing The Shame That Binds You*. Jacob hated that particular work. After struggling to around page 30, I finally said, "I don't blame you. If I were fifteen I wouldn't find this interesting either."

I asked Jacob to write with his non-dominant hand, which was supposed to open the pathway to the inner child. I brought pencils, pens and markers for him to draw with, though I hadn't a clue as to how to interpret his artwork. Almost daily we discussed his dreams, though my most common comment was, "Hmmm. I wonder what that means?" I even tried an amateur version of ink blots. Generally we both saw the same thing, which probably says something about the both of us!

Hoping to trigger memories, I showed him the few family photographs that were made available to me via the defense. Once I handed Jacob an 8x10 picture of Kermode holding his infant son, Cameron. Silently congratulating myself on a clever idea, I asked Jacob to write his feelings about Kermode on the photo itself.

Jacob wasn't so easily reached that he would suddenly scrawl, 'I hate you. You molested me.' Such things might happen in movies or with real therapists, but they never happened at CJC. Instead, Jacob drew horns and a devil's beard on his stepfather and wrote things like 'dumb, annoying, a pervert.' No grand revelations there. If I was going to get anything from my "client," I would have to dig it out inch by painful inch.

In the beginning, after working with Jacob for about a week, I decided to see whether I could stir some memories of his lost childhood years. What would be the best way to accomplish this? Another sleepless night. Why not approach the past as if it were a scene from a novel? To make writing come alive, an author must put himself into another time and place. I did this by asking myself a bunch of questions. What did the character smell? What did he see? What did he hear? What did he taste? What did he touch? What had Jacob Ind's world

been like as a five-year-old in San Jose, California?

The next day in the contact room, I started asking him a series of innocuous questions, "What did your house look like on Woodmont Ave? Did you walk to school? Did you carry a lunch pail? Did you have a favorite outfit? What shoes did you wear? Who were your friends?"

After a short time, Jacob said, "I'm getting a headache."

"Maybe we should stop."

"Go ahead."

While Jacob swore he had few specific recollections, he did recall certain details—the schools, his friends, various programs for the gifted and talented. He remembered his bedroom on Woodmont Avenue and Kermode playing dart guns when they were home alone. More frequently, he spoke in generalities. He had "bad memories" of Woodmont, which is the first place Kermode and Pamela lived after their marriage. He became frightened when he thought about the house. He might have felt okay in the backyard clubhouse, but he felt afraid everywhere else. The middle residence on Sidlaw Court, where the family lived less than a year, didn't seem dark or scary to him, but Arabian Street, their last home before moving to Colorado, was as dark and scary as Woodmont.

Were we onto something with Jacob's talk of light and dark? Why were those places scary? He had already said that his parents assaulted him from the time he was little. Was this what so frightened him? Or was it something else?

Jacob suddenly complained that his hands were clammy. He held them out and they shook as violently as if he were coming off a week long binge. He commented that the room seemed to be tilting.

"That's enough," I said. "We'll save this for the psychiatrists."

◊ ◊ ◊

Over the next few days Jacob's behavior changed. Initially, he'd reminded me of a frightened deer, approaching warily, not certain whether my presence held danger or rescue. Any sudden movements or unexpected noises and he might dash away. Because of my actions he now felt threatened and he had fled—if only psychically.

"I just feel sick, sick to my stomach, unclean, like I need to take a shower," he said.

I sensed his panic, as if he were trying to hold his sanity together with the emotional equivalent of baling wire and a handful of staples. Whenever he tried to remember the years between five and nine, he felt a quick rush of pain across his head. He didn't get clear flashes of memory, but something was stirring way down deep, like a restive dragon.

"Everything is foggy," he said. "There might be something but I can't focus on it. I guess it's something bad, but I just can't make it out. When I start

thinking about it, it's in my cell." He complained again about how sick he felt. "I don't feel like doing anything, just sitting. I've been spacing out."

I was alarmed. What was happening to Jacob? What monsters were threatening to bubble up from the quagmire of his mind? What had his stepfather done to him?

Jacob said that he felt cold, "the same way I did when Kermode called me a faggot. It's like my mind is trying to warn me away. I feel so fragile."

When Jacob was feeling thus, he preferred to be away from the other convicts and the constant agitation of prison life. But in lockdown there was all that time—all those hours and days yawning before him. And what lay ahead at the end of that tunnel? Who were those phantom figures flickering across his brain? What had they done to him?

I asked about counseling. The only people available were jail counselors and he didn't dare talk to them. The defense was supposed to send in psychiatrists, he thought, but months had passed since Drs. Caster and Barron's last visit. Jacob appeared to be disintegrating right before my eyes. What if he suddenly remembered and had some kind of psychotic break in my presence? I had no experience with anything like this. I could contact his attorneys, but after our initial consultation they never returned my phone calls. I was in way over my head. I had no idea what to do. And if I made a mistake, Jacob would be the one who paid.

On May 27, 1993, Jacob entered the attorney's booth where we were meeting. I knew immediately from the pain in his eyes that something was wrong.

"I've written something," he said. "I don't know whether I should show it to you. You'll think it's dumb."

When I assured him I wouldn't, he handed me a ten page journal entry through the opening beneath the plate glass. In the entry he stated that he was ninety percent sure that he'd been sexually abused, but he didn't have specific memories. He was afraid some day he would suddenly remember and it would all come rushing out. He called his mother, "The Dehumanizer." She had taught him that good emotions were things like hatred and the bad were love and compassion. Referring to Pamela, he wrote, 'Your love killed me. Your love killed you.' And later, 'Why can't you leave me? Why can't you die?'

After finishing his painfully eloquent missive, I just looked at him. It was impossible to comprehend what might have gone on between Jacob and his parents. Not only because I'd never been exposed to the harsher side of life, but because on a basic scale I couldn't understand Kermode and Pamela's treatment of their son. Of all children, Jacob was so easy to love.

124

"Do you mind if I take this to Shaun?"[28]

Obviously, Jacob was on the verge of remembering what his mind was 'screaming for me to forget.' Maybe Jacob had provided the breakthrough we'd hoped for--and only ten days into my visits. This was going to be far easier than I'd anticipated.

Jacob shrugged. "Do what you want."

I immediately drove to Shaun's office. After being shown the letter, he said, "Don't ask him any more questions about sexual abuse. We'll get the psychiatrists in."

He xeroxed a copy and sent one of his messengers to the doctors' offices.

We waited. And waited. Jacob never met with either therapist until nearly a year later. As always when dealing with Jacob, the fates seemed to be conspiring against him. There had been a mixup with his journal entry. Dr. Caster never received it. He and his colleague never knew that their patient was ready to open up. Subsequently, Jacob closed right back down tight as a fist.

And this time the memories went even further underground.

Another myth of American justice revolves around criminals' rights: They get everything, including free medical and dental care, and mental health treatment denied to a hard-working public. Sounds great in theory, but reality is far different. Jacob has never received any mental health counseling, not in regular prison and certainly not preceding his trial. Jacob's psychiatrists evaluated him for court, but beyond that no funds were provided by the state.[29]

Ignorant of this fact, I wrote Dr. Caster inquiring why Jacob had been left languishing at CJC. He was still emotionally fragile. There could be no trial if the defendant committed suicide or decided to retreat forever into limbo.

I met with David Caster in late summer of 1993. Caster, who is middle-aged and possesses a pleasant, mellifluous voice, explained that in a murder case a suspect might get as little as one hour of psychiatric evaluation.

"Jacob's already had eleven. The state will never pay for therapy. It just doesn't happen."

So if I was willing, the defense would use me to further work with their client. Only this time our focus would be on the sexual abuse. When I told

---

[28] I do not have a copy of the journal entry. The defense has the original. At one time Charles had a copy.

[29] Ultimately, Jacob's father relinquished guardianship in order to expedite treatment for his son. Approximately five months before the trial Judge Jane Looney released the necessary funds, but Jacob never met with anyone but me.

Caster I had absolutely no qualifications, he replied, "Nobody knows for certain how to uncover it. One of the most important things is that the patient has to trust his therapist. Jacob trusts you. The rest is pretty much guesswork."

I was far from perfect, but our options were limited. Each day brought us closer to Jacob's trial.

"Respect your instincts," Caster said. "You know more than you think. In your letter you came up with the answer. Remember? You spoke of the mother. Pamela is the key, just like you said."

The doctor explained that Jacob was one of the most severely depressed patients he had ever seen.

"He's repressing buckets full. There's no doubt that he's been sexually abused, but we would never dare hypnotize him. As an abused child, he's highly suggestible. We can't risk being torn apart in court."

We discussed Jacob's psychological tests. He showed a small degree of sociopathy. We also talked about what made a serial killer.

"A lot of it has to do with what happened to them in infancy, even doing toilet training. Formative years are critical. If the mother is extraordinarily cruel, the child can be well down that path before he ever enters kindergarten."

Caster felt strongly that Jacob should not walk free. Rather, he needed three to five years in a "cat house."

"What is that?" I asked, thinking of a house of prostitution. Was Caster advocating the love of quite a few good women to bind Jacob's wounds?

"It's a treatment center. There inmates are forced to face their pain and their actions. If Jacob doesn't deal with his past and a similar set of circumstances arise—such as he's approached in prison by a rapist—he could kill again."

Caster explained how I should deal with Jacob.

"Be firm. Get tough. If he's playing games with you, tell him, 'Cut the bullshit! I don't believe you.' Make him nervous. If he thinks he's losing you, he may open up. Ask him the same question dozens of times and in dozens of different ways. When he tells you he doesn't want to see you any more, you'll know you're making progress."

Caster's words went against everything I believed as a parent. If you love your children unconditionally, you don't manipulate them into obeying. Some of Dr. Caster's tactics sounded too much like Kermode and Pamela's.

The good doctor gently reminded me, "You're not Jacob's mother. This isn't about unconditional love. It's about uncovering memories."

◊   ◊   ◊

brain refuses to. That's why some therapists believe so strongly in touch therapy. If someone was always touched a certain way on his stomach, or his neck was twisted just so as he lay beneath his abuser, the mere touch five, ten, twenty years later can bring back a flood of memories. The mind can lie, but it's there in the body. Jacob had talked about how an electric shock sometimes went through him. Was that some sort of body memory?

I learned about all the various symptoms that can occur in a child—bed wetting, vomiting, anal bleeding, high temperatures, stuttering. I read about denial and disassociation, and how these kids over time often become like their abusers. I learned that there are many forms of abuse. Some, which society finds perfectly acceptable, such as an older woman initiating a boy into sex, can be extremely damaging. And that abuse often sets up a twisted reversal of roles between the perpetrator and his victim. By the very nature of their predilection, pedophiles must become masters at the art of manipulation. They woo their intended, seducing the child by lavishing an unusual amount of attention upon him. A predator carefully chooses his victims. He seeks out all the Jacobs in all the playgrounds, backyards, summer camps and shopping malls across America. He becomes a "friend" to these lonely children, perhaps the first friend they've ever known. Because of these dynamics, an odd thing happens when the crime is exposed. The victim frequently takes responsibility for actions the perpetrator refuses to acknowledge as wrong. And, all too frequently, society allows him.

Jacob wasn't as unhappy as I was about my new role. In some ways he was relieved because he wouldn't have to face someone new. Still, he wasn't particularly eager to explore this new unknown. He said, "I don't want to remember. People would look at me weird."

I, in my naivete, responded, "Of course they wouldn't. You were just a little boy. A child. Nobody blames a child. Besides, statistics say one in six boys are molested."

"No. That would mean that one of my friends had also been molested. That can't be."

Jacob had already given me a myriad of clues concerning the incest. Every conversation contained at least one allusion.When discussing Woodmont Avenue, the first home following the Jordan marriage, Jacob could remember every room, albeit vaguely, except the bathroom. That drew a complete blank, and when I asked him questions like, "What color was the floor?" "What color were the fixtures?" he became extremely irritated. I knew that Kermode had bathed him and Jacob made so many references to showers and water and memories "like soap scum," that I wondered what had happened in those bathrooms...

Off-hand comments such as, "For as long as I can remember I always knew how to have intercourse. Only I thought people did it exactly like dogs..."

Situations and behaviors that might have been lifted from a case book.

Jacob always felt that somebody was watching him when he was in bed, but when he opened his eyes, nobody was there. While he attributed that to the house being haunted, he remembered similar incidents before Colorado. He had no idea he was describing a common sensation among incest survivors. The child remembers the beginning, when the parent first enters the room or is standing in the doorway, pondering his intended prey, and simply blanks out the rest...

Early on, I began wondering whether Jacob had been molested by Pamela, as well as Kermode. He had so many bizarre notions such as "If a mother molests her son, the son has to share partial responsibility for the act. He knows what he's doing."

He often mentioned watching others having intercourse, in the sense that if he had a child, he wouldn't see anything wrong with that child watching him and his wife make love.

"That would be a positive way to teach them. It's only society that considers it wrong."

"How would you have felt watching your parents?"

"That would be disgusting!"

He said other things that didn't add up. For example, he saw his mother naked in the weeks before the murders.

"But only by accident. I just happened upon her in her bedroom. She laughed and got under the covers."

How peculiar, I thought. In a house of locks, in a place where Jacob was afraid of the manner in which he looked at his parents for fear of inciting their rage, what was he doing barging unannounced into his mother's bedroom? And why would someone who hit him for splattering bacon grease on the stove, merely laugh at such an invasion?

Over the weeks he recalled other odd incidents. One time when he was approximately six years old, Kermode was either away on a business trip or sleeping on the couch. He remembered his mother saying, "You can sleep with me tonight."

He started to go into his bedroom to get his pajamas.

"No," Pamela said. "You don't need your pajamas. Just get undressed now and get into bed."

He undressed in front of her, but when she saw he wasn't wearing underwear, she told him to go put some on and not to do that again.

"That's all I remember," he told me the first time he recounted the story. Later he said he crawled in bed with her and went to sleep...

Up until the time Jacob was twelve or thirteen, he sometimes asked if he could sleep with Kermode and Pamela. They would say, "Go get your pillow," and he'd spend the night between the two. Pamela complained that he kicked and often exited the bedroom, leaving him alone with Kermode.

"Nothing happened," Jacob said.

I always felt so strange listening to such stories, as if I'd just entered the theater in the middle of a movie. I had no idea what had transpired before or what would take place after, but I figured there was more to these anecdotes than Jacob was telling me. I just didn't know how to get him to tell me.

◇ ◇ ◇

On August 24, 1993, Charles called me. He was leaving for an out of state college. He sounded tired and drained and expressed guilt over abandoning his little brother. He didn't want to leave Jacob. He loved him and worried about him, and asked me to please take care of him. And, since I was in constant contact with Jacob, to let him know how his brother was doing.

Charles paused. "Since you're the investigator, I have something to tell you," he said. "Kermode did molest us," he said.

Finally, Charles had opened the door and allowed me a peek inside. Finally, I had my first terrible glimpse of what Kermode Howard Jordan had done to Pamela's boys.

The Grizzly Bear is huge and wild,
He has devoured the infant child.
The infant child is not aware
He has been eaten by the bear.

~A.E.Houseman
" Infant Innocence"

Chapter 18

Kermode took Jacob's hand and helped him out of the red van. Kermode had picked his stepson up from Action Day Care, where he spent half a day. A month after Kermode had moved in with Pamela, the couple had married in Las Vegas. Charles had told his mother, "You're making the biggest mistake of your life."

"Shut up," said Pam.

Jacob had been happy about having a daddy as nice as Kermode. Kermode was so big and friendly and he paid so much attention to him. The wedding was fun, too. Jacob spent much of the ceremony trying to look up the minister's robes and had asked his mother, "Why is a man wearing a dress?" Kermode had laughed. He laughed a lot when they were together. And he held Jacob a lot. Jacob sometimes fell asleep in his arms. It made him feel safe and warm inside, falling asleep to the sound of Kermode's heartbeat.

Jacob really had a daddy now. This was the first time Kermode had driven him home from day care, but he and Mommy had only been married a few days. Jacob couldn't remember how many. He could count and his teacher, Miss Budlison, always told him how bright he was, but it was hard to remember days. It was fun having Kermode home. Mommy said something about him having a business and they had moved things around in the den so that Kermode would have a place to work. Mommy warned that he and Charlie must be very quiet so Kermode could concentrate, but when Jacob came around, Kermode always stopped to talk to him. Jacob liked that. And he liked the way Kermode pulled him up in his lap. Kermode had a deep voice which rumbled in Jacob's ear when he burrowed against his chest. Jacob also liked the way he smelled—of cigarettes and alcohol rather than his mommy's overwhelming lavender perfume. Sometimes, when Jacob and his mommy bathed together, she also smelled of Calgon Bath Oil. He hated that, too, as well as the slimy feel of the bath oil in the water. And he got scared when he saw the look in Mommy's eyes when she washed him, just the two of them, alone in the bathroom. He guessed it felt good, but he didn't know why she had to lock the bathroom door. The only other time she paid attention to him was when she let him crawl into bed with her, but sometimes he got an odd feeling when he touched her. And even though she was gentle with him, not the way she usually was at all, she looked so odd and that confused him. Still, he wanted his mommy to be nice. The best part

about having a new daddy was now he had somebody to be nice to him all the time.

Kermode fumbled with the keys to the front door. As he fit one in the lock, he swayed and mumbled to himself. When the bolt clicked, he looked down at Jacob and winked. Jacob had been practicing winking back, though he wasn't very good at it. But it made him feel special, having their own private signal. Jacob liked feeling special. He also liked the way Kermode had him walk between his legs. Jacob was just tall enough that he could brush the crotch of his stepfather's trousers. Kermode grinned when he did that. Jacob felt happy when he pleased Kermode so they played that particular game a lot.

Kermode opened the door. They entered the darkened house. Charles wouldn't be home from third grade until after cartoons started and that would be a long time yet. After slipping off his tennis shoes and placing them beside the door the way he was supposed to, Jacob walked along the hallway to the kitchen. He put his latest school project on the kitchen table near an empty bottle of vodka and an ashtray full of cigarette butts. Mommy would be mad that Kermode didn't put things away. Jacob hoped she wouldn't yell at his new daddy like she yelled at him and Charlie. Kermode might just disappear the way Al had and that would make Jacob sad. He wanted his new daddy to stay.

Jacob heard the sound of running water from the bathroom. Woodmont had two bathrooms. The one off the master bedroom was for Mommy and Kermode. The other one was for him and Charles.

Jacob yawned. Sometimes he stayed with his Tia after day care and they took naps together. He liked sleeping with Tia. They snuggled and he told her stories and they just talked and talked until his eyes drooped and she stroked his hair and he nodded off. He'd like to do that now, take a nap. Maybe Kermode would take a nap with him.

Kermode emerged from the bathroom. His shirt sleeves were rolled up. "Come here. See what I have for you."

Jacob trotted over. Kermode picked him up. Jacob slipped his arms around his stepfather's neck. Kermode carried him into the bathroom. Nothing special about the area—white linoleum on the floor, white tile around the bath, white fixtures. Only in the tub bubbles were piled up like a snowy mountain. Mommy never let him have a bubble bath.

"Bath time," Kermode said.

It was awfully early for a bath. He always got one after Mommy came home, before supper. And Jacob really wanted to take a nap. But he also wanted to please his new daddy.

After squeezing him hard, Kermode set him down. Jacob crossed to the tub and scooped up a handful of bubbles. He turned and patted them on his face like a beard. Kermode laughed.

"I'll help you get undressed," he said.

Kermode sat down on the commode. Jacob stood between his legs.

131

Kermode slipped Jacob's t-shirt over his head. He tickled Jacob's belly button and Jacob laughed. He ran his hands along Jacob's shoulders and down his arms. Then he began fumbling with Jacob's leather belt. He was having a hard time with the buckle. He chuckled when he finally loosened it. After unsnapping the button on Jacob's pants, he opened Jacob's zipper. He brushed against Jacob's front as he did so. Jacob just stood there, allowing Kermode to slip his jeans down over his ankles. He was big enough to undress himself, and he was proud of his independence. He liked being able to comb his hair and brush his teeth and get his clothes on right side out most of the time. Well, he knew he'd better or he'd get in trouble with Mommy, but he'd have to remind Kermode that he was four years old and didn't need help undressing.

Kermode bent over to remove Jacob's socks. His head rested against the front of Jacob's underwear. He was breathing heavily, the way he did sometimes when Jacob sat in his lap. His bushy hair tickled Jacob's stomach, but Jacob didn't feel like laughing.

Kermode slipped off Jacob's underpants and lifted him into the bath.

"I can do it myself," Jacob said. Kermode hadn't been around long enough to realize what a big boy he was.

"I wouldn't want you to get hurt on the glass shower doors."

Kermode placed Jacob carefully amidst the bubbles and watched as he played. Jacob forgot about being tired. Mommy never let him have this much fun.

Kermode tossed in a rubber ball and a battle ship. Jacob could hardly believe how lucky he was. Mommy was usually in such a hurry, but Kermode actually seemed to enjoy sitting on the commode, observing him.

Jacob couldn't say how long he stayed. It just seemed like a really, really long time. The temperature began to cool and Kermode let him add more hot water. Mommy never allowed him to do that. "You've been in long enough," she'd say. Or, "I've got better things I have to do. Time to get out."

Kermode finally stood. "Let's get you clean now."

"...Kermode grabbed the white washcloth and soaped it up with Ivory.

Of all the different kids he's had and all the different acts he's done to them, this has got to be his favorite. Taking the rag, he starts by washing Jacob's back and shoulders, caressing them while getting excited. Little children are the greatest—so pure and clean. Not like adults. Not like all the sluts and whores he's been with. All women are nothing but filthy whores. But no, not this wonderful, beautiful child here before him—pure, clean, fresh. His penis got unbearably stiff in his trousers so he had to rearrange it. He started to soap Jacob's buttocks, roughly soaping the crack.

Seeing the look of confusion in Jacob's eyes only made things better... So naive! It is almost time.....

Jacob couldn't understand what was wrong. Something was different. Kermit (as in the frog. He couldn't pronounce it right.) did this different than his mom. She was gentler and always paid attention to his pee-pee, putting a subconscious thought that it was a filthy thing. Kermit was paying attention to his butt. Was that real dirty also? He just couldn't understand why this seemed wrong.

Kermode lifted Jacob out of the tub and slapped him. "Why?" was all Jacob could think as tears welled up in his eyes and confusion added to his physical pain. Kermit was bending him over on the tub... Oh, the pain...

Now! Kermode lifted Jacob out of the tub and bent him over the edge. He pulled out his erect penis and plunged it into Jacob. A shame he had to ruin a clean thing, but wasn't this the whole purpose, destroy in others what he could not achieve? Yes, this was the ultimate achievement, to destroy this sickening pureness, and he had the power to do it.

After what seemed like a long time, Kermit was done. Jacob was glad it was over. The terror just turned to overwhelming pain, emotional and physical, with lots of questions. What happened? Why? What did I do wrong? I didn't leave my toys out, did I?"

"Stop crying, you dirty bastard. Only babies cry!"

Okay, yeah, I'm a big boy. Big boys don't cry. But he couldn't stop and received a blow. Finally he slowed and eventually stopped sobbing, wondering where his Tia was..." He was too numb to be truly frightened. He was just glad that whatever had happened to him was over.

Jacob couldn't know that his horror was just beginning.

The violation began as soon as Kermode and Pamela were married. "From the very first moment," Charles said. It escalated over time, but in the beginning Kermode pulled Charles on his lap and made him fondle him. "You tell anybody and I'll break your neck," he warned.

Charles hated Kermode. Always had, always would. And Kermode reciprocated. Because Charles was a stocky eight-year-old, Kermode made fun of his weight. He also ridiculed him for a learning disability which made him slower in school than Jacob, his "old woman ways" and his serious nature. Jacob was all male, the perfect boy. Charles was defective. There was never ever anything remotely gentle about their sexual encounters. Jacob was the one. Now and forever.

Kermode was obsessed with Jacob. For the first two years of the Jordan marriage, Kermode didn't work. Oh, he pretended that he was busy starting his consulting firm, but he had one thing on his mind. Staying at home allowed him

to drink and provided him nearly unlimited access to Jacob. Each day they spent several hours alone, where Kermode could do to him exactly as he pleased.

"Generally he concentrated on shaping me, teaching me all of his views and how I was to see the world. Only when I started to get "pure" again in his eyes would he repeat "the act.""

Kermode was determined to mold Jacob into a smaller version of himself. No, more precisely, Kermode wanted Jacob "to become him." Calling Jacob his prodigy, he often said, "There is so much power in that mind." Kermode taught him about various philosophies and religions and even read to him out of the Koran. He taught Jacob to play chess.

Far more desperate for affection than intellectual stimulation, Jacob responded. He crawled up in Kermode's lap and Kermode held him, stroked him and kissed him—often in front of Pam and Lupe and other relatives and friends. Kermode couldn't get enough of Jacob. He wooed him like a lover.

Jacob explains, "He loved himself and I was him so he loved me as himself."

Kermode brought him gifts and they went out on dates, just the two of them. They spent hours together at night, outside on the lawn. Kermode showed him the Milky Way and they studied the stars, though with the city's glow little of the night sky could actually be seen.

Kermode's love was not unconditional. Jacob remembers when he was four and Kermode was trying to teach him to tie his shoes.

"I couldn't get it right and Kermode kept yelling at me and slapping me because of it. We were in the master bedroom and I can see it was dark. The bedspread was the greenish one with the Monarch butterflies on it. "Stupid" and "son-of-a-bitch" are associated with this memory.

"'You're old enough to tie your own goddamn shoes, you stupid son-of-a-bitch. No, like this...Why can't you get this fucking right?'

"At first he was kind about it, but then he got frustrated and mean."

Nor was Kermode's corporal punishment any less brutal than Pam's. After they were married, he felt free to "discipline" Jacob and Charlie. Sometimes he beat them while Pam watched. Sometimes, it was the other way around. Often they made the boys count out each stroke of Dr. Stick or Billy Belt. Once Charlie counted "thirty-two" before they stopped. Thinking to circumvent the beatings, Jacob cut up a switch his mother had hacked from an apple tree in the back yard. Pam made him cut off another one and punished him all the harder.

Initially Kermode was pleased that Jacob had destroyed the switch. It showed he wasn't weak or dumb. Jacob "saw a happiness in Kermode" at what he did. But when Jacob destroyed a second switch, he became angry. Instead of pleasing his stepfather, Jacob had shown stupidity because he hadn't learned the first time.

"I learned after the second."

Kermode drank all the time. Without a job he was able to indulge his

addiction, and his shame over his molestations caused him to drink all the more. The sexual abuse was almost a daily affair. Kermode had never been able to so indulge himself and he was like a sex addict in a harem. But he had spent a lifetime constructing his macho image and hiding his secret. Jacob and Charlie had seen behind the facade and he hated them for that. So he beat the living shit out of them.

Kermode's unpredictability was extremely confusing to Jacob. One minute Kermode cuddled him and the next minute he threw him across the room. Once when Kermode was hot and drunk, Jacob tried to put some ice on his forehead. Kermode cursed at him and slapped his hand away. Jacob never knew what to expect. Would he be kissed or would he be killed?

Jacob and Charles do disagree as to the frequency of Kermode's assaults. Charles remembers them as constant, at least until he reached puberty. Now that Jacob is in prison, the "safe place" psychologists said was necessary for him to fully recover memories, he is at least willing to talk about the molestations. "It only happened a few times (with Kermode). After I wasn't pure, what good was I to him, as far as that went? Now he was concentrating on molding me."

Which boy is lying? What IS the truth? Perhaps the answer lies in the relationship each child had with each adult. Kermode despised Charles, but "loved" Jacob—so he only anally raped him a handful of times? Pamela "loved" Charles—which meant she verbally and physically assaulted him, but saved the ultimate for the person she hated most? Whatever the answer, we know the person Pamela Jean hated most in the world. And that was Jacob.

Pamela was obsessed with Kermode—at least his money-making potential—and wouldn't admit that their marriage was a mistake. Still, it was obvious that her hundred thousand a year man was a fraud, and she was mighty unhappy about his drinking. When Kermode was on a binge, the house stank from him, his cigarettes and booze. Bottles were scattered in every room. Cigarette butts were extinguished on any available surface. Tables were overturned; lamps broken. Her elegant businessman had stains on his clothing, a five day growth of beard and smelled of vomit. Kermode was a belligerent drunk, as well, though he seldom fought with Pam. Rather he took his moods out on the boys. And Pam, rather than directly confront Kermode, also used her sons. In more ways than just as her whipping post.

Pamela had always equated sex with power. Kermode was the clear authority in their relationship. He had the physical prowess, the education, the earning potential, the age, and the commanding personality. While she could bully Frank, there was something about Kermode that caused her to hold back. She respected him for being tougher than she was. But she also hated it. Because she could not control Kermode she could not use sex as a weapon, the

135

Who saw him die
I, said the Fly
With my little eye
I saw him die.

~Nursery rhyme

A child's a plaything for an hour.

~Mary Lamb
Parental Recollections

Chapter 19

"I remember it was at Woodmont, shortly after Mom and Kermode got married," Charles said. "I remember coming home one day, right after school. I remember Jacob crying, yelling, 'Don't! Stop!' and Kermode saying, 'Shut up! Just relax.' I knew it was coming from the bathroom and I knew what was going on. So I shut the door really loud, hoping he'd stop it. I went into the family room, and one of the rules was when you get home you don't watch t.v. I went in the family room and turned on the TV and put the cartoons on really loud.

"And then Kermode came out and he zipped up his pants. And he was... he looked really pissed off. His whole face was red and his bottom teeth were showing the way they did when he was really pissed.

"'What the hell are you doing watching cartoons? You know better than that.'

"And I just looked at him like, 'I know what you're doing,' and I did it on purpose. He shut off the TV, came over, grabbed me by the shirt, pulled me up and let me go, and hit me.

" 'You know better than that shit.'

"Because he knew I'd caught him in the act. And I said, 'Fine. I'll just go to my room.'

" 'Yeah, you'd better.'

"Then I was walking to my room and Jacob was coming out of the bathroom. He looked really sick, really pale, and really tired. His eyes were swollen from crying. I just closed my eyes and I went to my bedroom. Jacob got to his bedroom and Jacob started crying some more. And what could I say? I couldn't have said anything. And not to Kermode. And not to Jacob either. Because I knew what was going on... and he did it to me. We knew what was going on and I knew what was happening to Jacob but we didn't talk about it. Because we were embarrassed as it was. It was kind of like conversation through looks, through the eyes.

"Before I went into my room I just put my hand on his shoulder. And I looked at him, and I just directed him to his bedroom and I heard him crying.

137

There was nothing I could have done."

◇ ◇ ◇

According to Charles, he and Jacob initially fought Kermode. [32] They
fought him so hard that, after Kermode stripped them naked, he tied their hands
and feet to the commode before attempting to enter them. He did many things
to the boys. He made them masturbate him and occasionally ejaculated in their
faces. Sometimes he made Jacob watch him and Charles. Sometimes he tied the
both of them and violated them, one after the other. Afterward, he slapped them
and ordered them to take showers.

"You're so fucking dirty," he said.

He kept the rope in the bottom of the sink cupboard. Pamela had to see it
when she cleaned but she never mentioned it. Charles couldn't believe that his
mother knew or she would have protected him, wouldn't she? He was her little
man, wasn't he? He was super responsible and helped around the house and
cooked and baked, knowing that such girl things pleased Pam. On the other
hand, Jacob fought her all the way. He wasn't going to do sissy things, not when
he was four and not when he was fourteen. So Charles could understand
Pamela's antipathy toward her youngest, but HE had done everything right. He
had been the dutiful son. Surely, she wouldn't have allowed Kermode to violate
HIM, would she?

Charles wanted to tell Pamela about the bathroom sessions. Not daring to
blurt out the truth, he hinted, but she ignored him. Did Pamela know about the
molestations? Of course she did. Sometimes at night, when the bathroom
sessions were in full swing, she heard Charlie and Jacob screaming. She knew
each time Kermode left her side for the boys. Often, he would assault her sons
when they were sleeping. He would wake them up by hitting them with their
pillow "just before he fucked us."

Throughout, Pam stayed in her bedroom and pretended to be asleep. She
bought an enema kit in order to clean Jacob up after Kermode was through with
him. When Lupe noticed the contraption and questioned her, Pamela explained,
"Jacob has trouble with constipation."

But the real trouble was what might happen if Kermode tore Jacob's anus
beyond repair. Pam didn't dare risk a visit to a doctor so she took care of the
matter herself. Jacob scoffs at the notion that his mother didn't know. "She
didn't have to. She was doing the same things herself."

Charles denies that, clinging to the fantasy that she wasn't a child
molester. That despite things he "heard" between her and Jacob, sworn

---

[32] Jacob says no. "Maybe we fought him a little, but subduing a kid is easy. And I
don't remember any tying up."

testimony that she fondled a young male, and an eyewitness account that she did the same thing with both her sons under the guise of "cleaning their penises." Charles continues to maintain that he only tried to tell her once about the molestations.

"It was when Kermode was supposedly laid off, but he was fired. Kermode was really drunk. It was when he started working on our screen room on our house at Arabian, and Mom came home. Kermode had gone somewhere. I think it was to the liquor store. Jacob and I were both upset because Kermode told us that we basically were leeches, we were spenders, we didn't pull our weight, we didn't do anything.

"Mom said, 'If anybody's a leech around here it's Kermode.'

"When she said that, I was tempted. I said, 'He touched us.'

"She said, 'What do you mean? Did he hit you?'

"One of the things Kermode did before he did anything sexual with us, he would hit us to break us, to let us know, 'Don't try to stop me.'"

"She said, 'Did he do anything else?'

"I remember the expression on Mom's face. She grew really pale. She was pale as it was, and she got even more pale. 'Oh, he just hit you with the belt.' I knew I couldn't tell Mom that, what he was doing. Because I knew it would devastate her. So I knew in the back of my head, 'Don't tell her because it will just make the situation worse.'"[33]

Kermode did generally confine his sexual escapades to weekdays. According to Charles, they watched for the danger signs. If he'd had a bad day at work, the next afternoon Jacob and Charlie would get it. Charles also remembers that Kermode often wore hats. When he donned a black one, they knew what was going to happen. A white one and they were safe. They could also gauge his desire by the amount of booze he was drinking, and what kind. Wine meant one thing, scotch something else. If he came into their rooms to help them undress or to watch them, they understood that the nightmare was imminent.

Jacob was probably the cleanest kid in California. All boy, he was forever getting dirty. He liked to dig holes in the back yard, play in the mud, wrestle with his dog, and go exploring. Any man thing, any boy thing and Jacob was for it. Which meant Jacob's face and hands got soiled and his clothes stained and his shoes caked. Ever fastidious, Pam hosed the boys outside before allowing them in her house. Kermode sprayed Charlie, but if Jacob had so much as a smudge on his cheek, it was bath time. Jacob spent more time in the water than a fish. The procedure was always identical—the running water, the

---

[33] Jacob also remembers that incident. But he interprets his mother's impression differently. "It was the one that said, 'Oh, shit! We're going to get caught!'"

bubbles, the locked door, the washcloth, the hour long sessions, the noises and sobbing. According to Charles, Jacob always cried when Kermode bathed him. As he always cried when Kermode took him into his bedroom. Charlie could count almost to the second from the time that Kermode locked the door to when he would hear Jacob's sobs.

Charlie wanted to protect his little brother, but he didn't know how. He hated himself for not being able to help Jacob. He tried to make things easier on Jacob by secretly doing some of his chores and allowing him to be a kid. Sometimes Charles even deflected Kermode or his mother's anger away from him.

But, no matter whether only one was being picked on, the other was affected. Charles remembers one particular incident in the sixth grade.

"I think I got caught lying, and Mom said...she made me drop my pants. I was really embarrassed because my voice was cracking everywhere and I was starting to develop.

"I said, 'No, I'm not.'

"So she slapped me. And she took the belt and hit me with the belt five times. One time after the other. Kermode was there, standing between the living room and the dining room. It was an open area with a guard rail. He was laughing. And then he came up and then he hit me for five more minutes. Pam was just watching. For sassing or lying. I never told many lies, just small little white lies that wouldn't make any difference anyway. 'Yeah, I ate a cookie.'

"Jacob was in the kitchen. After I was done I was crying because it hurt so much. Jacob's entire face was pale, and he was really scared.

" I said, 'They're not after you. They're after me. Just go to your room and stay there.'"

Jacob remembers that—or perhaps it was a similar incident—a bit differently.

"Actually, I don't remember Kermode hitting him that time. Mom hit him a bunch while Kermode and I peeked around a corner and snickered. Charles had a string of bruises BECAUSE of Kermode."

Charles would rather take a beating sometimes than watch his brother face the monsters. There was just something so bewildered, lost and vulnerable in Jacob's expression. He simply didn't understand that you had to be tough and wary and guard your heart. Each day when he awoke it was almost as if he had wiped out his previous four-five-six years, that he really believed the world was a wonderful place and his parents were terrific people. Crushing Jacob's innocence would prove a daunting task. But Charlie hoped it would happen soon. Jacob needed to learn that grownups could not be trusted, that life was rotten. Jacob was always retreating into a fantasy world, and he told the most charming stories, but for the sake of Jacob's own survival he needed to realize the truth. And the truth was he and his brother were no different than prisoners of war. Charlie was old enough to understand about the hostage situation in

Iran, where Americans had been held by terrorists. He identified with those hostages, because that's what he and Jacob were. Only Kermode and Pamela were their captors.

Jacob turned five and started kindergarten. After school Godmother Lupe often watched him and Charlie. She still laid down with Jacob and loved listening to his chatter. He told such funny, imaginative stories that she couldn't help but laugh. But after Kermode came into his life, his tales took a violent turn. He talked about men in black hats and white hats who were trying to kill him. He spun tales of people hiding in the bushes that he'd kill with a gun, or shoot with an arrow into their legs. He recounted dreams about bad witches and how only the good witch could save him. He told fantastic stories about his former teachers at Action Day Care. He swore they were witches who tied him up, put tape on his mouth and made him sit in a corner.

When Lupe expressed doubts, he said in his soft little voice, "It's true, Tia."[34]

He spoke with such urgency that Lupe was worried. This wasn't the Jacob she knew. She expressed her concern to Pam.

"There's something wrong. Jacob's never talked like this before. You need to check it out."

Pam shrugged. "He's just not getting enough stimulation at school."

Jacob began stuttering. He'd never previously had a speech problem, but suddenly he could hardly talk—at least around the house. When he was at school, Lupe, who worked as a school aide, noticed that the stuttering disappeared. What did that mean? Was something going on in the Jordan household? The boys were so guarded and Kermode was still a touchy subject between her and Pam so Lupe could only surmise. Lupe didn't spend much time with Pam anymore, but at her friend's request she sometimes checked out various bars to see whether Kermode was drinking. Once Pamela even left Kermode for a month, but she went back, much to Lupe's dismay.

Lupe just couldn't understand the attraction. Kermode cleaned up nicely. When he wasn't drinking, you could take him out in public without being ashamed of him, but he was such an obnoxious drunk. Several times he stripped to his underwear and collapsed on the front lawn, shouting, "I am God." And he was always talking about the Greeks, as if anybody cared. Lupe knew enough about ancient history to understand that, democracy to the contrary, the Greeks were a barbaric society with a low opinion of women and a lot of pretty bizarre sexual practices. What was all this talk about the aristocratic males taking

---

[34] Jacob still insists it's true. "After I pulled the tape off, they tied my hands. I was being disruptive at a magic show."

young boys as lovers? When the older man mentored the younger, the mentoring always included initiating the boy into sex. Kermode hated homosexuals. Explain how diddling children was any better?

Still, though Lupe saw the "unnatural way" Kermode kissed and stroked Jacob, she dismissed her suspicions. Pamela loved her boys. Despite Pam's harsh discipline, Lupe had to believe that her friend was a good mother. Nobody told her what to do with Jacob and Charlie and nobody better say anything bad about them. They were HERS. Someone so fiercely protective wouldn't allow any harm to come to her children.

Kermode's real son, Cameron, visited every other weekend. Pam detested Cameron. He would not mind. He would not respond to her standards of discipline and Kermode allowed him entirely too much freedom. Pam was jealous of his mother, Shannon, who had married the wealthy owner of a day care franchise and had a fur coat and a San Francisco mansion on the waterfront. Pamela never lost an opportunity to denigrate her and her child. Cameron returned Pam's hate, calling her—not surprisingly—"The Bitch." Pamela dared not say too much in front of Kermode, so she saved her vitriol for his absence.

I personally believe that Kermode (and possibly Pamela) molested Cameron, but he was never interviewed by the defense so I am surmising from very limited evidence. (Somehow the prosecution and probate attorneys had no trouble contacting Cameron, but Jacob's attorneys could never track him down.) I saw photos of Jacob's stepbrother, taken at the age of seven or eight, in which Kermode had scrawled such phrases as "Cameron trying to hide from me," and "My (underlining the my) Son." Cameron was a possession, a belonging to do with as Kermode pleased. Neither he nor Pam ever looked on their progeny as people. With such a dangerous attitude, it would be easy to cross the line with Cameron, just as they crossed the line with so many others.

Cameron has long had severe psychiatric problems. He never did well academically, got into drugs early, and finally dropped out of high school. In one of the psychologist's reports I read at Ridge Drive, the therapist commented that Jacob and Cameron were very similar, "almost two sides of the same coin." Both boys look alike too, with dark hair and dark eyes. Knowing Kermode and Pam's history and the black hatred Cameron expressed toward both of them, I cannot help but wonder.

In some ways Kermode was a good absentee father. He did a lot of things with Cameron. They went camping, fishing and skiing (Cameron was an excellent skier}, but by the time of the murders, the two were almost completely estranged. On a trip to Nebraska Kermode got so drunk that Cameron later told Jacob, "He was swerving. I called him a drunk, so Kermode pulled over."

Cameron was so angry that he started hitting his father. The fight escalated until Kermode ended up with cracked ribs.

That was only one of several brawls. While going through the family room

following the murders, I found a napkin where Kermode had written in huge, slashing letters,"Cameron" and "Tough Love." Beneath it he had drawn a pistol, complete with the trajectory from an imaginary bullet. At the funeral, Cameron, who appeared to be high on drugs, wept copiously and proclaimed his love for his dad. Later he collected a substantial amount of insurance money, as well as most of Kermode's possessions. Charles swears that, if interviewed, he would have lied on the stand, but it's puzzling why such an important witness was never interviewed by the defense.

When I asked Jacob whether he thought Kermode might have sexually abused his biological son, Jacob responded, "Why wouldn't he molest him? Look at how screwed up Cameron is." Kermode used to talk about bandaging Cameron's penis after he was circumcised and when I showed Jacob a picture of Kermode in bed with Cameron as an infant—both of them were naked, at least from the chest up—Jacob said, "Look at him. Doesn't he look like a pervert?"

On the other hand, Charles doesn't believe that Kermode would have violated his own flesh and blood. Cameron's severe emotional problems stem as much from his flaky mother, who treated Cameron like a street kid. Charles doesn't believe that Kermode was a pedophile who preyed on a host of boys. Jacob and he were the only ones and he abused them more to taint them and keep them docile than for his sexual pleasure. It was about power, not sex, according to Charles.

"For me," says Jacob, "it was to make me like him. For Charles because he hated him. I can't say what he might have done to anyone else. I just don't know."

When Jacob was seven the Jordans moved to a white stuccoed house on Arabian Street. After Jacob became a full time student, Kermode had abandoned his consulting business and found employment with various engineering firms, which meant a jump in salary. Arabian Street was quiet and the two story house was spacious, with a swimming pool in the back yard. Pamela had long defended Kermode on the basis of his potential, and it finally seemed that, thanks to the love of a good woman, Kermode was turning "potential" into "money." When he went on drinking binges he wouldn't show up at work for weeks so he bounced around from job to job, but California's economy was good and he always managed to find another.

The Jordans lived well. For recreation, they went fishing, rafting, to the beach and on camping trips. On Jacob's seventh birthday, Kermode bought him a seven hundred dollar bike. Another time he and Pamela presented Jacob with a five hundred dollar cat—to replace a five dollar hamster.

Such extravagances seem suspiciously like bribes. The sexual abuse at Arabian was particularly bad--more frequent and brutal than before. Perhaps

working for a living had made Kermode more tense. He and Pam weren't getting along well either, so marriage number five might soon be history. Whatever the reason, when Kermode was at his most abominable, he sometimes tried to make amends. Pamela never showed remorse but Charlie remembers one time when Kermode returned from a business trip with a mound of presents for him. The sexual abuse had been unusually horrific and Charles understood the unspoken message, "I'm sorry."

Jacob began carrying around a .22 rifle with a missing bolt. He even slept with the weapon.

"When Kermode was drunk he gave me permission. One of the neighbors saw it and sent me home where Kermode took it back. Then the cops came."

Unfortunately, the .22 couldn't protect him from panic attacks, which began around this time. Jacob vividly recalls one, in particular. He had his own room, with venetian blinds on the window and an ancient radio on the chest of drawers beside his double bed. He awakened early one morning, when dawn had begun to creep through the slats. The house was quiet. It was summertime and Jacob felt as if he were smothering. He explained it as "a smoggy feeling. It was really hard to breathe, like in Des Moines, Iowa, when it's 100 degrees and you can't breathe. An oppressive feeling." Jacob's heart raced and he was terrified. He ran down the hall into the bathroom, flung open the window and gulped in huge amounts of air.

"I kept thinking, Fresh air. Get fresh air.

His stomach hurt and later in the day he vomited. (At Action Day Care, soon after the Jordan marriage, Jacob vomited a lot. The aides would take his temperature but they could never find anything wrong, no matter how often he complained.)

Jacob had much to feel panicked about. The abuse was almost non-stop.[35] He was still Kermode's prodigy, but Kermode's love was mixed with a hefty dose of sadism. One time when Reagan and the contras were in the news, Kermode came home from a bar ranting against the president and his policies.

"I'm going to go down to Nicaragua and fight for Daniel Ortega and to hell with being a member of the establishment."

Jacob and Charles had set the table, but Pamela hadn't yet arrived. A pound of hamburger meat had been left to thaw on the counter. Because Kermode was angry at Ronald Reagan he took it out on Charlie and Jacob. As they tried to tiptoe out of the kitchen he suddenly swept all the tableware onto the floor.

"You wanna be a real man?" he yelled at the frightened boys. "I'll show you what a real man is."

He scooped up a handful of raw hamburger meat and crammed it into his

---

[35] Again, Jacob insists, not the sexual, at least for him.

mouth.

"All right. Now you two eat the rest."

After Jacob and Charles did as ordered, he made them clean up his mess.

Meal times were generally unpleasant. Lots of lectures and fighting. Sometimes, especially when the boys were older, Kermode would read to them from Greek philosophers or about the ancient Greeks and quiz them afterwards. If Jacob or Charles didn't display the proper manners, either parent would spear their hand with a fork. If they failed to eat everything on their plates, the leftovers would be served until the boys finished them.

Charles remembers another incident when Pamela was preparing dinner. Kermode was at the kitchen table teaching his stepson math via flash cards. Charles's learning disability made memorization difficult, and Kermode's ridicule didn't help his concentration. The more nervous he got, the more mistakes he made. Charles could tell Kermode was upset, but only the right answers would defuse the situation and Charles's mind was blank.

Pam entered from the kitchen, carrying a steaming casserole. Charles made the mistake of glancing up from the flash cards as she placed the dish on a hot pad amidst the plates and silverware.

Kermode yelled at Pamela, "Do you mind? I'm trying to teach your son his fucking flash cards."

He yanked the tablecloth off the table, sending food and utensils crashing to the vinyl.

Pamela didn't say a word.

The beatings continued. Generally, Kermode and Pamela picked on one boy at a time. "Divide and conquer," was their motto. Whoever was the anointed scapegoat would strip naked from the waist down, bend over the couch and the ritual began. Charles remembers his mother laughing when Kermode took his turn. Once Charles made the mistake of putting his hand behind him to ward off a blow. Pam accused him of trying to hit her. She tied his hands with the cord of her bathrobe and beat him. Jacob also remembers her tying him.

While Jacob tried to fade into the background or retreat into a fantasy world to escape the abuse, Charles turned to food. He began putting on weight. Kermode and Pamela hated fat people and they weren't about to have an obese son. They initiated a diet of Carnation Instant Breakfast for breakfast and lunch, and a baked potato or salad—sans dressing—for dinner. They also chased Charles around the house and up and down the street with a belt to "run the fat off of him." Both parents bragged about doing this. They kept a chart of his progress on a calendar. Sometimes Charles dropped two pounds in a day.

When I asked Jacob about his worst childhood memory, he said, "Charles bought some candy from the ice cream man. He was in the middle of his diet and when my mom found out she beat him until he was black and blue."

The neighbors' most vivid recollection is of Charlie mowing the lawn in the middle of summer, wearing long pants and a long sleeved shirt. Why would

145

he do that? They wondered. The boys say to help Charles sweat off the fat.

Despite Kermode's improving work record, Pamela appears to have decided that her second marriage was a bust. One evening she called the boys into the living room.

"Kermode and I might separate." She mentioned something about Kermode's drinking. "What do you think about him moving out?"

Jacob, who even at seven had a rough mouth, said, "I hope you divorce the motherfucker."

Kermode also talked to them. "I really love your mother. I hope we can work things out."

Perhaps Pamela was only bluffing. Kermode landed a steady job at Digital and their money situation improved dramatically. Talk of divorce died. Instead, they began contemplating leaving San Jose. Recently, Lupe and her family had moved to Minnesota, and California no longer seemed all that desirable. "Too many fags," she and Kermode lamented. Pam also hated the smog and the rat race, and crime was a constant worry.

"I want to move some place safe," she said. "Somewhere up in the mountains."

Around this time, Charlie called his real father and told him he might want to come and live with him. Charlie had never been close to Frank, but he didn't know how much more he could take of Arabian Street.

"All right," Frank said. "If it's okay with your mother."

The next time his son called, Frank thought Charlie would say, "I'm moving in with you."

Instead, Pamela came on the line.

"We're moving to Colorado," she said.

146

And when she ceased, we sighing saw
The floor lay paved with broken hearts.

~Richard Lovelace
"Gratiana Dancing and Singing"

PART 5
COLORADO

Chapter 20

Having never met Pamela Jean Wallace, I am the first to confess that she is an enigma. Despite the hundreds of pictures I've seen, I can't even be certain about her physical appearance. Sometimes she is a real beauty with shoulder length hair, striking dark eyes and a slender figure shown off by stylishly tailored clothes. Other times her face is gaunt, she appears to have a hooked nose, and her expression is forbidding. Recalling the more flattering photos of Pamela, I've asked Jacob whether he ever thought his mother was pretty. He shudders. He uses many adjectives to describe Pamela Jean, but that would never be one of them.

Pam was 5'4", and generally wore petites. For work, she favored expensive attire—silk blouses and Pendleton suits, accesorized by conservative jewelry. Kermode, so much older, treated her as something of a trophy wife and often bought her extravagantly expensive apparel. Pam seemed to alternate between being womanly and cropping off all her hair, donning masculine attire, and divesting herself of any trace of femininity or beauty. In fact, Pamela often looks like a man. Other times she looks like a boy. When she was angry she looked like a witch. The more I study her pictures, the less I can decide who or what she was.

I am haunted by how normal Pamela and her life seemed, and how it paralleled mine, at least in outward appearance. We were both the same age, same dark hair, approximately the same height and weight, same middle class lives. We got married in the same year, and to our high school sweethearts. Even our wedding albums look remarkably similar—same sixties hairdo, plain wedding dress and perky veil. Her photo albums remind me of my own, for we both had children at approximately the same time, and we both lived in California. The palm trees and beaches look familiar, as do the beautiful baby boys with their deep-set brown eyes. It gives me an uneasy feeling, as though my life could have been hers if I'd taken a few different turns or we'd experienced similar childhoods.

I often told Jacob that, had I met Pam, I probably wouldn't have liked her—she was too serious to interest me—but I would have been intimidated by her. A career woman with two perfectly behaved teenage sons, an immaculate

home, who, despite a full time job cooked regular meals, attended her sons' football games and other activities and helped out at school? Call her Wonder Woman.

Pamela was the kind of woman who always did the "appearance" of the right thing. She kept a perfect house so that if a stranger entered, he would know that Pamela had it all together. She was actively involved in her sons' lives and mouthed the appropriate phrases to teachers so that they would think she was concerned for her boys. She was not an absentee mom, at least to the outside world. Her children were not so much an extension of her as her possession and Pamela took great pride of her possessions. Charles and Jacob had better wear the right clothes, make the right grades, treat her and Kermode respectfully around their elders and reflect a proper upbringing to the public. Pam polished, cleaned and arranged her boys the way she would a fine piece of furniture. And they had as much meaning to her.

Sometimes I worry that the brutalization which Jacob suffered occurred when he was so young that his central core, "the real Jacob," is way, way down inside—perhaps no more than a baby. Maybe he'll never come out, the Jacob Ind that would have been had he developed in a loving, nurturing environment. Still, I have never doubted that that core is pure, or that Jacob himself is a good, decent person.

But who was Pamela Jean Wallace? What was at her core? Was she essentially amoral, someone who reflected back what she thought others wanted to see? Kermode strikes me as more of a sad monster. Despite his rages, perversions and cruelties, he appeared to have a depth that Pamela lacked. Pam seemed to delight in being cruel simply because she felt like it whereas Kermode's brutalities seemed to originate from unresolved demons. Was pedophilia his dark secret? Was his agony rooted in his childhood, in his relationship with his mother? In events that Kermode took to the grave with him? In the disease of alcoholism? Kermode was a soul in torment, whereas Pamela didn't appear to have a soul at all.

When interviewing people about Jacob's mother, three words never mentioned in their descriptions are "gentleness, kindness, compassion." Even the pictures of her, especially as she ages, convey no hint of softness. To borrow from the duped attorney's comments about his psychopathic paramour in the movie, *Body Heat*, "She was relentless." And Pam was. As well as cold, angry, manipulative and selfish. Pamela Jean just didn't seem to quite get it, this business of being human.

That verdict may be unfair, however. Her parents certainly loved her. Grace Wallace called her the light of their lives. And Charles mourns "the real Pam, the Pam before Kermode."

But Pamela was never nice to Jacob. Nor can her animosity be blamed on a man who didn't even come into her life until her son was four years old. And while I believe that Pamela and Kermode both systematically set out to murder

Jacob's soul, in my opinion his mother is more responsible.

What would it be like to live in a household where your flesh and blood isn't there to nurture you, but you are there to service her needs, desires and neuroses? Children aren't stupid. As an infant, Jacob may not have known what the words, "I hate you," meant, but he heard the loathing in her voice, he saw the hatred in her eyes, felt the roughness of her hands as she picked him up, and the stiffness of her body as she held him. "Experts" used to assert that infants were largely blank slates upon which all of life's experiences could be written. They come into the world knowing and feeling nothing. That is ridiculous, of course. If Pam didn't want Jacob in the womb, if she resented him even then, if her life was in turmoil, all that was transferred to him. Jacob's soul must always have known the truth about Pamela Jean. She could lie to the entire world, but she could never lie to her son.

When I inspected the school papers, drawings and mementoes at 120 Ridge Drive, I marveled at how normal everything appeared. Granted, the prosecution had long ago swept in with their bags and fingerprint dust and experts, removing everything from Sheetrock to a dictionary and a painted dog skull that Jacob kept atop his headboard. Nor were they the only ones who enjoyed access to Ridge Drive. Charles had a key, as well as every realtor in town, and the executors, including teacher Lucinda Reed, who was one of the star witnesses for the prosecution.[36] Unlike some crime scenes where the site is preserved for years, the master bedroom was re-done as quickly as possible. Jacob's defense might have spent next to no time there gathering evidence, but that didn't mean that the house was closed off from the public. If there was any evidence of the Jordans' debauchery, plenty of interested people could have removed it at their leisure.

Still, judging from the paraphernalia I found four months after the murders, Pam appeared identical to millions of other proud mothers. I read a card congratulating Jacob on his eleventh birthday, in which she tells him how much she loves him and expresses the hope that their next eleven years will be as wonderful as the first eleven. Those words certainly sound like the expressions of a doting parent. (One possible explanation might be that Jacob's grandparents visited on that particular birthday, so Pamela was playing to an audience.) And I did notice that most of the school projects of a personal nature—the ubiquitous Valentine and Mother's Day cards from elementary school—came from Charles. Hand prints of Jacob, a kindergarten project, hung among the gallery of photos. Pam had the obligatory pictures from Olan Mills, though again, there are far fewer of Jacob.

---

[36] Although Reed passed herself off as an executor of the Jordan estate and Charles referred to her by that title, probate documents make no mention of Reed in any capacity.

But it's in the photos themselves that Pamela--and Kermode, as well--slip up. They, the ultimate narcissists, were forever chronicling their lives. And in some of those snapshots other truths emerge.

Kermode had several expensive cameras and took thousands of pictures. I went through hours of negatives and boxes of photographs. (I always figured that somebody as perverted as Kermode would have had to take perverted photographs, but if he did I never found them.) He did so love to capture Kodak moments, especially when he was drinking.

At the trial, Kermode's cousin, Doug Kermode recounted one incident when Jacob was five. The two Kermodes had "had a beer or two." At one point, Jacob and Doug began wrestling. Jacob bit Doug.

"Kermode was in a rage," Doug Kermode testified. "He said, 'I hate a man who bites,' and slapped Jacob way too hard.[37] I remember Kermode's dad would become enraged and slap Kermode the same way. It was way too rough for a five-year-old. Kermode was out of control. Then he wanted to take Jacob's picture as he was crying but Pam and I talked him out of it."

The prosecution also repeatedly showed a lovely picture of Pamela and Kermode, heads together, smiling for the camera. What a handsome, loving couple, prosecutor Bill Aspinwall intimated. Those who knew Kermode and Pamela laugh at the photo. "It's obvious that Kermode was drunk out of his mind," they say.

While at Ridge Drive, I studied the gallery of pictures and all the albums depicting birthdays, Christmases, swimming and rafting trips and family outings to Disneyland and Yosemite National Park. Every household in America must have similar photographs.

Not quite.

Every once in a while a peculiar snapshot, a glimpse of something rotten beneath the bucolic facade, slips through.

* Jacob, around the age of five, at the kitchen table with Charles. Jacob is licking a wicked-looking carving knife covered with frosting while Charles smiles into the camera. Charles has a black eye.

* Jacob at four, seated on the kitchen floor, trying to remove his one piece pajama suit. The camera angle directly shows his genitals.

* A third picture, taken off to the side, showing Kermode in the bathtub, most of his body fully exposed, washing his hair. When I showed it to Jacob, I, who had never met the man, recognized his stepfather. He swore he had no idea who the figure was.

* A series of pictures of Jacob, at around twelve years of age, standing with his mother on the deck. He has his arms around her and is kissing her on

---

[37]In another version, Kermode said, "Real men don't bite," doubled his fist and hit Jacob, knocking him down.

the lips. She appears to be trying to draw away. (He said, no. She was protecting him from her cigarette.)

 * Six-year-old Jacob cowering in a chair, clutching a Kleenex and crying, while Pam bends over him, her face only inches away. She is obviously yelling. Jacob says it must be after one of their altercations because who would take a picture of two people fighting?

 But who would take pictures of a naked three-year-old either? Pamela Jean, that's who. Jacob, the little wild man, enjoyed taking off his clothes and running around outside. Several pictures show him grinning at the camera, with his blond beatle haircut, stocky little body and genitalia fully exposed. While Jacob himself is all innocence, there is something cruel about the pictures. Every mother knows that when her children become teenagers such photos will mortify them, so why do such a thing? Jacob's unsuspecting smile and openness is somehow marred by the sly, even sinister knowledge of the photographer. Pam even placed one of these pictures, of a naked Jacob standing by a water fountain, in the gallery. After the murders, the psychiatrists asked their client to visualize something and explain his reaction. Jacob closed his eyes and envisioned that specific picture. The word "fear" flashed through his mind. When I tried to show Jacob that particular sequence of photos, he refused to even glance in their direction.

 "Look at them. Don't you think they're disgusting? What kind of person would take something like that?"

 He makes the same comment about another picture of himself, again at three, urinating against a tree. I agree. To me, it is as if an evil troll has just put in its first appearance and is inching forward from the edges of the fairy tale, readying to devour the unsuspecting child.

 Seven months before Jacob's trial, Lupe Thorson flew to Colorado to try to help the defense jog Jacob's memory. One evening Lupe, Jim Dostal, (Jacob's then attorney) and I spent three hours in the contact visiting room showing him a myriad of pictures, including several of him in a bubble bath. By September 1993 I knew that whatever had happened to Jacob, some of it involved the bathroom. He repeatedly referred to bathing, showers and body functions. Charles said cryptically, "Ask him about his hour-long baths." For my part, although I realized that confessions of sexual abuse might strengthen the defense's case, a part of me really didn't want to hear them. I preferred to believe that Jacob's parents would never have so brutalized him. While I understood Jacob should be pressed for any and all graphic accounts, I was content with oblique references.

 Maybe his "Tia" would get more out of him.

 Lupe and I showed Jacob a stack of photographs. We saved the bathtub ones, which were the most important, for last. Beforehand, Jacob swore he'd never had a bubble bath in his life.

 "Never. Ever," he said emphatically.

We triumphantly displayed our evidence, several pictures of Jacob in the tub surrounded by foam, mugging for the camera.

He stared blankly at the photos. "No, that never happened."

We spent a good fifteen minutes badgering our increasingly nervous hostage. Suddenly he got an image of someone pouring Calgon bath powder into the water.

"They were fighting about who would bathe me. My mom said, 'I'll bathe him,' and Kermode said, 'No, I'll bathe him.' She said Kermode kept me in dirty water so when I got out I'd still be dirty. Kermode told her the water wasn't dirty. It was Calgon that made it appear that way."

And that's all he remembered, no matter how we tried to stir the memories.

For Jacob, life really began after the family moved to Colorado. Before that most of Jacob's past continues to be buried in the protective blackness of his mind.

The blow of a whip causes a welt,
but a blow of the tongue crushes bones.

~(Ecclesiasticus 28:17)Apocrypha

Chapter 21

The Jordans moved to Colorado in the spring of 1987. Jacob was in fourth grade. Kermode had been transferred from Digital. The Jordans were in good shape financially. That year they made $130,000 and they had sold their California home. With the difference in property values they were able to purchase one of the nicest houses in Sunnywood Manor. They paid cash for a Dodge Ram and bought a lot of furniture. Pamela was finally able to achieve her dream of being a housewife. For approximately one and one half years she stayed home, enjoying her spacious residence, her soap operas, and a life devoid of work schedules and outside pressures.

Jacob was dismayed by the change in Pamela's routine. She only made his and Charles's lives more difficult. All that extra time didn't make her a more loving mother. It simply gave her more opportunity to meddle. For example, the first year they moved to Colorado, Jacob got in trouble on the school bus. Pamela refused to sign the "down slip" so the driver no longer allowed him to ride. For nearly half a year Jacob pedaled his bike to and from the elementary school, which is approximately four miles from the Jordan home. Part of his punishment took place during the winter when ice covered the road and huge piles of snow obliterated the shoulder, making any journey dangerous. Pam wouldn't let him cross the street or go to a neighbor's house supposedly for fear of what might happen, but she ordered an eight-year-old to travel eight miles a day because she was mad at a bus driver? No wonder Jacob lamented that she was totally inconsistent. To him, her actions made no sense. But they didn't have to.

During Pam's vacation from work, Jacob felt he couldn't breathe without her looking over her shoulder. Throughout the school year she volunteered at the elementary building just to watch him, he was sure. The teachers loved her, but the kids said, "Your mom's a bitch." Jacob and Charles had always gotten spankings for any unsatisfactory grade, but now Pam was so close with the teachers that she knew Jacob's grades before he did. Thus, his hell stretched out for weeks instead of just report card day.

Summers were worst because he couldn't escape to school. Pam even chose what books he and Charlie could read. Children's books were unacceptable. Rather they had to read something from Kermode's collection and write reports on them. They weren't allowed to go to the local library because Pam said it was too much trouble to drive the 2.5 miles and get them a library card. Forget about friends coming over. Every time Jacob did something to displease Pam, he was grounded for the entire summer. At this rate he'd be ninety years old before he

could do anything.

There was another reason that Jacob didn't like having his mother home. Charles swears that the sexual abuse with Kermode stopped for him after Colorado. He believes it did for Jacob, as well, because he no longer heard him crying in his bedroom when he and Kermode were together. Jacob vehemently insists that nothing could have happened to him on Ridge Drive.

In a curious statement, he told me, "Don't you think I would have blown *them* away right then? Kermode knew better than to approach me sexually because when Mom and he read about homosexuals in the paper or talked about them, I said, 'I'd blow them away.' Kermode would have had to consider that a warning."

"How did he respond?" I asked.

"'You don't have the heart to kill anybody.'"

But there are indications pointing to continued sexual abuse. Jacob still sat in Kermode's lap until he was twelve or thirteen and "it just didn't seem right." When Pamela's mother visited, Grace was appalled to see how Kermode cuddled Jacob, the "hooded look" that came into his eyes, and how he abruptly hurried to the bathroom. During a Colorado visit when Jacob was nine or ten, Lupe also observed Kermode and Jacob's odd interaction. Kermode stroked his stepson's thighs and buttocks the same way he did Pamela's when she sat on his lap.

"It was as if Jacob was his wife," she said.

But whether or not Kermode quit molesting Jacob in Colorado, one thing is certain. His mother didn't.

◊ ◊ ◊

"This is a memory from early Colorado when Mom wasn't working, Charles was somewhere. It was summer, late morning, one of the few times I actually penetrated her. I was 11 ½ to 12 years old.

"I was downstairs, (I don't remember what I was doing) and my mom called me upstairs to her room. When I got there, she was naked, standing in the middle of the room, about four feet from where I'll kill her later on. I knew instantly what was going on. I embraced her and we kissed. She got on the bed. I undressed and started to caress her and eat her. (I know this stuff is unpleasant to read. I don't like thinking about it, but it happened and I have to be as truthful about my life as I can be.) Anyway, I was hard, so I did what came natural, and stuck it in. After I was done, she lost her 'loving motherly sweet voice and manner,' so things went back to normal. Not too many times after this time, the sex stopped."

Outside corroboration of Pamela's perversion and predilection for young boys is provided by Lupe Thorson's own son. Before the Jordans settled in Colorado, the Thorson family had re-located to Minnesota, where Chet Thorson opened a lumber yard. That summer Lupe and her family visited. Her son Eric

was fourteen. Lupe had long sensed that Pam disliked Eric, but she couldn't figure out why. How could you not like a child? So she dismissed her feelings, and when Eric made derogatory remarks about Pamela, she insisted that he treat her best friend with respect. Lupe even ordered him to call her "Aunt," something Eric refused to do.

Eric hated Pam. He had never forgiven her for slapping his mom right in front of him when he'd been small. And she was so mean to her sons. He'd also seen other things, like the time when the two families went camping together in the Jordans' motor home. Charlie and Jacob, who would have been around eleven and seven at the time, had been out playing in the sand. Before being allowed back inside her immaculate motor home, Pam ordered them to strip down outside and get cleaned off. She insisted on personally cleaning their genitals. Perhaps because Pamela always disregarded children, she felt comfortable doing this in front of Eric. And what Eric saw was not someone cleaning genitals but fondling them.

During that same vacation Lupe also observed some disturbing behavior. Kermode got drunk and stripped down to his jock strap. He lounged on the motor home's couch in front of the boys and made lewd comments to everyone. Pam didn't seem bothered by his behavior—though why Lupe expected better she didn't know. Only hours previously, Pam and Kermode had made noisy love separated from the other six people by a few feet and a flimsy door.

"Why do you put up with him?" Lupe asked Pam, after scooting her children safely away from Kermode's grotesque display.

"He doesn't drink that much," Pam responded. "He just has a chemical imbalance that affects him differently."

Eric kind of liked Kermode but he really, really didn't like his mother's best friend. If Pam was in one room, Eric always made it a point to be in another. So imagine his surprise when during the Thorsons' trip to Colorado, he should have his own personal encounter with Pamela Jean.

After he entered the guest bathroom one afternoon, Eric unzipped his pants and readied to urinate. At that moment the door opened and Pam entered. Without a word she walked over, reached down and grasped his penis.

"I was stunned," Eric told me later. "I didn't know what to do. She was so mean and I was afraid of her. So I just finished my business."

Pamela then ordered him to fondle her chest, which he did. They were interrupted by someone coming up the stairs. She ordered him never to tell anybody and walked out.

Eric kept his secret until six weeks before the trial, though the event so

155

traumatized him that he went into intensive therapy soon after.[38]

Lupe noticed something else during their infrequent times together. Pamela's increasing regimentation. Pam had always been structured, but even though she wasn't working, she didn't relax her rules one bit. She had a time for everything. Weekends were taken up by cleaning, and the boys had chores every evening after school. Pamela was proud of the fact that the kitchen closed promptly at eight p.m. The boys had better not even enter afterward. Every morning she laid out their vitamins and orange juice. She told them what to wear, how to comb their hair, when to speak and what to say. The boys reminded Lupe of automatons. While Pamela echoed her earlier comment about Lupe's own parental laxity, "Someday you're gonna be sorry," Lupe was stunned by the look of absolute hatred that flitted across Charles's face once when Pamela corrected him. Charles's expression chillingly fit the saying, "If looks could kill." Lupe never saw that look from Jacob. He just hung his head or disappeared. Like the magician, David Copperfield, her little Jacob-beaner could vanish right before your eyes.

Kermode's job at Digital, while good, couldn't afford a $1300 a month house payment and a $500 motor home payment, in addition to other bills. The Jordans were living beyond their means. Pamela tried to ignore their negative cash flow. She loved staying home. Although she had always refused to touch her investments, she started cashing in her stocks and bonds from Pacific Bell. Maybe the money could last until Kermode received enough raises to support them.

Finally, however, Pamela had to face the truth. Another dream shattered. It wasn't fair. She had done everything right and they'd been in such great financial shape when they'd moved to Colorado. She had relished writing huge checks—six thousand dollars for furniture, twelve thousand dollars for the Dodge Ram, and even that hadn't depleted their savings. How could it all go to hell in less than two years? Pamela was furious, but she knew she had no choice. She had to go back to work.

---

[38] Looking back, Lupe believes that that wasn't the only incident with her son. She fears Pam molested him from the time he was two, when Eric suddenly developed severe speech problems. She and Eric also differ as to whether he ever told her about the incident. Lupe swears he didn't. He believes he did. He definitely did tell his therapist, who, because of confidentiality, kept the incident a secret from Lupe and Chet.

Must we go to bed indeed? Well then,
Let us arise and go like men
And face with an undaunted tread
The long black passage up to bed.
~Robert Louis Stevenson
Northwest Passage, 1, "Good Night"

Chapter 22

Pamela had a hard time keeping a decent job. She went back to school for a short time and then quit. She was overqualified for everything. Nobody wanted to hire someone with her background for $5.00 an hour, but they weren't about to pay her a livable wage. This was Colorado Springs and the movers and shakers in the community figured that the gorgeous view of Pikes Peak made up for pitifully low wages—at least for everybody but them. Fifty thousand dollar jobs for women in El Paso County were as rare as snow in June--not unheard of, but certainly unusual. Pam even took a job as a manager of McDonald's for a while, but ultimately ended up at Care & Share. She didn't even make twenty thousand a year. Increasingly, she felt trapped. According to Charles, she wanted to leave Kermode, but she couldn't afford to. She needed his health care. How could she support Jacob and Charles on such pitiful wages?

Pamela did have options, however. She had five years after leaving Pacific Bell to return, with only one step down in pay. She just didn't want to give up her lifestyle. Nor did she want to give up on Kermode. She remained obsessed with him and in denial about all his faults. He wasn't drinking and he wasn't too rough on the boys and they had a perfect marriage.

But now Kermode was making triple her salary and the balance of power had shifted. She was more completely under his domination. Amazingly, he kept his job at Digital and was considered a good worker. He confined his drinking to moderate during the week. He and Pamela would purchase a six pack a night—two for her, four for him. On Fridays he drank a bottle of wine plus a twelve pack and when he was on a bender, hard liquor. Pamela maintained he wasn't an alcoholic because he primarily drank beer. She actually insisted to Lupe during one of the Thorson visits that Kermode wasn't even drinking though he fell twice going down the hill to the van, which he drove to the liquor store.

When Lupe pointed out his condition, Pam responded, "I'd be concerned if it wasn't beer."

Jacob entered fifth, sixth, seventh grade. He began keeping a diary. In it he said things like, 'I would kill Kermode except he pays the bills.' While his stepfather was the only one who was ever nice to him, Jacob still wanted him, rather than his mother, dead. In fact, as a seven-year-old he'd made the statement that if anything happened to his mother, he'd kill himself.

157

During this period Jacob also drew a picture of Kermode with a knife sticking out of him, and wrote, 'I don't want you punishing us. If you do, you might not wake up.' He pinned the note on Kermode's pillow.

He told his mom what he had done.

She said,"Don't be silly."

Kermode was furious. "I've divorced people for shit like this. I'll take your house and divorce your mom and I won't give a damn."

Jacob and Charlie fervently hoped that he would make good on his threat. Charles so he could have his old mother back, and Jacob because he was beginning to believe if Kermode wasn't around, maybe he could control Pam. Or as he once said, "Maybe I could make her love me."

Pamela and Kermode insisted that their sons play sports. Jacob played football and some baseball. He didn't really like baseball. His worst memories were of him and Kermode out on the baseball diamond, all alone, at twilight. Jacob couldn't do anything right. Whether throwing or hitting, it was wrong. He threw too hard; he threw too soft. Kermode screamed at him and hit him on the head. Jacob was either uncoordinated or he hit the ball too far. During the games Kermode ranted about conspiracies against him and his stepson.

Once Pam acted as the football team nurse. The kids identified her by her inevitable moniker, The Bitch. One little leaguer got so mad at her he threatened to kill her. She was so mean to another that he actually hit her.

Jacob was now allowed to ride the school bus. Often, especially toward the end, he listened to Heavy Metal through his earphones and wrote, "Brutally kill all fags" on the fogged windows. He continued to do well in school and was in accelerated courses. He continued to get pummeled for any grade that was below perfect. Pamela's mental and physical abuse got worse. She took out her unhappiness on her boys. She hit them for anything—for mumbling or speaking too loudly, for looking mean, for not feeding the dogs or not walking them. It didn't matter what Charles and Jacob did. If she was in a bad mood she would find something.

During Jacob's first eighth grade summer, Pamela exited for a two week Mexico vacation. She was happy to get away and enjoyed herself by picking up a couple of young men. While she was gone Kermode, who fancied himself a Hell's Angel, bought a motorcycle. After drinking and driving he wrecked it and spent the entire time in bed. When Pamela called to check up on him he ordered the boys to lie. He and Pam were deep into the game, "Alcoholic and Co-dependent." The boozer lies. His spouse tries to catch him in the lie. He was the naughty boy. She was the disapproving mother.

Caught in the middle, the boys did as they were told.

"Nothing's happened," they told Pam. "No, Kermode isn't drinking. He's going to work every day. Everything's fine."

Actually, Kermode had cracked a couple of ribs and broken his collarbone. He went to the hospital, but convalesced at home, drowning his pain with booze.

He made the boys wait on him constantly. Even when he was asleep one of them would have to sit by the bed in case he should wake up and want something. Whenever they sneaked out, he had a bell beside his bed which he rang interminably. Once, when Charles didn't move quickly enough, he threw the bell at him.

Kermode and Pamela were increasingly locked in a struggle for control. Kermode had the monetary power, but when he was drinking, Pam sometimes got the upper hand with her disapproval. When she was gone or he was away on business trips, the drinking and whoring around really got bad.

Little by little Pamela Jean gave up. Until the Jordans put the house up for sale months before the murders, she hadn't even decorated it. Only then did she put up wallpaper and the homey touches that she had always insisted upon. Kermode chose the wallpaper just as he chose the furniture and many of the art pieces. Increasingly, Pam just didn't give a damn.

Jacob doesn't remember his parents fighting much at all. He remembers Kermode hitting her once. Charles remembers him throwing a chair, but generally they seemed "very much in love." For a short time, Kermode and Pamela worked together at Digital and fellow employees certainly thought so. They ate together, rode to work together, and preferred each other's company to the exclusion of company workers. Jacob does remember one occasion when Kermode got Pam drunk.

"Mom went on about her mother. I was up in my bedroom, but when I heard Mom crying, I crept downstairs to the living room."

The lights were dim and the stereo was on. They were dancing and Pamela was sobbing in Kermode's arms.

"I really hated Kermode for hurting Mom like that, for making her cry. I only saw my mom cry twice. Both times was involving her mother."[39]

Jacob does have good memories of his stepfather, though. Kermode still paid far more attention to him than did his mother. And since Kermode had molded Jacob, their views pretty much coincided. Jacob especially enjoyed their political discussions. Kermode hated the word "hippy."

"I'm not a hippy," he said."I'm a revolutionary."

Up until the time of the murders Kermode believed that he was being watched by the F.B.I., that his phones were being tapped. He bragged that he was an honorary member of the Black Panthers, and that he knew people in the mob. During his acting days he'd even been involved with illegal gambling and murder in New York. He often spoke of wanting to run guns for the contras and

---

[39] At other times Jacob said she also cried over Charles's leaving.

the blacks in South Africa.[40]

When the KKK marched in Denver in the summer of 1992, Kermode and Jacob spent hours planning to attend the rally, where they would assassinate the Grand Wizard and other Ku Kluxers. Jacob first decided they should disrupt events by throwing stones at the KKK. Kermode countered with Molotov cocktails. The scenario, which took place over two nights, became increasingly complex and deadly.

Jacob, caught up in their fantasy, asked, "Why don't we shoot them?"

"What are we going to shoot them with?"

"The .357."

He was referring to the .357 magnum that eventually became the murder weapon. Kermode purchased the revolver the last year of his life. Supposedly, Pamela hated guns and wouldn't allow them in the house, but after a heated disagreement which she lost, she never brought up the subject again. Kermode also had a .22 and a twelve gauge shotgun. Whenever the fighting got really bad and the boys were afraid for their lives, Jacob or Charles scrambled to hide the guns, often in the secret room. A drunk Kermode was a mean drunk. You never knew when he was going to try to blow away some guy at Jan's or Tres Hombres, or go after Charles and Jacob. Sometimes, when Kermode got really nasty and started hitting or yelling at Charles and called Pamela a bitch, Jacob grabbed the shotgun. He wanted to protect his mother however he could. During one altercation he retreated to his bedroom and loaded the .357. Pamela spotted him.

"I'm going to kill him," Jacob said. "I don't want him to hurt you."

"Just put it away."

Pam seemed pleased that Jacob was willing to defend her.

Increasingly, guns played a prominent part in the Jordan household. Jacob often loaded bullets into the chamber one at a time. Sometimes he fantasized killing Kermode, and sometimes himself. One time he put the .357 to his head and his hand froze. He didn't want to pull the trigger. Finally, he managed to lower the gun, but he was afraid he couldn't let the hammer down without shooting. He yelled for Charles, who entered the bedroom and removed the weapon.

Charles was never as interested in guns as Jacob. He wasn't at all mechanical and he considered guns to be just a bunch of macho bullshit. But the .357 found its way into Charles's life one night, as well.

---

[40] Curiously, after their deaths, agents from Alcohol, Tobacco and Firearms appeared at the Jordan residence. Supposedly, they were there to investigate "gun running." Considering Kermode's background and the fact that my source knew nothing about him, it's an interesting charge which I haven't been able to document.

"I was fifteen.[41] I was a freshman in high school. You know how male adolescents get these surges of testosterone. I started lifting weights and started noticing other things, and started becoming infatuated with women. And of course I wanted to impress them by flexing my muscles. Well, apparently, with me lifting weights, I started getting more of a backbone. I started standing up against what Mom and Kermode were doing, physical and mental.

"And they didn't like that, that I had some self esteem. Kermode got drunk one night off of some cheap wine, a one liter bottle of some cheap stuff. He started becoming really, really pissed off. It almost seemed like he was against me getting a backbone, so he wanted to put me in my place. And he came up to my room. It was about three o'clock in the morning. Mom was downstairs in the kitchen. They'd been fighting. It wasn't fighting among themselves. It was...it seemed like Mom was trying to defend me at first, and then she started siding with Kermode, saying that I had an attitude problem. I needed to be set straight.

"So I'm up in my bed and Kermode comes into my room, turns on the light and tells me to get up.

"'It's three o'clock in the morning and I have school tomorrow.'

"'I'm tired of your goddamned attitude.'

"He came over to the bed and punched me and ripped the sheets off. And I was just in my underwear so I was really embarrassed. And he said, 'Get down. Right now.'

"I said, 'Fine. I'll be down.' He just stood there. I said, 'Kermode I'll be down in just a bit.'

"He came over and smacked me. 'Don't give me that attitude.'

"So I put on a bathrobe and went downstairs. Then they started yelling at me about my attitude.

"Kermode said, 'Just because you feel your balls dangling between your legs doesn't make you a man. You have no idea what a man is.'

"I said, 'Oh, and I suppose you know?'

"He said, 'You're goddamned right!'

"And he slammed his two fists on the table and stood up and hit his head on the lamp, which I kind of laughed at. Which wasn't a good move. He pushed

---

[41] This is taken directly from a tape Lupe did with Charles over Christmas break 1993, which she later turned over to the defense. Jacob swore much of the incident could never have happened because, "My parents would have killed Charles." He dismisses it as an example of the "Lucinda Reed Syndrome," meaning Charles's supposed penchant for embellishing a story.

161

the table to his right and Mom said, 'Hey! Just sit down.'

"Kermode wouldn't stop. He put his hand on the kitchen table chairs—the captain chairs. Put his hands on the arm rest and got into my face.

"He said, 'Listen here, you damn motherfucker. I can kick your ass and break your neck and you wouldn't know what was going on.'

"And I was just scared because that look on his face was the same look that he gave me before he molested me. Before he hit me and while he was tying me up. The same exact expression. For some odd reason it seemed that the TV just went on and I was just watching everything happen. It was like a TV scene for the first hour. Them constantly yelling at me, and I would see myself just sitting there and I'd just be nodding my head. Pamela was yelling at me too.

"She said, 'You lousy fucking bastard. Look what we've given you. You've got a nice house. You go to a nice school. You have friends, you play football. You're able to do all this shit and look how you treat us.'

"And it really hurt. That's when I decided that she had just become Kermode. From that night on, I treated her just like Kermode.

"For some odd reason, we moved downstairs. I had just started lifting weights. Kermode wanted to prove to me that he was stronger than I was. He failed at that attempt. But it wasn't that funny. When he lifted his weights I got mad and I pumped more than he did. Twice as much. He did it four times. I did it eight times. So he put more weights than I knew I could handle. And I got underneath it and I pumped it once and he said, 'Do it again!' So I did it. And as he was coming down he was supposedly spotting me. When I had it on my chest he held it down there.

"Pam was sitting at the couch, watching. She looked at me like... When this first happened, I said, 'Mom, have him take it off me!' I was yelling. I was almost out of breath. I was suffocating, and she just sat there. She just looked at me like, 'That's what you deserve, you little shit.'

"And Kermode lifted up the bar and I doubled over, trying to catch my breath.

"He said, 'There you go.'

"I was doubled over on the floor. He took his fist, and kicked me over. He didn't kick me. He kind of shoved me with his foot. He walked over to the couch and he started laughing. I got up, and I was in a complete rage. I was so pissed off. I started yelling, calling him an asshole, and motherfucker.

"And I pointed over to my mom and said, 'You fucking bitch. You just let that happen, didn't you?'

"She got up and she said, 'Never call me a bitch,' and she came over and slapped me.

"And Kermode, he just sat there. I knew he was building up, becoming enraged. Mom sat back down. He got up and started shoving me and shoving me and shoving me. He grabbed me by the neck with both of his hands clenched around my neck as if he were going to suffocate me with his thumbs, in that

162

kind of grip.

"He said, 'You think you're such hot shit, calling your mom a bitch.'

"As he was getting more and more angry, his grip was tightening and tightening and I slapped his hands away and I ran upstairs to the bedroom and I locked the door. The door had a lock and a phone. I called 911.

"I said, 'My stepdad is totally out of control. He's drunk, he's really hurting me. Just get someone over here and have him stop it.'

"She said, 'Okay, okay. Where do you live?'

"And I told her, '120 Ridge Drive, Woodland Park, Colorado.'

"Then my mom knocked on the door and she said, 'Charlie. He's calmed down. It's all right now.'

"And she used that voice. This time she jumped from Kermode back to the old mom with that voice. It sounded so genuine and caring. But I was making the call and the operator was saying, 'What's going on? What's going on?'

"'Hang on, just a second.'

"Mom said, 'Listen, he's calmed down. Let's just go downstairs to the kitchen and talk. He's downstairs in the kitchen.'

"And I said, 'Listen, Operator. Everything's fine. The situation's under control. Thank you.'

• "The operator asked, 'Are you sure you don't want us to send someone over?'

"And I said, 'No. I'm sure, thank you.'

"I hung up the phone and unlocked the door. Kermode was right behind my mom. He took me by the robe and shoved me into the wall. She used the phony voice to lure me out because they obviously knew what I was doing and didn't want to bring the cops in. They knew they'd get arrested. It was really betraying. I felt like from that day on, ' Don't count on Pam.' When she started yelling at me, and saying, 'You fucking bastard,' it was after that that Mom actually died.

"It was after the fight, and I said, 'Listen.' I started acting tired, looking like I was dozing off. And then most of the nerves were calm. I was still pissed off. My head started thinking, just kept on thinking, Get rid of the bastard. Get rid of the bastard. If you kill him, it'll be just one less bastard in the world. I just started acting tired.

"They said, 'Why don't you just go off to bed?'

"I started getting up and they said, 'Oh, you're not going to kiss us goodnight?'

"And I said, 'Okay.'

"I kissed Mom on the side of the cheek and she said, 'No, no, no. On the mouth.'

"I said, 'Fine.' And I did. And Kermode wanted it too. And I said, 'Fine.' And I got upstairs. They had their backs turned. So I went into the bedroom and got Kermode's .357 from his top shelf. I took it out and made sure there weren't

any bullets in there. I brought it down and I had my hands behind my back. I used the same voice, like an innocent child's voice.

"I said, 'Mom, Kermode!'

"They said, 'What?'

"I took out the gun. Kermode and Pam were sitting at the kitchen table. I pointed it at Kermode, and the look on his face was worth it. It was worth all that shit. I could never forget that face. It was shock. And I knew his life flashed before his eyes. Pam was in shock. Her face just went pale. She grabbed the sides of the captain's chair. Her hands were just straining from the grip. And I cocked it and I swear to God, I thought I heard someone take a piss. And I smirked, slammed the gun on the table. They jumped from the chair to the ground, thinking it was loaded and it was going to discharge. And it didn't. And I just stood there with a smirk on my face and they just got up and they were filled with so much hate.

"And I said, 'Thanks for a nice night.'"

If you strike a child, take care that
you strike it in anger, even at the risk of
maiming it for life. A blow in cold blood neither
can nor should be forgiven.

~George Bernard Shaw
'How to Beat Children'

Chapter 23

Jacob repeated eighth grade. Pamela had insisted that he was too immature to enter high school. On the witness stand, self-proclaimed family friend/teacher Lucinda Reed said that she'd been involved with the decision, but Reed hadn't had anything to do with Jacob since sixth grade so he angrily disregards her comments.

"She just has to be the center of attention, no matter what. She had nothing to do with anything."

Jacob's second eighth grade was a breeze. His grades were excellent and his friend Mondo had also repeated so he insists he was happy.[43] Digital had started laying off workers. Kermode grew increasingly nervous about his job. 120 Ridge Drive was probably more than the Jordans could afford, especially in this market and with Kermode's shaky future. He and Pamela discussed downsizing.

"Maybe we should buy some acreage farther out where land is cheaper. We might even put a trailer on it, at least until the recession's over and the market improves."

To get Ridge ready for the market, Jacob and Charles were commandeered to paint the outside. Jacob, who was afraid of heights, was ordered to paint the peak of the three story structure.

"Will you hold the ladder for me?" he asked his mother. "Hold it tight. Don't let go."

"I won't," Pam promised.

As soon as Jacob reached the top, Pamela walked away. He was literally paralyzed with fright. He started crying and shaking and calling out for somebody to help him. Kermode finally came along and talked him down inch by inch.

That's the way it was. Pam was always mean to him. Kermode was more unpredictable. Jacob remembered another time, when he was around twelve, when the family went on a camping trip. He wasn't usually a bed wetter, but one

---

[43] Other kids remember teasing Jacob mercilessly because of being held back. One recalled piling on him, along with several other males, hoping to break his leg. All for the "sin" of repeating eighth grade.

night he wet his sleeping bag. The next morning Kermode hung out Jacob's gear to dry. Pamela and Charles began taunting him, but Kermode covered for him.

"We slept under a tree. Moisture dripped onto the bedding, that's all."

On September 26, 1991, Jacob's fourteenth birthday, his parents gave him a dress watch. He had already started his hippie phase and the watch was just another indication that they wanted him to be anything other than what he was. He alternated between feeling rebellious and wanting to please Kermode and Pamela. Sometimes he and Kermode got along great, though beyond the bedroom Jacob had never had any rapport with his mother. He always felt her rejection. But what was so maddening for both him and Charles was that much of the condemnation remained unspoken. Thus, their feelings could be—and were—dismissed. Kermode and Pamela's entire attitude conveyed their antagonism, but how to explain it? It might have been blatant but it was seldom verbal."I don't know what you mean," Pamela would say if Jacob tried to question her, which caused him to wonder whether he was indeed misinterpreting the message.

But even when Pam mouthed the proper words, their meaning was twisted. She said things like, "Of course we love you. Look at all the things we buy for you. Look at your nice house." "You know we're not so bad. We take care of you."

Jacob would feel guilty and think, Yeah, I really am a butt, even though her every action screamed her disapproval.

As he matured, he wasn't so easily confused. Pamela hated him, no matter how many times she said, "I love you." She wasn't interested in the things that interested him. She didn't care that he was mechanically inclined or that he had a crush on Lila or that he had a wicked sense of humor or that he liked King Diamond or dreamed of starting a revolution. She didn't care about JACOB PATRICK IND. She never even saw him. She insisted that he be somebody else--anybody other than who he was. She wanted him to be a preppie son like Charles. She wanted him to be the daughter she'd never had. She wanted him to be anybody but Jacob Ind. That message, at least, came through loud and clear.

Pamela often compared Jacob unfavorably with other people. "You're a bum. You dress like a bum," she said, especially after Jacob became a recycled hippie. That last year, he was torn between trying to live up to her expectations and to rebel. Nothing he ever did was right anyway, so why bother? But he had to bother, because if he didn't there'd be hell to pay. And Jacob still needed her approval.

Pamela had long lamented to Jacob the fact that she had never had a daughter. She, the least feminine of women, would look across the street to the Smiths' house, and say, "I wish I had a daughter like Laurie." Laurie just happened to be Jacob's age and Pamela had once fixed her hair before a dance. Pamela often brought that incident up, bemoaning her supposed loss. A

daughter would have helped her "relive her childhood." Jacob took this as a personal rejection. If only she hadn't had him. If only he'd been born a girl maybe everything would have been better. It wasn't her fault that she was such a bitch. It was his. He was the wrong gender. Pamela would have been a completely different person if she'd had a daughter to cuddle.

Actually, Pamela was playing head games with him. Lupe had a very feminine daughter. Pamela never expressed any interest in Sonia or any other female.

Lupe says, "I never ever heard Pam utter any supposed desire to "do girl things." I never heard her express any regrets over not having a daughter."

Such regrets were reserved for Jacob's ears. Just another of a million cuts etched into his soul. Jacob believed he was damaged goods, no doubt about it. His defiant side made him rebel every time his mother wanted him to do something remotely feminine, like decorate the Christmas tree or bake cookies. He would prove to her he was all boy. Yet, unless Jacob is different from most victims of sexual abuse, he inevitably has some gender identity problems. The damage is greater if the child has been violated at a very young age and by both parents. If Jacob would have had one parent to turn to, one parent who hadn't raped him, perhaps he would never have killed them. But he was like a man in a box--trapped on one side by the physical abuse, on another by the emotional, on the third by the sexual, and on the fourth side by the total absence of what ordinary people define as love. He could see no way of breaking out, so he turned to violence. In this he was emulating his teachers.

Age fourteen was important to Jacob for another reason. In addition to Pamela's secret perversions with her sons, she had always made provocative sexual remarks. Those increased with Jacob. When he was in the bathroom she always tried the knob. If he failed to lock the door she barged in on him and stared at his nakedness. She made lewd comments about his genitalia.

"Do you still have that cute little mole on your ass?"

After Jacob talked to his girlfriend, Lila, on the phone, Pam asked him at the dinner table about "the bulge in his pants." Jacob was mortified and denied it, but Pamela said, "A mother knows these things. I used to change your diapers."

She said, "Your butt has dimples," and when he went upstairs after a shower, hollered, "I can see your balls." Several times during those last months she came into his bedroom in her nightshirt. She bent over so that her posterior faced the mirror. Jacob couldn't fail to notice that she wasn't wearing underwear. He was embarrassed by her behavior but he was also titillated. After all those years of her forcing herself on him, he had reached puberty and sex was constantly on his mind. Now he actually wanted to be intimate with his mother. She had initiated Jacob into sex. He knew all her secrets, and when the act would finally give him pleasure, he fantasized about having intercourse with her. She teased him, showing off her nakedness and openly ogling him. Pam

167

knew exactly what she was doing to her son, and she was delighted. It brought back those old feelings of power, of control, and there was so little that Pamela controlled these days.

All his life Jacob had dreaded the sound of her voice, saying, "You can sleep with me tonight," and shuddered at the touch of her hand. She knew he hated having to do those things with her so she made him perform. Perversely, now that Pamela knew sex was something he actually wanted, she did a typical Pamela thing.

She denied it to him.

◇ ◇ ◇

Christmas 1991, the Jordans' last Christmas, was a big event. Since moving to Colorado, Christmas had become more of a chore, less of a holiday. Only if guests were expected would Pamela bestir herself to put up the fake tree, the plastic wreaths and the other decorations. She'd fix a decent Christmas dinner but that was about it.

This particular Christmas family members from both the Wallace and Jordan sides agreed to meet in Woodland Park. Kermode and Pamela purchased a whole shopping cart full of booze from Cheers Liquor in Colorado Springs. When family members arrived, including Pamela's parents, Kermode started acting as if he was going to drink the entire stash himself. He stayed intoxicated throughout the holidays. Pamela pretty much ignored his behavior but her mother, Grace, was appalled. Kermode was so drunk and revolting. Once Grace made a derogatory comment, which angered him. He came after her as if he meant to hit her, but she didn't back down.

"If you were a man I'd hit you," she said.

Grace hated what was happening. Kermode was a filthy, disgusting pervert and the boys slunk around the house like whipped dogs. Pam was so thin and her demeanor so strained. As she had repeatedly over the years, Grace begged her daughter to leave Kermode.

"You can live with your dad and me. We'll take care of you and the boys. But you must leave him."

Grace held her daughter. She could feel the bones in Pam's shoulders and her heart broke. Pamela wouldn't confide anything to her and she wouldn't leave Kermode. Grace didn't know what to do.

Stepson Cameron also arrived for Christmas '91. He and Jacob tried to stay away from the guests, holing up downstairs. Cameron played with the Nintendo in the family room so he wouldn't have to view his dad's stumbling around and obnoxious good cheer. Jacob retreated to Kermode's study, which had two computers.

Sometimes Pamela called him upstairs. "You're being rude. Pay attention to your guests."

In Jacob's presence she recounted stories about what a rotten kid he was,

168

or launched into "colorful anecdotes." Once Jacob couldn't suppress the urge to correct her butchering of the facts.

"That's not how it was, Mom," he said.

Pamela went insane.

"How dare you contradict me. Who do you think you are, calling me a liar?"

In front of the guests, she slapped Jacob across the face. Pam was physically strong for being so slight, and her "discipline" hurt like hell. Jacob slunk back downstairs to his computer game. Their visitors pretended that nothing had happened.

Kermode took a shine to four-year-old Galahad, (*) the son of Dan Wallace, Pam's younger brother. Although he was stinking drunk, Kermode whisked Galahad off to the guest bathroom for a leisurely bath. Jacob and Charles both observed what he was doing. Charles was angered that no adults even questioned Kermode. Galahad wasn't even related to Kermode and Kermode was obviously intoxicated and the Wallaces entrusted their son to him?

After Kermode took Galahad into the bathroom, Jacob retreated to the study, where he tried to block out his uneasiness by plunging into the fantasy world of Conan the Cimmerian. An hour passed. An hour and a half. None of the adults lounging at the kitchen table commented on Galahad's absence. Finally, Jacob went upstairs. He carefully opened the bathroom door. Galahad was standing in the tub, surrounded by toys. Kermode was crouched beside him. Jacob quickly fled back downstairs to the study and buried himself in his make-believe world. After two hours Galahad emerged. The only people who ever remarked on the incident were Jacob and Charles.

Kermode started drinking early each morning. By afternoon he was blitzed. By evening he was disgusting. One evening he decided that he was going to take the motor home and everybody at the house on a sightseeing expedition to Durango, a five hour trip. Nobody could dissuade him. He got nasty when Grace said, "No way." Finally, everybody conspired to hide the keys from him. Otherwise, Kermode would have endangered his guests' lives on a kamikaze expedition over several snow covered passes. As drunk as he was, it is amazing that everyone save Grace either ignored or accepted his behavior.

Charles was so miserable and humiliated that he confided in his favorite aunt, Beth, about Kermode's physical abuse. He even told her that he and Jacob had been sexually abused. Beth never mentioned the conversation to anyone.

The worst event of Christmas '91 occurred near the end of the holidays. Cameron had stayed glued to the Nintendo, which infuriated Pam.

"He's being rude," she said to Kermode. "He doesn't have any manners. He doesn't know the meaning of the word "discipline..." It's all his bitch of a mother's fault. Shannon doesn't know how to raise her son. His disrespectful behavior is making us look like fools."

Pamela nagged Kermode until he too started getting damned angry. The

nerve of Cameron, behaving like a little shit, embarrassing him in front of a houseful of people. Finally, after hours of drinking and brooding, Kermode staggered downstairs.

"Turn that damned thing off," he yelled, referring to the television. He was so drunk he swayed on his feet.

Sensing a fight, Jacob snuck to the study door, where he had a clear view of the action. Cameron made a derogatory comment about Kermode's drinking. Kermode swung at Cameron and nearly fell over. Cameron hit him. They started fighting right there in the family room. Only the stairway and the foyer separated them from the rest of the guests, congregating in the kitchen. Pamela hurried downstairs. Yanking off her shoe, she began hitting Cameron.

"Let go of him, you little bastard!" She screamed. Finally, the pair was separated. Further mention of the incident, other than to castigate Cameron, was forbidden.

At the trial Pamela's brother, Dan, said that Kermode was a happy drunk and a good father. Pamela was not too hard on her children and Dan vowed that he intends to raise his children the same way she did.

Charles was a junior in high school. He stayed away from 120 Ridge Drive as much as possible. He was active in forensics and football and anything else that got him out of the house. He felt bad that he couldn't really protect his brother, but his own survival depended on distance. Jacob was such an expert at fading away that Charles hoped Kermode and Pamela would forget all about him. He knew that was a vain hope but Charles had problems of his own. He started drinking heavily. Life was just so horrible. He needed to escape both Kermode and Pamela. He no longer really loved his mother. He loved "Mom" but he hated "Pamela Jean," and she was more and more in evidence these days.

With her independence gone, Pam grew increasingly bitter and hostile. As winter drifted into spring, a friend spotted her at a forensics convention and was shocked over the change in her. Her eyes looked lifeless, dead. It was as if any spark of joy, of vitality had been sucked out of her.

Kermode did try to give the boys more freedom those last months. Charles figured it was his way of making up for the past. It didn't mean that Kermode was nice. He could be nice; he could be cruel—all in the space of five minutes. Jacob remembers one incident where he entered the house. The wind caught the door, causing it to slam shut. Kermode barged down the stairs.

"What the hell do you think you're doing?"

Jacob tried to explain.

"Shut up! I'm gonna stand here and you're gonna open and close that goddamned door right, do you understand?"

He ordered Jacob to do it two hundred times—and counted each one.

The amazing thing about Pamela and Kermode is how much energy they wasted playing the game of "Gotcha." Before leaving for work Pam would sometimes place one or two of the dots torn from the edge of a spiral bound notebook in a certain position on the kitchen floor. She would also take a grain or two from the litter box and place it nearby so that when Jacob said, "Yes, I did my chores," she could ascertain whether he was lying. If the dots or the granules hadn't been swept up, she would triumphantly point that fact out to Jacob before administering her punishment. The question has to be asked. Why would Pam waste so much energy trying to trap Jacob? Wouldn't it have been far easier to sweep the floor herself or accept her son's word?

Despite the fact that Jacob was turning into a handsome young man, he remained extremely shy around girls. Rosa Falu, a friendly, outgoing senior that Charles met through Forensics, remembers Jacob as being so bashful he couldn't even look her in the eye or carry on a conversation. Sometimes when she called for Charles, Jacob would answer. Rosa, who figures she can carry on a conversation with a doorstop, was determined to draw Jacob out. [44] Instead of asking immediately for Charles, she generally made small talk with Jacob. After a few minutes, Kermode would pick up the phone and order him to get off. Jacob obeyed without question.

Rosa is a Christian and the few times she went to the Jordan residence, she talked to Pam about God. Pam had always scoffed at religion, but when Rosa asked whether the older woman would like to attend her church, Pam responded, "Yes, I'd really like to." Several times they made plans. Each time Pam would cancel, saying, "I'm sorry. I can't. Kermode won't let me."

Pam had started using Kermode as her scapegoat. Before she had always protected him, but increasingly she blamed him when making excuses for something she herself didn't want to do. She would like to be more open, but he prevented her. She would like to go out, but he wouldn't allow it. She would like to do more for her boys, but Kermode was so difficult. Pam was friends with Yvonne Smith, a petite Puerto Rican native with a mass of greying hair, who lived across the street. They often walked the dogs together, and Yvonne, a charismatic Christian, swears that Pamela had entered a bible study before the murders. But Yvonne also swears that she never heard or saw anything amiss in the Jordan household. The Jordans weren't abusive. Parents should be strict with their children. Yvonne and her husband were stern with daughter Laurie, but that wasn't called abuse. It was called being a good parent.

Jacob was seldom allowed to go anywhere without Kermode and Pamela. One of his happiest teenage memories occurred during Charles's senior year, soon after his older brother received his driver's license. He and Charles were

---

[44] Rosa is one of several who say that the murders changed Jacob for the better. He is far more self confident and has more self esteem than before.

given permission to go alone to the mall. As Charles drove, Jacob gazed out the window into the passing night, and dreamed of them just driving forever and never coming back.

More often the mall was a source of embarrassment for Jacob. Whenever Kermode spotted some cute teenage girls, he stopped them.

"Wouldn't you like to go out with my son here? Don't you think he's cute?"

Jacob just wanted to disappear. The girls giggled or hurried away and Kermode laughed, as if he'd just done something extremely funny. When they ate out, he'd call the waitress over to the table. "Waitress," he'd say, "can't you make this little boy behave?" Jacob hadn't been doing anything. He'd just been sitting there or sipping his tea.

Jacob did everything in his power to keep from going out in public with his parents. If Kermode wasn't trying to embarrass him, his mother made a big phony show. After a football game she put her arm around him, kissed him on the cheek and told him how proud she was of him, which infuriated Jacob. She was so insincere. Couldn't anybody else see what she was doing?

When Jacob wasn't grounded, he was occasionally invited to spend the night at a friend's house. Kermode and Pamela seldom directly said no. That was too simple. Rather they laid down impossible ground rules like "We need a week and a half advance notification." A spur of the moment thing, such as, "Jeremy asked me if I could spend the night tonight," led them to say, "You know the ground rules. That's impossible." They made everything so much harder than they had to. If for some reason they relented, upon Jacob's return they complained about how dirty everything had gotten in twenty-four hours, and doubled the usual chores. His parents always acted like they were doing him a huge favor so the payback wasn't worth the bother—though the last summer they did let him spend more time with Mondo. whom they liked.

More frequently, however, "Friends" remained a game whereby Jacob's parents played by whatever rules struck their fancy. Sometimes Kermode and Pam complained about the boys going out; sometimes they said, "Why don't you have your friends visit?" Such dishonesty enraged Jacob. Worse, if he was so stupid as to believe them and asked, "Could Jeremy come over?" the complaints started up again.

They said things like, "We'll have to watch TV in our bedroom." "You're disrupting our entire evening." This was another example of words contradicting the message.

On the few occasions when guests actually visited, the atmosphere totally changed. Kermode and Pamela were model parents. "Would you like us to rent some movies?" Can I make you some popcorn?"

They were super nice to the kids although they trashed them the moment they left.

"Don't ever invite him again," they warned.

172

Charles and Jacob didn't.

◇ ◇ ◇

In June 1992, following the end of the school year, Charles and Pamela drove to North Dakota and the annual forensics convention. Charles was to give a presentation of 'Dr. Jekyll and Mr. Hyde,' for which he won an award. Jacob was left alone with Kermode for an entire week. Since their move to Colorado and Kermode's steady job, he and Jacob hadn't spent any extended period of unsupervised time together.

Charles was relieved to be leaving. Alone with his mother, she reverted to "Mom" and any reprieve from Kermode was cause for celebration. Tensions in the household escalated, almost by the day. The fighting was louder and more physical, especially since Charles had started hitting back. Money was a constant problem. The family savings was totally depleted. Charge cards hovered in the six-seven thousand dollar range. Sale of Ridge Drive would have netted the Jordans a cool $120,000.00, but in the current market serious buyers were about as rare as whales in a swimming pool.

Whenever Pamela went away, Kermode acted like a naughty boy freed from his mommy's watchful gaze. June 1992 was no exception. Jacob remembers that they went camping. Kermode was drunk and they slept in the same tiny tent. Jacob placed the .357 in the overhead netting within easy reach, but he swears nothing out of the ordinary happened. On the way back from Cripple Creek, a drunken Kermode nearly plunged the Ram over thousand foot drops. Maybe he was too preoccupied regaling Jacob with stories of his sexual escapades to pay attention to driving. Kermode was forever pressing Charles for details about his sex life, but Jacob was too young to provide much of a titillating nature. So, as they drove, Kermode confessed that the best lay he'd ever had was a woman with thirteen children, and talked about his ex-wives and their proclivities in the bedroom. He also discussed Pam, saying what a magnificent woman she was, as if he were trying to make Jacob jealous.

Over the weekend, Kermode went to Tres Hombres, a local bar that specializes in Tex Mex food. Tres Hombres sits on the corner of a string of connected buildings constructed in the frontier style, with false fronts. This particular Saturday was Reggae night. Kermode had always had Jacob accompany him to bars. As usual, Jacob was the youngest one there. He spent the entire evening watching Kermode grope a much younger woman who worked in the bike shop that had sold him his motorcycle. Afterward, Jacob had to help his extremely drunken stepfather to the Ram. Tres Hombres' parking lot is tiny, sandwiched between the Pony Tail beauty salon and a paint store. The area was deserted save for Jacob and Kermode. Kermode lost his car keys.

"Where are my goddamned keys?" he said to Jacob. "You stole them."

"No, I didn't," Jacob said. "I don't know where they are."

173

Kermode grabbed him in a headlock and slammed him against the car. Jacob was afraid he would have to use his knife, the bear mace or the .357, packed away in the camping gear, but Kermode abruptly quit hitting him. Finally Kermode found the car keys beneath his jacket.

Jacob can't remember whether any other incidents occurred, though he once said Kermode drank every night.[45] In a curious statement, he commented, "I was Kermode's wife that week." As far as details, he doesn't supply any, except that he cooked and cleaned. He became angry when I pressed him.

"I would remember if something else happened," he insisted. "If Kermode had tried to touch me, I would have killed him on the spot."

Nevertheless, something happened. At least, Charles believes it did. On his and Pam's return from forensics, Charles took one look at Jacob and thought, You bastard. What have you done to my brother?

Jacob had the same look in his eyes as when he was four years old—right after Kermode had finished molesting him.

---

[45] In my notes I wrote that Jacob was so frightened during that week that he slept with the .357 beside his bed. Jacob swears I'm mistaken, that I confused that incident with the one when he was little and slept with the broken .22. Jacob's memory can't always be trusted. With the passage of time he tends to minimize anything his parents did. I stand by my notes.

Nothing begins, and nothing ends
That is not paid with moan;
For we are born in other's pain
And perish in our own.

~Francis Thompson
"Daisy"

Chapter 24

"Jacob really changed after Forensics," said Charles. "I couldn't place my finger on it at the time. It's hard to give an outside observation when you're in the picture. I knew what was going on, but I wasn't sure. I didn't want to see it happen again. I didn't have the inclination to do anything about it anymore. At that point I was so drained with everything else... Whatever happened when we were in North Dakota, (Jacob) blocked out, but not the feelings. You can't block out feelings."

Before the trial, Charles would awaken to the sound of Jacob screaming in his brain, the same way he'd screamed when Kermode raped him. But throughout summer '92 it was Jacob's face that haunted his older brother.

"That's when I started planning to kill (Kermode). It fluctuated on my part, how I would plan it. And that's after I'd be drinking. I'd be writing down all the details. I even started doing time lines. I started getting really depressed. I thought about killing them both. Pamela because she should have known. I mean, come on! She was our mother! It was her fucking job to protect us! I tried to protect Jacob but I couldn't do it. I mean at the age that I was at (when so much of this began)—what could a nine year kid do? When this happened at forensics I felt weak again. I felt incredibly weak. No matter what I did it wouldn't change anything. It wasn't the punishment. It always came across, the hatred is what we'd really discuss. I never told Jacob that I sat up drunk plotting their deaths. Never told him that.

"I had to get out. I started getting really violent thoughts. I started visualizing throwing them out windows, something like that. Kermode...it just seemed like it almost obsessed all my time. Every time I was in the house. Like right now, every second, How can I kill Kermode? I'd be sitting down, watching TV and it was in the summertime and I just got off work and sometimes it would be one or two in the morning, and I knew they'd be sleeping in the house and I'd be thinking, How can I kill them? Then I started thinking that. Every time I was in the house I started thinking about it."

Charles and Jacob never discussed their plans. According to Charles, the most Jacob said was, "I just wish they would leave, go away."

"And I would say, 'Unfortunately Jacob, we have to stay. There's nothing we can do.'

175

"I never, never heard Jacob say, 'I'll kill them,' but I did hear him say, 'I wish they were dead.' And I said that once. But when I made those plans, I passed out right after. Then when I woke in the morning and saw those sheets of paper and then I'd throw them in the fireplace. I'd wake up and I'm hung over but I'd just shake my head and say, 'It was all a dream. That didn't happen.'"

◊ ◊ ◊

Jacob started suffering from insomnia. With David Mabie he began breaking into houses. Jacob also started smoking pot and anything else he could get his hands on. Hoping for a cheap high, he and his friend Jeremy even smoked some kinnikinnick they picked in his backyard. He also began playing Russian Roulette. It certainly seemed that something had happened to precipitate Jacob's self-destructive behavior. However, Jacob doesn't believe in cause and effect, at least when it comes to his own actions.

"Nothing happened. Summer '92 was the best summer of my life. For one thing, I was depressed all the time, and I like the feeling I get when I'm depressed. Also, I had my first job so I was away from home a lot more."

He was thrilled to have his own money, even though it was in a joint checking account so he couldn't touch the funds without his mother's signature. Though Jacob really enjoyed working at Jan's he tried not to act too happy or Pamela would have made him quit.

"Any time I had something I liked, my mother would take it away from me. That's why I never wanted any privileges."

In July Kermode and Jacob and Pamela spent a week camping in Cortez. Jacob loves to fish and he cherished any opportunity to indulge his passion. Kermode and he fished together, or Jacob would wander off on his own. He enjoyed sleeping out under the stars, watching the moon inch across the sky, and tracking the clouds, listening to the whisper of insects and the nearby stream.

This time, however, Pamela pretty much spoiled everything. Her ulcer had started acting up, and as usual she took her frustrations out on Jacob. If he wanted to go downstream, she said no. "You might get lost." If he wanted to sleep outside, she said, "Who do you think you are, Davy Crockett?"

It really embarrassed him when she continually told relatives, "He's just in a Davy Crockett stage."

As the week progressed, Jacob grew increasingly irritated with Pam. "Everything she did bugged me." Kermode allowed him to go do "man things" and didn't hassle him, but Pamela wanted to treat him as if they were back in the kitchen at Ridge Drive. No allowances for the fact they were on vacation. She constantly accused Jacob of talking back and being disrespectful. She slapped him often and belittled him continually.

Jacob also spent one or two weeks that last summer with his real dad, but

he never confided anything to him. As far as they were concerned, he wouldn't help them so both Jacob and Charles kept their mouths shut and suffered in silence.

Kermode's drinking worsened. For five years he had controlled his binging to the extent that few outsiders were aware of his behavior. He largely stayed away from bars and confined his public displays to business trips. But Kermode seemed to be losing control. He started frequenting Jan's. Jan's is a two story cafe with family dining downstairs and a bar/lounge on the second floor. A couple of times Kermode was kicked out of the lounge for being belligerent. One night while Jacob was washing dishes, he heard the help discussing some old drunk who had just fallen down the stairs. He later discovered it was Kermode.

The fighting between Kermode, Pamela and Charles escalated. Charles threw Kermode's drinking in his face and held his ground until the house reverberated with the trio's shouting. Jacob was like a ghost in the house. Whenever there was any sort of altercation, he disappeared into the computer room or his bedroom.

Near the end of August 1992, the Lofthouse Incident occurred.[46] Kermode had all his teeth pulled. When his dentures were put in, they weren't the right pair and the dentist was forced to chip away some of his bone. The procedure was extremely painful. Kermode loaded himself down with pain killers. With the weekend he started mixing alcohol with the pills. He began early Saturday morning. He, Jacob and David Mabie were going to go fishing. Waiting for the boys to finish football practice, he spotted Charles outside WPHS's commons. Much to his horror, Charles was wearing an earring. One of the Jordan rules was, "No earrings." While the eighteen-year-old wanted one for fashion reasons, a furious Kermode said, "Only homos have earrings. Either you give that thing to me or I'll rip it out. You can't follow fucking directions."

Humiliated, Charles obeyed. Afterward, his coach, Victor Smith, saw the teen walking along the road and picked him up. Charles poured his heart out to Smith, telling how miserable he and Jacob were, about Kermode's alcoholism, and both parents' emotional abuse.

Meanwhile, Kermode picked up Jacob and David to go fishing. As the mixture of drugs took effect, Kermode's driving became increasingly erratic. He nearly veered into a ditch.

David screamed, "Look out!"

At the last minute Kermode over-corrected and headed for the opposite shoulder. That's how it went throughout the eight mile trip. After reaching their

---

[46] The following is a combination of Jacob's and Charles's recollections. Charles testified to the incident at Jacob's trial. Others, such as teacher Victor Smith, mentioned portions of that day.

destination, the trio fished for a while but Kermode's behavior worsened. He began playing with one of his hunting knives.

"This goddamned thing probably needs sharpening," he said. He tried unsuccessfully to pull a hair out of his head in order to prove his point. After finally managing to remove a small clump, Kermode attempted to cut an individual hair. Instead, he sliced his finger. As he stared at the oozing blood he reminded Jacob of a small child who'd just skinned his knee.

After dropping the boys off at 120 Ridge Drive, Kermode drove to Jan's Cafe where he continued drinking.

Meanwhile, back at the Jordan residence, Charles returned from his job at Wendy's. Kermode had left a note to Pam, telling her about Charles's earring, and that he was off fishing.

Before Pam could really question Charles about his disobedience regarding the earring, he deflected her attention with, "I smelled whiskey on Kermode's breath."

Now Pam would have to deal with a drunken husband. She and Charles went to Jan's. The bartender told them Kermode had already left.

"He tried to pick a fight with our customers," the bartender said. "I gave him a choice. 'You either take a cab or I'm calling the police.'"

Charles drove Kermode's white Ram home, while Pam followed in the other vehicle.

Once the Jordans were all together, events turned ugly. While trying to maneuver the stairs from the bedroom level to the main floor, Kermode missed the landing and tumbled down the seven steps. He sprawled at the bottom, bleeding from a gash in his head.

Jacob and Charles looked at Kermode. He didn't move. They both thought he was dead. They hoped he had broken his neck. Charles kind of smiled.

Pamela said, "Just get a towel and some ice and give them to me. I'll try to staunch the blood."

At that moment Kermode groaned and shifted position. Jacob thought, Oh no, he's alive. Charles thought, Shit.

Kermode started yelling, "Where's Charlie? Where's Charlie?"

Charles was overwhelmed with hatred. The feelings of killing Kermode were so intense that he couldn't deal with them. At that moment he made up his mind. He could no longer live in that house or ever again associate with his parents.

"I'm outta here!"

Charles stalked to his room where he threw a bunch of clothes into a bag. By the time he returned, Pam had helped her husband to a recliner and Jacob had retrieved ice for Kermode's cut.

Charles slammed the door on his way out.

When it was just the three of them, Pam helped Kermode up to the bedroom. Once there, the trio rested on the bed until Kermode suddenly jumped

up, yelling, "I know what you're trying to do!" He staggered back downstairs to the kitchen.

Jacob and Pamela followed.

"We're leaving," Jacob said to his mother.

"No. Just hide the knives."

Jacob whisked the knife block off the counter. Then he hid the .357 and the other weapons in the secret room.

Kermode noticed that the knives were missing. "I'm gonna crush your head in," he screamed at Jacob.

"Bitch!" he yelled at Pamela before collapsing in a kitchen chair. While muttering to himself, he groped in his pants pocket for his pocket knife, which he flourished in front of them.

"You forgot one!" Kermode threw the knife at the window. It fell harmlessly to the floor.

"Mom, let's get out of here!"

Pamela refused. "He'll calm down soon."

But Jacob had endured enough. His number one priority was to protect his mother. Kermode was worse than he'd ever seen him. What would he do next?

Finally, Pamela agreed that Kermode was going to have to fend for himself. Taking the knives with them, she and Jacob checked into the Lofthouse, Woodland Park's only motel.

The Lofthouse is located downtown, a block off the highway, and three miles from the Jordan residence. The rooms are dated but serviceable and Jacob and Pamela rented a single.The police arrived and filled out a report. (Kermode had called in that the family guns were stolen.)

"Maybe I should go back and check on Kermode," Pamela kept saying. "No."

Jacob thoroughly relished his role as Pamela's defender. For the first time he felt like a real son. His mother was uncertain, vulnerable. She needed him and he wouldn't let her down.

They turned on TV. Pamela paced the room while Jacob sprawled on the double bed. Alternately she worried about Kermode and cursed him. "If he doesn't quit drinking I'll leave him. I promise you I won't go back to him."

Jacob felt wonderful. He had long dreamed of this moment. Pamela was manageable without Kermode. She was also beginning to bear some resemblance--though not much--to a regular mother.

After dark, Jacob decided that he'd like to walk down to McDonald's, approximately a half mile away, for something to eat.

"No," Pam said. "Kermode might come along. He might see you."

"Mom, I'm going. That's how I have to deal with this. Don't worry."

"Well, be careful."

He couldn't believe how easily he could assert himself. Pamela didn't say another word. Jacob strolled along the dirt roads behind the highway toward the

golden arches and with each step his heart lightened. He'd never dared say no to his mother before. Now he had and she hadn't done anything about it. Things were going to get better. Finally, his mother was going to leave the bastard and he and his mom would be a family, just the two of them.

Once at McDonald's Jacob's euphoria increased. He'd never been allowed to go anywhere by himself. He watched customers enter and leave and it felt so good because he didn't have to account to anybody for his time and he didn't have to worry about getting in trouble for some real or imagined wrong. He ordered a coke and a Big Mac. That felt good, buying his own food with his own money. And being able to sit in a booth alone and eat just like an ordinary person.

For the first time in his life, Jacob felt as if he had something in common with other people, that he was actually connected to the human race. For the first time, he felt normal.

"I already started to daydream about helping, to carry my weight, and pay rent on where Mom and I would live and... But it didn't end up how I wanted it to."

The next morning Jacob went to a friend's house and then to work. Pamela returned to Ridge Drive. It was as if nothing happened. The incident was never mentioned again. Kermode swore he would quit drinking, Charles moved out, and the countdown to murder began.

There's no better way of exercising the
imagination than the study of law. No
poet ever interpreted nature as freely as a
lawyer interprets truth.

~Jean Giradoux
Tiger at the Gate

PART SIX
JUDGMENT

Chapter 25

By the time Jacob went to trial on May 2, 1994, I had known him less than
sixteen months and been professionally involved with him for a year. We had
spent nearly a thousand hours together, talking about his life, digging through
the layers in order to uncover every facet of his character and personality. I
maintained then, and I still maintain, that I know Jacob better than anyone. Of
course, I might be deluding myself. Pop-style psychologists, those who don't
know Jacob or me but have seen enough talk shows to "understand" the human
mind, are always psychoanalyzing the two of us.

One of their favorite questions is, "How do you know this kid was even
abused? What if he just made up a bunch of stuff to save himself from prison?"

The inference behind their remarks is that I'm a gullible woman, too stupid
to realize when someone is lying or manipulating me. I'll let others decide
whether that is a fair characterization. But the fact is, at least ninety percent of
Jacob's story HAS been corroborated. Jacob sometimes provides more detail, but
all of it, including his mother's perversions, have been at least partially backed
up by family and/or friends.

Critics have dismissed those incidents because they came from "friendly
witnesses." Such attitudes show either a monumental lack of insight or wilful
ignorance concerning the reality of abuse. Abusers can only survive in secrecy.
Since they understand what they are doing is against all that is moral and
decent, are they going to beat or castigate or molest their charges in public?

Some are also skeptical about the memories of sexual abuse because Jacob
initially said he "didn't remember." A more accurate phrase would be he didn't
WANT to remember. But it is true that he recalls more now from the safety of
his prison cell than he did immediately after the murders. Does that make his
recollections suspect?

The current vogue is to talk about False Memory Syndrome vs. Repressed
Memories. One school believes that if you can't remember something outright,
it must not have happened. Another that memories can spring up out of nowhere
fifty years after the fact. All I can say is that after watching Jacob over the
months I saw how quickly he could dump the past. Sometimes he had awesome

recall, parroting back to me my exact words from a previous conversation. At other times he erased entire incidents, such as my initial visits with him at CJC. He couldn't recollect ever talking to me before I walked in as an investigator, yet we'd met face to face at least six times.[47]

So to depend on the shifting sands of Jacob's memory is tricky business. Because he also has a wondrous capacity for denial. It wasn't that he ever disavowed his part in the murders or tried to mitigate his responsibility. Quite the opposite. Jacob never said he was abused. He didn't believe he was.

"Physical abuse isn't beatings. It's breaking limbs... I wasn't ever really molested if Kermode never totally penetrated me..."[48]

Jacob believed himself to be a "bad seed." That, rather than his parents' behavior, explains his crime.

Another criticism, which I find particularly disingenuous, is leveled by those in law enforcement. It goes like this. "We know he wasn't abused. His story changed. In the beginning, he said he wasn't abused. Then he was."

When I pointed out that some of Jacob's first words to authorities were, "They beat me, they beat me and I couldn't take it any more," the response was, "Why wouldn't he allow us to interview him then? If he had nothing to hide he should have talked to us."

Which neatly sums up my problem with so many people on either side of this issue. While I have been criticized for my lack of objectivity by those who prefer to view a complex case simplistically, I have always stated that Jacob committed a heinous act. I understand those who have no sympathy for him. Such equivocation has no part in the thinking of most law-and-order-enthusiasts, however. Rules are rules. Black is black. White is white. There is no such thing as grey.

This thinking is doubly frustrating because not only was Jacob forbidden by his attorneys to speak to the prosecution, but if he had, his statements would have been used against him. A defendant is damned if he speaks, "You admitted to the crime...You were inconsistent in your first statement..." etc. and damned if he doesn't. "He won't talk to us because he's guilty."

In the courtroom, it is the prosecutor's job to make the defendant's most innocuous act appear damaging, just as it is the defense attorney's task to do the exact opposite. In the process, truth and justice are irrelevancies, something we give lip service to but don't actually seek. Increasingly, the only people who still believe in America's criminal justice system are those who have never been involved in it.

---

[47] While editing this manuscript from prison, Jacob wrote cryptically, 'I remember a lot more these days.' Including those meetings.

[48] Initially, Jacob only admitted to his stepfather's masturbating against his body.

While I would assume law enforcement should be well versed in human nature, I was also disturbed by the ignorance of those I interviewed, both directly involved in Jacob's case and those who spoke in more generic terms, regarding the effects of abuse. Although at least ninety per cent of those inside prison have been abused, with the incidence of sexual molestation far greater than in the general population, these black/white thinkers all too often saw no correlation between a convict's early mistreatment and his subsequent aberrant behavior. Their attitude toward children like Jacob is particularly appalling.

"He could have gotten out of the situation. He could have told a teacher or gone to live with his brother. He had a lot of options. Instead he chose murder."

Such people know nothing about child abuse or parricide, though they are in positions where their lack of knowledge can thwart justice, rather than serve it. In his classic, *When A Child Kills*, defense attorney, Paul Mones, describes the typical teen who commits parricide, as well as that teen's home environment. He could have been describing Jacob and the Jordans. Everything from their social status to the botched murder plan to Jacob's lack of remorse sounds as though it was directly lifted from 120 Ridge Drive. (I contacted Mr. Mones early on at CJC. He was very interested in Jacob's case. He received no cooperation from Jacob's attorneys, and no family member was willing to come up with his $10,000 fee, even though there was far more money than that in the Jordan estate.)

Those who speak so blithely about Jacob's "options," possess a second flaw in their thinking. Their statements pre-suppose that even if Jacob hadn't considered alternatives—which he did—a fifteen-year-old has the mind set and maturity of an adult. Yet, all too often men or women in similar situations are paralyzed with fear. Why do we expect a youngster to be capable of greater rationalization than a grown-up? Children who are abused don't develop normally to begin with. Their perceptions are stunted and distorted by the terror of their environment. For example, prisoners of war or hostages who are in captivity even for a short time experience distortions in their thinking, especially if they are isolated. Imagine fifteen years of terror. Studies have been conducted on animals who are punished when they eat a certain food or approach a particular exit to freedom. Even when the shock is removed, the animal doesn't dare reach for that bone or head toward that particular exit. This condition is called "learned helplessness." We know it works in the animal kingdom. We have seen it occur during times of war. But somehow it doesn't apply to a child. No excuses for a kid, by God.

As I would soon find out in Jacob's case.

◊   ◊   ◊

Although I visited Jacob at the Criminal Justice Center anywhere from two to six days a week, very little else appeared to be happening with his defense

183

until less than four months before his trial. That was when Tom Kennedy entered the scene. Shaun had split from his former partner and Judge Looney had appointed Tom as co-counsel in early 1994.

Kennedy is tall and thin, with a gentle smile and more than a passing resemblance to actor Bruce Dern. Tom had spent ten years in the D.A.'s office and ten years as a defense attorney. An unpretentious man who doesn't seem to have the ego so omnipresent in the legal profession, Tom had no desire to be involved in such a high-profile and heart-wrenching affair. But once called in, he was committed to giving Jacob the best defense possible.

Kennedy was concerned about our lack of time. "We should have a year to prepare a case like this," he said and threw all his effort into whipping the defense into shape.

Previously, Jacob's defense had seemed chaotic. If Shaun was doing anything, he was doing it behind the scenes and not bothering to keep anybody, particularly his client, informed. Tom Kennedy brought in Jeanette Shick as his private investigator. P.I. #1, Candace Delaney, had only contacted a couple of witnesses and was far more interested in her deli business than in Jacob Ind. Jeanette, a petite, hard-working blonde with a pleasant manner, scrambled to begin an interviewing process that, with less than three months to go, should have been largely completed.[49] Kennedy organized Shaun's files and made a point of visiting Jacob every week in order to keep him apprised of events.

"I have kids Jacob's age which makes this too emotional," Kennedy said. "But now that I'm here I'm going to do the best that I can by him."

As hard as Tom worked, however, it is virtually impossible to put together a capital murder case in a few weeks. Almost all of Jacob's family and friends, with the possible exception of Charles, had long expressed misgivings concerning Kaufman's handling or mishandling of Jacob's case. Ignorant of the system, we kept hoping that more was happening behind the scenes, or that Shaun was one of those who worked best in the face of a deadline. And, to be fair, juvenile cases are always difficult. Like so many communities, Colorado Springs imparts a double message to its children. "Do as we say, not as we do." When children have the temerity to flout adult rules, their punishment is generally swift, harsh, and in my opinion, overly punitive. Only lip service is given to rehabilitation and education. The emphasis is on "teaching them a lesson." Increasingly, our solutions involve wrath, rather than reason.

So perhaps Shaun was another Don Quixote, tilting against windmills. Someone must be a voice for juveniles, no matter how unpopular or unwinnable

---

[49] Upset that she had been terminated, Candace Delaney refused to turn over her notes, causing Jeanette to lose even more time re-interviewing people. Other attorneys have told me, "She couldn't do that. That's illegal." My response: "She did it anyway. Who was going to make her conform to the law?"

their task. Unfortunately, at least in his high profile cases, Shaun's voice either went unheard or was ineffective.

In 1988, Kaufman had reached a plea bargain in the case of another Woodland Park youth, Richard Mijaris, 17, who killed his mother. The normal term for second-degree murder is eight to 24 years. Mijaris received 36.

A second plea bargain involved the 1991 beating death of soldier Layne Schmidtke. Schmidtke died of a rare brain injury after being kicked repeatedly in the head by several youths. Dominic Peres, Shaun's eighteen-year-old client, received 16 years.

(I've heard different versions as to whether Jacob was offered a plea bargain. Shaun was quoted in a newspaper article as saying the D.A. never offered them one. Jacob said Suthers proposed one count of first degree murder, which would still have meant life in prison without the possibility of parole.)

In a case that went to trial a year after Jacob's, seventeen-year-old Dameon Nicholas received a first degree murder conviction for killing a tourist. No one even charged that Dameon had pulled the trigger, but he still received life under the law of complicity.

Because of the conservative local climate, it is impossible to say whether another attorney could have done a better job or received more lenient sentences for his clients. But in Jacob's case, those most intimately involved had definite concerns regarding Shaun's competency.

As one attorney/family friend maintained, Kaufman appeared to be "building a great case for misrepresentation." In addition, Shaun seldom engaged in such basic courtesies as answering phone calls. For example, when trying to get into Ridge Drive in July 1993, I found that the locks had been changed. While I was concerned about completing my investigation, I was even more concerned about the evidence we'd already gathered.[51] I phoned Shaun's office at least twenty times explaining about the evidence and reminding his secretary to tell him that it had to be removed before the forthcoming auction.

No one ever returned my calls. After cornering Shaun at a pre-trial hearing he assured me that a couple of "big burly guys" would be going in over the weekend to remove everything. Didn't happen. The evidence was never gathered. Some was thrown out. Other items, such as the butcher knives that Kermode had threatened the boys with, were auctioned off. "Billy Belt" was picked out of the trash by Lupe Thorson and attorney Jim Dostal on a hurried evening trip to Ridge Drive in October 1993, only days ahead of the garbage men.

It is important for the reader to remember that there are many sides to

---

[51] Candace told me to throw all possible evidence we found into a big box in the study closet. She never labeled any items, nor did she instruct me to do so. Concerned over such obvious sloppiness, I began cataloguing them on my own.

every "truth." My truth about Shaun must be colored by my life experiences. Perhaps Shaun's troubling behavior, only a tiny portion of which I've documented here, is typical of attorneys. Being unfamiliar with the justice system I might have been shocked by actions that are actually the norm. But if that is the case, the system itself is badly flawed and the guarantee of a fair trial is worthless.

Shaun has had counter-charges of his own to level. In an August 1996 article that appeared in the weekly news magazine, *The Independent*, he complained to reporter Greg Worthen about my "lack of objectivity," and the fact that when I spoke to witnesses, "She always interpreted what they said in a light most favorable to Ind, colored by her own perceptions of him and her sympathy for him."

That was an interesting comment for Jacob's attorney to make. My assumption was that when readying a case, the prosecution honed in on everything that made the defendant culpable, while the defense did the opposite. I assumed the truth probably rested somewhere in between, but being a total novice I could not have known. If I was performing my task incorrectly, Kaufman should have communicated his concerns to me. The truth is that no one ever told me the proper way to file a report, what to write about, or whether written communication was even necessary. Shaun never gave me any sort of feedback on my work, whether to disparage it or praise it. I only had one meeting with Kaufman during the entire year I worked for the defense.[50] Yet, suddenly, he was an expert on my motives, my views, my ability to interpret facts, and also upon the veracity of this book, which he had never read.

Initially, the defense had asked me to interview possible defense witnesses beyond Jacob. This I was very reluctant to do. I had never been involved in a court case, knew nothing about the law or legal matters, and had never formally interviewed anyone in my life. No one would ever ask a dentist to fly a commercial airplane or a secretary to construct a skyscraper, so why were they leaving Jacob's defense to a neophyte? Where was Candace Delaney? Why wasn't she interviewing anyone?

After a few months, the attorneys instructed me to concentrate solely on Jacob, which was a great relief. I knew Jacob. I was comfortable with him. And

---

[50] Whenever I wanted to talk to Shaun I would appear at his office. If I was lucky, he would grant me a couple of minutes on his way to court or riding down on the elevator. Otherwise, I never received any counsel or feedback from him. Nor was I ever paid for my time. Initially, Kaufman had told me I would be paid $35.00 an hour. At the end of the first month I submitted a bill. Shaun never mentioned paying me or referred to compensation again. I figured the important thing was not the money, but spending time with Jacob. Mistakenly I believed that the information I gathered would make a difference.

we had enough time that I figured any errors on my part could be corrected in a subsequent meeting. If I were out in the community interviewing strangers, what if I asked the wrong questions? Asked them incorrectly? Didn't solicit helpful information? Inadvertently did or said something that jeopardized Jacob's entire case? I had no formal training in this, and as the months passed without a real investigator, all of us who were sympathetic toward Jacob asked each other, "What is wrong with Shaun?"

Shaun was right about one thing. Jacob's defense shouldn't have had to rely on me or any other amateur. Yet, all too often, that was precisely what happened. Over 1993's Christmas vacation, Lupe Thorson was the one who interviewed Charles about familial abuse. She also interviewed Al Gonzales and his kids about life with Pam. I was the one who talked to Lupe. If our efforts weren't compiled in a professional, lawyerly manner, I plead guilty.

One of the biggest complaints from people like Lupe and Charles is that Shaun and Tom never bothered to interview them beyond incidents that I or others had initially gathered. In the weeks before the trial, the attorneys did visit some out of state witnesses, but all agreed that there was no further probing. The defense merely went over previous testimony.

Another common, and far more serious, complaint that has surfaced since the trial comes from Jacob's classmates and members of the community. It goes like this. "Everyone knew Jacob was abused. We even knew about the sexual abuse. We couldn't understand why no one from the defense ever contacted us. We could have told them things that we saw, but no one ever asked."

Considering the short time frame available to investigator Jeanette Shick, it is no surprise that so many people were never approached. I believe that the most important component of any criminal case is "detail." If a lawyer knows his case thoroughly, and is familiar with even the most seemingly trivial fact, he will win. For whatever reason, Jacob's defense appeared to be put together as an after-thought.

The results speak for themselves.

The jurors at the Ind trial will have much
evidence to consider. Is there anything
wrong with asking them to evaluate the
caliber of the defendant's life as well
as his weapon?

~ Raymond McCaffrey, columnist
Gazette Telegraph

Chapter 26

Tom Kennedy was a conscientious co-counsel. He always found time for
Jacob, and he always found time for me. During one of our initial meetings, he
explained how Jacob's plea of self defense would be presented. If jurors viewed
Jacob's actions through Jacob's eyes, through his distorted perceptions rather
than from their own—as the law stated they must—then Jacob had indeed been
in "imminent danger" when he pulled the trigger.

"We're confident Jacob's story will be told," Kennedy said, after
interviewing his client and going over my multitudinous reports. "I'm just not
sure Jacob will be the one to tell it." (Whether Jacob was denied the opportunity
to testify is an issue that will surely be raised in a future proceeding. This is a
basic fundamental right. Yet Jacob swears that he was not allowed to testify. His
assertion is backed up by other witnesses.)

Tom believed that Bill Aspinwall, a seasoned prosecutor of some twenty
years, would tear the sixteen-year-old apart. Jacob's brother agreed.

Charles said, "If he gets on the stand, he'll just shut down."

But if Jacob didn't speak, who would tell about his many suicide attempts
and the last seven months of his life when his state of mind had been so
precarious?

Still, Tom worried, there was the little matter of Jacob's emotions. Problem
was he didn't have any. Most children in Jacob's situation aren't remorseful over
killing their parents. That's just a fact. They view their abusers as Satan
Incarnate. How can you feel remorseful over destroying the devil? As Jacob
explained, "When the cops kill somebody bad they give them a medal. I killed
somebody bad and they want to put me away for the rest of my life."

But the jury needed tears. If Jacob appeared callous and cold, his testimony
would be the only one considered. Jurors would convict him on the basis, not of
his words, but on how skillfully and/or sincerely he projected emotion.

Another problem, however, was that Jacob's story changed. While most
defendants come up with more horrific tales nearer their trial dates, Jacob was
just the opposite. He minimized. Everybody gets hit. Everybody gets called nasty
names.

"My parents didn't always yell at me for four hours at a time. Sometimes
only two. And it only happened a couple of times a week... I quit eating and

sleeping because I was depressed over my break-up with Lila rather than Kermode and my mom."

He hadn't gotten the belt the murder night after all. He hadn't killed Kermode and Pamela because he was abused. He'd killed Kermode and Pamela because he hated them.

"But WHY did you hate them, Jacob?" I asked repeatedly.

"I don't have to have a reason. I just did."

During the months I'd spent with Jacob, I'd seen so many transformations. Initially, he'd reminded me of a frightened deer. As he became more comfortable with me and his incarceration, his self confidence had returned--or perhaps manifested itself for the first time. Among the Jordans' closest acquaintances, as well as some family members, there was remarkably little sympathy for the deceased. "Those killings were the best thing that ever happened to Jacob," said one. "Finally, he's free."

Jacob was extremely mercurial. He seemed to re-invent himself as often as Madonna. One time he would have long hair; the next it was shaven. Sometimes he sounded like a philosopher; occasionally, a gangbanger. When I walked into that attorney's booth, I never knew which Jacob I was going to meet. I became familiar with depressed Jacob, tough Jacob, sweet Jacob, punk Jacob, seductive Jacob, vulnerable Jacob, limbo Jacob, intellectual Jacob, fundamentalist Jacob, argumentative Jacob and probably a dozen others.

But no matter who Jacob decided to be on any given day, he was always perceptive, discerning—and entertaining. When he really kicked his intellect into gear, he could also be extremely logical and persuasive. Forensics, plus years of interrogation by his parents, had sharpened his debating skills until he could twist me like a pretzel. I found all of Jacob's personas fascinating, many challenging, and some incomprehensible.

Perhaps I found him so confusing because we occupied different emotional planets. What I, who had enjoyed a happy childhood and was largely ignorant of the dark side of humanity, didn't realize was that Jacob Ind is a textbook abused child. He merely pretended to inhabit the land of the living. Attacked by both parents, Jacob had long ago been soul murdered.

We couldn't even agree on the definition of words.

"What are feelings?" I asked.

"I don't know. I really don't have any."

"What does rage mean to you? How does your body react?"

"I can't say. I'm not sure. Nothing ever seems quite real or genuine."

Love meant a different thing to Jacob than it did to me. As did physical pain. Happiness, even fear, had to be re-defined. So did prison. To me, prison is what Jacob is locked up in. To Jacob, prison was life with his parents. So, despite the iron bars and all the unspeakable indignities of incarceration, Jacob considers himself to be free.

I was amazed that Jacob managed to survive, even to carve out a life for

189

himself. Was he being truthful with me? Was he really indifferent or did he want his freedom so badly that he dared not even hope? Did he really believe imprisonment was preferable to his parents?

Or could there be another reason?

When I asked psychologist Frank Barron whether he thought Jacob would ever really relate the extent of his abuse in order to help with his defense, Barron responded, "It depends on how badly he wants to be punished."

I guess now we know.

◊   ◊   ◊

Jury selection began May 2, 1994. It lasted one week. The defense was surprised by how pervasively abuse seemed to touch people's lives, and thought they'd assembled a sympathetic jury. They were also hoping that lead prosecutor Bill Aspinwall, who has an abrasive courtroom manner, would alienate the jurors. With his aggressive voir dire, he'd made one woman cry. Another asked, "Why are you doing this to me?"

In his mid-fifties with a Richard Nixon nose and a penchant for cheap suits, Bill Aspinwall has a reputation for being shrewd and intelligent. When running unsuccessfully for District Attorney in August 1996, the Gazette Telegraph called him the 'Rambo of the District Attorney's Office—a temperamental commando of the court.'

Aspinwall agrees. "It's a battle and it's a war and you better be willing to fight any way you can."

His adversaries have characterized him in less flattering terms. One attorney labeled him "one step above dishonest." He was reprimanded by the Colorado Court of Appeals for his behavior in two high profile murder cases. Jennifer Reali killed the wife of her lover, Brian Hood. Aspinwall tried and won both cases. In 1991, appeals judges ruled Aspinwall's conduct in the Reali trial was "inappropriate, unwarranted and unprofessional." In 1992, they commented on the chief prosecutor's behavior in the Hood trial.

"We agree that some of the prosecutor's comments were ill-considered and that his facial expressions and whispered remarks were both unprofessional and offensive."[50]

In order to elicit sympathy from the jury and overcome his sometimes obnoxious personality, Aspinwall often comes across as a bumbler, though he is anything but that. The defense strategy to handle Aspinwall: Ignore him. Let him hang himself.

While Shaun and Tom were pleased with their jury, members of the Woodland Park community couldn't understand why the defense didn't insist

---

[50] Aspinwall was also later reprimanded for his behavior in Jacob's trial.

upon a change of venue. A gag order had been invoked early on, but that was after all the details of the crime had been splashed across the newspaper and on the nightly news. The prosecution had largely had its say while the defense had effectively been muzzled.

"Everybody's already made up their minds," said a local postal worker. "All they want to know is why."

One potential juror, who did not make the final cut, later told me, "As I waited to be called in, I knew this kid would get convicted. Eighty five percent of the people had already decided upon first degree murder."

Colorado Springs, where the trial was actually held, is one of the most conservative cities in the United States. It is home to the Air Force Academy and Fort Carson, a huge army base, not to mention tens of thousands of military retirees. As in all professions, the Armed Forces tends to attract a certain type of mind set, which could most succinctly be labeled anti-liberal. Colorado Springs is home to Amendment Two, an anti-gay measure that had triggered the "Boycott Colorado" movement following the 1992 election. It is a pro-business community where a beautiful view of Pikes Peak is supposed to compensate for low wages caused by weak unions and retirees willing to work "for a little something extra." As evinced by its horrendous sprawl, cookie cutter housing tracts and endless shopping malls, the city council considers developers a notch below God. *The Gazette Telegraph*, Colorado Springs' lone newspaper, is proudly conservative. A moderate or dissenting viewpoint seldom reaches its editorial pages. More than one hundred religious organizations, many of them fundamentalist in nature, make their home in the area. Focus on the Family is only the most famous. With Dr. James Dobson's Biblical principles of family values and child rearing so much in evidence, it may come as a surprise that the area has some of the highest child abuse statistics in the state.

As a child therapist lamented following Jacob's conviction, "Those statistics never come out in the *Gazette*. It doesn't fit with the sterling image they want to convey. Just as our letters in support of Jacob, saying he was only a symptom rather than the problem, were never printed."

On the first actual day of testimony, Courtroom 403 was packed. Two cameras had been set up and reporters could observe proceedings on monitors located in a cubbyhole across the way. Several seats were reserved for the press and public defenders. The rest had to scramble for what few available spaces remained. Frank Ind, who had taken leave from his city job in Rockford, Illinois, was totally barred from the trial. He spent the entire six weeks pacing outside in the hallway. Prosecutor Bill Aspinwall also denied access to several other friendly faces, including me, on the grounds that we might be called as "rebuttal witnesses." None of us were.

As a member of Jacob's defense said, "Aspinwall has no intention of calling anyone. He just wants to make life more difficult for everyone involved with Jacob. He's just being an asshole."

Later, at Gabrial's trial, actual witnesses were allowed to sit in during the entire proceedings. For whatever reason, Aspinwall appeared to have a personal vendetta against Jacob. Or maybe his animosity can be explained from a different perspective. From a layman's view, I would assume that the defendant who would receive the most vilification would be a Gabrial Adams. What possible rationale could there be for killing someone merely for money? Jacob had an excuse. You didn't have to believe it or accept it, but I considered it a mitigating factor. Not so the law. The law generally goes after the "conspirator" more forcefully than his hired gun. Jacob was the mastermind. Didn't matter the reason. He was the most culpable.

The defense was hoping Aspinwall's obstreperous manner would backfire. A couple of jurors did develop an intense dislike for the man. "I wanted to kill him," said one woman. But several had problems with Shaun. He didn't really seem all that engaged and they were not charmed by his courtroom manner.

"He just wasn't right for that jury," said one attorney who observed several sessions. "He came across as too "eastern," maybe, too different."

On the other hand, Tom Kennedy collected a clique of admirers, who pumped me for information about his marital status, and whether he was as nice in person as he seemed to be in court.

Although the courtroom that first day was primed for the "star" attraction, it was Gabrial Adams rather than Jacob who first entered. There was almost an audible sigh of disappointment from onlookers. Throughout, Gabrial had seemed an incidental. Most people dismissed him as a psychopath. It was Jacob Ind whose story they wanted to hear. What would drive a kid to murder his parents? One Woodland Park newspaper had compared his case to the Menendez brothers, whose trial had recently ended in a hung jury. What sensational secrets would Jacob and his brother offer up to the public? Colorado Springs wasn't in a forgiving mood, but it certainly wanted every salacious detail.

Gabrial's attorneys requested and received a new court date, October 24, 1994. After Major was ushered out, everyone's eyes remained glued to the doorway through which Jacob would emerge. The tension was palpable. Those unfamiliar with the justice system, at least in El Paso County, didn't know that trials never start on time, so they kept nudging each other and asking, "What do you think is happening? Why is this taking so long?"

Finally, Jacob walked into the courtroom. For the first time since his arrest, he was wearing street clothes—an aquamarine sweater and matching shirt with brown pants. His hair was neatly parted and he wore glasses, which added to his preppie look. This Jacob didn't have much in common with the Jacob I knew from CJC. That Jacob was actually kind of a slob. Sometimes he would come in with his hair all slicked back, and other times as if he hadn't combed it in days. (In fairness, a lot of times I woke him up.) This Jacob was trying manfully to do what he thought was expected of him--though he wasn't

quite sure what that might be since Shaun hadn't offered many tips on courtroom demeanor.

Jacob even tried to monitor his body language. The Jacob I knew was always waving his arms or fiddling with something—a perpetual motion machine. This Jacob did his best to "behave," though he couldn't resist occasionally turning to smile at one of his friends, and his attempts at dressing himself weren't entirely successful. His collar wasn't all the way out of his sweater, and his pants were too long. Much ado was made in the press over the fact that his clothes—the sweater was an extra large—were too big, making him appear like a little boy lost. Some acted as if this were a calculated move on the defense's part. The truth of it is, Nancy Overmyer, one of Jacob's most faithful friends, had bought his clothes without ever being allowed to measure him. And, as far as his glasses, another "fashion prop," I had been fighting for months to get Jacob's vision checked. Finally, Tom Kennedy had arranged to have him visit an optometrist while handcuffed and in chains.

"Maybe we should make defendants wear their prison uniforms to court," said one member of the D.A.'s office in a television interview. "Or the clothes they were arrested in."

Which would have been quite a trick for Jacob. He had grown nearly two inches during his incarceration and put on twenty pounds. Apparently, growth spurts and weight gain are common traits of abused kids after they're taken out of their harsh environments. As one child psychologist said, "I've seen it happen time and again. It's as if their bodies are saying,'It's safe now. You can concentrate on something other than the fear.'"

The jury, ten women, four men, paraded into the jury box. So these were the people who held Jacob's life in their hands. Most were middle aged and casually dressed. The men preferred T-shirts and blue jeans. One older woman favored suits and always looked the part of the professional. Jurors' occupations ranged from psychiatric nurse to housewife to a museum operator to a construction worker. Some appeared to take their duty seriously. More seemed to consider this trial a personal inconvenience.

The prosecution consisted of two seasoned attorneys. Bill Aspinwall's co-counsel, Gordon Dennison, is short and balding and a former military prosecutor. Jacob, who liked Dennison and applauded his professionalism, commented, "He seems to have an iron rod up his butt." With his intense, harried style and jerky movements, Dennison reminded one spectator of "a munchkin in the Wizard of Oz."

Opening statements began. Aspinwall addressed the jury first. "This is a sad case for me to bring to you, and I take no pleasure or joy in it." According to him, the prosecution would prove that Kermode and Pamela had given their sons an upper middle class life, only to be rewarded with death. Experts had analyzed the scene, and their analysis told a horrific tale of murder and mayhem.

193

"In the early morning hours of December 17, 1992, Kermode was sleeping on his side of the bed, and Pam Jordan was next to him, sleeping on her stomach, when Gabrial Adams entered the bedroom, armed with a .22 single action revolver. He pointed it right at the head of Kermode and shot him above the left eyebrow. The bullet didn't penetrate; it bounced off to the side.

"Pam Jordan woke up, and the next shot was fired at her. She got out of bed and stood facing her attacker. The next shot entered her shoulder. Kermode must have sat up because the next bullet was shot into his face. He must have reached out to the attacker, a couple of feet away, with his hand warding him off, because the next shot entered his arm.

"Both Kermode and Pam must have gone towards the exit, but they were met by Gabrial Adams with a knife and they couldn't get to the door. They fought him. Pam's hands were cut, and the webbing between her thumb was sliced.

"They must have gone to the bathroom door then, tried with all their might to get in that door, desperately trying to get away from the knife attack of Gabrial Adams. Their backs are now toward him, and he's hacking at them with the knife. Pam got the worst of it. She was hacked a number of times...her skull was opened up.

"But they can't get in because on the other side of that bathroom door is Jacob Ind, holding the door shut while his conspirator is hacking away at his stepfather and his natural mother.

"When he does open the door, in his hand is a can of bear mace, a hot pepper spray that is used to ward off bears. He sprays them right in the face, then takes a .357 Magnum revolver and shoots his stepfather in the head. Kermode Jordan dies, falls in the doorway between his bedroom and the bathroom. Then the defendant shoots his mother in the head and she falls on top of her dead husband.

"Afterward, the two boys wash up in the same bathroom in which the bodies are lying. Then, taking his weapons with him, Gabrial Adams left, and Jacob Ind went to bed, then got up in the morning and went to school."

When Aspinwall described the murders, Jacob flinched, and his hands trembled. The prosecution's version differed from Jacob's in several respects—when and why he was in the master bedroom, the sequence of events involving the bear mace, the murders themselves, as well as the placement of the bodies. Nor had Jacob ever said anything about washing off blood in the sink. (Blood tests never actually determined who, besides Gabrial, might have washed themselves off. Aspinwall can't have it both ways. He made a point of saying, Jacob "didn't have a bruise, cut, or scratch on him," and conversely that Jacob washed off HIS blood.)

Aspinwall concluded, "When the police got finished they said, 'Why? Why does a teenaged boy kill so coldly, so viciously?' Ladies and gentlemen, you'll find this is a killing done out of hate. The defendant wanted his mother dead

and he killed her himself."

Before the defense's beginning, the courtroom took a break. Throughout the day, people had stopped to look in the windows, though a sign warned not to open the door while court was in session. Even in the elevator people talked about the trial and their impressions of the case. Jacob could properly be called "notorious." Everyone seemed to have an opinion of Jacob Ind—a boy they'd never met.

After court reconvened, Tom Kennedy stood and faced the jury.

"When we think of home, we think of a place where we are safe, secure and loved--a place we go to be safe from the world. When Jacob thought of home, he thought of a place of humiliation, abuse and degradation. When he killed his abusive stepfather and his cold and controlling mother on December 17, that was only the end of the story, ladies and gentlemen. The story began when Jacob Ind was born.

"To understand why this happened, you must understand that he saw no alternative. He saw no escape, and he resorted to desperate acts."

Reminding the jury that the case was not a "who-done-it," Kennedy said that the real question was one of what could have happened in a home to allow something like this.

Kennedy led the jurors through Jacob's life—Pamela's divorce from Frank Ind, her marriage to Kermode and all the accompanying abuse. After the Jordans moved to Woodland Park in the mid-eighties, "Now there was an added factor: isolation. Their support group and friends were gone. They didn't know a soul out here. And their house was distant from other houses.

"The abuse was this family's dark secret. The boys were schooled, 'This is our secret.'"

Tom has an engaging but still intense way of speaking. He appeared to be speaking directly to the man in the back row with his arms folded, his body language saying, "I'm closed to all of this."

Despite the fact that opening and closing statements are pretty much considered to be sacrosanct by the opposing team, Bill Aspinwall stood and objected when Tom mentioned that Charles had been given weight-lifting equipment to help him with a weight problem. Judge Looney, who never once raised her voice during the six week trial, said she would rule on Aspinwall's objection later and motioned Kennedy to continue. Tom did not speak for nearly a minute, silently letting the jurors know that his opponent had been out of line.

Tom concluded, "Jacob's life really began to fall apart in the summer of 1992 when his brother Charles left home. Charles got himself emancipated. He couldn't take it any more and moved out. Up until that point, Charles had tried to protect Jacob. When he left, Jacob's only ally was gone. Life went from bad to intolerable.

"After December 17, Jacob told his friends. He didn't take off. He admitted freely what occurred. He said, 'I couldn't take it anymore.'

"The one thing he said that sticks out is, 'I just wanted to be safe. I just wanted Charlie and I to be safe.'"

Later, after the jury was removed, Judge Looney expressed her displeasure over Aspinwall's interruption. Aspinwall, who appeared to believe that he was in charge of the courtroom, would not be cowed. He called Tom's remarks "lies."

The trial was off to an acrimonious start. Problem was Tom and Shaun never fought back. Thinking Aspinwall would self-destruct, they tried to concentrate on the case itself. But this jury, judging from their verdict, liked Aspinwall's theatrics. Courtroom spectators did not, but they, after all, were not in a position to vote life or death for Jacob Ind.

There was a time when most Americans—
especially parents—lived by the credo:
Spare the rod and spoil the child.
If kids got out of line, they got a "good
spanking." If they said a bad word, they
got their mouths washed out with soap.
That's how children learned what was
right and wrong. Of course parents—
at least the good ones—made sure their
kids knew that they loved them too.
But defense attorneys say love was
missing from Jacob's home. Instead,
discipline was used to intimidate the boy.
Jacob and his brother lived in fear, never
quite sure when the rod was going to come...

~Raymond McCaffrey/columnist
Gazette Telegraph

Chapter 27

Principal Jim Taylor and Counselor David Greathouse were the first prosecution witnesses. They detailed Jacob's confession in the initial hours after the murders. Those familiar with Jacob's defense expected Shaun to hammer away at Greathouse's credibility. Why hadn't the counselor reported the abuse immediately? Knowledgeable about the law, Greathouse was careful to state that the boys hadn't mentioned PHYSICAL abuse in their meeting a week prior to the tragedy. In separate interviews, both Charles and Jacob insisted they had, specifically mentioning the piano recital when Kermode slammed Jacob against the car. Since their meeting at the police station, the boys hadn't spoken to each other about the case, yet their stories were remarkably similar. Rather than take either boy's word, the truth could easily be proven. All phone conversations at CJC are monitored, including those during weekly visits. Charles only visited his brother a handful of times, anyway, and they seldom communicated via the mail. (Mail can also be monitored.) Greathouse was bound by law to report all physical and sexual abuse. If Jacob was going to successfully plead self defense, Shaun had to start making the case that the brothers had gone to professionals for help, but that none had been forthcoming, leaving a desperate Jacob forced to take the law into his own hands.

Shaun's cross examinations of both Taylor and Greathouse were perfunctory. He did question the principal about who is supposed to report abuse to Social Services, but never followed through on that angle.

According to observers, "Shaun would get up like he was going to really give the witness a piece of his mind, kind of throw his arms out to his side as if

197

readying to do battle, say, 'No questions,' and sit down. It got to be a bad joke."

◊   ◊   ◊

For the next two weeks the prosecution presented its case—the sheriff's officers receiving the call, entering 120 Ridge Drive, finding the bodies, taking Jacob into custody. By the time the state rested, they had shown three hundred fifty exhibits, including 115 photos of the victims and the crime scene. In addition to hard evidence such as the .357, they presented such things as the screen from Gabrial's window and a couple of bayonets that had nothing to do with the murders. Aspinwall and Dennison laid forth their case diligently, if not always in an entertaining fashion. But no one could accuse them of being less than thorough. If necessary, they would drown the jury in evidence. No matter that some of it was bogus or irrelevant, or that they blurred the line between Jacob's crimes and Gabrial's. If they fudged a little bit, well, it was up to the defense to point that out. Which they didn't. The prosecution was actually surprised that their witnesses were not more frequently and closely cross-examined. From the beginning rumors had circulated about how badly botched the crime scene had been and how poorly Teller County's deputies had done their jobs. If true, however, the defense was not pursuing that angle. Nor did they attempt to cast "reasonable doubt" upon any other aspect of the prosecution's scenario—including their interpretation of the murder scene, which presented Jacob in a far colder light than he had presented himself. Perhaps Shaun had decided to concede the prosecution everything since his client HAD confessed. Maybe he would save his firepower exclusively for the defense portion of the trial.

On the first Friday of testimony, the prosecution moved to show the murder scene. Shaun objected. "The facts about how the Jordans were murdered is not an issue," he said. Since Jacob was "physically, sexually, and emotionally abused," going over the grim details would only prejudice the jurors."

"This may not be a whodunit, but it doesn't mean I don't have to prove my case..." Aspinwall responded. "[The pictures] show how vicious and hateful this act was. He [Ind] wasn't putting the Jordans out of their misery. He was torturing them."

It might be instructive for those who are unfamiliar with the law and believe the current wisdom that defendants have too many rights and "get away with murder," to attend an actual trial. By the end of Jacob's, his supporters were embittered by court rulings which almost invariably favored the

198

prosecution.[53] The prosecution argument prevailed. The Jordan slideshow was allowed. While Aspinwall pushed the button on the projector, Detective John Falton, who had videotaped the crime scene, explained the photographs. They began with the perfectly manicured Jordan residence.

One observer said, "Everything was just too perfect—not a speck of dust anywhere. The floors were so highly polished you could see a mirror reflection of the hall tree. In the living room the magazines were spaced precisely one half inch apart. Though this was the middle of the week, there wasn't even a glass on the kitchen table."

Those sympathetic to the defense thought that such perfection showed pathological neatness on the Jordans' part. To the prosecution, which dwelt on the family's material goods, what wonderful providers they were. The majority of the slides depicted bloodstains on the carpet, bed sheets and wall, bullet holes and, of course, the bodies. The more graphic pictures headlined the evening news. Wearing flowered pajamas, Pam was sprawled atop her husband. Kermode's bony ankles, looking curiously vulnerable peeking out from the bottom of his sweat pants, were prominently displayed.

Obviously wanting the crime scene to be imprinted in the jury's skull, the prosecution lingered over every photo, whether it be of a broken ceramic duck or a nearly invisible bullet hole. Throughout, Aspinwall/Dennison never distinguished between Gabrial and Jacob's actions. Skillfully, they obscured the line between the two boys, often insinuating that the stabbings and the gore were attributable to Jacob, though all available facts totally refute that.

During the presentation Jacob sat with his hand over his eyes and his head down. He appeared shaken. But after months of media buildup, some spectators were unimpressed by the actuality.

"You see so much blood and gore on TV the fake stuff is far more gruesome than the reality."

A volunteer for the police department agreed."Suthers (The district attorney) is grandstanding if he says this is one of the most gruesome scenes he's ever investigated. I was at a suicide this past weekend that was far worse."

It soon became apparent that Kaufman was not nearly as aggressive as Aspinwall. Spectators sympathetic to Jacob worried that he had either conceded his client didn't have a chance, he was waiting for the defense portion to bestir himself, or he wasn't very familiar with his own case. For such a horrendous crime, Jacob had better convince those ten women and four men that he had been in imminent risk of being killed—quite a feat considering his parents had been asleep and the murder was premeditated.

---

[53] Defense attorneys who daily deal with judges cite Jane Looney as one of the more impartial.

Research shows that in such cases the victim has a warped sense of danger. He is always hyper-vigilant, always attune to danger, real or perceived, because that's the only thing he's ever known. At CJC, Jacob had certainly been that way. While I remained totally oblivious, he would hear guards approaching far down the hall. He could tell when he was being watched even though the observer was beyond his direct vision. Outwardly relaxed, he would suddenly tense at seemingly imperceptible changes. His antenna was always out, checking for hidden threats--a raised hand, a quick movement, a narrowing of the eyes, a certain posture. A "normal" person's sense of impending harm, of safety and danger, does not apply to the Jacob Inds of the world. All psychologists agree on that. But that point had to be hammered home to fourteen people largely ignorant of the dynamics of hyper-vigilance, soul murder, and abuse when perpetrated by BOTH parents. The jury had much to learn. But Jacob's supporters were beginning to wonder if they had the proper teachers.

Charles Ind testified on the fourth day. Charles would take the stand twice--initially as a witness for the prosecution to recount Jacob's confession. In May of 1994 Charles had just completed his freshman year at Cornell College in Iowa, where he planned to major in psychology and sociology. He was twenty years old, but with his dark-rimmed glasses and serious demeanor, looked much older. Unlike Jacob, Charles is obsessively neat from his perfectly moussed hair to his highly polished wing tips. For his first day of testimony he wore a black double breasted blazer, gray pants, white shirt and conservative tie.

Bill Aspinwall guided Charles through his childhood, asking specifically about visitation arrangements following Frank and Pam's divorce. Initially, Charles and Jacob had seen their father every other weekend. After moving to Colorado, they visited Frank for two weeks in the summer and every other Christmas--when the logistics could be worked out.[54]

Charles discussed his high school activities—football, wrestling, drama. Throughout he maintained a tolerant, almost patronizing attitude toward Aspinwall. Unlike Jacob, Charles's movements were controlled to the point of verging on robotic.

"When did you move out of 120 Ridge Drive?"

"I believe it was the last week in August. School hadn't started yet. Two months later a friend, Michelle Mendez, and her infant son moved in." When

---

[54] The prosecution emphasized the airline ticket that would have taken Jacob to Illinois the day after the murders. The defense never pointed out that such a vacation would provide only a temporary reprieve. They said, "We're going to have to rough up Frank on the stand for being an absentee father," but he was never called.

Aspinwall pressed Charles on the relationship, he stressed that it was friendship. "She didn't help with the rent. I paid it. I've been working at Wendy's since ninth grade."

Often referring to his mother as "Pam," he said, "She didn't want me to move out. She was real upset and let me know. We fought about it once before moving out."

Following Charles's departure, he and his parents had had very little contact. In fact, Pam had only gone to the cabin twice, though she had tried to get him to return home.

"Did she cry over your leaving?" Aspinwall asked.

"Not in front of me. Jacob later told me that she had."

Charles made no secret of the fact that he had moved. He first talked to Counselor David Greathouse about his decision in early September at registration. School officials all knew the Jordans and were aware of the senior's decision.

Charles drove an ancient Volkswagen that he'd been given upon receiving his license at seventeen.

"Was the Volkswagen taken away when you moved out?"

"It wasn't mine. I didn't use it after I left."

"Who's decision was that?" Aspinwall asked.

"It was agreed upon," Charles said warily. With his meticulous way of speaking, he seemed more like a college professor than a student.

Aspinwall asked whether Charles still carried health insurance, insinuating that his continued coverage on Kermode's plan was proof of the Jordans' love. To further press his point, Aspinwall asked whether Pamela ever brought groceries to the cabin.

"Once. She called me and said she was going to Sam's [a discount warehouse] and asked if I needed anything. I gave her a list and she returned with three times the amount of things I needed."

He was also invited three times to Sunday dinner. The first time was soon after he'd moved out and the last had been on Thanksgiving. Pam never gave him money.

Aspinwall segued to the family finances.

"I wasn't aware of any financial problems, but I knew the house was for sale. That decision was made before I moved out... They never discussed family finances with us."

The prosecution had repeatedly made allusions to the fact that the murders were executed for monetary gain. While the boys' inheritance would have been negligible under the best of circumstances, Aspinwall pressed Charles about his schooling, which was nearly $20,000 a year. Immediately following the murders, Jacob had babbled something about money for college, which was four years away for him but imminent for his brother.

"How do you plan to pay for school?"

"Largely through loans and grants."

Aspinwall continued zeroing in on money. Charles talked about Kermode's thirty-two year old daughter from his first marriage, Justine Jordan. Kermode seldom saw her and Charles could only remember visiting her once or twice when they were growing up.

"She came out to Colorado in the summer of '93, maybe six months after the murders. I had dinner with her and her mother in Cripple Creek. We discussed the estate."

Either at dinner or at the hotel room, Charles mentioned that Kermode had not had a drink for three months before the murders. "Mom told me that on three separate occasions."

If the prosecution was trying to maintain that Kermode had reformed and was on the wagon, they were ignoring their own toxicology reports. According to the coroner, Kermode could have ingested up to twelve ounces of alcohol in the hours before he died.

"How often did you see the defendant after you moved out?"

"Only in passing in the hallway. We didn't have any classes together, though our lunches were the same, fifth hour. Students are allowed to go off campus and we had different friends. We didn't eat together."

Aspinwall moved Charles to December 16, 1992.

"I got home after school, about 3:30 p.m. I didn't work that day. It was my day off...I didn't talk to Jacob, though he had called me in the past. I had the flu and didn't go anywhere. My roommate was also with me at the cabin."

"Did you take any medication for the flu?"

"No."

Aspinwall asked Charles his opinion about Gabrial Adams.

"I couldn't stand him. I did not like him. I told Jacob he was a psychopath, to stay away from him."

Listening to this testimony, one of Jacob's friends felt a chill. To her it seemed that Charles' admonitions might have had the opposite effect intended. Instead of warning him away, Charles might have been planting seeds.

Aspinwall had Charles recount the morning after the murders, the telephone call informing him "something has happened with Jacob," and their ten minute meeting in the presence of a police officer. Principal Jim Taylor tried to get Charles a counselor from DSS, but saying, "I already went that route," he left.

Aspinwall questioned him about the family guns, with particular emphasis on the .357.

"We had that since approximately two years before the incident. It was moved around a lot by Jacob or me. Generally, it was kept in the night stand on Mom's side of the bed. When Kermode would come home drunk he sometimes wanted to take the gun and shoot someone with it. We had to hide it from him. A shotgun was kept in the Master Bath closet, along with some shells. None of

the guns were loaded. Jacob kept a .22, which was broken, in his closet."

"Were there knives in the house?"

"Yes. Kitchen, steak, and hunting knives. The hunting knives were kept in my parents' night stands. Jacob had a Swiss army knife, but no samurai sword."

"How about a bayonet?" Aspinwall asked.

"I don't know."

"Military swords?"

"No."

Aspinwall asked Charles about his father. As of December 1992, Charles couldn't remember the last time he'd talked to Frank. Jacob was supposed to spend Christmas at their dad's, but Charles had chosen to work instead. Frank had only recently moved from California to Illinois, and Charles made it very clear that the trio was not close.

Aspinwall began questioning Charles about an interview he had given Detective Jim Rocco on the day of the murders.

"I told Officer Rocco about Kermode's drinking and about how he was always getting drunk. The last time was in August just prior to my moving out... I don't know about Kermode's drinking after that.

"Kermode would come home drunk at two or three in the morning and make me sit at the kitchen table. I had to discuss philosophies with him-- Socrates, Plato, communism, socialism. Sometimes he'd make me read, knowing how hard that was with my learning problem. These discussions only took place when Kermode was drunk, which was often. The last time was a couple of months before I moved out. I always humored him because I was afraid of him and because I wanted to calm him down, to keep him away from Jacob. Jacob knew what was going on... Kermode never hit Jacob except for discipline, like the time he slapped Jacob in the face because he told a lie. Mom was the one who usually punished him."

According to Charles, the worst part about Kermode and Pam's punishment was the verbal put downs.

"As long as I did what they wanted me to do for a living, they would praise me for that. Otherwise, they taunted, 'You're no good. You'll never amount to anything.'"

Charles then discussed the recital incident both boys swear they related to David Greathouse. Jacob had begun guitar lessons. He and Pam were readying a flute and guitar duet for the Christmas program. Jacob didn't like to wear ties and Pam and Kermode wanted him to. He preferred a turtleneck. Pam finally allowed him to wear a sweater, though she was angry about a tiny hole in the sleeve.

In an uncustomary flare of defiance, Jacob said, "There's nothing wrong with this, Mom."

Pam didn't respond, but when they were in the garage, Kermode slammed

203

Jacob up against the Ram and screamed at him for "having an attitude."

Court was recessed for lunch.

◇ ◇ ◇

In the afternoon, Bill Aspinwall directed Charles to the murder night.

"Jacob told me he left the front door unlocked and went to bed. He took some painkillers and Nyquil to help him fall asleep. He heard six gunshots and screams. He heard some wrestling around and Gabrial called out, 'You hypocritical bastard.' Jacob got up and opened his bedroom door. It was dark in both bedrooms. Gabrial was trying to do a brainstem snap on Kermode with the knife. Jake said he was in the bedroom looking down the hall when he saw that."

Charles recited all of this without moving anything but his eyes. His voice, while a monotone, still effectively conveyed his emotion.

"There was a lot of wrestling. Kermode fell. Then Gabrial went for Mom and threw her to the ground. Gabrial came up to Jacob's bedroom door. He was covered in blood, with one glove missing, and Jacob said, 'You fucking bastard, you fucked it all up. You said it was going to be quick and painless.'

"Jacob still heard screaming so he went to the bedroom, got the bear spray and sprayed them with it because they were screaming. He stayed in the bathroom and covered his ears to block out the sound. Then he decided to get the .357 magnum, loaded it and Kermode stood up or looked at him and he couldn't forget what his face looked like—it was all mangled. Kermode's face distorted before Jacob shot him.

"Jacob shot Kermode. Mom was standing up. He fired and missed. Then he loaded the gun again and shot her in the head. Mom fell to the ground and she started twitching. Then he went back to his room, got the alarm clock, some clothes and a blanket, and went downstairs. He heard Gabrial leave. He stayed up all night wanting to commit suicide with the shotgun."

Charles spoke about the mental torment his brother was living with. "Jacob just wanted that pain to stop—the emotional pain."

Charles's version differs from Jacob's in many respects, as well as with forensics'. Such discrepancies are commonplace. They can be explained by Charles's emotional state, Jacob's incoherencies and the chaos surrounding the event.

"Did the defendant tell you how he planned to pay Gabrial Adams the two thousand dollar fee he promised?"

"Yes."

"Did you have paintings that were worth a lot of money?"

"One was worth over ten thousand dollars. Or at least we were told that. I later discovered it wasn't that valuable. When Mom and Kermode were drunk they bragged about it in front of us."

204

Charles looked down. By this time he had been on the stand much of the day. Aware of his dyslexia, Aspinwall had initially succeeded in flustering him by repeatedly asking him to refer to his testimony. Charles had indeed had difficulty finding the proper passages. But after a lifetime of adaptation, both boys could arrive at an adversary's destination before he did. When Bill Aspinwall emphasized a particular page, Charles began reading it verbatim—a practice which visibly annoyed the prosecutor.

Aspinwall again pressed him about a possible motive.

"One night Mom and Kermode didn't yell at Jake and he almost called off the plan. But the evening of the murders he got the belt for taking an extra $1 to school for lunch. He decided not to call it off then."

"Who used the belt on him?"

"Jacob didn't say."

"Where was the bear spray kept that Jacob used?"

"Generally it was kept in the drawer in the bathroom. Also, pepper mace was kept in the bathroom, in Mom's purse and there was one in each vehicle."

Aspinwall returned to the subject of the family dogs.

"Jacob told me they ran off about a week before the murders. He believed it was because Kermode was kicking them down the stairs. When they ran off, it was Kermode who had been taking care of them. This is speculation on my part, but I believe that Kermode opened the gate and the dogs ran off."

"Why did you make the comment at the funeral that the dogs were history?"

"Because everyone was asking about them and I had more important things to deal with."

Aspinwall insinuated that Jacob had deliberately let loose Pike and Chaka.

"No," Charles said flatly. "He would never have run them off. They were the only source of affection that Jacob and I had."

After a break Shaun began his cross, emphasizing a few points such as if the Jordans were contemplating moving to an even more isolated spot, Jacob would have been completely at their mercy. When asked why Charles didn't talk to his brother that much, Charles replied, "I needed to get my own space for a little bit. Then I could get closer to Jake."

Shaun questioned him about the phone call from school on the morning after the murders.

"I knew something serious had happened. I was shocked when I heard. When I saw Jacob he started crying and kept saying, 'I'm sorry.' I told him, 'It'll be all right. I'll take care of everything. Just sit tight and answer the questions.' I put my hands on Jake. I remember they were very cold and I was shaking really bad. Jacob was crying the entire time. That was unusual for Jacob, not to

be under control. My brother is introverted and always under control."

One or two more questions and Shaun was finished. Bill Aspinwall wasn't.

"Did you cry during your conversation with the defendant?"

"No, I was too numb."

When Charles once again asserted that Kermode and Pam never showed any genuine affection, Aspinwall produced several family snapshots. After each photo he threw the back of the sticker he was using to label it on the floor. Charles leaned over, picked up each scrap and placed it neatly in a pile. Throughout, Bill Aspinwall edged closer to the obviously fatigued young man.

Shaun finally stood. "Objection! The prosecution is making the witness uncomfortable."

Aspinwall asked Charles directly, "Am I making you uncomfortable?"

"Yes."

Aspinwall stepped back.

Charles stared dutifully at each picture—photos of his prom, of the entire family together, and of him, his mother and Jacob. By this time his face was pale, his entire body rigid. Despite the fact that he hadn't moved, he somehow gave the appearance of being plastered against the back wall in an effort to distance himself from Aspinwall and his exhibits.

"There were a few happy moments from outward appearances," Charles said, struggling to control his emotions. "Most of those pictures were taken after Kermode's drinking binges because everyone was trying to entertain him. They may say, ' I love you,' but there was no feeling behind it."

Soon after, Charles was excused.

Outside in the hallway, he vented his frustration.

"That fucking bastard," he said, referring to Aspinwall. The photographs in particular had shaken him. Despite his support of Jacob, he still sometimes missed the mom he'd known before Kermode. The pictures had been a powerful reminder of what his brother had taken away from him.

Eric Glanzer, the emergency room physician at Langstaff-Brown Medical Center, testified after Charles. Glanzer took blood samples from Jacob, but was questioned primarily about the extensive number of cuts on Gabrial's hands. The prosecution was allowed to show slides of Gabrial's wounds, which surprised spectators. Since Jacob had no injuries, why was the prosecution allowed to show GABRIAL'S wounds?

"I thought Jacob was on trial for his deeds," said one. "How come they're being allowed to crucify him for his partner's actions?"

On May 18, 1994, the fifth day of testimony, teacher/friend Lucinda Reed was sworn in. She began by relating her friendship with the family, emphasizing Pam and distancing herself from any interaction with Charles, at least before the murders.

"Pam acted as a judge in Forensics and she couldn't watch her sons compete. The family was private and hid its feelings. As Charles once told me, 'We were taught not to tell.'"

Aspinwall questioned Reed about the last time she had seen Jacob before the murders.

"It was at a novice Forensics tournament at the end of November. I complimented him on winning his debate round. He said it wasn't bad for not having any sleep. He said he was only sleeping two, three or four hours. I attributed it to nervousness over his performance."

Reed had taught Jacob in 6th grade and liked him, but he showed "a lack of maturity."

"It wasn't typical behavior," she said, often directly addressing the jury with a half-smile. "He would slam his books down, and he wouldn't raise his hand. If kids bumped into him he would retaliate aggressively. He wasn't disrespectful to adults, but had difficulty dealing with his peers. I would call him a loner, but not reclusive. He didn't know how to make friends."[55]

Pam discussed with Lucinda her decision to make Jacob repeat eighth grade. Pamela felt that Jacob was too immature for high school, despite the fact that all of Jacob's teachers, save one, urged her to allow him to go on. (The exception was neutral.)

According to Reed, "Pam was concerned about other kids picking on Jacob. She didn't want him to get hurt or to hurt someone else."

While Jacob's behavior didn't raise any warning signs, Reed did tell Pamela, "Sometimes I feel your parenting is too strict. Charles is angry and I think it would be beneficial if you got counseling... Later, at the police station, when I asked about their family counselor, Jacob was surprised. He asked, 'What counselor?'"

He didn't know what Reed was talking about. Charles was even more shocked.

"This was the first time I really knew of any problems," Reed said. She was "extremely upset" because Pam had lied to her about the counseling, saying that they had been going when they hadn't.

---

[55] As Shaun pointed out in his cross, some of the signs of child abuse are lack of maturity, inability to relate to peers, and a lack of understanding of consequences. Although Reed had taken courses in abuse, and reports about two cases of abuse a year, she didn't suspect a possible connection between Jacob's behavior and mistreatment.

In the spring of 1992, nine months before the murders, Reed asked Pam to meet her after Charles told her, "Kermode goes on drinking binges and passes out." Reed suggested they meet in the lounge at Jan's Cafe, a curious choice considering the role alcohol played in so many of the principals' lives. Kermode also put in an appearance, ordered a drink and Lucinda's "frank discussion" never materialized.

Aspinwall asked Reed about Jacob's statement that he'd "got the belt" the night of the murders.

"I thought he meant he had gotten beaten. I think Charles interpreted it as meaning Jacob got ahold of the belt to defend himself."

Then Reed recounted Jacob's confession, which was fairly similar to Charles's recollection. Throughout, Reed batted her eyes, cocked her head, and gestured often with her hands. Some courtroom observers were disgusted by what they considered the drama coach's "histrionics." Her performance must have been effective, however, because a photograph of a tormented appearing Reed made the newspapers, and she was the lead story on the nightly news. All of Colorado Springs saw her rolling eyes and distressed expression, and heard her dramatic inflections as she recalled Jacob's words as he shot his mother. With a catch in her voice, Reed said, "Blood and brains went everywhere."[56]

After Reed completed her appearance, the dramatic quotient decreased considerably. Several neighborhood teenagers testified regarding the family in general. Jacob was quiet, the parents seemed strict, but not too strict, and they had heard Jacob say that he hated them.

Stephanie Endsley was sworn in. A sturdily built sixteen-year-old with cropped, curly hair and an upturned nose, Stephanie had been Jacob's girlfriend for a short time. Approximately a week before the murders, they had broken up, but remained friends.

"Jacob and I would talk at school, lunch and before or after school. We would talk on the phone nearly every evening. Jacob had to walk the dogs and do chores and then we would talk. Our conversations lasted from a few minutes to 3 or 4 hours."

Sometimes Jacob would do other things while on the phone with her, like listening to music and playing Nintendo.

"We did homework together quite a bit. When his parents came home, he would say, 'I have to go. My parents are here or are coming home.' I heard his parents sometimes. They would tell him to get off the phone—and when they did he usually obeyed right away."

"Was Jacob afraid of Kermode? "

"Yes. He was afraid of being hit. He said Kermode slugged and punched

---

[56] Jacob denies he ever said this. Forensics backs up his version.

him. He didn't like to tell anyone about his bruises. Many times he showed me the marks on his neck, shoulder, and upper back. I saw a fist-like bruise on his upper right arm that had four circles like knuckle marks. I also remember a large, dark, one-color bruise on the back of his neck. His bruises were visible when he wore a cutoff shirt or tank top. They were different from the bruises he got during football which were on his legs or lower arms. Jacob said that his parents were unfair about the chores, that he had to do everything, that since Charles left they were really emotionally and physically abusive. His mother slugged him with rings, leaving marks. His parents often told him he was worthless and going to be a nothing. Jacob told me that and I also heard his mother say that to him. Jacob would get embarrassed and apologize."

"Did Jacob ever say he hated his parents?"

"Yes, maybe 2-3 times a week. Jacob felt that it was his mom's fault that she had divorced his dad and he hated her more because of that."

"Did he ever state that he hated one more than the other?"

"No," Stephanie said, contradicting herself. "The same."

"When did Jacob talk about killing his parents?"

"After Charles moved out—near the end of October, early November. He blamed his parents for his brother's leaving. He felt that they took it out on him and blamed him for Charles' departure. He didn't say how he would kill them and I didn't take him seriously."

"Did you tell anyone else about the excessive chores, the killing or the abuse?"

"No."

Aspinwall asked to submit into evidence a letter written one week before the murders. In the letter, which Stephanie had written to Jacob, she communicated her desire to kill HER parents. Aspinwall questioned Stephanie about her personal problems.

"I didn't feel like I fit in at school. I did make statements about killing my parents. They were unusually strict and wouldn't let me date until I was 16."

The prosecution turned to Gabrial Adams. Stephanie had met Gabrial after a band concert. He offered Stephanie and one of her girlfriends a ride home.

"We declined. He was pretty weird."

Stephanie recounted a telephone call she'd had with Jacob on the night of the murders. "I can't remember who phoned who or if one of us called and had the call returned a little later. The conversation lasted a long time--from 8:30 or 9 until 10:30 or 11. Major was there. Gabrial only said "hi" when Jacob went to the bathroom and he said, 'Here. Talk to Gabrial.'"[57]

---

[57] Jacob swears this conversation never occurred, and evidence brought out at Gabrial's trial effectively refuted at least Major's involvement In addition, one of Pam's sisters talked to her on the phone that evening, further calling into question any

Stephanie recalled that Jacob discussed killing his parents that night. He was not depressed, but rather seemed easy-going. "I asked him how he was going to kill them. He said,'I have a gun and I'm going to shoot them.' He told me that Gabrial was a good marksman. That he did target shooting."

Jacob ended their conversation when he heard his parents coming up the stairs. This was perhaps forty-five minutes after being told to get off the phone—and, according to Stephanie, only a few hours before Jacob murdered them.

---

extended conversation.

[The jurors] may believe that Jacob Ind was
abused, or they may not. And even if they
believe the boy was abused, they still might
feel that it's no excuse for the act he has
committed.

~Raymond McCaffrey/columnist
Gazette Telegraph

Chapter 28

On Thursday, May 19, 1994, Jacob's former friend, David Mabie, took the
stand. Mabie is tall with long, dishwater blond hair, parted in the middle. That
morning he sported a scraggly moustache and his eyes were glassy. Both Jacob
and a counselor in the courtroom familiar with substance abuse commented that
Mabie appeared to be stoned.

David testified that he had known Jacob since 6th grade and saw him on
a regular friendship basis.

"Sometimes we would spend the night together or do things on weekends.
After Jacob was held back a year, we weren't as close."

Jacob was always quiet and very polite at David's house. He never
complained about being abused.[58] David had met Kermode and Pamela and they
seemed pretty normal when he was there. If he phoned Jacob and Kermode or
Pam answered, he didn't sense anything unusual.

"Did you ever witness any arguments between the defendant and his
parents?"

"Once. His mother had just cleaned up the kitchen. Jacob was cooking
bacon and splattered grease. She yelled at him. There was a lot of verbal abuse.
After the bacon argument, we wanted to get the sled out of the garage and
needed the keys and his mother ragged on Jacob for not knowing where they
were... I never saw bruises on Jacob or heard him complain about injuries."

"Did you notice their relationship going down hill?"

"Yes, about three years ago. I saw more arguments and he was always
getting into trouble. They kept Jacob caged and wouldn't let him do things.
Once they grounded him for the summer because he didn't go to the store for
milk.[The store would have been a six mile round trip.]"

Two months before the murders, Jacob started complaining that he wasn't
getting along with his parents and wanted them dead.

"He would say that a couple of times a week. I talked to him at lunchtime

---

[58] At a pre-trial hearing I spoke with Mabie's stepmother. She said she'd loved Jacob
and could have adopted him. But, because of his crime, she now hoped he would rot in
hell.

211

or after buses had dropped us off before school. Jacob didn't really say why he needed someone to help him kill his parents. I said no."

"Why did Jacob ask you to help him kill his parents?"

"I don't know."

This conversation about the Jordans' murders occurred in October 1992 around 12:45 p.m. David and Jacob were returning to the campus after lunch. At first, Mabie didn't believe his friend was serious.

"Jacob wasn't himself at this time. He had a short temper and he wasn't bathing. He said he didn't like his parents, and didn't want them there to tell him what to do any more. They were always telling him that they didn't like the way he dressed, especially his bellbottoms. He said he hated his parents more times than I can count. And every time he spoke to me he'd mention that he wanted me to kill them. He'd say that maybe three or four times a day."

One day after getting off the buses, Jacob said he had found someone else to help him kill his parents—Major Adams.

David and Jacob had two in-depth conversations regarding the killings with a two-week lapse in between. During the second conversation, near the beginning of November, Jacob said that Major was making a silencer for a .22 pistol or he was going to talk to Gabrial about making a silencer so no shots would be heard.

Mabie testified that he likes guns. He collects them and hunts. Yet when the prosecution held up the .357 that David said he had seen in the Jordan household, Mabie didn't recognize it or the nylon holster and ammo pouch. He identified the .22 revolver as the one he saw in Jacob's room.[59]

"Were you over at 120 Ridge Drive after Charles left?"

"Twice. That was after Jacob moved into his brother's room."

David then recounted Jacob's confession before school on the morning of the murders. "Jacob said, 'I will never forget my mother screaming.'"

"Have you had any contact with the defendant since December 17, 1992?"

"A couple of telephone conversations. And he wrote me a couple of letters."

David had reported Jacob's conversations, which took place during his stay at Zeb Pike Detention Center, to the police. Mabie asked if he should tape these conversations. They said yes so Mabie used his answering machine. Afterward, he turned the tape—as well as Jacob's letters—over to the D.A.

One taped conversation was played for the jury. In it, Jacob told David that he had heard Major had been released on bond. Jacob was worried that the "psycho" would turn on Charles to get back at him for telling police of Gabrial's

---

[59] Actually, it wasn't. That had been the broken .22 that Jacob had carried around since childhood. The murder weapon the prosecution displayed was the one Jacob and David had stolen that previous summer.

involvement in the killing. Jacob also added that getting rid of Major would improve his defense. He said that Principal Jim Taylor had missed half the conversation and David Greathouse would not be able to testify--presumably because of counselor-student privilege.

"So If Major disappears, they have nothing on me. I'll say he either told me to do this stuff or that Major did everything. I need to find someone to get Major."

"What do you mean?" asked David on the phone.

"Think."

"Oh, yeah, I don't know."

"Find someone to do it."

"What do you think the defendant meant when he said "to get" Major?" asked Bill Aspinwall after the tape was shut off.

"I thought he meant to find him and kill him."

When asked to identify to whom David was speaking on the tape, David did not recognize his former friend's voice. Only after he was shown the tape could he verify that it was the one he'd made.

The impact of the tape was devastating. As it turned out, the only time the jury would hear Jacob Ind's voice was when he sounded like a punk. As is required by law, the prosecution had long ago shared their content with the defense, so the conversations were nothing new. But afterward Shaun acted as dazed as everyone else. And he did little to mitigate their impact. He never raised the question of Jacob's mental state in the days following the tragedy, or why Jacob would feel comfortable discussing murder with a supposedly innocent bystander, or why David Mabie felt compelled to turn on his friend, or whether David had cut some sort of deal with the state. Shaun never confronted David with Jacob's assertion that it had been David, rather than he, who had first mentioned killing Pamela and Kermode, who had given Jacob the .22 that was used in the murders, or about David's possible participation in the murder plot. Shaun mentioned very little about David's personal problems, which also include major abuse, and which must be weighed when assessing his credibility. Especially when his 6'5" father sat in court during his entire testimony. (As did David's attorney.)

The defense was reluctant to tear into David because they were trying to paint Jacob as a terrific kid and Mabie could have testified to the contrary--that they had smoked pot and had broken into a couple of houses. But any aberrant behavior on Jacob's part would be explained by the defense psychologists. Anti-social behavior, often in a far more serious fashion and far earlier than in Jacob's case, is typical of abused children.

In the elevator after the end of the day's testimony, Shaun said, "Keep smiling," as if the prosecution had delivered a bombshell. Because of the defense's reaction, indeed they had. And Aspinwall knew it. During a recess he went over and stood beside Jacob. He grinned down at him, as if to say, "Gotcha,

punk." At another time he stared at Nancy Overmyer, the tall grey-haired lady who Jacob considers "family," and smirked.

The following day, Shaun tried to exercise some damage control.

On the morning of the murders in the school hallway, Jacob had expressed concern over his brother's safety.

"Gabrial had a reputation for being dangerous," Mabie testified. "Jacob said, 'Inform my brother, man, that Major may go after him.'"

"I asked, 'So he's threatening you? Why would he go after your brother?'"

"'I don't know. The kid is psycho, you know that. To try to get to me.'"

Shaun asked, "Did you ever see any bruises or injuries on the defendant?"

"I saw one on his arm. Jacob put a tattoo there, and he was afraid because of his parents. Jacob took a wire brush and scrubbed it off which left a scar... He told me there was physical and verbal abuse, that his stepdad beat him."

As far as Jacob's relationship with his parents, when he was thirteen, Mabie said it was fine. It took years to deteriorate. By the fall of 1992, "He told me about his sleepless nights. The last six weeks Jacob wasn't eating, sleeping or taking care of himself. I knew toward the end there was a lot of verbal abuse. He had really bad mood swings, which increased after Charles moved out." They had a conversation about going to Social Services. Mabie, speaking from first hand experience, told Jacob, "They don't always help kids."

In Mabie's deposition, he had mentioned Jacob being beaten. Now Shaun zeroed in on that statement. He held up a piece of paper on which he'd written in blue magic marker, "BEAT."

Displaying the word to jurors and spectators Shaun said, "He was beat, Beat, BEAT!"

Soon after, Mabie sheepishly left the stand.

Jacob later charged that David had lied seventy-six times. That plus the discrepancies in Lucinda Reed's statements caused his supporters to wonder about possible perjury charges against the pair. Again, that showed our naivete. Witnesses, defense and prosecution, professional and ordinary, lie on the stand every day in every courtroom across America. That's accepted practice. Only a newcomer to the system believes otherwise. Only someone like me or Jacob's friends actually assumed that taking the oath "to tell the truth and nothing but the truth," meant something. In Jacob's case, the prosecution had no interest in bringing perjury charges against two of their own witnesses. And, for whatever reason, neither did the defense.

Jacob's best friend, Armando Lee took the stand next. They had been pals since 7th grade. Several times they'd had sleep overs at each other's houses.

Mondo said, "At our house one of us would throw a sleeping bag on the floor while the other slept in the bed. We could stay up all night if we wanted

214

to."

Which contrasted with spending the night at the Jordans.

"We were immediately separated in different bedrooms and made to do our homework. At supper time his mother took the phone off the hook so that dinnertime wouldn't be disturbed, we ate and then Jacob and I went to our separate rooms for the night."

"Did you ever witness any arguments between the defendant and his parents?"

"No, though I do remember one incident when Jacob expressed fear of them. We were going to go hiking behind the high school. It was winter. Jacob borrowed Kermode's ski pants without telling him. As we were coming back down, we slid. Jacob caught the pants on rocks and tore them. He got really scared and asked if there was some way they could be sewn up, but there wasn't because they were made out of nylon."

The prosecution questioned Armando about his friend's chores.

"Jacob had to clean the house, clean up dog dung in the garage, and feed the dogs." Armando also had chores and he didn't think Jacob's were unusual.

"Jacob talked about how much he hated his parents for as long as I knew him. He said his parents beat him a lot and put him through mental head trips. He told me about being hit by a belt buckle across the face one time."

"Did you ever see any evidence of that?"

"No."

Nor did Mondo see any bruises or marks even though they had gym class together.

"Jacob said he wanted his parents dead and wished he could find someone to do it."

"Did you see Pam and Kermode strike or use violence? What about yelling? Arguments?"

"No."

"Against Charles?"

"No."

Aspinwall directed the witness to the morning after the murders. Mondo had seen his friend between second and third hour. Jacob said he needed to talk. They walked outside the freshman hall.

"He told me that Major screwed everything up big time and that his parents were dead. Jacob kept pacing back and forth. He kept asking me, 'What should I do?' He felt so bad he was ready to kill himself...I mentioned calling the police.

"Jacob said, 'I don't think I could do that.' He was speaking in half sentences, really down and really scared. I told him I'd make the call."

After a fifteen minute break, Shaun began his cross. Armando testified that Jacob was "kind of a geek" and didn't have many friends. Mondo was shunned by some because of their friendship. Jacob could be loud and obnoxious, but he

215

was different at the Lee place, an isolated homestead of two hundred acres. There Jacob was happy. The two teenagers hunted, hiked, and camped. With his parents some 50 miles away, "Jacob felt safe."

Shaun asked whether Armando noticed any changes in Jacob's behavior.

"Yes. For example at lunch Jacob and I would walk to Cactus (A local fast food place similar to a Taco Bell) and he would eat five burritos. By mid-fall, early December, he simply stopped eating."

Mondo couldn't recall whether that was a gradual thing or quite sudden.

Shaun finished his questioning by discussing the fact that Mondo had never noticed any bruises.

"Teenage boys don't make a point of looking at other teen-age boys, do they? Not even in gym class?"

"Right."

"That's part of teen-age boyness, isn't it?"

"Yes, Mondo replied. He also agreed that there were no meetings at school where an authority figure told kids it was okay to tell if they've been hit.

"Kids don't boast about parental bruising, do they?"

"No, they don't."

Several expert witnesses followed, testifying about fingerprints and ballistics and hair samples, most of which came from Gabrial Adams. None were found from Jacob and several strands appeared to have come from someone other than the victims or the defendants. Kenneth Van Cleave, a lab agent specializing in latent fingerprints, testified that Jacob's right thumbprint was found on the bear mace, and Gabrial's right thumb on the .357. Gabrial's print was positioned in the same place that the thumb would be if the weapon was being held to shoot. But the fact that Gabrial's prints, rather than Jacob's were on the .357 didn't necessarily mean that Gabrial had fired it.

According to Van Cleave, "Prints are only found in eight to ten per cent of items submitted."

As it turns out, other than the bear spray which witnesses saw Jacob handle many times before the murders, there is no evidence linking him to the scene of the crime. There are no powder burns or fingerprints. Nor can any bloodstains be conclusively attributed to him. The prosecution's serologist testified that blood samples could either be Gabrial's or Jacob's, (and during Gabrial's trial that they could have been Charles's, as well). The tests were "inconclusive." Throughout the proceedings, Aspinwall stressed the fact that Jacob didn't have a scratch on him. If that's true, the bloodstains still cannot be attributed exclusively to Gabrial Adams. The serologist also testified that he didn't think the bodies had been moved after death or "there would have been pooling of blood."

216

Tom Griffin, a lab agent for the Colorado Bureau of Investigation, admitted that there was no "residue from a firearm" on Jacob's hands. However, That did not mean that it hadn't been there at one point.

"Rubbing one's hands together or washing them will remove much of the residue, as would four to six hours of normal activity."[60]

In Jacob's case, he wasn't swabbed for perhaps ten hours after the murders.

On May 24, 1994, the ninth day of testimony, Kermode and Pamela's autopsy photos were introduced. The defense objected, charging that they were "inflammatory and cumulative." Out of dozens of slides, Looney finally disallowed one. For more than two hours, jurors saw photos of the victims' heads and torsos while El Paso County Coroner David Bowerman painstakingly explained each mark, abrasion and wound.

Kermode was displayed first. "Mr. Jordan could have survived the three .22 shots to his head," Bowerman said, as the first photo of Jacob's stepfather was displayed. Kermode's eyes were closed. His hair, due to the coroner's ministrations, lay in short wet strands against his skull. Before photographing each body, Bowerman had scrubbed away all the blood and debris.

"Mr. Jordan would not have bled to death from his wounds, though his wife could have died from loss of blood."

While Kermode had been shot three times in the face, the wounds were surprisingly small, no bigger than a fingertip. They seemed more like blemishes than anything that could kill a man. The prosecution lingered over each picture so spectators had plenty of time to gaze into that face, to study the full straight nose, the thin lips, the rather puffy eyelids. Kermode looked as if he were concentrating on pretending to be asleep. In the various pictures his skin looked mottled, reminiscent of a rhinoceros's hide, though that was due to death rather than age. In one photograph detailing the cuts on his hands we clearly viewed the hairless chest and the slightly bloated belly, tapering down toward his genitals.

Although I wasn't allowed in the courtroom until closing arguments, I did see the photos during Gabrial Adams's trial. I found them disturbing. Not so much because I was looking at two dead bodies, or even because of the violence perpetrated upon them, which did not match the horror of press reports or of my imagination.

---

[60] Other experts say gunpowder would have HAD to show up. Since Jacob was in his underwear, he should have been covered by it. A more comprehensive test should have been conducted. There are those who believe that Jacob didn't even kill his parents. Discrepancies such as these lend credence to their assertion. Despite Griffin's testimony, I've talked to other knowledgeable men who maintain something should have shown up on those tests. Another question. Why didn't the defense question such a possibly important discrepancy?

But because I correlated the corpses to their actions in life. Viewing Kermode, I found myself thinking, This is what a pedophile truly looks like. Too bad there wasn't some clue in that lifeless flesh, in those merciless photographs that would explain the origin of Kermode Jordan's perversion, some scarlet letter warning the world that a monstrosity walked among them.

Or maybe there was a clue, after all. If not to Kermode's perversion, at least to Jacob's final act—the bullet to the brain.

As Jacob's psychiatrist once explained to me, "Every crime scene reveals a lot about the reason for the murders and the nature of the abuse. There are many clues in the deed itself, as well as in the chosen weapon."

In Jacob's case, he had used a .357. One squeeze and there is complete, instantaneous extermination of the personality, of billions of memories--both inconsequential and profound. If you can demolish what made Kermode and Pamela functioning, thinking, feeling human beings, can you somehow eradicate their deeds? And by destroying them, does that mean that one is free of the past and their influence? Did their power explode simultaneously with the bullets entering their brain? Jacob believes so, though he scoffs at the notion that his choice of weapon was relevant. The .357 was the closest thing available and the deed had to be done. But the same could be asked concerning Jacob's proposed method of suicide on the morning after the murders. Place a barrel between the eyes and pull the trigger. Why not slit your wrists? Take pills? Drive off a cliff? Place the barrel against your heart? Why do so much violence to his brain?

After many more close-ups of various parts of Kermode's body, it was Pamela Jean's turn. In the first picture we see the back of her head, her hair falling away from her scalp in snaking tendrils, and a portion of her shoulder and back. Pam's wounds are far worse than Kermode's. Amid the coiling hair are two wicked cuts, four to six inches in length, that reach to the skull. A third cut penetrates near the base of her neck, as if Gabrial Adams had indeed been trying to "pith" her.

Click!

The coroner has positioned the body so we can see a particular graze-wound. Pam's skin is fish-white and wet. More photos, several of her face in profile. (Pamela's "good" side. Where the .357 entered the entire area is almost completely blackened by tattooing.) Pam's hooked nose, the chin receding into her neck does make her look like a witch. Her mouth, unlike Kermode's, is open, showing her strong teeth. Kermode's face was neutral, but Pamela looks angry as hell.

Another slide focuses on an abrasion on Pam's shoulder. Upon glimpsing one of her breasts I cannot escape the thought, How could two people have so perverted sex and love? Pamela's breasts hadn't been used to nurture. They had been used to violate. Her womb hadn't given life. It had snatched away all chance at anything save a faint echo.

218

There are other photos I need to see of Pamela and Kermode, photos that will never be shown in this courtroom to awaken my pity. Perhaps if I could view images of Kermie and Daddy's Little Girl that were taken from childhood-- when their eyes are as bright as the promises of their future and life beckons them with hope and love, rather than the defeats of their childhood and their own deeds. Perhaps then I could feel for these two dead people, these two "victims" on display for all the world to see.

◊ ◊ ◊

In the afternoon, John Peters Jr., an aerosol chemical and self-defense expert, was scheduled to detail the effects of BearGuard, the spray that Jacob had used on his parents. Jacob's supporters hoped that Shaun would question the expert as to why, if the mace was deadly enough to totally incapacitate Kermode and Pamela, it hadn't immobilized Jacob and Gabrial. One observer, familiar with mace, reminded Shaun that pepper spray is often far less debilitating than advertised. Shaun promised that he would question Peters on that point.

The defense never had the chance to raise that contradiction or anything else. After stating his credentials, Peters "accidentally" discharged the mace in the courtroom.

As reporter Deborah Correll of the High Mountain Sun wrote, 'One little spritz may be worth a thousand words.

'Especially when the spritz in question is one of pepper gas, and especially when its aimed straight at a courtroom of people sitting in judgement of a 16-year-old-boy who blasted his parents full in the face with the stuff before killing them with a .357 Magnum revolver.'

"Oops! It went off...I'm sorry...I didn't know there was anything left in the can," Peters said. Some witnesses claimed he looked surprised, others stunned, still others as if he knew exactly what he was doing.

Reporter Correll continued, 'Having your throat close up, your eyes water, your nose fill up, and not being able to breathe has a way of giving new perspective to what Kermode and Pam Jordan encountered just after being shot and stabbed repeatedly and just before being sent to their deaths.

The prosecution could not have done a better job of putting jurors in the Jordans' shoes if they'd planned it.'

Jacob's father claims that's exactly what happened. Barred from the courtroom, Frank Ind had spent every minute in the hallway. Before Peters' testimony, Frank overheard co-prosecutor Gordon Dennison and the expert discussing the possibility that some liquid remained in the can. Supposedly, one said, "I wonder what would happen if this went off in the courtroom." (Other members of the defense also believe it was a fix, but so what? Nothing can be done about it.)

Coughing and wheezing, former spectators congregated in the hallway.

Several mentioned that Aspinwall and Dennison kept grinning, as if well-pleased with themselves. Frank Ind, hardly a hothead, was so infuriated he threatened to punch Aspinwall, though not to his face. Frank tried to talk to Judge Looney about what he'd heard. Looney refused to see him.

Once the spray was dispersed, the defense moved for a mistrial. Looney denied their motion. She did order Peters' testimony to be excluded from the record. Nor did she allow him to return as a witness.

Which was hardly a blow to the prosecution. Aspinwall simply brought in another mace expert.

The prosecution rested.

Parents kill their children all the
time. It's seldom that children strike back.
When they do, of course, it is the stuff
of tabloid dreams.

Raymond McCaffrey/columnist
Gazette Telegraph

Chapter 29

On the afternoon of May 24, 1994, the ninth day of the trial, the defense began presenting its case. Before the first witness was called, several people joked about the pepper spray. Aspinwall arrived wearing a mask over his mouth and nose. He had certainly gotten his point across about the mace's debilitating effects so he could afford to joke about it. But, although jurors were told to disregard the incident, a basic law school maxim is "Once you ring a bell, it can't be unrung." If jurors obeyed the judge's dictums and wiped the incident from their minds, they would be one of the few juries ever to do so.

The incident with the pepper spray was just one of several sleazy tricks pulled by the prosecution. Many of Aspinwall's antics seemed to be right out of first year law school. They were so transparent they would surely alienate a jury, wouldn't they? He hammered each point ad nauseam. He assassinated characters on the stand and acted as if he owned the courtroom. At one point, he told Judge Looney, "These witnesses will not testify in this courtroom."[60] When Charles was called to testify a second time, Aspinwall kept the court waiting for nearly two hours while he drove his family to the airport. He said he had gotten the times "mixed up." Of course the jury didn't know the reason for the delay. Other attorneys termed it a tactic to unnerve Charles, who was going to testify publicly for the first time about sexual abuse.

Aspinwall also blamed the defense psychiatrists for not turning over certain documents and held up court proceedings because he himself hadn't prepared for their testimony. He was sarcastic to witnesses, Judge Looney and defense attorneys. He even tried to have Jacob's friend, Nancy Overmyer, barred from the courtroom for nodding her head during testimony.

One juror, who was not charmed by Aspinwall's demeanor said, "He was so vicious I kept wondering how he treated his own children. Maybe he saw himself in Kermode and Pamela."

As the defense began, Jacob's supporters hoped that the defense would prove as aggressive as the prosecution. Jacob's private investigator, Jeanette

---

[60] They did. Not only did Looney never raise her voice, she never chastised him. She very quietly performed her duties, but to many spectators, Aspinwall seemed to run the show.

Shick, had told me she thought he had the strongest case for self defense she'd ever seen. She had interviewed the witnesses. She should know.

Doug Kermode, Kermode's first cousin was sworn in. Doug testified that he had once seen Kermode haul off and hit five-year-old Jacob for biting. He also tearfully testified that Kermode had been kind to a child with a severe facial deformity. Doug had not seen his cousin since the early eighties, when they'd quarreled during Kermode's mother's funeral.

During cross exam, Bill Aspinwall asked Doug whether he was an alcoholic.

"My ex-wife thinks I am, but I believe I have the problem under control now."

Barbara Blackwell Jordan Turrentine, Kermode Jordan's second wife, was next. Although in her late fifties, Barbara remains a striking blonde. She was pregnant with her son, Christopher, when Kermode and she met in 1962. They moved in together and were married four years later. The marriage ended in 1969 and Barbara hadn't seen her ex in nearly a quarter century. Her opinion of Kermode's "domestic attitude: "One of "violence."

Barbara testified that Kermode loved her son Christopher and never hurt him. Kermode sometimes sent him money and Barbara had requested that her son, now 31, be included in Kermode's estate. Christopher is in prison and could not appear to represent himself in probate matters, which was the main reason Barbara had come forward, but she had not put any conditions on her testifying. Nor, as of May 1994, was she any longer pursuing a claim to the Jordan estate.

"Kermode was a mama's boy. He and his mother spent a lot of time together. Kermode took Thora many places, and they enjoyed traveling together."

When Kermode and Barbara were together, Kermode, who "never disciplined Christopher," preferred Thora's treatment of Christopher to her own. Barbara recalled one time when she wanted to give her son an aspirin. Thora advised against it. Barbara went against her wishes and gave Christopher the pill.

"Kermode dragged me out on to the porch, hit me and said, 'How dare you talk to my mother like that?' I saw stars after he hit me, and I cried. I felt angry, fearful, and chagrined."

Barbara recalled another incident when they were walking across the parking lot at Long Beach College. She walked into a broken antenna from a car and Kermode hit her.

They often argued in their apartment. "We had a very small living room so we were only five to six feet apart. Kermode threw a heavy glass ashtray at my head and missed me. He burst out laughing, leaned back and said, "You have the fastest reflexes of anyone I've ever seen.' I remember driving down Long Beach Blvd, this was in 1964 or 65. Kermode was driving while hitting

222

me continuously with his right hand... Another time in 1965 we were in Long Beach one afternoon. We were standing on the street corner waiting for the light to change. Kermode raised his arm and I instinctively ducked."

Barbara testified about a Christmas party that had taken place in 1966. They were with Kermode's friends, none of whom she knew. "On our way home Kermode was very drunk. He got verbally abusive. I started crying and tried to get out of the car. He grabbed me and pulled me back in."

After Kermode and she separated, Barbara became involved with his best friend. Kermode invited them to visit, but then disappeared on a days' long binge. When they returned home, Kermode threatened to shoot them. He kept a gun in the house so they took the threat seriously.

Barbara did not testify about Kermode's revolutionary activities. Nor was she closely questioned about other incidents of abuse or asked about the possibility that her son was molested by Kermode. All testimony beyond that concerning her interest in Kermode's estate was taken outside of the presence of the jury. They never heard any of it.

On the second day of the defense's presentation, Jacob's godmother took the stand. Wearing a bright turquoise dress and with her black hair falling softly around her face, Lupe Thorson was sworn in. She was extremely nervous and did not feel that she had been sufficiently prepared. Other than a breakfast appointment with Tom Kennedy, wherein they'd only perfunctorily gone over her testimony, Lupe had no idea how to act.

Lupe testified that she met Pamela in 1972 through a mutual friend. Pam was married to Frank but the Inds didn't yet have children. The two families would see each other often, and do things together on weekends, though Frank seldom joined in. Lupe and Pam became best friends when Charles was born on December 20, 1973. Lupe babysat Charlie at her house so the women saw each other daily. Pam would have a couple of beers and stay for dinner. They also shared a nanny.

Lupe babysat Charlie until he went to kindergarten. Pam's marriage was not going well and she constantly complained about her husband. Then she got pregnant with Jacob.

"What was Pam's attitude about her pregnancy?"

"She was not happy with it."

Pam moved out when Jacob was somewhere between 1-1½ years old and rented an apartment in Campbell, California. She then left Charlie and Jacob with their father. Two-three months afterwards, Frank said he couldn't handle the responsibility so Pam moved back in with her sons.

Jacob was almost two when Pam returned. Lupe was regularly in their home and witnessed Pam's interaction with her children.

223

"Pam was very regimental and controlling. She had a set pattern. The kids were in bed by 6 p.m. Pam would spank Jacob if he got up after six. If Charlie or Jacob used certain gestures or words of disobedience, they would have to bite into a bar of soap (Charles was 6 at the time; Jacob 2½). I saw her do that to Charlie when he was 3. He didn't want to take a shower so out came the soap. The boys never used profanity, but were disciplined if they didn't react fast enough to go to bed or take a shower."

Pam was not demonstrative with her sons. There was no holding or cuddling unless for a very short time. When they cried, Pam got irritated. One time, when Jacob was crying in his crib, Lupe overheard Pam say,"I just hate you. I wish you'd never been born."

"Were the boys ever paddled?" Shaun asked.

"Dr. Stick was kept near the refrigerator. The boys were always aware it was there." [61]

Shaun pointed to a large tablet on an easel. "Would you draw the paddle for the jury?"

Lupe drew a rough oblong shape six to seven inches wide and eighteen inches long.

"Did you ever see Pamela use Dr. Stick?"

"Once. Jacob came out of his room after being put to bed. Pam made him drop his pajama bottoms and whacked him. He was past the diaper stage and was struck on the bare bottom."

"After Pam moved back, how did she treat Charles?"

"The same. Pam was sometimes harder on him."

"How did Pam meet Kermode Jordan?"

Lupe recounted the story of the pair meeting in a bar and Pam's excitement over his education and "$120,000 a year job."

"Kermode moved in four days after they met. They were married 1½ months later."

Pam and Lupe, who lived close to each other, still saw each other frequently, four to six times a week.

"Did you spend time with Kermode?"

"Not really. I was introduced to him about a week after he moved in. I didn't like him much. I could tell he had been drinking beer. Kermode drank a lot. A month after their marriage, Pam came to my house because Kermode had gone on a binge and she wanted her kids and herself to get away from his drinking. They stayed with us for a couple of weeks.

"Pam and I returned to her house because we were concerned about Pam's phone stocks, that Kermode might somehow cash them. We snuck in. We were

---

[61] Jacob clarified that Dr. Stick was actually a switch. They're talking about two different implements.

afraid and really quietly opened the living room door. The first thing I noticed was a stench from the house being closed up. Kermode was passed out on the couch. Ten to twenty bottles of liquor were on the floor. Furniture was upturned and the house was in disarray. We hurried and got Pam's stocks. After a couple of weeks, Kermode sobered up and convinced Pam he wouldn't do it again. She took him back. During the time the Jordans lived in San Jose, Kermode went on a lot of drunks. When he was on the wagon he'd confine himself to one or two drinks. But eventually, he would go on a binge that would last anywhere from five to six days. Pam would ask my husband and I to try to find him at the bars. I would tell Pam where he was."

"Would you try to take him home when he was out drinking?"

"No, he was too belligerent."

"What was Kermode's employment record after marriage?"

"He lost a job soon after Pam met him and decided to start his own business. That lasted for one year. Pam remained at the phone company."

Although Pam had always been a strong disciplinarian, she got worse after Kermode. Lupe mentioned Charlie's weight problem.

"I remember inviting them to dinner. We had hamburgers and fries. Charlie was given celery and carrot sticks. Pam and Kermode made jokes about it. They taunted Charlie with, 'Isn't this hamburger good?'"

"Did Jacob have a problem with stuttering?"

"Yes, especially in kindergarten. I babysat him in the afternoon and then half days for kindergarten and all school year. I noticed that he didn't stutter at school or around me. It was mostly when he was around Pam and Kermode who would taunt him and tell him to grow up."

"What was Kermode's relationship with Jacob?"

"Kermode was very affectionate. The school considered Jacob a gifted child. Kermode wanted to mentor and mold him. I remember one incident when Jacob was sitting on Kermode's lap. They were playing chess. Jacob sat on one of his knees. Kermode's legs were open and Kermode would fondle Jacob's buttocks the same way he would fondle Pam when she sat on his lap. Kermode would get real touchy when he was drinking—too touchy—with sexual overtones toward Jacob."

Throughout Shaun's questioning, Bill Aspinwall objected repeatedly. Every time Lupe tried to relate an incident or seemed to become more comfortable on the witness stand, Aspinwall jumped up, breaking her concentration and distracting the jury from whatever anecdote she was recounting. After each objection, Lupe became increasingly flustered.

In July of 1983 the Thorsons moved to Minnesota. The families still remained close, enjoying beach outings and visiting three-four times a year. They talked frequently on the phone.

"We also visited Colorado several times. I still considered Pam a close friend until a year and a half before she was killed."

Once Lupe convinced Pam to come back to Minnesota with her for a vacation. Stepbrother Cameron, Jacob and Charles were with her. That was when during a trip to the beach in the Jordans' motor home Kermode stripped down to his shorts and bellowed, "I am the Power."

"Another time at our house, Pam and Kermode were over for dinner and drinks. Kermode got real drunk and went outside. Pam had to prevent him from taking his clothes off. He still managed to remove some of them."

"Did the parents ever show any affection?"

"Not with the children. They showed it to each other. When Kermode wasn't drinking he was totally different.

"Sometimes Kermode would quit drinking for awhile. Pam would drink but Kermode would not. During one of our Colorado visits I noticed that Kermode had the shakes. I was surprised that Pam was drinking in front of him. I said, 'Let's get out of here. It's not right to be drinking in front of him.' Pam often seemed to taunt him with her own drinking."

When Lupe and her family visited Woodland Park, they stayed at the Jordans. They generally made a ski trip to Colorado and then a couple of other trips in the summer or fall.

In the winter of 1989-90, Lupe and some other friends planned a ski trip to Breckenridge. They were driving a motor home and stopped in Woodland Park on their way. Lupe brought their own food and liquor. She brought all the supplies into the house. Charles barged in and said, "You gotta get rid of this," (referring to the liquor). "He's already drunk."

Charles, who was fourteen or fifteen at the time, "was very scared, terrified."

In 1991, Jacob's thirteenth summer, Lupe took him back to Minnesota with her. During his three week vacation, "Jacob was in heaven, staying up late, going fishing, riding go-karts with a neighbor and playing golf... That trip was the last time I saw Jacob."

Lupe concluded her testimony by saying, "Pam changed from 1983 to 1991 when she was married to Kermode. When I first met her she was smart, bright and in control of her life. Twenty years later, she wasn't the same person. She had lost herself. She had no energetic ability. The life had been sucked out of her."

In what would prove to be the fiercest cross-examination of the trial, Bill Aspinwall questioned every aspect of her relationship with Pam. If Pam was such a terrible mother, how could she have been her friend?

"I liked the Pam that dealt with me, but not the Pam that dealt with her kids."

English is Lupe's second language and knowing that he was confusing her, Aspinwall hammered on tiny discrepancies in her story. He also accused her of being an alcoholic because of her testimony that she and Pam sometimes shared a few beers. Stunned by the fury of his cross, Lupe grew increasingly

bewildered. She had expected the defense to grill her far more extensively on incidents of abuse, which were more numerous than what she'd related, on Pamela's abortions, and to ask about incidents involving Pam's sexual deviancy with Jacob in infancy. That would have laid the groundwork for the testimony of her son, Eric, who later asserted that Pam had molested HIM. None of that was done. Uncertain of her purpose, feeling that she was basically "thrown to the wolves," Lupe grew more frustrated and inarticulate.

Aspinwall questioned her closely about who she had talked to concerning her testimony. On March 17, 1994, six weeks before the trial, defense attorneys had met with her in Minnesota. A week later she had talked to the prosecutor's investigator by phone. She had talked to Jacob on the phone periodically, but believing the phones were bugged they never discussed the case. In October, 1993, she had also visited Jacob in jail for four days. The defense had flown her in to try to jog Jacob's memory.

"Did you tell the defense about the paddling on the butt?"

"I don't remember."

"Did you tell the defense about Charles and the Breckenridge incident involving booze, and about Kermode's playing with Jacob's buttocks?"

"I can't remember. One of the investigators, Mary Ellen Johnson, called and asked about the past."

"Did you tell our investigator that you wanted to 'help this little boy as much as possible?'"

"Yes, I did."

Aspinwall questioned her closely about Kermode's relationship with Jacob. Upset by her remarks about the sexual nature of their contact, Aspinwall raised his voice during his questioning of the time Kermode fondled Jacob's buttocks, as Lupe phrased it, "as if Jacob were his wife." He tried to make the stepfather's actions seem like ordinary affection.

"Kermode did dote on Jacob," Lupe said. "Kermode and Pam both sometimes directed more warmth toward Jacob. Sometimes Kermode would intervene on behalf of the boys and allow them to do more. If he wasn't drunk."

Aspinwall questioned Lupe as to why Charles was held back in third grade. At that time Lupe worked at the school as a volunteer. Knowing Lupe was Pam's friend, both the principal and Charlie's teacher asked her to try to persuade Pam to change her mind.

"Charles didn't need to repeat. Pam's attitude was, 'It's my choice. I'll decide whether my son goes into 4th grade.' Charles did not have a voice in the matter. Pam was very adamant. So he repeated third grade. Nobody told Pam what to do concerning her boys...

"In that family there was a lot of hurtful taunting. Many times I saw Charles almost in tears." Lupe clarified the difference between teasing, which is playful, and taunting which is hurtful.

Aspinwall asked her about her statement to the prosecution investigator

that Pam "treated the boys as though they were her puppets."

"I witnessed some things but I didn't want to talk on the phone about them to the prosecutor's investigator."

Nor did she want to talk to the investigator about sexual abuse. Her feeling was that the prosecution investigator was hostile toward Jacob, so why should she confide anything in him?

After Lupe was excused, Judge Looney called a short recess. Lupe walked out in the hallway, where several spectators and even a reporter expressed commiseration over her rough treatment. Her testimony regarding Kermode fondling Jacob's buttocks and treating him like a wife headlined the evening news.

To this day, Lupe remains bitter about her experience.

"Those boys went through hell. From the incidents related on the stand, you'd think it was no big deal. But it was. I know how mean Pam could be. And Kermode? He was nothing but a drunken pervert. Yet in court you'd think the Jordans were the typical American family. If they were, well, all I can say is God help us."

Shaun also expressed unhappiness over Lupe's treatment. He counted twenty-eight objections during her testimony and told reporters that throughout the prosecution's entire case, the defense had objected only fourteen times.

Shaun told reporters, "I have very little respect for Mr. Aspinwall right now."

Spectators who considered Aspinwall's behavior rude and his objections spurious wondered why Judge Looney did not reprimand him.

"He would object over the silliest things," said one. "It was obvious that all he was trying to do was break the witness's train of thought. I can't understand why the judge didn't tell him to sit down and shut up."

But she didn't. Which allowed the prosecution to succeed in diminishing or totally destroying the impact of one of the defense's key witnesses.

After a lunch break, two of the Gonzales children were sworn in. The Gonzales family had lived with Pam and her children when Jacob was an infant. Sonny Gonzales, a tough looking twenty-six year old, spoke first.

When questioned about Pam's parenting, he said, "She was strict and mean, a disciplinarian. She was real rough on Jacob, who was two at the time. If Jacob wasn't prompt, Pam would grab him and whack him. Charles too. This was a common occurrence. They did something she didn't like and she was instantly mad.

"I saw her discipline Jacob with a ping pong paddle a couple of times on the bottom. She was mean toward me and my brother, too, though I was thirteen at the time and she knew better than to try to hit me. She was bossy, sarcastic,

and demanding, and loved to nitpick, but not all the time. When my sister, who is 2 years older, or my dad were around, she acted different."

Sonny spoke of the boys' fear of their mother, and of Pam's regimentation.

"Was Pam ever affectionate to Jacob and Charles?"

"If everyone was together and Jacob or Charles did something cute, she'd hug them."

In his cross, Aspinwall, who insinuated throughout that perhaps Jacob wasn't being disciplined enough, asked whether Sonny's father had ever hit him.

"Yes. Sometimes my dad used a belt on me; sometimes on my bare bottom."

"Do you feel that you were abused?"

"No." But later Sonny added, "When J.J. got hit he wasn't doing anything wrong. When I did, I was doing something wrong."

Lorraine Gonzales followed her brother to the stand. In a soft voice, she spoke of life with Pam and her boys. When Lorraine was around, she pretty much assumed the role of mother. Upon being asked about the discipline, Lorraine responded,

"I don't remember anything being broken, but they were often spanked. If they didn't respond fast enough, Pam would drag them to bed. Jacob's feet wouldn't even be on the ground."

Lorraine remembered Pam lathering up soap and sticking it in his mouth. She also remembered Jacob crying in front of his mother's door in the middle of the night.

"I got up to help him but he didn't want to have anything to do with me. He just wanted Pam. She never responded."

"How did the boys react to their mother?"

"If she raised her hand, they would flinch and cringe. Pam popped a blood vessel in her finger from spanking them once."

After a short cross-exam, Lorraine was excused.

[Charles] testified that he came home
from school one time to hear his brother
screaming in the bathroom. His stepfather
emerged shortly thereafter. But what
Charles remembered was the look on his
brother's face."As I passed by the bathroom,
Jacob just stood in the doorway pale...
just completely out of it."
Ultimately, jurors might have to stare
into the face of Jacob Ind and determine
if they can see that look still.

~ Columnist Raymond McCaffrey
Gazette Telegraph

Chapter 30

On May 31, 1994, the twelfth day of Jacob's trial, his brother took the
stand a second time. Dapper in a green double breasted suit, white shirt and
print tie, Charles appeared composed, though inwardly he was nervous. Still, he
was determined to tell the extent of the abuse. The previous evening he had
expressed his anger toward his mother to Lupe, calling Pamela a "fucking
bitch." As always, Charles was ambivalent about his mother, sometimes
expressing love and hate in the same sentence. Now he was going against a
lifetime of training, of warnings to keep the secrets. He just wanted to get his
testimony over, to tell the entire truth, as painful as it might be, and then erase
the trial, his entire past from his life.

Tom Kennedy questioned Charles. First he had Charles list all of the
family's addresses since Pamela's divorce from Frank on the easel. He then
instructed Charles to talk about life at each address.

Sebastian Street in San Jose had been the residence they'd shared with Al
Gonzales. There, Charles remembered, Pam had been the chief disciplinarian.
Her weapons had been soap, wooden spoons, and paddles.

"If a bar of soap wasn't handy, she would get the liquid soap under the
kitchen sink and put it in our mouths."

He recalled a particular incident when she had hit him with a wooden
spoon. "It broke. That made her even madder so she continued hitting me with
the cutting board...

"If Mom felt we deserved it, she would hit us. We would get hit for things
like whining, leaving our toys out, watching the wrong TV station or being in
the back yard without her knowing. Even though Jacob was four years younger,
he got the same punishment."

"How frequently were you punished?"

"Consistently. "

"Any time outs?"

"She would lock us in our rooms with the doors shut and the shades drawn. We had to sit in a corner in the darkness. Jacob was scared and would cry."

Tom Kennedy pointed to Woodmont, the next address on the easel. Pam and the boys moved there after she broke up with Al Gonzales.

"I was in the second grade. Kermode moved in a short time later. Jake and I came home from our dad's and we saw a red van with gray stripes. When we came in the door, Kermode was there. Mom introduced us, saying, 'Boys, this is Kermode.' We said, 'Yup.' Two weeks later Kermode moved in. Mom asked us, 'How do you like Kermode?' Jacob was indifferent. I said I didn't like him and Mom told us they were getting married."

"Did things change after Kermode?"

"Very much so."

Everything seemed more separate, independent. The atmosphere was far more covert and secretive. The boys were told, "What goes on in this house is nobody else's business." It was a constant theme.

Kermode took over the punishment and discipline. Before Kermode, the three of them had worked together to get things done.

"At first it was us—Mom, Jacob and me, and then it was them—Kermode and Pam."

The family relationship was colder, more distant. According to Charles, Kermode was the one who came up with Billy Belt and Dr. Stick. Kermode would send Charles or Jacob to get it with instructions as to the proper qualities. It couldn't be dried out, but had to be flexible.

"We would have to pull down our pants and Kermode would switch us. It would leave marks... Billy Belt was a belt that Kermode usually wore. He would say, 'Well, its time for you to get the belt.' We would have to drop our pants, bend over and we would be hit on the backside [buttocks]. Sometimes Mom would use the belt, but usually it was Kermode--and it was a frequent occurrence."

The brown-tooled belt, minus the buckle which was an Aztec calendar, was admitted into evidence.[62]

"Kermode also taught us table manners. If we had an elbow on the table or used the wrong fork, he would stab us with a fork on the arm or the shoulder... The reflexive flinching intensified. If Mom or Kermode would stretch a hand across the table we would back up. We always tried to stay at arm's length so that they would have to lean over and we would have more time to react. Mom would also slap us with the back of her hand. Sometimes she would slap us across the face. Still, Kermode was generally the worst. I didn't

---

[62] This was the same belt that Lupe and Jacob's former attorney, Jim Dostal, had pulled out of the trash during their hurried trip to Ridge Drive.

like his discipline and tried to tell Mom that. She told me to shut up and take it."

Tom asked about Kermode and Pamela's verbal forms of correction.

"They would make fun of us—me basically for my weight and Jacob for stuttering. They would tell Jake to slow down. They would make "You're not worth it," type of taunts. They'd say things like, 'Are you just stupid? Can't you just talk?' Then his stuttering would worsen."

As far as Charles's weight, Kermode put him on a diet of carrots and celery. "He would wake me up at 6 to run. Then I would run again after school."

"Was this positive encouragement?"

"No. Kermode would say I was too fat and 'I don't understand how you would allow yourself to get like this.' He would call me a walrus. He would chase me around the block with the belt."

"Were you afraid of Kermode?"

"Yes."

"Were you afraid of Pam?"

"No."

"Was Jacob afraid of Kermode?"

"Yes."

"Was he afraid of his mother?"

"Yes. Even more so because she punished him more severely than she did me. Her words were harsher. This became more noticeable after she and Kermode were married."

Tom questioned Charles about flash cards.

"Because of my learning disability, it was difficult for me to give quick answers in math. Kermode would use flash cards while I dressed in the morning or after dinner. If I gave a wrong answer, he would slap me and tell me to go back to my room to study it again."

"Did Kermode have outside employment while you lived at Woodmont?"

"Most of the time he stayed at home. Sometimes he talked about going to law school. We would be home with Kermode quite a while before Mom came home from work. She didn't get home until 6:30 or 7 so we were alone with him for several hours after we got home from school."

Tom shifted to Kermode's drinking.

"He was always on the couch asleep. I thought he was sick. When he got up he would be angry and he would generally drink some more. He was more violent to Jacob and me when he was drinking. The punishments were more severe."

Kennedy then approached the heart of the abuse. He said, "Describe for the jury the "Bathroom Sessions."

Charles paused and sighed deeply. This was the moment he had long dreaded, the time that he would have to tell the TV cameras, the reporters, the

whole world, in essence, one of the most painful family secrets.

"It normally happened when we got back from school. We didn't know if it would happen that day or not or who to."

Usually it would happen to one or the other of them. Only once was it both. They could tell by the look on his face what was about to occur. Charles described it as "seeing you in a different way."

"He would basically rape us," Charles said flatly. "He would have us get undressed, tie us so our hands and feet...we couldn't move our hands and feet. We would be tied to the toilet. Then he would get undressed..." Charles choked and struggled for composure. "He would hit us around, though not with an open hand. Then he would start to masturbate, keep calling us names, putting us down, keep on hitting us. Then when he had an orgasm he would hit us and ejaculate all over us. After he was done he would get dressed and say, 'You're so fucking dirty. Go take a fucking shower.' Then he would untie us, we'd go take a shower and he would leave. Sometimes he would watch us in the shower. He would return to his desk and continue doing whatever he was doing before we came home from school and act like nothing was wrong."

Jacob closed his eyes and lowered his head during part of this testimony.

One day school got out early and Charles came home. Jacob usually got home before he did. "I heard Jacob screaming. He was pleading for him [Kermode] to stop. I knew what was going on. I had heard the same words."

Hoping to distract Kermode, Charles went over and turned the TV on loud, which was against the rules.

When Kermode finally came out, he walked very fast over to Charles, hit him, yelled,"What the fuck are you doing watching TV?" and sent him to his room. As Charles walked past the bathroom door, he saw Jacob just standing there.

"He was pale, in shock, completely out of it."

Charles guided his little brother to his bedroom and told him, "Do what you need to do. Knock on the wall if you want me."

"What did you mean by, "Do what you need to do?"

"I would kick the bed and cry for a long time to get the anger out of me. I don't know what Jacob would do but I did hear him cry for a very long time, longer than I would cry."

"When did these sessions begin?"

"Soon after the marriage. Mom was always gone. I was in third grade. Jacob was in kindergarten."

"How often did they occur?"

"At Kermode's whim, though we were afraid that it might happen daily. There wasn't any pattern."

Tom asked for more detail about the rapes.

"We were tied with a rope that was kept under the bathroom sink..." Charles then broke off. "I can't answer any more questions." He asked for a

233

break which Judge Looney granted.

When court resumed, Tom returned him to the bathroom sessions. "Were they related to Kermode's drinking?"

"Not always. Usually he was sober."

"How many times did you see that look on Jacob's face? (Meaning that he was pale and in shock.)

"Several times. I don't remember how many. This was one of the family secrets. There was no need for Jacob and I to talk to each other about it."

As Charles's testimony became increasingly graphic, Jacob appeared to be in another world. He sang to himself, as if to block out the words, and tapped his pencil to an imaginary beat, seeming to transport himself away from the events at hand.

Tom directed Charles to the family's next residence, Maree Court.

"Sometimes Kermode would hide behind the doorway and scare us when we came in. I never knew why Kermode would be home. Sometimes we would get a bathroom session. The bathroom sessions were more intense and sporadic. Jacob and I were constantly nervous and scared."

Tom asked about any changes in discipline at Maree Court.

"It was only the belt. No more switches."

This was the time that Kermode instituted a calendar upon which he monitored Charles's weight, as well as such disciplines as Jacob's groundings.[63]

"Kermode wrote down my weight every day. He'd watch me weigh myself and then taunt me. 'Only lost five pounds today. I think you need more exercise.' I would feel ashamed."

The calendar was also used to keep track of how many times Charles and Jacob got the belt so Kermode could increase it each day.

"For example, if we got hit twelve times on Monday, on Wednesday we would get twelve plus five for our infraction. We each had our own separate numbers. The most I ever got was thirty two. That was for looking at Kermode the wrong way."

"Was your stepfather drinking that day?"

"No, he was relatively sober. Mom stood in the doorway, watching--and grinning.

"Generally, at that time Mom and Kermode would have a six pack after work each night. Then Kermode would have his binges on hard liquor--Jim Beam, gin, vodka, Jack Daniels or Cutty Sark. He always went on binges at Thanksgiving and Christmas. The shortest was a week. The longest was 2½-3 weeks. This routine occurred at all the places we lived."

---

[63] That was another piece of evidence I found that was rescued at the last minute. It was never introduced into court.

234

As Charles reached puberty the bathroom sessions dwindled. They stopped altogether before moving to Colorado. Jacob's were also less frequent, but they still occurred. Whenever one was imminent, Kermode would take off work early to be there when Jacob came home from school. There was a one hour difference between the time Jacob and Charles returned from school. Charles always knew what had happened because of the "look" on Jacob's face.

"Did you and Jacob ever have privacy?"

"No. Mom and Kermode could walk into our rooms or when we were in the bathroom any time they wanted to. It bothered me a lot. The bedroom wasn't so bad, but the bathroom was a total invasion of privacy."

Charles testified that he'd only tried once to tell his mother about the sexual abuse. That was on Arabian Street, right before they moved to Colorado. During that time, Kermode and Pamela's marriage was in turmoil. One day Jacob came home and saw Kermode passed out on the living room. This was during a 2½-3 week binge. Jacob called Pam and she came home. Pam took him and Charles to the guest room downstairs. She told them she was thinking of divorcing Kermode. "I'm tired of his drinking."

"Jacob said, 'Yes, get rid of him.' I said, 'No give him another chance -- I still blame myself for this--maybe he'll change this time.'"

Then Kermode got the job with Digital. The company told them they were going to move either to Boston or Colorado. Finally, they got the news. Colorado would be their new home.

◇ ◇ ◇

Because of scheduling conflicts and court maneuvering, Charles's testimony was interrupted for more than a day in order for Jacob's psychiatrist and court appointed psychologist to take the stand. When Charles was called back to the stand, Tom Kennedy hurried him to Colorado. The deliberate pace of Tom's questioning seemed to have been shaken. He was not as detailed as he had been over the previous two sessions.

The belt buckle from Billy Belt was introduced into evidence.

"Were you ever struck with the buckle?" asked Kennedy.

"Yes, on the bare bottom. The belt was doubled over and we were struck with the buckle end. We were also struck on the back of the legs and the lower back."

Several report cards belonging to both boys were introduced. Then Tom zeroed in on the family's five years in Colorado.

Charles reiterated that the sexual abuse had dwindled for his younger brother. Despite the fact that by this time Jacob was telling his attorneys, "I may have been molested by my mother," and me that he HAD been molested by her, Tom never explored the possibility that the real danger no longer lay with Kermode. Rather, it lay with Pamela.

Tom asked about the physical abuse in Colorado.

"It was less severe and frequent. They still used the belt and their hands. More often we got lectures, nitpicking parties. They would tell us how stupid our activities were. Generally, they would gang up on one of us. During dinner they would humiliate us and put us down. Jacob got more of the lectures."

"What was his reaction?"

"He'd sit there but not be there. He'd look at them but tune them out. He'd get slapped for not listening."

"How often?"

"Whenever they wanted. It was constant putdowns. Every morning we would be criticized about our hair, the way we dressed. We felt degraded, that we could never satisfy them because the rules changed every day. One day it would be, 'Take care of the dogs first and then the cats.' The next day, it would be reversed."

"What consequences did you receive when you disobeyed them?"

"Lectures and punishment."

Tom asked about their assigned chores, which they completed "while Mom and Kermode drank beer and listened to the news while we cleaned. Mom made her own bed. Sometimes they would help shovel the driveway... If the chores weren't done right we had to redo them all. After I moved out, Jacob had to do everything."

"Why didn't you tell your real father or go live with him?"

"He was passive and not really caring. It was not a close relationship. When we had the custody discussion at jail on the night of the murder, Jacob was scared, terrified."

Tom moved Charles along to the months before the murders. He related an incident concerning Jacob and football. As usual, Woodland Park's freshman team had lost. Afterward, Kermode yelled at him."What the hell were you doing out there? You weren't doing your job." Kermode decided to show Jacob how to block. He took a three point stance. Kermode charged and knocked him back a foot or two.

"What was Kermode's drinking like in the months preceding the murders?"

"It never really stopped. We always had alcohol around. The binges were separate, spontaneous. We never knew when he would go on one."

Charles then related his version of the Lofthouse Incident in August 1992, which had precipitated his moving out.

Tom returned to Jacob's "Look."

"The last time I saw it was in 1992. Mom and I had gone to a national forensic tournament in Fargo, North Dakota. We left Jacob home with Kermode. When we returned, I saw it again. Jacob looked horrified, scared, extremely pale. Mom had called home a few times and Kermode was drunk again. I know Kermode and Jacob got into a fight over the car keys."

236

Tom asked, "Why didn't you tell about the sexual abuse?"

"After the first bathroom session, I vowed I would never tell anyone. Kermode said he would snap our necks or we might never wake up again. Telling is still too painful, humiliating, and embarrassing. I don't ever want to relive it. I try to keep it out of my head."

"How do you feel about Jacob?"

"I have mixed emotions. I was taught to defend my family. I love him as a brother, but I hate the decision he's made. It's made me too scared to have a relationship with a woman or to make plans to participate in school events because I never know if I'll have to come back to Colorado... I feel a lot of anger for taking my mother away from me. I don't miss Pam. I don't miss her at all. But I knew my mother before Kermode. She could be warm, caring, and loving. I admired 'Mom.' By the time we moved to Colorado, she was cold, hateful, spiteful, and seemed not to care. The change was gradual, but over time she became 'Pam' to me. Still, I saw 'Mom' a few times, like when we were at the Forensics Tournament and when I decided to leave after the Lofthouse Incident. I always hoped that if she just left Kermode, the old Mom would reappear."

Tom finished his questioning.

Onlookers felt that he had pretty much discredited Kermode, but Pam was another matter. While cruel, she often seemed more an onlooker than an active participant in the abuse, which was demonstrably false. Afterward, Charles expressed frustration over the defense's failure to pull out more incidents of abuse regarding his mother.

Bill Aspinwall stood to cross examine. He began with Charles's therapy. For nearly nine months following the murders, Charles had gone to DSS counselor Renae Delacroix twice a week.

"Why didn't you tell her about the sexual abuse?"

"I did tell her what happened, but I said I wasn't going to talk about it."

Aspinwall asked about the interview Charles had given to Detectives Falton and Adamovich on Christmas Eve 1992. "They adamantly asked questions about abuse. You only mentioned chores and put downs."

"When I really realized that Pam and Kermode were dead and couldn't come back to hurt me I felt I could tell about the sexual abuse. I remember Mom telling Jacob, 'What goes on at home stays at home.' We both lived by that."

Aspinwall asked about the various family doctors and about physicals for football. Charles stated that, like Jacob, he did not shower with the other football players.

Charles said that the first person he had really told about the incest was his godmother, Lupe, before he left for college in August of 1993. She had asked him about sexual abuse in the weeks following the murders, but he had denied it.

"I also told Mary Ellen Johnson after telling Tia. In fact, I told her on the same day."

"How did you know Mary Ellen?"

"She got involved and we became friends. Then she became an investigator and I told her about the sexual abuse. I did not go into detail with Lupe or Mary Ellen or my therapist...The bathroom sessions were only one example of the sexual abuse... Sometimes when we were sitting on toilet, he'd hit us with the back of his knuckles on our faces and body."

Aspinwall started on a theme that would continue throughout his cross-- Charles' callousness and mercenary nature.

Five days after his parents' deaths he had taken the Ram to Utah to see a friend. There he wrecked the car. Aspinwall asked Charles why he had asked Ralph Morris, a caseworker at DSS, how he could get his parents to give him a car after he'd moved in September 1992.

"I never said that. I did tell Mr. Morris about [the Lofthouse Incident], saying that was an example of what was going on in the house. I thought that would be enough to get Social Services to investigate."

"What is the value of the Jordan estate?"

"I don't know."

"How much insurance money have your received so far?"

"Seventeen thousand dollars."

Aspinwall questioned him more closely about the others who were contesting the estate, which included Kermode's son, Cameron, stepson Christopher Turrentine, and his only daughter by blood, Justine Jordan. Pam's portion of the estate consisted primarily of an insurance policy. Kermode had been the beneficiary, followed by Charles and Jacob.

"Who gets the money from your mother's estate?"

"The lawyers probably," Charles said to the amusement of the courtroom. If convicted, Jacob, of course, would receive nothing.

Aspinwall insinuated that Charles was being vindictive toward his brother because of his ambivalent feelings. When Charles expressed anger at Jacob for what he had done, Aspinwall implied that he was being selfish.

"How do you feel about coming to Colorado to testify?"

"I hate it. I feel like I'm becoming a novelty item. It's not a price I want to pay."

Aspinwall brought out more photos—of Charles's eighteenth birthday, of Jacob in hippie clothes, of a camping trip, one of Jacob's football games and of Jacob throwing a shotput. He also showed various photos of Kermode and Pamela, cousins and uncles, and for whatever reason, the family cats.

Disturbed by what he considered a cheap trick, Charles said, "I feel it's an invasion of privacy to show family photos in court." When Aspinwall continued his display, as if this provided proof of the Jordans' exemplary parenting, Charles countered, "There were very few happy times."

Throughout, Aspinwall was aggressive and short. By his manner and the wording of his questions he made it very clear that he considered Charles's

version of events bogus. As the day wore on and Aspinwall hammered away, Charles became increasingly wooden, as if he were a puppet. Eventually, only his eyes moved, following Aspinwall. When the prosecuting attorney got too close, Charles visibly stiffened. He didn't appear to be afraid of his adversary. It was more as if he'd erected an invisible barrier. Easy to imagine him reacting similarly with Kermode and Pam—becoming very still the way an animal does when it senses danger, and measuring the pair with his eyes, calculating their moves, figuring out how to survive their latest salvo.

Repeatedly, Aspinwall asked Charles to elaborate on earlier answers, sometimes for no discernible reason. "I started seeing a therapist a week after the murders... The last time I was beaten with the belt was when I was seventeen... The last time the belt was used on Jacob before I moved out was when Pam hit him for forgetting to put away his chess set..."

And once again, "Why didn't you tell your mother about the sexual abuse?"

"She would have been horrified over the fact that she had brought in a man who sexually abused her sons."

"Why did you urge your mother to stay with Kermode after she mentioned divorce?"

"I was afraid of what might happen if Mom wanted to divorce him. Even with divorce, I didn't think I could escape Kermode."

Dr. Frank Barron, a licensed clinical psychologist, testified about Jacob's state of mind. Barron specializes in adolescent evaluations for those in the mental health field, as well as lawyers, judges, and sometimes the district attorney.

Barron, who with his long hair parted in the middle looks like an aging hippy, explained that he had evaluated but did not treat Jacob. The first time they met was at the Zeb Pike Detention Center two days after the murders. Over the following year Barron also administered several standard psychological tests.

Following the murders, Barron had found Jacob to be severely depressed and suffering from intense anxiety.

"He had feelings of helplessness, of obsessive worry. He felt a constant sense of nervousness and impending doom that he couldn't really identify. It was from an ill-identified source, and all pervasive."

Jacob's thought patterns were confused. When he pondered possible problems he couldn't reach any firm conclusions. He had "information process deficiencies." Jacob over interpreted his potential for harm. He was always on the lookout for danger, scanning his environment for it. He had a "constant expectation of harm." When Jacob was emotionally aroused, meaning

experiencing fear, anger or sadness, he would withdraw and shut down his feelings in order to neutralize or avoid his source of stress. Later tests found Jacob feeling jumpy, anxious, and depressed. He didn't believe that he could control his life or protect himself and suppressed his feelings as a way of coping. Because of his background, Jacob tended to have a narrower range of emotions than the norm.

On cross Bill Aspinwall tried, largely unsuccessfully, to ferret out more detail about the murders.

"Did Jacob leave the front door open each night?"

"I assume so." To most of Aspinwall's questions, Barron answered, "I don't know."

The prosecutor asked, "Can the defendant tell right from wrong and form "intent?""

"Yes." Dr. Barron agreed that Jacob was not legally insane.

"Jacob is a rather fearful child, who lived in a constant expectation of harm. Essentially, there was nothing he could do to alter what was going to happen to him. I consider that to be helplessness."

"Did the defendant tell you he was sexually abused?"

"He said he doesn't remember. I asked at each interview. On one occasion he said, "I can almost see it but I can't.""

"Did you talk to family members?"

"I didn't talk to Charles. Jacob's father and stepmother weren't really helpful since they hadn't seen him much for 6 years since they moved to Colorado."

Barron went on to say that Jacob was constantly stressed and overwhelmed by feelings of helplessness—which was defined as feeling frightened but not being able to do anything about it. After his parents were killed, his helplessness was relieved, which "speaks to defects in his reality testing. However, one incident doesn't negate a general feeling of helplessness."

On redirect, Shaun asked, "Can one have fear and still try to control his environment?"

"Yes."

"Can you give us an example of Jacob's helplessness?"

"Yes, his inability to determine when he would receive physical punishment. Fear and helplessness mesh. Fear creates a state of overwhelming paranoia about what might happen to you. If you do not have the tools for coping, nothing you can do will make any difference. Helplessness doesn't always mean inactivity or immobility. Sometimes you'll develop tactics that will cause you to be left alone--such as dressing weird, being loud and obnoxious."

"Do sexually abused children tell about their abuse?"

"Typically they will hide that abuse because of shame. Repressing is common, particularly in young males."

After lunch, Dr. David Caster, Jacob's psychiatrist, took the stand. Caster,

240

with clear blue eyes and a neatly trimmed beard, stated his credentials. His practice is geared toward dysfunctional families and abused children. He has treated adolescent murderers.

Caster had seen Jacob on four separate occasions. His instructions had been to gain as much understanding as possible as to why the killings had occurred and to explore the possibility of impaired mental condition or insanity.

"Jacob does not have a deficiency," the doctor stated. "He can determine right from wrong."

When asked to define abuse, Caster explained, "Abuse is always psychological, but it has many other components. The purpose is to denigrate the child, as in the bathroom sessions. In accidental abuse the child is not allowed to vent frustration or anger. Intentional abuse always contains anger as a component. It is consistent, persistent, and its goal is denigration."

"What is psychological battering?"

"An intentional, persistent, sadistic attack on a child's person, his soul, with the intent to control his thinking, feelings, and actions. It always demeans the child and that is its purpose." Caster paused. "Prisoners of war know about this. Jacob knew about it too."

Caster went on to say that there is a significant difference between a battered woman and a battered child. "With a spouse, it is one on one. When it is a child/adult that is not the case. If the child says, 'I'll call the police,' the adult replies, 'They'll believe me, not you.' A child's sense of reality is, first and foremost, the home. It's not the school. It's not the church. It's the home. Therefore, a battered child—even battered adults—do not flee their abusive environment because they feel there is no escape.

"It's because the control is so intense that people in this situation...lose their ability to make logical, rational decisions."

"What is the impact of battering on the self-concept of a child?"

"Children believe that everything that happens around them is because of them. The abuser also tells the child, 'This is because of you.' The child loses his perspective as this message is pounded into them. In Jacob's case, it was driven into him that he was a homosexual and that homosexuality is evil and that he was perverted."

"Why don't these children see a way out?"

"Fear. If Jacob did try to escape and it didn't work, there would be hell to pay. If he tried to run away, police would bring him back and believe his mother."

"What was the extent of psychological battering to Jacob?"

"Everyday life in the Jordan household was torment for the boys. Pamela was a sadistic mother who stood by and enjoyed Jacob's torment. Her lack of support was akin to putting a knife in the back, turning it and enjoying the process... It is very rare for a child to hate their mother, but Jacob did." Caster concluded, "I don't know why Pam was the way she was. That is what I would

like to know."

"What was the defendant's attitude toward his stepfather?"

"Kermode knew that Jacob was bright and there was an intellectual challenge between the two of them. They shared an interest in philosophical and political interests. There were times when he was gentle with Jacob and Jacob appreciated that a great deal. But Kermode could be explosive." Caster related the Lofthouse Incident. "Another time after Charles moved out, Kermode lost his car keys and blamed Jacob and rammed him into the barbecue grill."

"What was the effect on Jacob of Charles's leaving home?"

"He was more depressed. The weight loss, lack of hygiene, and sleep problems are all symptomatic of a deepening depression. He felt envy, anger. Charles had been a buffer. He felt he had to stay away from the family more and more and suffered increasingly from panic attacks."

"What are some of the concrete effects of abuse?"

"Such a child has severe issues of self-esteem. He feels like a jerk, a freak and will associate with children of other dysfunctional families. He exhibits a marked vigilance and a narcissistic attitude wherein he believes that everything that goes on is his fault. He keeps secrets. After Charles left, Jacob's level of safety decreased. He became increasingly aware of what his life was like."

Caster termed Jacob's abuse as "lifetime," and stated that as early as the age of seven he and his brother had considered killing to be a way out.

"Jacob suffered almost daily anxiety attacks. He was hyper- vigilant and had a chronic concern for his safety. Jacob also has a severe limitation in his development of coping behaviors. That points to the fact that the abuse happened early on. Also, the younger the child and the more severe the abuse, the more he or she represses the information. Early on, Jacob had no recollection before the age of nine. Over the last eighteen months some memory has returned."

"What triggers repression?"

"Fear of annihilation or rejection."

Shaun asked about the David Mabie tape.

"Jacob saw their relationship differently than David Mabie did. Jacob tried to hold onto that. Jacob was concerned about Charles, the last (caring) person left, his lifeline. He reacted in a desperate way based on misinformation. Such a reaction is related to hyper vigilance, wherein a person is excessively alert to even the possibility of danger."

When Aspinwall cross-examined Caster, the doctor elaborated on his earlier mention of Gabrial. Jacob felt betrayed by Major and by what people like David Mabie, whom he'd considered a friend, said at the preliminary hearing. "Jacob told me that it was important to pay Major, believing that he would keep quiet."

"Did the defendant "court" Gabrial Adams to murder his parents?"

"No. He simply asked him."

"Did you ask Jacob whether sexual abuse ever occurred?"

"His response was, 'It's impossible for that to have happened because it would have been my fault and I would have fought and I would have killed him.' My colleague, Dr. Barron, asked about sexual abuse on several occasions. Jacob said it would have been his fault."

"Did Dr. Barron talk to Charles about sexual abuse?"

"No. I talked to Charles approximately two months after the murders as part of Jacob's evaluation. From Charles, I better understood what was going on around the time of the killing. I was concerned about Jacob's mental state."

"Did Charles volunteer information about sexual abuse?"

"No. And its not surprising that he would not."

Aspinwall asked about physical punishment.

"Pam and Kermode would alternate hitting with the belt. Pam sometimes used her shoe because of arthritis in her hands. Sometimes she just watched when Jacob was being beaten. To not intervene in a child's beatings is sadistic."

When asked about the lack of bruises, Caster said, "The boys were seldom hit on areas of their bodies that were not covered."

On a visit to Jacob one month after the murders, Dr. Caster noted evidence of self-mutilation.

"Isn't it inconsistent to say physical abuse occurs but there is no physical evidence?"

"No. The abuse was ongoing. We had no information on when the last beating was."

Aspinwall asked about the "family secrets," and why the boys wouldn't tell. "Because Jacob felt he wouldn't be believed. Secrets were kept from authority figures. Charles did tell me he talked to DSS."

Aspinwall showed Dr. Caster exhibit 171, a letter from Pamela to Miss Miller, one of Jacob's junior high teachers. In the letter Pam complained about Jacob being picked on at school. Other kids had been punching him, stabbing him with pens and Pam wanted it stopped. 'Jacob has been instructed to inform us of inappropriate behavior,' she wrote.'To ignore physical abuse... we as parent do not instill that type of mentality.'

Aspinwall tossed the letter on his desk as if he'd just destroyed the defense's entire case. Caster remained unperturbed.

"Pam was intensely interested in her sons' education. Her self-righteous comments had nothing to do with her actions. The attitude of abusive parents is that "this property is ours." Nobody messes with their children unless they, the parents, say so. In addition, abuse victims are frequently scapegoats. In this case Jacob was being scapegoated by other children."

Aspinwall began painting several scenarios where corporal punishment or beating might be okay. Caster didn't agree. "Once a kid has reached the point where reasoning takes over, spanking should cease. There are alternate methods."

During one of his sessions with Jacob, Caster asked him to describe himself. His words:"Clumsy and a jerk." Trying to open up memories, Caster asked Jacob "to envision himself as a child."

Jacob saw himself at the age of [three], the same as in the naked picture Pamela took, watering the lawn. As he imagined this, his heart raced, his chest hurt, and he experienced an anxiety attack.

"Jacob had a long standing history of anxiety between three-six p.m., which included palpitations. People who are under the fear of assault become hyper vigilant and often suffer such attacks. Jacob was persistently terrified of future assault. He would never know when he was in danger and so always perceived himself to be at risk."

Day thirteen of testimony ended.

These contrasting arguments (as to whether
Jacob killed his parents out of hatred or
because of years of abuse) lead one to
view the snapshots of the Ind family like a hologram,
one of those postcards that show, say, the New
York City skyline, and then if tilted slightly,
a picture of the Statue of Liberty in the background.

~Columnist Raymond McCaffrey
Gazette Telegraph

Chapter 31

On June 3, 1994, day 15 of Jacob's trial, Grace Wallace testified. In early March Shaun and the team's private investigator, Jeanette Shick, had interviewed her at her home in Cottonwood, Arizona. Both Shaun and Jeanette had agreed that her testimony was the most powerful and moving they had ever heard. When she spoke of losing her daughter and of her agony over the murders, Shaun and Jeanette were in tears. But Grace was extremely volatile. Would she become so distraught she would disrupt the proceedings? Would she say too much? Not enough? She was still understandably protective of her daughter, blaming Kermode for everything, and if there was a connection between Pamela's adult behavior and her childhood, Grace was not about to reveal it. Shaun had to walk her carefully through her testimony. Two days previously she had threatened not to testify at all. Her health couldn't stand it. The defense wasn't paying enough attention to her. Did they have any idea of the psychic toll this was taking?

"I can't even get Shaun to return my phone calls!" she complained.

Grace, a slight, attractive woman with high cheekbones and grey hair done in typical "granny" fashion, was helped to the stand. Grace's health problems dated back to the 1960's. During that time she'd had three back surgeries plus a bout with cancer in the 70's. Subsequently, she'd suffered a multitude of ailments. Currently, she had to deal with a bad heart. After settling into the witness chair, Grace smoothed her blue and white print dress and surveyed the jurors through silver-rimmed glasses. She appeared fearful and hesitant, though family and friends knew how quickly her demeanor could change. When she stiffened her back and raised her chin, look out. That Grace, the parent that Pamela had so dreaded, could be cold, dismissive and concerned only with her own needs. In the days preceding her court appearance, another daughter had succinctly summed up the children's relationship to Grace with these words, "She was never a mother to us."

Shaun began his questioning by asking Grace about her daughter's marriage to Frank Ind. Grace spoke of helping Pam after the couple separated. During her visits, she would buy Pam groceries and try to lighten her burden by

driving the boys to school and helping with their baths.

After Pam and Frank divorced, Grace recalled her first meeting with Kermode Jordan.

"When they picked me up in the airport, Kermode made my skin crawl. That night they took me out to dinner to a fancy French restaurant, even though I don't care for that kind of food. Kermode ordered for me. He also ordered a bottle of wine to toast my arrival. He started drinking wine and went through four bottles during the meal. Pam and I had some, but he drank most of it."

"Did you ever see any interaction between Kermode and Jacob?"

Between sobs, Grace nervously fidgeted with a tissue. She had difficulty getting through much of her testimony.

"Yes. Jacob would pull on Kermode's moustache. Kermode would stroke Jacob all over, including his buttocks, smile, and get a hooded look in his eyes. Then he would put Jacob down and go immediately to the bathroom. It was sick."

"What was Charles's relationship with Kermode?"

"Charlie always had a desperate look in his big black eyes and he would wring his hands. Kermode mocked Charlie. When I visited in 1981 he would drive the boys to school. Charlie wanted to tell everyone something. Kermode would stutter like Charlie and wouldn't let him finish.[64] Charlie threw a ball at Kermode and Kermode's face became livid. He said, 'That's always your way of settling things.' I only saw his hatred of Charles."

"The following year, 1982, did Charles visit you in Rockford?"

"Yes. He was living in San Jose. His plane was supposed to arrive in Chicago, but Kermode insisted that he get off in Denver. Pam told Charlie not to get off the plane until Chicago. The airline was advised of a lost child and by the time he got to us, he was shaking and crying. He said,'I can't go back. They'll beat me. They'll beat me.' I said Kermode wouldn't do that."

Grace testified to another visit in 1988. The family had moved to Colorado and the Wallaces had arrived to celebrate Jacob's eleventh birthday. As soon as the kids came home they went to their room. Thinking this peculiar, Grace tried to talk to Charles. He said, "This is where they want me. I hate Kermode." Pam came up the stairs then and Charles shut up.

Grace's recollections largely revolved around her oldest grandson. Again, Jacob seems to be the invisible one, always floating on the edge of any gathering, trying to keep to the shadows. She told the court about a four day fishing trip they and Kermode and Pam had taken in the motor home. Kermode was half drunk the entire time.

"I never saw him without a bottle of beer or wine." When Pam took over driving, Kermode swore at her for going too fast. After they stopped at a

---

[64] She must have meant Jacob. He was the stutterer.

wayside, Kermode commented to Grace, "Your daughter is wound up like a clock."

"I said, 'No, Kermode. It's more like a time bomb.'"

Several times Grace dropped her head into her hands and sobbed loudly. In between, she managed to relay a series of small incidents—such as a time when Jacob was forced by Kermode to eat green peppers, even when he couldn't tolerate them, and a phone call that interrupted dinner. It turned out to be a survey of high school students. One of the questions was, "Do you believe in God?" Charles, who took the call, answered, "No," which pleased Kermode but upset Grace, who is religious.

"I said,'Pam was raised a Christian.' Kermode said,'What is a Christian? Do you consider yourself a Christian?' I was angry so I excused myself and went upstairs. When I returned, Kermode's elbow slipped off the table he was so drunk. I said, 'I've watched you over the years brainwash my grandchildren and abuse Pam. You're nothing but a drunken old bum.' I went upstairs. Kermode came after me real fast, as if he was going to "get" me. I was frightened. He doubled his fists, leaned close and said, 'Hit me, hit me.' I put my hand on his chest to keep him away. Pam pulled him away. Kermode said, 'The establishment killed my mother. Killer! Killer!' We left as soon as we could get our things together. Jacob pleaded for us not to leave."

Increasingly distraught, Grace turned to the jury at one point and sobbed, "Jacob has a good heart. Please help him. Please."

Concerned about the effect the grandmother's testimony might be having on her own heart, Judge Looney ordered a fifteen minute break.

Upon Grace's return she told about visiting the family during the Geoffrey Dahmer trial, which fascinated Kermode. He seemed to revel in every gory detail. Sickened by the talk, Grace retreated outside to the deck.

"Kermode followed, switching the subject to seventeenth century pedophiles. He asked me if I thought Charles was a homosexual. I asked, 'Why do you say that?' and went back into the house."

"How much time were you allowed to spend with Jacob and Charles during that visit?"

"Not much. Pam was always around. I played cards with the boys. Kermode followed their every move with his eyes."

"What sort of a daughter was Pam?"

Grace choked and twisted her tissue. "She was a loyal, loving daughter. After she married Kermode she became a different person. Each time I saw her she became more relentless with the boys. I tried to get her away from him. He had taken her soul, her mind. Quiet civil war was going on in that house. I wanted to take those kids out of there so badly but I knew when they returned they would get it even worse."

So Grace was added to the list of those who realized something was wrong, and had wanted to "do something," but did nothing. Her testimony also revealed

247

how little she really knew her grandsons—and how isolated she was from them—whether by Pamela and Kermode's design or circumstances.

After another break, Bill Aspinwall's turn came. Upsetting or badgering an old woman would not win him points with the jury, so Aspinwall only asked a few questions.

When Grace was dismissed, she again pleaded with the jurors to spare her grandson. Shaun and a son-in-law rose to escort her from the stand. Turning to the jury, Grace cried, "Help Jacob!" Then she tried to pull away from her "body guards." She reached toward her grandson, crying, "Jacob! Jacob!"

Sheriff's deputies rushed forward and removed her from the courtroom. *The Gazette Telegraph* reported that Jacob watched her "with a blank expression on his face." Jurors also later remarked on his seeming indifference. I knew better. After the incident, Jacob broke his pen in two, just the way he had the day that I'd told him during a conversation in the attorney's booth, "Yes, it's true, Jacob. Your mother never loved you."

◇ ◇ ◇

Grace was followed by a parade of teachers. The first was Cindy Meyer, who taught Jacob geometry. Cindy described Jacob as very studious, hard-working, energetic and enthusiastic, the kind of kid who would get "extra help when necessary." He would often sit near her. Cindy had an extra chair next to her desk for students to sit in and talk but Jacob preferred resting on the trash can. When asked why, he replied, "This is where I belong. My life is shit."

On fifteen or twenty different occasions he told her he was very unhappy at home, but didn't supply many details.

"Close to the time of the murders did you see any changes in Jacob's attitude or personal hygiene?"

"His attitude was basically he had no energy. He was subdued, depressed. He didn't give any specifics but he said he had difficulty sleeping. He told me he couldn't sleep at night, but he was vague about why. He said, 'I have a lot of thoughts going through my head,' but he didn't elaborate. Sometimes he would fall asleep in class. Two to three weeks before the incident, his hair was dirty and he wasn't clean smelling."

On cross, Cindy said, "I did ask him on several occasions why he was unhappy. He wouldn't say. At home, he stayed in his room a lot. That's where he went because his parents didn't bug him there." In an interesting choice of words, she added, "Jacob said he felt safe there."

Nobody asked the geometry teacher what might have caused Jacob to feel "unsafe," or why she hadn't questioned Jacob more closely as to why he believed he might be harmed.

Victor Smith, Jacob's drafting teacher, was next. In his late forties, Smith

is tall and muscular. Dark-rimmed glasses accentuate a plain, honest face. What little hair he has is brown and wavy and touched with grey.

Smith met Jacob through Charles, with whom he had a close relationship. He had coached Charles in football. Smith initially met Jacob when Jacob attended his older brothers games.

During football, Smith worked closely with Charles in his capacity as coach. Charles spoke of stress in his family life. Smith had been privy to part of the Lofthouse Incident, in which Kermode had yelled at Charles for wearing an earring. After the fight, the eighteen-year-old was walking along the road and Smith picked him up.

"Charles was really upset and mad at Kermode for embarrassing him in front of his friends. I talked with him for half an hour. Charles said Kermode drank a lot. He said that he and Jacob and Pam were going to leave Kermode and he felt good about it. Charles felt very alienated from Kermode."

He spoke of Jacob's behavior in drafting on the day of the murders. He had gotten in trouble and Smith had threatened to call his mother.

"Jacob became visibly upset. He did not want me to call her. I still called, but I told Pam that I had been pretty hard on Jacob and requested that she pamper him a little bit. Jacob cried after the phone call. He was nervous and emotional."

On cross, Gordon Dennison asked, "How did Jacob react when you spoke to his mother?"

"He was very attentive as to what I said to Pam... Pam had been a very supportive parent. Jacob made comments about his parents. He said he wasn't getting along with them and wished they were dead."

Another startling revelation that passed without comment. On re-direct no one asked why Smith hadn't followed up on the remark or questioned Jacob in more detail.

Dennison asked when Jacob said he wished his parents were dead.

"I'm not sure. Other students had been talking about why their parents had grounded them. Jacob made the comment in the context of that statement. I said, 'You don't really mean that,' and the subject was dropped."

Smith hadn't seen anything unusual in Jacob's demeanor on the day of the murders.

Dennison asked Smith to further clarify their conversation following the earring incident. In a line of questioning that could have opened up worlds of possibilities to the defense, Smith said, "I asked Charles if he was abused. He said yes and that he was getting ready to move out. Charles did not like Kermode. He said Kermode came down on him too hard and wanted him to be a better student. I asked if he was beaten. Charles said no, that he didn't consider it to be physical abuse, more like browbeating. If they didn't come home with the right grades, that sort of thing. Charles felt that Kermode was never satisfied."

Later on, Smith also spoke with Pam. Pam said they were moving out of the house because of Kermode's drinking and he offered his support.

"She appeared concerned, but not angry, though I did see her get irritated with Charles. After he moved out, Jacob was playing football, Pam was watching and Charles was talking to her. I came up and asked how she was doing. 'Well it's been kind of rough,' she said. I offered to help. 'If you need anybody to talk to...' Apparently, she knew that Charles had been talking to me about the situation and just said that she had a lot of friends."

In another statement that wasn't addressed and might have held a clue to Pamela's parental involvement, Smith said, "She was concerned about who Charles was telling things to."

Following Smith's testimony, the jury was dismissed and a statement from Beth Parentice, "an unavailable declarant," was read. Beth is one of Pamela's sisters, and had refused to come to Colorado, declaring that she was mentally incapable of testifying about Pam's death. Judge Looney expressed astonishment that an out of state judge had declined to force a witness to testify.

"I've never had that happen before," she said. "Miss Parentice is a rich and powerful woman."

The defense wanted her testimony "to rebut the prosecution's recent fabrication of Charles Ind that Charles never told any family member of sex abuse."

Beth had told the D.A.'s own investigator that Charles said Kermode struck them and sexually abused them. Beth believed that Pam knew about it and may have talked to Lupe Thorson about it.

Since much of the D.A.'s case was predicated on the fact that the boys were lying about the abuse, the statement of a witness hostile to the defense could have been extremely damaging. In rebuttal, Aspinwall brought up the fact that Charles said he did not tell any family members and that no report had been given by Beth Parentice to the defendant's attorneys. Shaun, who couldn't have had any detailed reports concerning Parentice or anyone else until mere weeks before the trial, responded that the defense had been relying on the D.A. investigator's interview. As to whether Beth would have possibly made up something favorable to Jacob, the answer lies in Beth's own statements. She considers Jacob Ind to be an "odd kid who liked to talk about torturing small animals and shooting them." In her opinion, "He is predisposed to being a psychopath and I would hate to see him get out on bail." Privately, she went further. She told family members, "I hope Jacob has to spend the rest of his life in jail and Gabrial Adams gets the electric chair."

250

Lupe's twenty-two year old son, Eric, testified in the afternoon. Eric, dark-haired and green-eyed and possessing a Minnesota cadence to his speech, hadn't finished high school, but was a successful carpet layer with his own business. Eric had called me in the weeks preceding the trial to confess that Pamela had molested him. I considered this to be important information because Jacob at that time had been hinting broadly that his mother had sexually abused him, but why would anyone believe such an outrageous charge? In the days before the trial, Jacob had started giving details as to his mother's molestations. Many would consider his hesitant revelations suspect. "Yeah, he just wants to save his butt so he's making things up." But if an entirely independent witness emerged with corroborating testimony Jacob's assertions might take on the weight of truth.

Friends of Jacob were excited about Eric's testimony. Jacob and Eric hadn't spoken to each other in years so there was no way the incident could have been planted, just as there was no way Charles's testimony could have been molded following Jacob's incarceration. Three different young men were telling tales of sexual abuse, and two of them—Eric and Jacob—were pointing the finger at Pamela. Eric Thorson's testimony could provide the first strong glimpse into what kind of creature Pamela Jordan really was.

Eric's deposition was taken outside of the jury's hearing. Lupe had told the defense about Pam fondling Jacob as a baby, but Tom had never questioned her in the courtroom about that. Eric had also told Tom and Shaun about seeing Pam "wash" her sons' penises. That incident was never brought up either, leaving the door open for precisely the ruling that followed Eric's deposition.

Eric related Pam's bathroom visit, which had occurred when he was fourteen.

"She played with my penis with her hands. I was totally shocked. I didn't know what to do. Then she asked me to touch her on her chest. I did. The entire incident lasted maybe 5-10 minutes until somebody called for her and she walked out."

"What was your reaction?"

"I was terrified of her. She's the kind of woman to be terrified of."

Eric did not tell anyone until three or four years later, around 1990. He confided in a doctor at the hospital and the doctor told his parents.

Upon cross, Eric testified that he had been in a rehab hospital for drug/alcohol related problems.

"I was there for a week. I was disturbed. There was no drugs or alcohol involved. I had started stealing from my parents to buy things for my girlfriend, who was the wrong kind of girl. I took rings, perfume, things like that. I took them to pawnshops with the intention of getting them back. My parents thought I was buying drugs."

251

Eric clarified that he had only been molested by Pam, not raped. "I never told my mother. I was ashamed and Pam was her best friend. Mom just let it go after the doctor told them. She didn't pursue it."

Because the defense hadn't laid the groundwork for Pamela being a pedophile, Eric's testimony was ruled irrelevant, and the jury wasn't allowed to hear it.

After the jury was brought in, Eric was "officially" questioned. He testified that Pam was a "very hard lady. She never allowed the boys to have any fun. It was just home or school, with nothing in between."

"How did Pam discipline the defendant?"

"She would hit Jacob with the belt for minor offenses... Pam was nice to adults, but she was different toward children. She exercised total control. You had to be an adult around her."

"Did Pam change over time?"

"No. I was always afraid of her. Jacob and Charles were always afraid of her."

Upon cross exam, Bill Aspinwall asked a few questions. Then he slipped in the knife.

"Does your mother have an alcohol problem, Mr. Thorson?"

"No."

Aspinwall didn't allow Eric to elaborate on his answer.

Following Eric's anti-climatic testimony, two more teachers were called. One, Richard Palmer, testified that he'd taught Jacob in sixth through eighth grade. Palmer couldn't understand why Jacob was forced to repeat eighth grade. He remembered an incident when Jacob became upset because he couldn't complete an assignment.

"Jacob cried and said he couldn't get a paper done. He asked me to tell his mother that the paper could wait. He was clearly upset because of his mother's possible reaction. I had a short conversation with Pam. This was our only contact... Jacob didn't talk much about home and there were no signs of physical abuse."

Carla Dolan taught Jacob Honors English. She also taught Charles during his freshman and sophomore year.

"What was Jacob's behavior in the weeks between September-December 1992?"

"Jacob was more outgoing than his brother. He was pleasant, no behavior problems, never sassy, not shy. If anything Jacob tended to be too talkative. He talked with his girlfriend, Stephanie Endsley, too much. That increased over time, though Jacob and Stephanie weren't your typical boyfriend/girlfriend. There were no longing looks, that type of thing. They just talked a lot."

252

Shaun questioned Carla about a journal she had assigned in the months preceding the murders. Students were supposed to write answers to questions such as, 'What Makes You You?' Jacob responded, 'His liberal views, clothing, his music, the fact that he played chess and football.' 'What Will You Be Doing in Five Years?' 'College.'"

In an entry penned five weeks before the murders, Jacob responded in typical Jacob fashion to Dolan's assignment, 'Reflect On Your Weekend.' 'I lost my self respect, I felt low and down. I never got it back and that pleases me.'

Dolan saw nothing in Jacob's journal to cause alarm.

On redirect, Shaun asked the English teacher whether she observed any changes in Jacob in the weeks preceding the murders.

"Yes. After Parent-Teacher conference in November, his distraction was noticeable. His clothes were unkempt, his grades were going down, he wasn't paying attention or functioning well. He was thinking but he had something else going on. It was a combination of being distracted and being intense. I knew things were not wonderful at home and that Charles had moved out."

"How did you know? Did Charles hint about problems?"

"It was more than a hint. Charles would say, "It's really bad at home.""

Every week employees from Department of Social Services, Woodland Park High School and the local police department meet to discuss problem teens in the system. With all the comments the boys were making about abuse and the changes in Jacob's behavior, it seems incredible that Jacob Ind was not discussed. Perhaps we'll never know. Shaun never followed up on that line of questioning and later, when individuals started pressing the appropriate agencies for access to various agency records, they were either denied access or told there were no documents involving either Charles or Jacob Ind.

Estate Attorney Bill Brown was the day's last witness. Following Jacob's conviction, a member of the sheriff's department provided the real motive for the Jordan murders. "Greed. The estate was valued at a half-million dollars." Interesting assertion, but it is not backed up by the facts. Shaun and Aspinwall led Brown through a tedious recitation of the Jordans' debits and assets. Even had the boys' inherited Kermode's portion, rather than Kermode's blood son, Cameron, there was no huge life insurance policy or estate. In the end, just as Charles predicted during his testimony, the attorneys got most of it.

Are people fed up with defendants
who blame everyone except themselves
for their crimes? Or are stories about
the effects of various forms of abuse
actually making people more sympathetic
to those who claim they are victims?
The answer for Jacob Ind will only come
with the verdict.

~Raymond McCaffrey/columnist
Gazette Telegraph

Chapter 32

Jacob's trial entered its final phase. The defense called Ann Tyler as its last witness. Tyler, a Utah psychologist, is an expert in child abuse and post-traumatic stress syndrome. She had recently been a witness at the Menendez trial, involving the two California rich boys who had murdered their parents. To prepare for her testimony, she had interviewed Jacob for several hours over the course of three days. Jacob had not been impressed, saying, "She treated me like a kid."

A professional looking forty-some year old with black hair and a gaunt face, Tyler was soft-spoken but firm. She testified that Jacob had told her he had taken non-prescription drugs and, according to an article in the Gazette Telegraph, "played a potentially lethal game of Russian roulette in an attempt to kill himself during the four days before he killed his mother and stepfather.

"Jacob didn't get any counseling, so the pressure continued to build. His options continued to die. When you are in a debilitating state, the way you see the world is so fearful anyway, you lose all ability to think you can get out of it... Jacob held onto a rescue fantasy that his brother could somehow get him out of there... When his brother left, that was gone.

"I can see how it happened that this boy fell through the cracks. The family system denies there's a problem. The community system denies there's a problem.

"Jacob also denied a problem. He preferred beatings to family arguments because beatings were swift and the verbal arguments lasted for hours."

All the warning signs of depression—sleeplessness, poor hygiene—were virtually ignored by school officials.

"And it's a kill or be killed, a strike or be struck. It's a stay in prison and die—and Jacob had been contemplating suicide since fifth grade—or get out of prison and live.

"The core of all abuse in not the scars you can see... It's the scars an individual carries inside."

Tyler labeled different types of abuse—isolation, terrorization, denial and corruption.

"But denying emotional responsiveness is the most terrible abuse of all. When a parent says, 'I don't care about you. I don't love you.' Refusing comfort when a child is crying or hurt, that is absolutely the worst thing you can do to a child."

Tyler gave a mini-lecture on how emotional, physical and/or sexual abuse affects various age groups.

—0 to 2. "A child's primary task is to learn how to trust. If they don't, they can't attach to anyone. When a baby is rejected or degraded the message they receive is that they are unlovable. When a child is terrorized, as Jacob was, he reacts with fear. The message from that is, 'I'm not safe.' Such a psychological response changes a developing brain. A child will become fearful in certain situations and perceive certain situations as dangerous that "normal" children will not. When a parent never allows a child to do anything other than what a parent wants that retards spontaneous and unique development. All the signs of deep-seated abuse are there in Jacob's case."

Tyler defined "corruption," as in pornography, the idea that it was okay to hit, to get drunk and generally set a poor example in the Jordan household. Nor, according to Tyler, was Jacob taken care of healthwise. No doctor was provided when needed.

"The ability to keep themselves safe is not there in children who have been psychologically maltreated. The entire controlling, rigid family system provides an extreme form of emotional neglect."

—Ages 2 to 6, when Jacob was being raped and beaten and emotionally battered, mark the beginning of autonomy, an increasing sense of one's self.

"If a child is not allowed autonomy, he will doubt his own capabilities. Verbal and thinking skills, his emotional maturity will all be adversely affected."

—Ages 6-11. "A child learns to relate to the outside world. His self-esteem develops. Trust and autonomy continue."

—Ages 12-18. The time span when children re-negotiate family roles, test limits, wrestle with concerns about adulthood and determine who they are, via their sexual and gender identity.

Tyler explained how Jacob's life had shaped his being.

"When a child has been treated as Jacob Ind was mistreated, the results will be that the child will live with an all-pervasive fear, which will affect the way he reacts to everything. He will experience terror so profound that he will fear for his life. This terror is emotional, as well as physical, as in he will fear he's going crazy.

"He will withdraw and suffocate any normal emotions in order to adapt, physically or mentally, to the environment.

255

"He will suffer from isolation, internal as well as external. He will not be in touch with who he is. He has an inability to relate. His feelings are severed. He is in a state both of confusion and hyper-vigilance. His environment is one of total unpredictability, so he is always in that confused and hyper-vigilant state... When a child is not rewarded for good, it is axiomatic that he will eventually cease doing good. Abused crawlers have already learned to scan their environment. Unlike their surrounding siblings, they don't move to explore. At school these children have problems concentrating. They spend all their energy trying to stay safe."

After a lunch break, Tyler discussed patterns of family violence and how they applied to the Jordan household.

—Isolation. "A child perceives that he does not have choices outside the home. Jacob had a very secretive family, as has already been related. Grandmother Grace told how she could never be alone with the boys. Grandparents are often perceived by the child as rescuers. When this is not allowed, the child can feel really alone."

Jacob and Charles had told Tyler that the family was going to move to somewhere even more isolated.

"Jacob was not allowed to have many friends. What friends he had were troubled—dealing with similar problems. In such an enmeshed family system as the Jordans, the family stuck together, no matter what. There was always an unwritten rule never to go outside the household, adding to Jacob's all pervasive sense of physical and emotional isolation.

"As a child enters his teen years he becomes more independent. He wants to make his own decisions and test limits. In such isolated, closed families as Jacob's, there is no negotiation of roles. During family fights, Jacob couldn't say anything. He would turn everything off, not even paying attention to the subject of the argument. Charles had counseled him to 'Let it go in one ear and out the other.'"

Having a girlfriend is another part of adolescence. When Tyler asked how close he was to Lila and/or Stephanie, Jacob confessed that they had never even held hands.

"Jacob doesn't know how to deal with closeness."

—Built up pressure was yet another contribution to the murders.

"An abused child is very fearful. Things happen that they have no control over and the pressure builds. When the buffer, Charles, left, Jacob lost hope of any protection. That's when the suicide attempts really came into being. When Charles asked Counselor Greathouse for help and it wasn't forthcoming, the pressure built inside Jacob. His options died. He lost all ability to think of how to get out of his situation."

—Weapons in the home are yet another commonality among children who kill their parents.

"And there is always that threat of violence. That is the way the stepfather modeled handling an argument—subtly using fear and intimidation against a child. When drunk and threatened, Kermode was the one who taught the boys to turn to guns or knifes as a method of solving problems."

—The Target Child. The role of the child is vitally important.

"Jacob was the scapegoat. Charles was the buffer. With him gone there was nothing or no one to protect Jacob."

—Finally, there is denial, not only by Jacob's parents, but by the community.

"There was a total lack of intervention. Many people who could have intervened didn't."

The Utah psychologist spoke of Jacob's options.

"He talked to David Mabie, who had been in foster placement. Jacob felt that when he went back to his parents—which he considered inevitable—matters would be worse. He could run away, but he believed he would be returned. Or go to the police, who once again would send him back home. Jacob's conclusion: Kill or be killed."

"Why didn't Jacob talk about the abuse?" Asked Bill Aspinwall during cross.

"Child abuse and secrecy go hand in hand, so I did not find it strange that Jacob didn't tell. There is so much fear, secrecy and threats surrounding any such family that it is very rare to get a direct verbal report. Some children are so badly abused their personalities actually split. They may remember their daytime persona, for example, and nothing about the evening, when sexual abuse occurs. Others disassociate. When the molestation is occurring, they mentally transport themselves to another world. Or they repress memories, particularly when the abuse occurs at a very young age. Abused women often don't get help until around forty and their unconscious mind finally tells them it's safe to remember."

When asked about therapy for parricides, Tyler replied, "Some youngsters have been followed for up to four years after their release. The data indicates that they had no further altercations with the law."[65]

---

[65] Lynn Bliss, the courtroom observer who so graciously allowed me to use her trial notes, observed, 'Aspinwall kept asking Tyler seemingly irrelevant questions about sexual abuse. He tended to focus on an extraneous issue and give it more importance than it deserved in an attempt to throw a verbal smoke screen over something else... The prosecutor asked Tyler questions regarding corporal punishment to establish her bias. Tyler doesn't believe a child should be hit. It is apparent she strongly believes that Jacob was sexually abused. Jacob has all the classic symptoms, including a racing heart, palpitations, anxiety, school problems—failing, poor peer relationships, aggressiveness... The psychologist has a tendency to try to mitigate Jacob's actions whenever possible.'

257

"If the defendant really was sexually abused as a young child, as you claim, where are the medical records?"

"Mr. Kaufman told me the pediatrician in San Jose no longer has the records."

For three more hours Aspinwall attempted to poke holes in everything from Tyler's credentials to her judgement.

The defense rested.

◊ ◊ ◊

Department of Social Services' caseworker, Ralph Morris was called as the prosecution's first rebuttal witness. Morris testified that a caseworker is required by law to investigate all forms of abuse—physical, sexual, emotional.

"Though emotional abuse is poorly defined by the Children's Code... The investigation usually begins with the victim. Then we talk to the parents. We look for injuries, talk to doctors or refer the child to a doctor. There is a Child Protection Team in Teller County. Citizens meet once a week to review DSS cases. This includes information from DSS plus police reports, doctors' reports etc. The team consists of representatives from schools, a retired foster mother, law enforcement, a DSS intake worker and supervisor."

No one ever directly asked Ralph whether Jacob's case had ever been discussed. All involved officials later denied that it had been. Others in the know swear that it most definitely HAD been addressed several times, and that they have the documentation to prove it.

Ralph, who has a caseload of some 30-40 clients, testified that he doesn't remember talking to Charles.

"I believe Charles came in sometime during August or September. He was a walk-in rather than an appointment. That's why his name isn't in my appointment book." (Other DSS workers say even walk-ins are logged.)

"He inquired about emancipation. I thought Charles's question was unusual since most kids know that as soon as they turn 18 they can leave home. Charles seemed naive. We talked "around" the issue of why. I did advise that it would be difficult trying to go to school and work and he wouldn't have medical benefits. I also suggested he try to work things out with his parents."[66]

According to Ralph the Jordan family was not in DSS records until Charles started receiving food stamps in November 1992.

Tom Kennedy did a short cross.

"Does DSS keep a sign-in sheet at front desk?"

---

[66] This contradicts Charles's testimony that he told Ralph about the Lofthouse Incident, which would have involved physical and emotional abuse. If Charles's account is true, Ralph broke the law by not investigating the eighteen-year-old's allegations.

"Yes. I didn't check to see if Charles's name was on it."

"Would that have given the reason for his visit?"

"Yes."

Ralph said he had checked the records from June to December 1992 and found no mention of Charles Ind.

Kennedy made the point that Ralph's job was to protect those under 18 and Charles was over 18. He then asked Ralph to recount his meeting with Charles.

"It was a brief conversation, 20-30 minutes. Since Charles was already getting out of the home, I didn't pursue any possible problems. Nor did I ask about younger members still at home."

"Does DSS investigate on the basis of only "conflict in the home"?

"Yes."

Soon after, Ralph Morris was dismissed. Those familiar with what really happened regarding Jacob's case were not surprised that DSS and the Child Protection Team had escaped close scrutiny. "That's just the way things work in Teller County," said one.

Only with Jacob they very nearly got caught.

◇   ◇   ◇

Ralph Morris was followed by a youth supervisor from Zebulon Pike Detention Center, who testified that he had found no bruises, cuts or rashes on Jacob during Intake. No, he hadn't personally done the physical. On the question, "Is child abuse suspected", Jacob answered yes. "Has it been reported?" Jacob said, "Yes, to the school and police." According to the supervisor, Jacob was referring to the day of the murders, though it was never clarified whether Jacob specifically stated that.

Twenty-two year old Michelle Mendez took the stand. A tall, attractive young woman with flowing brown hair and an abrupt manner, Michelle had been Charles's roommate at the time of the murders. Mendez testified that she and Charles often discussed his family situation. He told her his brother was being mentally abused and cited such things as name calling. Charles said, "I hate my parents. I wish they were dead."

Michelle also directly contradicted Charles's alibi, saying that he was NOT home the night of the murders.

"I went to bed about 8 or 9 p.m. Charles left and came back really late. He had to crawl over me to get to his room because we were living in a very small cabin. He came home at 2 or 3 or 4 a.m. The following morning Charles seemed very nervous. He said he felt sick and stayed home from school. He smoked a lot and hovered around the phone. I made some comment about he was smoking

259

like a chimney. Though Charles usually told me everything he wouldn't tell me why he was nervous."[67]

Michelle testified that she had moved out of the cabin on the day after the murders. When she returned to retrieve more of her things, she found Charles and teacher/friend Lucinda Reed there drinking. Judge Looney had earlier ruled that Reed's condition, as well as the pair's relationship, which Michelle described as sexual, was irrelevant, so she was not to allude to either in court.

Whether admonished by the prosecution or not, Michelle plunged on. Mendez, who later stated that she was desperately trying to let the world know that Charles, rather than Jacob had masterminded the murders, was asked to characterize her roommate's truthfulness.

"I wouldn't believe Charles even under oath."

Though Looney had warned the prosecution to stay away from all mention of insurance and a new vehicle, they failed to stop Mendez from talking about a conversation she'd had with Charles--about insurance and a new truck.

"Charles called me at the fire station where I volunteer after he had testified and asked if I saw him on TV. Then he said, 'I lost $54,000 to my brother.' He also told me he bought a truck, a Ford Ranger."

Shaun immediately stood and requested a mistrial.

"Either that or that Ms. Mendez's entire testimony should be stricken from the record."

Looney denied the mistrial but struck Michelle's testimony and ordered the jurors to disregard it in its entirety. This incident reminded observers of the previous one involving pepper spray. Again the saying was repeated, "A bell once rung can't be unrung." The prosecution had been able to damage Charles's credibility without having to endure any cross examination concerning Michelle's veracity or motivation. The *Gazette Telegraph* headlined,'Witness Contradicts Charles Ind.' As far as Looney's instructions to the jury, one juror later stated that Michelle's testimony had loomed large in their decision to convict Jacob.

One of Pam's co-workers from Care & Share took the stand. The co-worker had never seen Pam parent the boys at home, but she believed that Pamela had a good relationship with her sons and was proud of them.

---

[67] At the time of the murders, Michelle was keeping a diary. In the diary she detailed Charles's behavior throughout this time frame. Such entries might be considered important since they would call into question Charles's alibi and his possible role in the murders. According to Michelle, the sheriff's department knew about this diary. An officer asked to see it. She said, "No." Incredibly, no one ever again expressed any interest in the diary or even referred to its existence.

"Pam talked about Charles and Jacob at work and seemed responsive to their needs. I never saw her behave in an abusive manner or be harmful to Jacob, who worked for us for a few days over the summer."

The co-worker saw the family as normal but acknowledged that Pam was strict, expecting her sons to be where they were supposed to be and do what they were supposed to do.

The co-worker finished by saying, "I would have trusted her with my own kids."

◊ ◊ ◊

Prosecutors called Tomie Justine Jordan, Kermode Jordan's thirty-two-year-old daughter from his first marriage, to the stand. Justine, a plump attractive blonde, testified that her father was loving, fun, kind and had never sexually abused her.

"He taught me how to play the piano, play hide and seek and I never had a problem with him... He was not violent with me."

Justine also said, "Kermode and my mom divorced when I was two years old, so contact between us was minimal. In the early years I did spend time with my father. He visited once every six months until I was nine when he began another relationship. After that I saw him once every two years, but we talked on the phone in between times."

Quite a contrast to Kermode's relationship with his blood son, Cameron, who visited his father on weekends and for a month during the summer. Justine lived on Mariposa Street in Long Beach, which was only a forty-five minute drive from Kermode. She didn't offer an explanation for his infrequent contact.

Justine was shocked when asked whether Charles Ind had ever told her about the boys being tied to the toilet and sexually abused.

"Tied to the toilet?" Justine echoed. "That sounds like a B-rated movie to me. Tied to the toilet."

Justine also stated that during a meeting with Charles following the murders she asked Charles twice whether he had had anything to do with the murders.

Soon after, Justine was dismissed.[68]

Justine's mother, Elizabeth Bell, followed. Elizabeth knew Kermode from 1957-65. She characterized him as a wonderful husband and father.

"Kermode, or Kermie, as I called him, was intelligent, fun, and creative... I considered him to be peaceful at home."

---

[68] Lynn Bliss wrote in her private notes, 'Justine's testimony carried overtones of anger. She gave expanded answers, more than the question called for and not always related to the question. Perhaps has her own agenda.'

261

During the course of my investigation of Ridge Drive, I had read many of Elizabeth's letters to Kermode. They detailed an extremely unhappy marriage, filled with infidelity, charges of drunkenness and pleas for Kermode to pay attention to baby Justine, act like a husband to Elizabeth and as a father to his child. That certainly was not the Kermode Howard Jordan Elizabeth painted some thirty years later for Jacob's jurors.

◊ ◊ ◊

Sgt. John Falton, one of the sheriff's deputies, was recalled and asked about the Aztec belt buckle that had been part of Billy Belt.

"We found the belt buckle in Jacob's bedroom on a chest of drawers on the left side of the room, either in it or on it. It wasn't with the belt."

One question that has never been answered was why the detectives would have initially placed any importance on a broken belt buckle. Jacob was never interviewed by the police so he certainly hadn't described it to them. He had mentioned being beaten with a belt, but he had not specified which one. Nor had he mentioned anything about the belt buckle, which had been broken and separated from the belt prior to the murders. Jacob maintained that sometimes he had been hit with the buckle. "But only by accident. They usually hit us with the leather part."

In May of 1993 Jacob asked me to find the buckle. All personal belongings had been packed away in huge boxes within weeks of the murder. (By whom we never knew. That would have been teacher/friend/self-appointed executor Lucinda Reed's purview. Nor were these mystery packers ever asked whether they, who spent far more time at Ridge Drive than the defense, found any potential evidence.) I dumped the packing boxes out several times and went through everything in Jacob's bedroom searching unsuccessfully for the buckle-- whereas the prosecution had understood its importance within hours of the murders.

John Falton was asked whether a Bible had been found in the house.

"Yes. In Jacob's room. It was closed."

"Any pornography?"

"No."

"Any naked pictures of Charles or Jacob?" Aspinwall asked in a mocking tone.

"No."

Shaun and Tom looked at each other. I had personally handed over several pictures of a naked Jacob. I fully expected them to produce them the following day when court re-convened. They didn't.

◊ ◊ ◊

262

When David Mabie was called in yet again to testify, Shaun finally became aggressive. A nervous David verified that his dad was in the courtroom "watching over everything I say."

Shaun made a very big issue out of David's earlier testimony in which he said, "Foster care doesn't always help kids." He and Shaun went over the question, referring to it on the computer screen several times. David appeared confused and uncomprehending of what was being asked of him. David had often told Jacob that foster care was bad, though, according to the prosecution, David thought foster care was terrific. Shaun tried to get David to clarify which version was correct. He was unsuccessful. David seemed unable to grasp the simplest question.

Shaun finally asked whether David had a lot to protect.

"Yes."

Kaufman finished his cross by asking whether David was afraid he would be charged in this case.

"Yes," David replied.

◊ ◊ ◊

Closing arguments. Bill Aspinwall spoke first.

"This is not a case about parricide, the killing of your parents. Those are words that make murder palatable."

Aspinwall said child-behavior experts had not found that Jacob suffered from a mental illness or defect often associated with severely abused children. Nor did he have scars, bruising, or other physical signs of abuse.

Aspinwall told jurors to discount the question of abuse. Instead they were to ponder the legal definition of self-defense, which states that a person must believe he or she is in imminent danger of death or serious bodily injury.

"It's imminent. It's going to be happening soon. Not being spanked. Not being put in a closet. Not being slapped in the face. You have to be afraid of being killed before you can take someone else's life.

"The self defense theory is further eroded because Ind asked one classmate to kill his parents and hired another to actually commit the murders. This has to be the most straightforward case of first-degree murder that there is. There is evidence upon evidence upon evidence."

Aspinwall spoke for nearly two hours. He didn't discuss the evidence point by point. Instead, he left that up to co-prosecutor, Gordon Dennison, who would speak following Shaun Kaufman.

Courtroom observers believed that Shaun had to appeal to both logic and reason. "Self defense" would clearly be a difficult verdict for the jury to arrive at. Shaun would have to go over the evidence, each defense witness's testimony and weave them together in a seamless mesh. Yank those twelve men and women into Jacob's world. Jurors would have to see, taste, touch, hear and feel

Jacob's terror. Dr. Caster referred to him as a prisoner of war. Prove it. Ann Tyler testified that such a badly abused child would have a difficult time distinguishing the reality of imminent danger from the perception. Show the jurors exactly what she meant. Make them believe.

Shaun began, "This is a case about terror. About a lifetime of terror. You were shown only glimpses of the years of abuse done to Jacob and his brother. It would be impossible to present every incident that occurred in the boys' lives.

"Could you bring a fact from twelve years ago into this courtroom to save your neck without somebody criticizing it?" Kaufman said loudly. He slammed the prosecutor's table with Jacob's leather belt, causing Aspinwall to jump and angrily object.

"I don't think so. It's not easy. It's not easy to dig into the fabric of someone's life. The fabric that held together Ind's life was flawed.

"If you see the case as a snapshot of December 17, 1992, you may see things one way. You may see the blood on the wall. You may see the fact of human suffering and death. Human suffering and death is what you'll take back in the jury room with you... But your life and your family's life is far more a movie than an isolated frame.

"The complexity of Jacob Ind's life and what he went through and what his family was about is what is necessary for you to carry into the jury room.

"Self defense should be measured on the totality of Jacob' Ind's life."

In closing Shaun spoke of being in the delivery room with his wife when she gave birth, of bringing his own children into the world and how precious each baby's life was. He asked the jury not to throw away his client's life. "I leave Jacob Ind in your hands now," he said before sitting down.

It was a moving but conventional closing. There seem to be several standard arguments and tricks taught young attorneys in law school. As unfamiliar as I was with the courtroom, I recognized "putting the client in the jury's hands." And while Shaun was an energetic orator, too often he spoke in generalities. His entire summation might have taken two hours and appealed almost entirely to emotion. He'd seldom touched on fact. His argument was lopsided. Spectators had the feeling that it, like so much of the trial, appeared to have been slapped together.

Which left co-prosecutor Gordon Dennison. He went over the evidence piece by piece. Between him and his partner they had covered all the bases.

While Dennison had often seemed a bumbler during the trial, he gave an effective rebuttal. First, he dramatically allowed Jacob's own words to incriminate him. He played the Zeb Pike tape wherein Jacob asked David Mabie to "get" Gabrial. Those words, where Jacob was into his tough guy persona, were the only ones the jury ever heard him utter. Did he sound like an abused child or a punk?

After Jacob's voice had sunk in, Dennison detailed all the steps Jacob took leading to the murders. Dennison also used a standard courtroom tactic—the "not" argument.

"Ind was NOT in imminent danger when he hid behind the master bathroom door as Adams allegedly pulled the trigger on a .22 caliber handgun, shooting Kermode Jordan as he slept." Dennison ran through a series of "nots," showing how Jacob wasn't in any sort of danger during the entire sequence of events.

"In the ensuing battle Kermode and Pamela Jordan were chased around their room with the gun, and when the bullets ran out, with a large hunting knife," Dennison said, inaccurately but effectively acting out the murders.

During that struggle, Dennison continued, "Ind held the bathroom door closed, preventing the Jordans from seeking shelter from their attacker. When he did open the door, Ind assaulted his parents with a heavy dose of pepper mace."

Dennison even staggered around the room in a dramatic re-enactment of the Jordans caught in the throes of bear spray.

"After assaulting his parents with the spray, Ind assaulted them with bullets from a.357 caliber handgun. It was those bullets that ultimately killed the Jordans."

Dennison implored the jurors not to ponder lesser criminal charges.

"You have two choices. Guilty of first-degree murder or not guilty of anything."

And (God) said, Take now thy son...
Whom thou lovest, and get thee into the
land of Moriah, and offer him there
for a burnt offering...

~ (Genesis 22:2)

Chapter 33

Friday, June 17, 1994. O.J. Simpson is arrested for the murder of his wife and her friend. Jacob Ind is found guilty on all counts.

The jury had been deliberating for several days. As each hour passed without a verdict, Jacob's supporters kept hoping for a hung jury. We knew things hadn't gone well in the courtroom, but we were hoping beyond hope. One person would hold out. There were eight women on that jury, eight women with children. Surely, they wouldn't condemn a child.

After seventeen hours of deliberation, the jury reached its verdict. Around nine o'clock in the morning, Jacob and his family were assembled and the verdict read. "Guilty of two counts of murder in the first degree."

Jacob was the lead story on all the area television stations. Reporters, many of whom were privately sympathetic, noted that when the verdict was read, Jacob had looked more bored than upset. As each juror was polled, he smiled wryly and later murmured, "Good job," to Bill Aspinwall. Displaying a monumental shallowness, the media commented on Jacob's lack of emotion. As if he would break down and plead for mercy before the very people who had just slit his throat. How many of us would give our enemies the satisfaction of knowing they'd just delivered a mortal wound? Why did people think Jacob would? He had spent many months building a wall around Vulnerable Jacob. It was tall enough the public couldn't peek over it. Eventually, it will be so impenetrable no one will be able to dismantle it. Why should he want them to? Sweetness had gotten Jacob nowhere in life. Sweetness and vulnerability will not serve him well in prison, just as it had served him poorly at home. The jury's decision merely reinforced what Jacob had long been taught: There's no percentage in exposing one's soul.

"I guess my feeling about this case is that it's too bad somebody didn't react until it was too late," Tom Kennedy told television cameras. "Jacob Ind is a good kid. He just never had a chance.

"The problem is the law doesn't recognize the situation a child finds himself in. Self-defense is the bar-fight scenario, not years and years [of abuse] where you finally explode."

Tom seemed on the verge of tears. Reporters stated that one of the attorneys had been crying, but it was Shaun, rather than Tom, who wept in his

wife's arms for Jacob and for his own children whom he had evoked during his closing statement.

"This is not a life sentence," he said. "It's a death sentence. He will die there."

Bill Aspinwall agreed that the case was a tragedy, but felt that the abuse was overstated. In a comment loaded with unintended irony, he said there were times that witnesses described the Jordans' lifestyle as "typically American."Citizens of Colorado Springs largely applauded the verdict. In a letter to the *Gazette Telegraph*, Ryan Talkington wrote that the sentence wasn't harsh enough. 'I would prefer to see Jacob Ind strapped to a chair, electrodes attached to his limbs, and someone throwing a switch that would send millions of volts through his miserable body. That would have been a more fitting punishment for this punk.

◇ ◇ ◇

Immediately, those who loved Jacob began playing the "Why" game? Why hadn't the teachers been discredited? Why hadn't they been read the statute detailing their duty to report abuse? Why hadn't they been backed in a corner and ordered to explain why they didn't feel the boys' stories of emotional abuse, alcoholism and physical abuse were serious enough to be reported? Why hadn't Pam's molestations been used? Why hadn't the photographs been shown? Why hadn't the attorneys pressed Charles harder on his mother's cruelties? Why hadn't they discredited David Mabie? Why hadn't they called all the defense witnesses? Why hadn't they dragged out every incident of abuse that they'd had at their fingertips?

Then the "What if" game. What if Jacob had testified? That was a tricky question. Which Jacob would have taken the stand? Combative Jacob, Limbo Jacob, Emotionless Jacob, Gang-banger Jacob, Indifferent Jacob? The only Jacob that would have made a difference to that jury would have been Tearful Jacob, and that Jacob is not going to appear for anyone. As Shaun said, "[The jurors] would have expected him to sit up there sobbing. He has gone beyond sobbing."

Even from the grave, Jacob is heeding his mother's message to toughen up. He's not going to cry for people who are judging him, or around other inmates who will tear him apart if they sense weakness, and he isn't going to cry around those who love him. Why would Jacob even want to? Once he started he would probably never stop and there is no safe place for him to unload. Besides, tough guys don't cry and he's in a place with a lot of tough guys who had a lot of adults who gave them similar soul-killing messages.

Now that Jacob's future is prison, probably the worst thing that could ever happen to him would be to become "emotionally healthy." Here on the outside that seems to be our goal. Inside, it's ludicrous. Jacob should get in touch with his feelings when he's being raped by some Bubba? When a bunch of prisoners

are beating the shit out of him? When the guards are tormenting him? He's better off being Dark Jacob, keeping all the pain in the shadows and turning that blackness outward. Most inmates aspire to both physical survival and emotional death. For Jacob to achieve those goals he must obliterate all that is lovable and good and bright about himself and become bigger and badder and meaner than Pamela and Kermode and the baddest motherfucker in jail. And Jacob can do it if he's inside long enough and he's given enough pain and terror and he's not knifed in the showers or his throat isn't cut or he isn't thrown off one of the tiers or the guards don't club the life out of him. Tears won't do Jacob any good now. Perhaps they wouldn't have done him any good in front of those jurors either.

◇ ◇ ◇

Jacob's former attorney, Jim Dostal, once said that despite the flaws in the justice system, something almost magical happens during deliberations. Get twelve people alone in a room and somehow in 95% of the cases, they return the proper verdict. Dostal, a taciturn man, was almost poetic as he talked about juries. But he was wrong. Every day in every state across the nation poor people are sentenced to life imprisonment or receive a death sentence with only the most rudimentary attempt at justice. Trials might last a day or two, the defense is drunk or incompetent, and nobody involved really cares—not the judge, the jury or the attorneys. Maybe the defendant's grandmother or girlfriend, if he's one of the few who actually has someone who loves him. Maybe the defendant himself, if he's not too screwed up on drugs or stupid or institutionalized or emotionally numb. Jacob was actually lucky. His case took six weeks. He had public defenders who tried. Maybe they should have been better prepared, or more combative, or called more witnesses, but he received a better trial than many. Which doesn't speak very highly of our criminal justice system.

But maybe in the end, nothing would have made any difference.

Because it all came back to the jurors. I believe that case was lost the moment those twelve were chosen. Jury selection may be an art form and it may be voodoo, but whatever it was, that's where Jacob's attorneys erred. What they had in that courtroom was not a jury of Jacob's peers, but of Pamela and Kermode's.

Since the trial I have talked to some of the jurors and I found them to be compassionate, caring people. But those were the ones who remain bothered by the verdict. I doubt that the rest give the case or its defendant even a passing thought.

Jacob equates adults with punishment and he is right. Those twelve jurors gave Jacob the thumbs down, the way the emperor gave the thumbs down in the coliseums, the way Pamela sentenced him to death on the day he was born and the way Kermode set the process of his execution in motion in that white-tiled bathroom on Woodmont Avenue.

Afterward, in explaining their verdict, one juror said, "The way the law is stated, we felt there wasn't anything else we could do."

Another commented, "The main thing was that he confessed to doing it. It was all planned."

The jurors had a lot of trouble with the defense witnesses. They dismissed Lupe as a flake. Some loved Jacob's grandmother because Grace was dramatic, whereas others said that she didn't have a tear in her eye. They didn't believe Charles and strongly suspected that he had instigated the murders.

As the juror who held out the longest told me, "If only the defense would have given some evidence of Charles's involvement. We would never have held Jacob so responsible. We figured Jacob was taking the rap for his brother because at fifteen the system would treat him better."

They were bothered by the airline ticket. Jacob could have left, couldn't he? Why hadn't Frank Ind been called to the stand to explain? The entire defense seemed haphazard.

A couple of jurors complained that the abuse wasn't consistent. Sometimes it had been administered with a stick, other times with a board, yet again with a belt. Because Kermode and Pamela used various weapons some disregarded them all. And if there'd been one crowning incident in Jacob's life, one thing they could point to as the defining moment, they would have been more sympathetic. But, as it was, being tied to a toilet didn't do it, or being beaten with wooden paddles or being an emotional prisoner of war. At least for some. And several jurors were confused by the fact that if Jacob had indeed been abused, why hadn't he received counseling? Aspinwall kept bringing that fact up in court and the defense attorneys did nothing to explain that supposed discrepancy.

Not that all the jurors were unsympathetic. Three women in particular, who, not coincidentally, were abused remain anguished over the verdict.

"We didn't think it was right that he should be tried as an adult," said one. "We didn't know first degree murder meant life imprisonment," said another. In fact, this juror has lost all faith in the justice system and laments the fact that Jacob wasn't tried in front of Judge Looney instead of twelve basically ignorant people. When trying to convince the holdouts, other jurors said, "Trust Jane Looney. She's sympathetic. She'll do right by him." None of them knew that first degree murder carried with it a mandatory sentence with no room for maneuvering.

Following the verdict, several jurors spoke to the media. A few called the experience "traumatic," others "heartbreaking." One female complained of nightmares and of losing 15 pounds due to stress. Some of them took long walks. Others went to work on off days, attempting to take their minds off the trail. Juror Linda re-learned the Moonlight Sonata on the piano. "I hadn't played the piano for at least a year," she said. Several spoke of the difficulty of convicting Jacob, of how some broke down, of how boxes of Kleenex were used

before the verdict was reached.

"It was very, very hard on me," said Juror Anneke. "It broke my heart, but I'm a better person because of this."

Even a year later one juror remains haunted by Jacob. She, who at fifteen had thrown a knife at her own alcoholic father, is plagued by nightmares. She still cries, and despite extensive therapy, can't reconcile herself to the verdict.

"If only I'd been stronger," she says. "If only they'd given us better witnesses. If only they would have told us he would never get out of prison."

But the majority suffered no such qualms. They were satisfied with their verdict, as well as the entire judicial process. This is America, after all, the greatest country in the world with a legal system to match.

"I doubt very seriously anybody could come up with a better system," gushed Juror Mike.

Juror Linda said, "If I were on trial, I would like a jury like we were."

Juror Kent considered his selection to be an honor, and looked forward to sharing his experience with his eight-year-old daughter when she was old enough to understand the seriousness of the issues. "I'm sure that as things come up in my life," he explained, "this is going to be one of the things that jumps into my mind as part of the decision-making process."

Courtroom observers were not as impressed with some of the jurors as they were with themselves. Three of the four male jurors wore sunglasses throughout the trial, as if they were too cool or too bored or too iconoclastic to show proper respect. An attorney who attended several sessions told me that, in his 25 years of trying cases, he'd never observed a jury like Jacob's—and he wasn't being complimentary. One of the male jurors repeatedly fell asleep. When evidence was produced, some acted as if it was an imposition to even be told to look. And behind the scenes, one of the publicly sensitive jurors lamented the fact that her flowers were suffering because she had to spend all her time in Colorado Springs. A second juror told a neighbor she wished the trial would hurry up and end so she could convict Jacob and get on with her life. A third juror stated that, despite Judge Looney's admonition to disregard all of Michelle Mendez's testimony concerning Charles, Michelle's testimony had weighed heavily in their decision to convict. So we had jurors that followed the law when it pleased them and disregarded it when it pleased them.

Juror M.R. Keena, in a letter to the Ute Pass Courier, expressed unhappiness with the public for second-guessing the verdict. In explaining his decision, he stated that no signs of abuse had been observed. 'If one unbiased witness was able to come forward and say, "Yes, I treated Jacob for a dislocated shoulder; yes, I saw welts on Jacob; yes, I saw Jacob with a black eye; yes, Jacob missed a lot of school due to serious bodily injury; or yes, Jacob told me he did not want to go back because his stepfather and mother were beating him," then perhaps we would have found a different verdict.

'But no one did and the only people who could have proved or disproved

abuse are dead. Murdered by poor little Jacob.'

Keena's remarks are quite revealing. Strip off the veneer and we have truth. No sympathy there for poor little Jacob. No sympathy, I suspect, from the moment Keena received his jury summons. Had he been one of the 85% who had made up their minds to convict before the first witness had taken the stand?

Keena called for an unbiased witness, though in reality there is no such thing. People are either witnesses for the prosecution or for the defense. And generally family members or girl friends or people intimately involved with offenders will be the ones privy to the signs. In addition, unless there is a broken limb, how often do abusers take their children to doctors? Offenders are not stupid people. They have figured out when and where to hit so they won't be found out. But Keena didn't care. He was more concerned with ridiculing Jacob.

And sentencing him to death.

◊ ◊ ◊

Jacob's case ended on the same day as O.J.'s began. We all know the outcome of the Simpson trial, which had far more to do with wealth and fame than race. The O.J. experience has raised a multitude of questions in the minds of most Americans. My paramount question is, Who is more important, more worth our time, energy, and compassion—an aging athlete or our next generation? Let's get our priorities straight here. Or maybe we are being honest. Maybe a sports figure IS more significant to us than a child. But then it must be asked, Why do we so want to crush these, our children? Why are we so angry at them? So bent on vengeance, upon total control of their minds, their hearts, their bodies? Why are we so afraid?

Obviously, Jacob Ind touched some primal fear in the hearts of the twelve jurors who convicted him. Was it the dread of the bad seed, that creature without a conscience that is far more fiction than reality? Children aren't born bad. They're born into bad households.

And, therein, I believe, lies the source of our terror. The fear that we'll be held accountable for our actions, that the weak will ultimately turn on the strong, that there is something lurking in our home that could coalesce at some time and strike back at us. Some evil force—but it is an evil force that we, after all, created. Children like Jacob are only the shadow side of our society, the mirror image that we refuse to look at. Because if we do, we'll have to take a cold, hard look at ourselves and our failings and we're never going to do that. Jim Morrison sang, "I know your deepest, secret fear." Jacob Ind is our deepest, secret fear personified. So we choose not to deal with him. Rather, we'll destroy him.

Jacob Ind died for our sins. He died so that all the dirty little secrets in all the lovely homes across America will never be revealed. Our children are our possessions. We can do with them anything we damn well please and nobody

will stop us. Whip them, humiliate them, rape them, that's all okay. If they should cry out for help they will not be heard. If they protect themselves they will be annihilated. Nothing excuses killing a parent? Maybe not, but it's perfectly acceptable to murder a child's soul because that's more insidious and more unseen and he can still walk among the living and no one will realize he's a zombie. Yes, that's fine.

We Americans are not ready to deal with The Truth. And The Truth is we don't care about our children. Through the 1970's, the murder of a child in Colorado carried a sentence of two to four years. Though our Governor, Roy Romer, claims to have a heart for our next generation and has campaigned to "Save Our Children," Colorado ranks twenty-seventh in terms of how well we care for our offspring. When factoring in everything from low birth weights to children living in poverty to high school dropouts, those percentages have increased over the last several years—sometimes by as much as 70%. We are one of the top ten states in the number of juveniles arrested for violent crimes. How did Romer and our legislature choose to address the problem? Try children as young as twelve-years-old as adults. Which means that Coloradans are now allowing pre-teens to be thrown into adult prisons, the way Jacob has been thrown into an adult prison, where they will be subjected to the same brutality they "enjoyed" on the outside.

So the charade continues.

So many of us adults wring our hands and decry the brutality of this younger generation. But we never ask, "Why are these children the way they are?" Instead, we administer punishment. We lock them up, safely away, where they will quickly be forgotten, where no one cares "Why?" That is a question we, as parents, are terrified they just might answer.

"You created us," they would say.

Which is true. These "monsters" were fashioned out of the clay of parental abuse and societal neglect. So we don't dare open that particular door. Far safer to focus on the symptom—who speaks with a voice no one hears, whose tiny presence is easy to ignore—rather than the cause. We scream that the Jacob Inds of the world must be held accountable for their actions, though we refuse to accept responsibility for ours? We punish all the Jacobs for their violent deeds, but from whom did they learn their cruelty? Do they so petrify us because down deep, as we examine our own private shames at three o'clock in the morning, we realize that we may have acted like Kermode and Pamela Jordan?

Do some of us worry that our fate could be similar? That one day our victims might rise up and shout, "Enough!" Is that why we choose to imprison all the Jacobs? Why do we expect more out of our offspring than we do from ourselves? Courts have long excused crimes of passion. A male happening upon his wife *in flagrante delicto* with her lover is seldom held accountable when he blows one or both of them away. Courts have also come to recognize that a battered women can be so psychologically devastated that she can be driven to

272

murder her abuser. That magnanimity, however, does not extend to a battered child, who cannot possibly have the reasoning power of an adult. Our "justice" system does not recognize the difference in a youngster's reasoning, in how that mind can be shaped, his perceptions twisted from a lifetime of terror. "This is the law," judges say, as though it was our criminal code rather than the ten commandments that was handed to Moses on Mount Sinai.

The Law.

Books have been written, lectures given, documentaries produced about justice in America. The truth is simple enough. Justice, "The Law," wears the faces of whatever prejudices we Americans clutch to our bosom at any one particular time. The slavery of the blacks, the annihilation of the Indians are only the more sensational manifestations. When we feared females, we denied them their rights. When we feared unions, we hanged the Molly Maguires and the innocents of Haymarket Square. When we feared black men might be making love to our white women, we turned them into "bitter fruit." When we feared communists, we manufactured Joe McCarthy.

Now that we fear our children, we've created thousands of Jacob Inds. We can't shut them all away. We can't silence all their voices. We can't murder all their souls before we choose to honestly deal with them. Or can we?

273

"I wish Jacob hadn't killed them. I wanted to
see them go to jail, to pay publicly for what
they did to us."

~Charles Ind

"The law would never have done anything
to them. They would never have been
punished. Never."

~Jacob Ind

Chapter 34

Colorado Springs considers itself a law and order community. But in El
Paso County justice is as selective as it is across America. While Jacob was still
awaiting trial, Vern Smalley, a retired colonel was tried for blowing away a
seventeen year old. The two had been engaged in an angry game of bumper tag
during morning traffic. After the teenager motioned him over to the side of the
road, Smalley, who patrolled the highways like some aging Road Warrior,
removed a gun from his glove compartment and rolled down his window. The
kid walked up to him. Some witnesses say he punched Smalley. Others say he
didn't. Smalley testified that his pistol accidentally discharged into the
teenager's chest. Experts countered that the pistol couldn't possibly have
accidentally done anything. The youth, Carmine Tagliere, died instantly, along
the shoulder of that busy highway. The jury acquitted Vern Smalley and the
community applauded the verdict. "Smalley was just protecting his property,"
was the most common response. The prosecutor, who happened to be Bill
Aspinwall, lamented the fact that the jurors had held a mere teenager as fully
accountable for his actions as a fifty-two year old man. Interesting line of
reasoning. A seventeen-year-old can't possibly have the reasoning capacity of
an adult—unless he's fifteen and his name is Jacob Ind, of course.

Soon after Jacob's verdict, a fourteen year old girl plea bargained the
murder of her seventeen-year-old boyfriend. The shooting had been
premeditated. Angelique Thomas hadn't been in fear for her life so self defense
wasn't a factor. The court sentenced her to six years' probation.

Immediately following Jacob's verdict, co-prosecutor Gordon Dennison
declined to prosecute a seventy-one-year-old retired military man (Dennison
himself is a former military prosecutor), who, after an argument with his wife,
ran over her with a truck. When she didn't die, he backed up and ran over her
again. No charges were ever filed against the murderer, who was deigned to be
too old to be held accountable for his actions.

A year after Jacob's trial, Eugene Baylis was acquitted of walking into a
biker bar, killing two men and injuring several others. Following an earlier
altercation, Baylis had gone home, loaded himself up with grenades and enough
firepower to equip a militia and returned to open fire on his tormentors. Since

this involved the death penalty, Baylis had at his disposal a crack team of defense attorneys who spent two years working specifically on his case.[68] They proved that, despite police and eyewitness accounts to the contrary, Baylis had been shot at first and acted out of self defense. D.A. Suthers, who obviously believes that the only good jury is one that returns a guilty verdict, castigated the twelve for their contrariness—though more than ninety percent of local cases end with a conviction. If this were a communist country or a banana republic, we would scoff at a system so stacked against the rights of the individual. We would dismiss its proceedings as a "kangaroo court." Instead, we Americans call it "justice."

And as far as the idea that the law would have taken care of Kermode and Pamela Jordan, two examples will suffice.

One year after Jacob's sentencing, seventy-two year old Francis Everett, a senior volunteer at a local elementary school, went before Judge Looney on a sexual assault charge. Everett admitted to taking the hands of seven first- and second-grade girls and placing them on his penis while he read them stories in class. The acts took place over a two-year period and were witnessed by many of the other children. Everett also admitted sexually assaulting another young girl, a family friend, while baby-sitting her.

Looney approved a "stringent plea agreement." Everett will remain free so long as a therapist deems he can be rehabilitated. If he is found eligible for treatment, Looney will either sentence him to probation or a community corrections program. Under Everett's plea agreement, which was drafted by one of D.A. Suthers' prosecutors, the self-admitted child molester will also undergo a polygraph test to help determine whether he has sexually abused other children. If so, he is to name names in order that these additional victims will receive proper counseling. In exchange, the prosecutor will not file additional charges—regardless of whether Everett has molested one additional child or one hundred.

While Everett is required by law to stay away from children under the age of eighteen, including his own grandchildren, Looney said, "I will probably never agree to unsupervised visits. I might agree to supervised contact."

Another example of "child protection" occurred, yet again, in Woodland Park. Soon after Jacob killed his parents, one of his classmates, Lonny Smith (*) told WPHS counselors that his father had been raping him and his two brothers for years. The counselor reported the abuse and the boys, two of whom were underage, were yanked out of the home. One of the investigators told Lonny—as if he were to blame—"You're never going to see your father again." Although Lonny was sixteen at the time, he ended up living with a couple of other teens

---

[68] For example, more than 400 defense motions were filed. In Jacob's case, I've received conflicting numbers--anywhere from three to ten.

and eking out an existence until graduating. Nothing was ever made public about the father's crime. The family was not well off, but the dad was very active in the community. He received five years in a work release program—meaning that he works in the community during the day and returns to a facility at night. All of Lonny's classmates were aware of both the molestations and the subsequent "punishment," which they regard as a sick joke.

Recently my daughter, who is friends with all three brothers, told me, "As it turns out, Lonny's stepmother was also molesting the boys."

"Yeah? What happened to her?"

"She divorced the father and left town."

The saga of the Jordan murders entered its final phase with the trial of Gabrial Adams in October, 1994. From the outset, the proceedings possessed a totally different feel. For one thing, most of the spectator seats were empty, as were the spots marked "Reserved for the media." The press, watching from the same cubbyhole opposite the courtroom, complained that the Adams' trial was a dull imitation of its predecessor. News coverage was far less comprehensive. Jacob had generally been the lead both on TV and in the *Gazette Telegraph*. Columnist Raymond McCaffrey had written a series of insightful articles, devoting more space to the Ind trial than to any other event in his career. This time McCaffrey never even put in an appearance. Few people lingered in the hallway or asked questions or made comments. Jacob's case had possessed all the high drama of Christians being fed to the lions. Gabrial's trial seemed more a match of battle-weary opponents wanting only to slink away without inflicting mortal damage on anyone.

Gabrial Adams entered the room, wearing a cardigan sweater and pink shirt. His long brown hair was pulled back in a pony tail. Initially I mistook him for a girl. I was surprised by how small he was. At the time of his arrest Major had been 5'6" and 111 pounds. Since then he had put on weight and grown, but if I hadn't known, I would have pegged him at a shade over five feet and one hundred pounds. I kept wondering how someone so tiny could have inflicted such damage on Kermode and Pamela. His smallness made me uneasy, as if I'd discovered raisins in a package marked chocolate chips. Something unexpected and a tad unpleasant. A gun is a great equalizer, but the .22 hadn't immobilized either Kermode or Pamela. How had Major managed to keep one person at bay while inflicting damage upon the other? The bear mace hadn't put in an appearance until much later. And if the spray was as deadly as the prosecution maintained, why hadn't it incapacitated Gabrial and Jacob as well as Kermode and Pamela? Obviously, stress and shock can make people react in odd ways. Awakened out of a dead sleep by gunshots and a knife wielding maniac in the darkness of one's bedroom would be terrifying enough to paralyze

anyone, but I remained troubled by the same old question: How could Gabrial Adams have handled two people? Why hadn't Pamela bolted when Major had been struggling with Kermode? Why hadn't she raced out the french doors leading to the deck? That exit was only a few feet from the bed, and could not have been blocked by Gabrial, who would have been preoccupied with Kermode. Pamela could easily have negotiated the twelve feet drop and run to the neighbors. If nothing else, she could have screamed for help from the deck. Or she could have fled downstairs to one of the phones and called 911. She could even have dialed from the princess phone on the night stand beside her bed. Not for the first time did I feel uneasy about the entire scenario. The Jordan murders still didn't add up.

The trial got underway. The prosecution intended to prove that Gabrial had cold-bloodedly executed Pamela and Kermode Jordan, the defense that Gabrial was an innocent dupe in the hands of Jacob and Charles. The same parade of prosecution witnesses testified—sheriff's deputies explaining how they discovered the corpses, WPHS's principal and counselor recounting Jacob's confession, the arrests of the two teens. Bill Aspinwall was as thorough as always, though his manner was far less intense. Gone were the fireworks, the nasty comments, the petulance and viciousness so omnipresent during Jacob's trial. He even displayed an occasional spark of humor.

On Monday, November 7, 1994, Gabrial's tape recorded statement was played for the court, finally providing the media twenty minutes of drama. Prior to the recording the biggest excitement had revolved around whether Jacob would appear and what would he say. (His appearance was brief. He wouldn't snitch, and that was about the extent of his testimony, leaving reporters to comment that he had gained twenty pounds since sentencing.} Gabrial's defense claimed that their client hadn't even pulled the trigger, that he had been a pawn in the hands of Jacob and Charles. Would Major's story back that up?

Gabrial was questioned at the Woodland Park police department. As a juvenile, he had the right to make his statement in the presence of his parents and occasionally his mother and father could be heard interjecting a question or comment.

Once Officers Mike Rulo and Nick Adamovich and the three Adams's were seated around the conference table, Adamovich advised Gabrial of his Miranda rights and Major launched into his account of the Jordan murders.

On December 16 Gabrial had remained at WPHS until nearly eight p.m. He and his mother had worked the band concession stand. Then, after returning home and fixing himself a sandwich, Gabrial had helped his dad bring in the Christmas tree. While the two men strung colored lights, Gabrial's mother and sister began decorating. Around 10:15, Gabrial retreated to his bedroom, which was located on the first floor, off the open living area. After washing up in his bathroom, adjacent to his room, Gabrial shut his door. His bedroom was a typical teenager's rat's nest strewn with papers, clothes, food and other

unmentionable things that parents fear investigating too closely.

As Gabrial readied for bed, his parents heard him coughing—he had a cold—and moving around. Soon after, Danny, who worked graveyard at a Cripple Creek casino, also retired to the master bedroom, which, along with a second bedroom and bath, was located upstairs.

Gabrial had already promised Jacob that he would be over later that evening to teach the fifteen-year-old how to use a samurai sword. While the late hour might seem strange, Jacob's parents didn't know about the sword and would have confiscated it so the lessons had to be secret.[69] Gabrial didn't know Jacob Ind very well. They had been riding the same bus for about three weeks and Major, who was mechanically inclined, had gone to Jacob's house once in order to fix a radio. At that time, he had met Kermode and Pamela, though he couldn't identify them by name. Major also knew Charles, but only slightly. Jacob's older brother had told him he'd left home because of his parents and that had been the extent of their conversation.

Gabrial rested on his bed, which consisted solely of a mattress heaped with clothes and bedding, waiting for everyone to retire. He heard his mom and sister laughing and talking as they worked. Finally, around eleven p.m., the townhouse was quiet. After donning his trench coat and grabbing his swords, Major slipped out his bedroom window and headed for the Jordan residence.

Highway 67 was largely deserted. Gabrial walked swiftly, following Lovell Gulch Road through the development of Sunnywood Manor.[70] When Gabrial spotted Jacob's house, high on the hill, it was completely dark. That didn't deter Gabrial. Swinging around an upper road to the back of 120 Ridge, he approached through a field. Upon arrival he didn't even have to knock. The door was open and Jacob was waiting for him in the foyer.

"Hi," said Jacob. "Let me get my sword."

Gabrial deposited his own swords on the hardwood floor in the entrance, near the mirrored hall tree and the stairs leading up to the bedrooms and down to the rec room. He also removed his boots and trench coat. The house remained dark and still, but Gabrial never thought to question what many might consider a curious situation. He followed Jacob to the upper level, along the carpeted hall lined with wooden frames and plastic frames and metal frames displaying hundreds of photos of the handsome Jordan family. Major had no idea that he was being escorted to the master bedroom, flush at the end of the hall. He didn't

---

[69] In court it was brought out that Jacob's parents indeed knew about the sword. Kermode had actually been with him when he bought it, and I had seen the sales receipt for that and a couple of antique bayonets.

[70] Although the distance between the Adams' and Jordan' residences is less than two miles, Gabrial didn't arrive until around midnight and couldn't account for the hour lapse.

see any guns or anything in Jacob's hands. Never once did he suspect that anything was wrong.

They reached Pamela and Kermode's room. Jacob went in first but somehow Gabrial was pushed inside and the door suddenly slammed shot. Gabrial was standing right next to Jacob, whom he assumed had closed the door. But it was so dark inside with only the light from the french doors on the opposite wall. Major didn't know the room's layout, and couldn't see that Kermode rested only inches away in the four poster bed.

Before Gabrial's eyes could adjust to the gloom, "a lot...a group of" gunshots rang out. Major saw the muzzle flash right in front of him, but couldn't make out much of anything else. He was terrified.

"I thought (Jacob) was trying to shoot at me so I got down, and then I heard the moans and groans and somebody moving around me. It was like in the bed, so I wasn't sure...

"I remember my face was burning. I thought I was shot, and I felt a knife, so I grabbed the knife and I tried to get the knife out and I thought it was Jacob's hands, but it wasn't. Jacob wasn't strong enough."

It was somebody big and burly. Gabrial identified his assailant as Kermode Jordan.

"My hands were cut up." Major sounded excited as he recounted the night's events. "I felt it. I grabbed the knife."

At one point on the tape, he said he tried to grab "the blade of MY knife." When Officer Rulo pressed him about that particular adjective, he backtracked, saying, "THE knife. I grabbed the blade of the knife, that's what I said."

Throughout Gabrial's recitation, one or both of the officers occasionally interrupted with questions. Their voices were calm and neutral, as if they were discussing the plot of an uninspired television drama, rather than a real life murder. Danny Adams, Gabrial's father, also broke in, urging, "You need to tell the truth completely."

Back in the Jordan's bedroom, Gabrial felt the knife cut through his blue t-shirt and his hand. (No slashes were found in the shirt.)

Major said, "I tried to twist (the knife) but it kept just pushing and pushing and I was pushed up against the wall. When I heard another shot, my fingers started to hurt and I thought it was still Jacob after me."

He described a burning sensation on his hands, and attributed that to the heat of a gunshot zinging past, burning the air as it flew.[71]

Suddenly, Jacob turned on the bathroom light. "And I saw Jacob's dad and mom on the ground...I thought Jacob was trying to shoot me, but he was shooting his own father."

After it was all over, Jacob wrapped the weapons in one of his shirts and

---

[71] A physical impossibility, as a ballistics expert later testified.

thrust them at Gabrial. "Jacob gave [the pistols and the knife] to me. I didn't know why he didn't shoot me again."

Jacob said, "If you don't get rid of the guns I'll kill your parents too."

Gabrial obeyed, he said with a sob in his voice, because "I didn't want my parents to get hurt. He just killed his parents. He would have killed mine." Gabrial wanted to terminate Jacob, but he was afraid. "He said if I touched him that he would kill my parents, too, and I believed him."

Gabrial left immediately. He had spent a total of twenty minutes at the Jordan residence, so he places the murders around 12:20.[72] He immediately went home, running along the road, carrying the weapons, frightened out of his mind. He reached his bedroom sometime after three a.m. He couldn't be more specific because a piece of clothing covered up all but the three on the face of his clock. Which meant it had taken him nearly three hours to traverse that two mile distance.

Once home, Gabrial removed his trench coat, his jeans and old brown hiking boots. He went into his bathroom and tended to his hands, which had several gashes. Then he flopped down on his bed. His sheets only partially covered the mattress, and some blood dripped onto it. He lay in the darkness, beside the plastic chair where he'd buried the murder weapons, pondering everything that had happened. What had he been thinking and feeling?

"It's vague," he told the officers, concluding his version of events.

Just being caught up in the drama of the moment, hearing Gabrial's distraught tone, "the crying sounds, but without tears," as Officer Rulo later testified, it was easy to believe the defendant's version of events.

So long as one didn't probe too deeply.

Which Mike Rulo and Nick Adamovich immediately proceeded to do. They told Gabrial that evidence placed him at the scene, taking part in the crime.

"Tell us exactly what happened," one urged. "We need to know the truth. We're just looking for the facts."

Rulo said, "If you were being set up by Jacob, the evidence will show that. Physical evidence does not lie."[73]

Adamovich chimed in. "Certain things you've told us don't jibe. We need the facts."

"I'm telling you the facts," Gabrial said, sounding irritated.

The officers then examined his cuts. Gabrial displayed a wound on his chest that he said came from the struggle. While fending off the knife attack, he'd deflected the blade down, toward his chest. The officers noted that the

---

[72] Both Jacob and the coroner place them an hour later.

[73] That statement is technically true. But it can be misinterpreted.

280

wound had scabbed over, indicating it wasn't fresh.

When Gabrial again mentioned his fear of Jacob as the reason why he took the guns, Danny Adams interrupted. "You should have told us."

"If I had, Jacob would have killed me."

When the officers pointed out that Gabrial had the weapons, he insisted that he was still afraid. According to a curious statement he made near the end of the tape, Gabrial also indicated that he was fearful of yet a third—or even a fourth—party.

His father asked, "Why didn't you tell us?"

"If I would have told you that, they would have gone to HIM and DAVE would have killed you."

Was that a reference to David Mabie? That and similar remarks were never investigated by the prosecution or the defense, just as Jacob's charges of perjury were never investigated. It is apparent from the tape that Gabrial believed at least one more person was involved, though he wasn't certain who.

Which did not help his defense attorneys in their case against Charles. Because if Charles had been actively involved, wouldn't Gabrial have known? Since Jacob was asking everybody he came in contact with to murder his parents, could he have kept quiet to his co-conspirator about his older brother's involvement? He certainly wasn't discreet about anything else. And if Major had known, wouldn't he have gladly fingered a second Ind in order to save himself? Someone with his background and reputation would never fear Charles. Major had no reason to remain silent—unless he was already adhering to the prison code, which is, "Never snitch."

And if Charles had actually participated in the murders, as the defense speculated, surely Gabrial would have seen him restraining Pamela or firing the fatal shots. Unless it was dark the entire time, as he maintained. Gabrial was insistent that whoever came at him with a knife was too bulky to be Jacob. Ballistics later indicated that the gunshots might have come from someone taller. But wielding a knife doesn't seem like something either brother would do. And if Charles was the attacker, why wasn't he cut up? (Actually, no one checked him for anything because he wasn't a suspect.) Finally, when the lights came on, where would Charles have hidden?

No, if Charles had been involved, Gabrial would have told.

Or had he?

When Charles was called as a prosecution witness, spectators anticipated fireworks. Gabrial's defense was adamant that Charles was the puppeteer behind the puppets. Now was their chance to prove it. Bill Aspinwall began the questioning. This time around he was Charles's champion, gently leading him through events.

"There isn't one shred of physical evidence linking Charles to the crimes," Aspinwall later said. During Jacob's trial, he had inferred that Charles was a cold-hearted liar interested only in collecting the Jordan inheritance. Now

Charles was the courageous older brother and Jacob, formerly the monstrous schemer, was a dupe in the hands of a Ninja warlord.

When defense attorney Mike Warren's turn came, the courtroom braced for an explosion. Warren had publicly fingered Charles as the mastermind. Earlier, he had made a big deal out of a life insurance policy that had been found on top of a filing cabinet in the Jordans' garage a few days after the murders. He seemed to be implying that money-grubbing Charles had gone into the house looking for it. He had also mentioned something about a rock used as a doorstop for the french doors. Was he hinting that Charles had watched the murders from the deck? Or that he had entered through those french doors, and had been the one to hold his mother at bay?

Warren, a heavy-set man with a greying beard and intense manner, directly asked Charles about the missing dogs. During the funeral, Charles had commented, "They're history," and Warren theorized that he might have helped get rid of them. He then questioned Charles about a previous statement he had made, that he and Jacob had wanted their parents dead ever since they were little.

Charles answered calmly and carefully. "The family dogs were gone a week or so before... My comment meant nothing beyond the obvious."

And he and Jacob may have said they wanted their parents dead, but that was just talk. Warren never mentioned the life insurance policy or the makeshift doorstop.

"Where were you on the night of the murders?" Warren asked. Michelle Mendez, Charles's roommate, had been subpoenaed to testify once again that he had no alibi for the time of the murders. Warren appeared to be laying the groundwork for the time when they would call Charles back on the stand, and spring their trap.

Charles repeated that he'd had the flu and had never left his residence. He remained unruffled throughout and smoothly recounted Jacob's confession. Gabrial had initiated the killings, had shot Kermode and Pamela six times and had been the one to wield the knife. When Charles mentioned that Major later went into Jacob's room carrying "a blood-dripping knife," Warren pounced on him. No blood had been found on Jacob's carpet. From the very beginning, the defense had been trying to paint Jacob as a liar.

"Has he [Jacob] lied to you before?" asked Warren.

"He has," Charles replied, without elaborating.

Charles might have been on the stand for a total of two hours. Warren reserved the right to call him back and once he left, worried to Judge Looney that the oldest Ind might try to thwart the subpoena rather than face the defense. Maybe so, but if Charles was anxious, he had done an excellent job of hiding it.

◊ ◊ ◊

Closing arguments. Despite the fact that Bill Aspinwall had introduced the same three hundred pieces of physical evidence, as well as heard all the testimony only four months previously, he had remained doggedly attentive throughout the month long trial. Now, he methodically laid forth to the attentive jury all the reasons Gabrial had killed the Jordans, just as he'd done with Jacob. He and his partner re-created the murders, leaving Mike Warren to argue that the prosecution's case was based on a great deal of questionable evidence, including what Warren termed "Jacob said" evidence.

Warren tried hard. He charged that the various pieces of evidence were enough to cause jurors to reasonably doubt the prosecution's case. The knife cuts on Gabrial's hands could be defensive, rather than offensive. He COULD have been attacked by some unknown intruder. He mentioned problems with some of the physical evidence. But he hadn't proven his major assertion--that Charles Ind was the mastermind. His case had been so weak that he hadn't even bothered to have Charles return as a defense witness. Warren had thrown out a lot of threads, but he'd failed to tie any of them together. He was a good attorney. He'd fought hard for his client. But, either the evidence really hadn't been there, or once again the law had sidestepped the truth by disallowing it, as those close to the defense later maintained.

"I leave you with this," Warren said in closing. "I leave you with Gabe's life. I have protected him. We have throughout all of this time... This will pass out of your life, as it will pass out of mine. [We attorneys will] be down the hall butting heads again. But it's not going to pass out of his life."

The jury deliberated seven hours before returning with its verdict. Guilty of murder in the first degree.

When the verdict was read, Gabrial, who'd been singing a gospel song in the holding cell, blinked once. No other reaction, save for that eerie half smile.

The prosecution had once again triumphed. Co-prosecutor Dan Kay told reporters the verdict ended "one of the saddest, darkest hours in Woodland Park history... We've thought all along that Gabrial Adams was the driving force." Kay added that Jacob probably would never have killed his parents alone.

Bill Aspinwall also spoke to the cameras. "Frankly, I think both boys are real dangerous, and dangerous beyond this case. That was the concern from my standpoint--that they could hurt again and hurt again violently."

"I feel like hell," said Mike Warren. "I'm going to go up and sit by the river."

Afterword/ Mary Ellen

After Gabrial's trial I settled into Life After Jacob. Over the months we communicated sporadically. We had quarreled during the trial over a minor incident which, under less stressful circumstances, we both would have shrugged off. Now our relationship was strictly business, and I mourned the loss of my "best bud." Jacob was getting adjusted to life in prison and trying to decide whether to plunge into the system or keep one foot in prison and one foot on the outside. When somebody is looking at spending an entire life behind bars, a life without hope, soul searching is in order. What matters the most to me? How do I want to play out my hand? Jacob would have much more in common with fellow prisoners than with "ordinary" people. How can any of us understand what it is like to be in the system if we haven't experienced it? Jacob's world will never again be our world. Is it worth the effort to retain increasingly tenuous ties, or bury himself in the labyrinth of his new "home?"

Since our separation, Jacob had given a lot of thought as to what he was going to do about the outside world—and what he was going to do about me. Because of his past, Jacob definitely has more trust issues than most, and that June verdict had provided a host of new ones. Jacob had been stripped naked before those jurors, and in the style of Kermode and Pamela, been violated once again. How would a "normal" person react under similar circumstances?

One thing all authorities agree upon is that it is very difficult for an abused child *ever* to open his heart. They can swing from total, blind trust to absolute suspicion in the space of a few minutes. Since I had walked into Jacob's life, nothing had occurred to inspire confidence in grownups. "Trust the system," he had been told. "Don't question your attorneys. They know what's best." "Put your faith in the hands of twelve men and women." If Jacob had once been inclined to tear down the walls, the outcome of the trial, being surrounded by a sea of adults who were now either his jailers or potential predators, had caused him to erect ever higher barriers.

I had been the premiere adult in Jacob's life for more than a year. Why? What were my motives? Precisely why had I spent so much time with him? Because I cared about him? Because I wanted to exploit him? Write a book and make lots of money? Because I was like those gawkers at a car wreck and simply wanted to be attached to something sensational? Because I was in love with him and/or had sexual feelings for him? Going through a mid-life crisis? Amusing myself at his expense? Bored? In the course of our relationship, everyone from lawyers to Jacob's father to the guards at CJC had questioned my motives. They had also questioned Jacob's. I've heard endless speculation, invariably issued from people who never met Jacob and barely know me.

Their accusations involve some version of the following: "Jacob Ind is a psychopath who's conned you.." "You're a gullible woman, a bleeding heart

who's turned a cold-blooded murderer into a cause..."

Jacob spent nearly a year sifting through a similar cacophony of voices, not to mention his own doubts, before reaching his decision. Throughout the first half of 1995, we did our "Becoming Reacquainted" Dance via letters. It wasn't easy. Jacob was in a lot of pain and some of his words were extremely hurtful. There were times when I walked away for good--if only in my head. Far easier to do that than to endure the sight of Jacob doing hard time, worrying about him and standing helplessly by as he reeled from crisis to crisis. Better just to get *The Murder of Jacob* behind me and retreat once again into my safe cocoon. What I had already seen and heard about Colorado's Department of Corrections was troubling. DOC is marginally accountable only to the state legislature, and prisoners are certainly not THE most popular issue. Crime is. Inmates' families complain about injustices in the way their loved ones are treated, but who will listen? Certainly not our politicians, who have allowed DOC's budget to grow by 16% a year over the past 15 years. No one cares that programs for prisoners are being cut, that convicts get very little mental health counseling, that they are brutalized as much by guards as by each other, that rehabilitation is a bad joke. "Why rehabilitate?" families say bitterly. "You do that and the guards are out of a job." I had already been told by Jacob's warden that Jacob had an attitude, that they were going to teach him "either the easy or the hard way" that he could never beat "The Man." Who needed this? I had a very nice life without Jacob Ind.

Still, I couldn't walk away. More for myself than for Jacob. Jacob has many people in his life--his father and grandparents, Nancy Overmyer and her daughters, who have become a second family, dozens of mail friendships. He appeared to be surviving quite nicely. But I had promised him at CJC, "When people hear your story, they'll understand why you killed your parents." Well, the public had only heard a tiny portion. Perhaps as importantly, I needed to recount his life in order to for *me* to understand. I still could not comprehend how a child who had been so horribly abused had been sentenced to an entire life of abuse, and with the approval, not only of an entire community, but of our entire judicial system. What was Jacob being punished for? His years of endurance? The courage to finally stop the madness? Or simply to cover up the sins of our community?

No. My business with Jacob remained unfinished.

So we did our dance. The letters became more frequent and softer in tone. Gradually, we became friends again. All that remained was a face-to-face meeting, and the circle would be completed. Or would it?

The prisons in the East Canon Correctional Complex rise out of the dun-colored earth like castles, complete with towers and fortress-like walls. They sit

in the middle of sagebrush, sparse wild flowers and desert—slabs of concrete and steel that house thousands of Jacobs. At the entrance stands a booth beyond which ordinary people aren't allowed to go. We are entering what I refer to as the Land of the Dead. It is July 30, 1995, and in a few hours I will see Jacob for the first time in more than a year. As eleven a.m. nears, a parking lot directly opposite the booth begins filling with family and friends. The automobiles are of every make and description. Nothing about them provides a clue that the people who own them are different from the vast majority of "good" Americans. This could be the parking lot of a grocery store or church or senior center. The people getting out of their cars appear identical to mall shoppers and neighbors and business associates. But we are indeed different. Each of us is here to spend some time in a human zoo, where the animals will be allowed out of their cages to interact, for a few short hours, among the free.

The Visitor's Center is a modular surrounded by asphalt and dirt. No one is permitted to enter before eleven and not so much as a tree or an overhead cloud is available to break the heat. Many of the people standing in line are elderly. Upon my arrival, the first thing I notice is the others' clothing. I have already been warned that I can be turned away for "inappropriate dress." No neckline below the collar bone, nothing too short—meaning five inches above the knees when sitting—no jewelry, including watches and sunglasses, no sleeveless shirts or shorts. Disobey these rules—it depends on the guards' discretion as to what is acceptable and what isn't—and you will be denied your visit. Some have been turned away after driving many hours. (The system, of course, does not try to be compatible with loved ones. The system only seeks to be compatible with the system.) Other regulars, more familiar with the procedure, bring several changes of clothes. Jacob suggested a T-shirt and jeans, which is what I'm wearing.

Once inside we sign a form consenting to allow "any search of my person or of the person of any minor children accompanying me." Our vehicles can also be searched. Anyone violating a long list of Department of Correction rules, which include bringing to an inmate "any uncancelled postage stamp" or anything that "might pose a threat to the security or operations of the Colorado State Penitentiary" such as batteries, cameras, film, flashbulbs, flashlights, chewing gum, pets or plant life "may be barred from the institution and institutional property, and may be subject to prosecution." I've already heard horror stories from relatives who say they have been denied visits on trumped up charges.

"DOC lives to break up families," they say. "If they can make it difficult on you, they do."

I feel vaguely uneasy throughout the sign-in procedure. I keep expecting to be castigated for my dress, my hair, my makeup, anything, though the guards are invariably pleasant and helpful.

A person can't just decide to "drop in" at prison some Sunday afternoon.

Before visiting, the inmate must put us on a list. After the computer ascertains that we are in compliance, a guard inspects our driver's licenses to make sure we are who we purport to be. Next step, we empty our pockets. We're allowed to keep our licenses and quarters for the vending machines. Our car keys, another security risk, are placed on a board in exchange for a silver marker with an engraved number. Afterward, we move to a guard holding a wand who orders us to open our mouths, extend our arms, turn around, and lift our hair. Security is a lot more stringent than at CJC. I've entered the big leagues.

Once the wand finishes its tour of our bodies, we're loaded onto an ancient bus that is the same color as the surrounding sand. The seats are torn or loose and a handful of windows are cracked. Someone jokes about "Our taxpayers' money at work."

Following a short wait, we are driven perhaps an eighth of a mile to our destination. My bus stops at Centennial. Depending on who I talk to, either one in three or one in six of Centennial's inmates are doing time for murder. Out of a population of some 330 men, thirty to fifty are juveniles. Jacob was placed here for security reasons. It is one of the few facilities that has private cells. In theory that provides an added element of safety for youngsters. In actuality, as the warden told me, "The only way we can completely protect someone like Jacob is to weld his door shut."

After unloading, we pass through automatic gates. The sidewalk leading to the prison is wide and neatly tended. A patch of grass rimmed by flowers gives it the feeling of a school, perhaps, so long as I don't raise my eyes to the tower or the wall of razor wire. Off in the distance is a flat patch of barren earth where prisoners work out or play basketball. A far cry from all the terrific amenities the public complains about.

Inside are steel doors and more steel doors before we descend into the visiting area, which is reminiscent of a campus lounge with several small tables and vending machines. There are major differences, however. The seats are assigned, a guard sits at a dais, and behind smoked glass another guard watches the room via a monitor. If more than one person is visiting, you have to get permission in order to move tables together. The prison personnel are friendly, but rules are rules. A kiss and an embrace are allowed at the beginning and end of each meeting. In between, you can hold hands—so long as you keep them on top of the table. Anything more and the visit can be terminated.

I will not be allowed a contact visit. Jacob is in trouble again so we'll meet behind plate glass. In all the time I've known him, I've hugged him once and touched his hand maybe a dozen times. Soon, we won't even have the privacy of a closed booth. Jacob was found with a shank in his possession. Given Jacob's youth, the reality of prison rape and his past, it is hardly surprising that he had chosen to thus protect himself. But The Man isn't interested in Why. Nor is he interested in seeing that one of its more infamous prisoners gets any sort of mental health counseling. Although Judge Looney recommended that Jacob be

sent someplace where he could receive therapy, her request was ignored. No, if Jacob is going to "get well," he is going to do it on his own. So far the results of his judgment and choices are discouraging. Jacob is headed for the baddest of the bad, Colorado State Penitentiary, CSP, maximum security, where he will be confined for twenty-three out of twenty-four hours. He will be handcuffed and shackled any place he goes, even to shower. Depending on the level, inmates are allowed one to four visits a month and one to four phone calls. The minimum stay is around a year. Despite DOC's official policy that prisoners can "earn their way out," some will never leave. I've been warned that if Jacob doesn't behave, he'll come out in a pine box.

As I await Jacob's arrival, I am extremely nervous. The surroundings are oppressive enough, but I'm more concerned about how our visit will go. Because he's "in the hole," he'll be brought out in irons. All of this is one step above a waking nightmare. How did I ever get here, at a state penitentiary, waiting for someone I love to be brought to me in chains? This was not part of my life's plan. Will I cry when I see him? Will we have anything to talk about? What will he look like? How will a year have changed him?

The other prisoners emerge one by one to meet their families. Easy enough to figure out who each con belongs to. This Friday there are only a handful of visitors. The young black man will be paired up with the tall, sad-looking lady, whose pretty four year old daughter smiles shyly at his approach. The middle-aged con with shoulder length grey hair and beard hugs an aging blond. The Hispanic with tattoos on his arms stops to comb his hair in the reflection from the monitoring booth before heading for a brightly dressed woman with a small oxygen tank clinging to her shoulder and a five-year-old clinging to her hand. To the outside world, each one of these convicts would be labeled by his crime. They are murderers, burglars, armed robbers, outlaws all. And it's true. They are that. Just as Jacob is. But in a society that loves to label, I believe Jacob is much more than that. He is my friend and I've missed him terribly.

Because he's being "Ad-segued," Jacob is one of the last to be brought out. I've been pacing in front of the visiting booths. All the while in the back of my mind I'm thinking, Something's going to happen to louse this up. In fact, one of the guards motions me inside, picks up a phone and tells me, "Sorry. You can't see him today." Several seconds pass before I realize he's joking.

Suddenly, Jacob is outside the booth. As the guards pat him down, I have time to collect my thoughts before meeting him face to face. My initial reaction is shock. What happened to my little boy? They've brought me a man. Jacob is 6'3" and 200 pounds of muscle. If it weren't for his complexion, which still breaks out, he could easily pass for someone in his mid to late twenties. Where is Jacob?

When he smiles at me, I know. He's still there. And when I hear his voice, I begin to relax. Within five minutes, it's as if we'd never been separated.

We argue politics. His have changed, which leads to a lively disagreement regarding how to "fix" what's wrong in Washington.. We segue into rock music, spiritual matters, what he's thinking and feeling, what I'm doing and thinking and feeling.

As we talk, my mind whispers, This is Jacob's home. This is how it will be for him the rest of his life. I can't comprehend it. I can't bear it. I try to tell him that—to speak of all he's lost. I fumble for the words, though over the past year my heart has made endless lists. Jacob will never walk in the woods or feel the petals of a flower or hold his child or drive a car. He will never see a full moon rise over the mountains or pet an animal, or stand in a check-out line, or fill out a job application, or enjoy a first date. He will never go to a movie or out to dinner or bake a birthday cake or decorate a Christmas tree. He will never walk on a city street in the rain or board an airplane. He will never go to England or Australia or the little bakery down the street. He will never play baseball with his son or tuck his daughter in at night or nestle in his wife's arms. He will never sleep in a regular bed or buy a suit of clothes or wear a pair of blue jeans or eat from fine china or wonder what career path he should choose. Jacob will never know a day without fear, without the threat of sudden death or violence, a day where he can sleep or eat or go to the bathroom completely, serenely alone.

Watching this child who is now a man, this Jacob who is so precious to me, I try to tell him these things, and how angry I am, how unfair life is.

But Jacob will have none of that. "You always focus on what I don't have. I focus on what I DO."

"And what do you have?" I ask, thinking of the shackles, the iron bars and the plate glass between us.

"Love."

God's love, the love of his father, the respect of his peers, new friendships inside and outside the system. He even has a girlfriend, which immediately brings out my protective instincts. Who is she? What does she want from you? Is she good for you? Will she cherish you for who you truly are? Will she appreciate the "Sweet Jacob" that I have come to love?

"My life is enough," he tells me.

"He's in denial," experts tell me. I don't know. Jacob has always confounded me. He has survived a life I can't imagine. He has asked for very little and received very little. Or so it seems to me. But we all yearn for love. It is the building block upon which our universe was created, our *raison d'etre*. For the first time Jacob has it. I can argue about the form of his God, who appears more vengeful than compassionate, or the beliefs of some of his companions or his choice of a girlfriend, but I can't argue with the fact that Jacob loves. And is loved in return. He has at least been freed from that most hopeless of prisons—the prison of the heart.

We say good-bye. As the guards lead him away I smile and wave, though

inside I'm crying. I know that I'll never again have my friend back save for a few hours a few times a month, that the life I had built for Jacob in my dreams must remain forever that. Simply a dream.

It's okay, I assure myself, during the hour-long drive home. If it's enough for Jacob, it has to be enough for me. Someday maybe I'll actually believe that. Someday maybe I'll even understand why Jacob Ind was brought into my life. But for now all I can do is return to my loving family and my quiet, ordinary life.

And count the days until Jacob and I are together again.

Afterword/Jacob

Jacob did this series of drawings for a Healing Images Art Fest,
which is held for survivors of incest.

Inscription written on the wall in the final panel:
There is one who breaks any prison walls
Be they pain, hate, present or past.
There is One who redeems us and frees us
from the prisons we erect.
No wall's too thick, no bars too many
His grace is for any.
Just ask and He will come.
Ask and He will heal
Answer His knock on the door of your heart.
He knows your pain,
He knows your struggle.
He was murdered and raised again for me and for you,
With Jesus in Heaven, our lives can begin anew.

WHAT YOU CAN DO TO HELP.

An African proverb states, "It takes a village to raise a child." In Jacob's case, it took an entire community to allow his parents' abusive behavior, to turn its back on his cries for help, to convict him, and to allow his incarceration to continue. If the public began speaking out on Jacob's behalf, the powers-that-be would offer their explanations as to why they can't do anything, as to why Jacob's sentence is just, as to why the author of his story is wrong or misguided, etc. Still, if the voices were not silenced, but instead grew louder, changes would eventually be made. One voice is a whisper. Ten thousand are a movement.

I have done everything that I can do. When talking to Mark Noel, our governor's advocate for clemency and pardons, Mr. Noel told me, "In order to help Jacob, we need more evidence of sexual abuse." My initial reaction was, How am I going to come up with that? I'm not a trained investigator. Besides, as we all know, incest takes places in the hidden places of the night. As I continued to ponder Mark Noel's instructions, I finally realized that, for those who are sympathetic to Jacob, I have told enough to convince them. For those who are not, even if I uncovered videotapes of the molestations, their reaction would be, "So what? Unless it took place in the seconds before he killed them, it has no relevancy to his crimes."

I will never convince the skeptics and I do not have the money, the energy, the expertise, or the time to continue being all things to and for Jacob. I have tried to be Jacob's voice. I will continue speaking out on behalf of my friend. But my voice must be joined by your voice, and that of your neighbors, and your friends and your city councilpersons and your state legislators. If I am the only one who cares, Jacob will soon be forgotten, save by a few visitors and a few family members. He will die in prison.

With the ending of this book, "my Jacob" ceases belonging to me. He belongs to everyone who reads his story. You can never again claim ignorance, or say, "Isn't it a shame what happened to that kid?" With knowledge comes responsibility. I am asking that you help me help Jacob.

It won't take much time. But it can make a tremendous difference, not only for Jacob but for others in his situation.

If you would like to help, there are several things you can do.

1. Buy a copy of *The Murder of Jacob*. Ask your friends to buy a copy. (Order form in the back of the book.) Half of all proceeds go to a Justice For Jacob fund. I believe I have uncovered enough new evidence, and that enough mistakes were made regarding Jacob's representation, that Jacob could be granted a new trial or win an appeal. Questions range from the investigation and prosecution to whether Jacob's civil rights were violated to the shredding of documents to the private conduct of at least one member of the jury. Whether these are important enough to gain Jacob a new trial or overturn his verdict

would require the expertise of a topnotch trial, appeals, or post conviction attorney. That takes money.

2. If you have any new evidence regarding Jacob's case, or any aspect of Jacob's life, please contact me through:
Voices Publishing
743 Gold Hill Place
Suite 243, P.O. Box 220,
Woodland Park, CO 80866-0220
(719)687-7450
Doesn't matter whether the evidence seems insignificant. Nor does it matter whether it is "anti-Jacob." I am not afraid of the truth, regardless of the form it takes.

3. Write to the El Paso County District Attorney's Office, asking that Jacob's case be re-opened and all new charges investigated by an impartial investigator or agency.
El Paso County District Attorney Smith
326 So. Tejon
Colorado Springs, CO 80903

4. Write to Governor Romer, asking that Jacob's sentence be commuted, or that Jacob be pardoned.
Governor Roy Romer
c/o Mark Noel
Governor's Advocate on Pardons
136 State Capitol
Denver, CO 80203
1-800-866-2880
Pardons in Colorado are akin to Bigfoot sightings. You hear about them. The public discusses them. We have all heard of someone who knows someone who has glimpsed one, but when the rumor is tracked down, it's found to be just that—a rumor. Truth is our governor doesn't grant pardons. In his entire tenure, he's only given a handful. His predecessor granted around 80 annually, and even that is very low. States such as Louisiana grant in the thousands. Colorado wants its governor to be tough on crime—and Roy Romer is. The governor gains no political capital by showing compassion toward convicts—especially juvenile murderers. For Governor Romer to take a positive interest in Jacob Ind would be a miracle indeed.

Those who would help determine whether Jacob should be pardoned also are an interesting group. They consist of people such as Ari Zavaras, the head of Department of Corrections, and prosecuting attorneys. Now, imagine this. A riot breaks out in Colorado State Prison. A guard kills a prisoner. Was it self-defense or murder? The guard is brought before a tribunal to decide whether he should be punished or go free. The tribunal consists of the prisoners who started

the riot, the family members of the dead convict, prisoner rights' advocates, and convicts who have had run-ins with the particular guard who now stands before them. Do you think this guard would be found innocent, or would he be voted, "Guilty?"

Unfortunately, if Jacob is to be pardoned or his sentence commuted, he will have to face a similar audience. The board is largely composed, not of sympathetic—or even neutral—individuals, it is composed of people such as those who convicted Jacob in the first place. Can they be fair? Can they be impartial? Will they grant pardons to fifteen-year-old murderers? Particularly when they've spent their careers convicting and incarcerating other Jacobs? When their livelihoods depend on perpetuating the present system?

Still, other states have granted pardons to other Jacobs. Our own Governor Lamm pardoned another Jacob in the 1970's. That juvenile killer went on to become a doctor. My dream is that a similar opportunity will be granted to my Jacob.

Please tear the following out and send it to Governor Romer's office.

WE, THE UNDERSIGNED, ASK THAT JACOB IND, BECAUSE OF THE MITIGATING CIRCUMSTANCES SURROUNDING HIS CRIME, BE GRANTED A PARDON OR COMMUTATION OF HIS SENTENCE.

Name   Address   Phone#

1.

2.

3.

4.

5.

6.

7.

8.

9.

10.

11.

12.

If you would like to contribute to a Justice For Jacob Fund, please send your donations to:

Justice for Jacob,
Box 2070,
Woodland Park, CO 80866

Or to:
Voices Publishing
743 Gold Hill Place
Suite 243, P.O. Box 220,
Woodland Park, CO 80866-0220

You can also contact Jacob through Voices Publishing. He enjoys receiving letters and will respond.

FOR ALL THE JACOBS.
INFORMATION ON SEXUAL ABUSE

WHY REAL GUYS DON'T TELL.

1. YOU CAN HANDLE IT.
REAL GUYS ARE TOUGH.

It refers to sexual assault by an older male or adult female.

Since our society expects any male to rise above his feelings and overcome difficulties, many male children and adult survivors of sexual abuse are reluctant to tell. The attitude that sexual victimization is less traumatic for males than for females prevents many males from seeking help. Fear of appearing weak, needy or frail leads to avoidance of self-disclosure with other males.

2. IT'S YOUR FAULT.

Males are supposed to be able to protect themselves from any danger. Male survivors of sexual abuse report self-directed anger at having failed to inflict serious physical harm on the offender. The male survivor may conceal his anxiety by using macho behaviors to re-establish a strong male image. He also may develop intensely anti-homosexual feelings or behaviors in reaction to sexual victimization.

3. YOU MUST BE A PUNK!

The male victim may assume that his failure to resist his assault shows passivity, and/or homosexuality. The molester of a male child is likely to be of the same sex (the majority of offenders are male) and any arousal or physical pleasure that was experienced may be misinterpreted by the victim as homosexual feelings. Normal male physiological responses during any sexual interaction (even a same-sex encounter) may conflict with the social message that sexual arousal should occur only in a male-female interaction.

4. MEN DON'T HAVE FEELINGS, ONLY ANGER.

Our society encourages males to ignore feelings. It is okay for a man to act on emotions, but dangerous to feel them. It is also okay for a man to act out his feelings which often include abusing others. Thus, certain male survivors have an increased risk to sexually offend. The risk for abusive behavior is further increased when the survivor feels extreme isolation--for example when he lacks a friend to whom he can confide his own abuse experience or when he fears that if he confides his victimization, other people may doubt his masculinity.

Low self-esteem related to the failure to protect oneself may cause attempts to control all other aspects of one's life. Whereas a female often withdraws because of her victimization, a male is prone to use his energy to rigidly control others.

5. NO BIG DEAL. I'LL WORK IT OUT OR DRINK IT OUT OR...

A lack of permission for men to display emotions may prompt some survivors to mask feelings through repetitive or compulsive behaviors. Although compulsive behaviors around work, materialism, sex, sports and competition are generally socially acceptable for men, such behaviors may indicate distress for the male survivor.

As with female survivors, males who have been sexually victimized often abuse food, alcohol and other chemical substances.

6. I DON'T NEED ANY HELP.

Many men will not readily use mental health services. Most male survivors of sexual abuse experience considerable conflict with the fact that a man can be a victim. Often a male survivor who asks for treatment will have been pushed to do so by a friend.

HOW TO REALLY PROTECT YOURSELF

*   Use the buddy system. Go to activities with a friend and don't allow others to separate you. Use prearranged signals to indicate you want to leave.

*   Always let family members know where you are and when you expect to return. If walking, call home just before leaving to let someone know.

*   Pay attention to your inner voice. When you have a bad feeling about a person or situation, leave immediately. Don't worry about being paranoid. Being safe is more important.

*   Be cautious of adults who are overly friendly and try to isolate you. Remember the buddy system.

*   Don't drink or use drugs. Using alcohol or drugs doesn't make you grown-up or macho. It does make you vulnerable to being abused by an adult or older adolescent. Alcohol and drugs also impair your judgment and decision-making skills.

*   Make a phone call. Always carry change for a call to family or friends in an emergency. Calls to 911 from any pay phone are free. Don't hitchhike. Even if it's late, call home or call a cab.

*   Make your own decisions rather than just going along with the crowd or an adult. Trust your judgment to know if certain behaviors are appropriate or safe. Don't be afraid of being called "chicken" or worse.

Reprinted with permission of Victim Witness Services/705 So Nevada Avenue, Colorado Springs, CO. (719)444-7538.

TIPS ON RECOGNIZING CHILD ABUSE

The Child:

* Shows sudden changes in behavior or school performance:
* Has not received help for physical or medical problems brought to the parents' attention;
* Has learning problems that cannot be attributed to specific physical or psychological causes:
* Is always watchful, as though preparing for something bad to happen;
* Lacks adult supervision;
* Is overly compliant, an overachiever, or too responsible; or
* Comes to school early, stays late, and does not want to go home.

The Parent:

* Shows little concern for the child, rarely responding to the school's request for information, for conferences, or for home visits;
* Denies the existence of—or blames the child for—the child's problems in school or at home;
* Asks the classroom teacher to use harsh physical discipline if the child misbehaves;
* Sees the child entirely bad, worthless, or burdensome;
* Demands perfection or a level of physical or academic performance the child cannot achieve; or
* Looks primarily to the child for care, attention, and satisfaction of emotional needs.

The Parent and Child:

* Rarely touch or look at each other;
* Consider their relationship entirely negative; or
* State that they do not like each other.

Signs of physical abuse. Consider the possibility of physical abuse when the child:

* Has unexplained burns, bites, bruises, broken bones, or black eyes;
* Has fading bruises or other marks noticeable after an absence from school;
* Seems frightened of the parents and protests or cries when it is time to go home from school;
* Shrinks at the approach of adults; or
* Reports injury by a parent or another adult caregiver.

Consider the possibility of physical abuse when the parent or other adult caregiver:

* Offers conflicting, unconvincing, or no explanation for the child's injury;
* Describes the child as "evil," or in some other very negative way;
* Uses harsh physical discipline with the child; or
* Has a history of abuse as a child.

Signs of neglect. Consider the possibility of neglect when the child;

* Is frequently absent from school;
* Begs or steals food or money from classmates;
* Lacks needed medical or dental care, immunizations, or glasses;

* Is consistently dirty and has severe body odor;
* Lacks sufficient clothing for the weather;
* Abuses alcohol or other drugs; or
* States that there is no one at home to provide care.

Consider the possibility of neglect when the parent or other adult caregiver:
* Appears to be indifferent to the child
* Seems apathetic or depressed;
* Behaves irrationally or in a bizarre manner; or
* Is abusing alcohol or other drugs.

Signs of sexual abuse. Consider the possibility of sexual abuse when the child:
* Has difficulty walking or sitting;
* Suddenly refuses to change for gym or to participate in physical activities;
* Demonstrates bizarre, sophisticated, or unusual sexual knowledge or behavior;
* Becomes pregnant or contracts a venereal disease, particularly if under age fourteen;
* Runs away; or
* Reports sexual abuse by a parent or another adult caregiver.

Consider the possibility of sexual abuse when the parent or other adult caregiver:
* Is unduly protective of the child, severely limits the child's contact with other children, especially of the opposite sex;
* Is secretive and isolated; or
* Describes marital difficulties involving family power struggles or sexual relations.

Signs of emotional maltreatment. Consider the possibility of emotional maltreatment when the child:
* Shows extremes in behavior, such as overly compliant or demanding behavior, extreme passivity or aggression;
* Is either inappropriately adult (parenting other children, for example) or inappropriately infantile (frequently rocking or head-banging, for example);
* Is delayed in physical or emotional development;
* Has attempted suicide; or
* Reports a lack of attachment to the parent.

Consider the possibility of emotional maltreatment when the parent or other adult caregiver:
* Constantly blames, belittles, or berates the child;
* Is unconcerned about the child and refuses to consider offers of help for the child's school problems; or
* Overtly rejects the child.

Reprinted with permission of THE NATIONAL COMMITTEE TO PREVENT CHILD ABUSE/
332 S. Michigan Avenue/ Suite 1600/ Chicago, Il 60604
Hot line: 1-800-55-NCPCA

ORDER FORM

Mail to: Voices Publishing
           743 Gold Hill Place
           Suite 243, P.O. Box 220,
           Woodland Park, CO 80866-0220

Phone: (719)687-7450

Please send me   copy(ies) of *THE MURDER OF JACOB*. I have

enclosed $16.95 per copy (Includes shipping and handling).

CUSTOMER'S NAME:

ADDRESS:

PHONE NUMBER:

THE MURDER OF JACOB is always in stock at Eon's Books, 601 W. Midland Avenue, Woodland Park. If you would prefer to charge your order, Beth O'Neal, owner of Eon's Books, would be happy to accommodate you. Eon's phone number is (719)687-8920.